The Collected Courses of the Academy o[...]

Series Editors: Professor Philip A[...]
University School of[...]
Professor Gráinne [...], European
University Institute, Florence; and
Professor Bruno de Witte,
European University Institute,
Florence

VOLUME XIII/1

Human Rights: Between Idealism and Realism

The Collected Courses of the Academy of European Law
Edited by Professor Philip Alston, Professor Gráinne de Búrca, and Professor Bruno de Witte

This series brings together the Collected Courses of the
Academy of European Law in Florence. The Academy's mission is to
produce scholarly analyses which are at the cutting edge of the two
fields in which it works: European Union law and human rights law.
A 'general course' is given each year in each field, by a
distinguished scholar and/or practitioner, who either examines the
field as a whole through a particular thematic, conceptual or
philosophical lens, or who looks at a particular theme in the context
of the overall body of law in the field. The Academy also publishes
each year a volume of collected essays with a specific theme in each
of the two fields.

Human Rights
Between Idealism and Realism

CHRISTIAN TOMUSCHAT

Academy of European Law
European University Institute

OXFORD
UNIVERSITY PRESS

OXFORD
UNIVERSITY PRESS

Great Clarendon Street, Oxford ox2 6dp

Oxford University Press is a department of the University of Oxford.
It furthers the University's objective of excellence in research, scholarship,
and education by publishing worldwide in

Oxford New York

Auckland Bangkok Buenos Aires Cape Town Chennai
Dar es Salaam Delhi HongKong Istanbul Karachi Kolkata
Kuala Lumpur Madrid Melbourne Mexico City Mumbai Nairobi
São Paulo Shanghai Singapore Taipei Tokyo Toronto

Oxford is a registered trade mark of Oxford University Press
in the UK and in certain other countries

Published in the United States
by Oxford University Press Inc., New York

British Library Cataloguing in Publication Data

Data available

Library of Congress Cataloging in Publication Data

Data available

ISBN 0-19-926861-4 (hbk)
ISBN 0-19-926862-2 (pbk)

1 3 5 7 9 10 8 6 4 2

Typeset 11 on 12pt Garamond
by Kolam Information Services Pvt. Ltd, Pondicherry
Printed in Great Britain
on acid-free paper by
T. J. International Ltd,
Padstow, Cornwall

Preface

The present book reflects the lectures which the author delivered in June 2002 at the Academy of European Law of the European University Institute in Florence. The text was completed in light of the discussions with the students attending this course. Documentary references have been taken into account until December 2002, the closing date for the manuscript.

It is not the aim of this publication to provide an overview of international protection of human rights concerning both its substantive as well as its procedural aspects. As the reader will see, the emphasis has been placed on issues of principle (such as the history of human rights or their universality) and on the reality of human rights. How human rights are enforced, and what they mean in practice for the human being, are the pivotal orientation marks of the following reflections.

CHRISTIAN TOMUSCHAT

Contents

Tables of Cases

EUROPEAN COURT OF HUMAN RIGHTS

HUMAN RIGHTS COMMITTEE

INTER-AMERICAN COURT OF HUMAN RIGHTS

INTERNATIONAL CRIMINAL TRIBUNAL FOR RWANDA

INTERNATIONAL CRIMINAL TRIBUNAL FOR
THE FORMER YUGOSLAVIA

INTERNATIONAL COURT OF JUSTICE

PERMANENT COURT OF INTERNATIONAL JUSTICE

NATIONAL COURTS

France

Germany

Greece

Tables of Legislation

TREATIES AND OTHER RELEVANT INSTRUMENTS

NATIONAL LEGISLATION

All the constitutions currently in force are reprinted in:
Gisbert H. Flanz and Albert P. Baustein, *Constitutions of the Countries
of the World* (Dobbs Ferry, New York: Oceana Publications), Binders
I to XX (last release 2001–2, issued March 2001).

Belgium

Burundi

Czech Republic

Dominican Republic

France

Germany

Greece

Ireland

Portugal

Spain

Soviet Union

United Kingdom

United States

Abbreviations

ACHR	American Convention on Human Rights
ACP States	African, Caribbean and Pacific States
AfChHPR	African Charter on Human and Peoples' Rights
AfHPRCion	African Commission on Human and Peoples' Rights
AJIL	American Journal of International Law
ATCA	Alien Tort Claims Act
BVerfGE	Entscheidungen des Bundesverfassungsgerichts (Federal Constitutional Court Reports, Germany)
CAT	Convention Against Torture and Other Cruel, Inhuman or Degrading Treatment or Punishment
CATCee	Committee Against Torture
CCPR	International Covenant on Civil and Political Rights
CEDAW	Convention on the Elimination of All Forms of Discrimination Against Women
CEDAWCee	Committee on the Elimination of Discrimination Against Women
CERD	International Convention on the Elimination of All Forms of Racial Discrimination
CERDCee	Committee on the Elimination of Racial Discrimination
CESCR	International Covenant on Economic, Social and Cultural Rights
CESCRCee	Committee on Economic, Social and Cultural Rights
CJEC	Court of Justice of the European Communities
CRC	Convention on the Rights of the Child
EC	European Community
EC Treaty	Treaty establishing the European Community
ECHR	[European] Convention for the Protection of Human Rights and Fundamental Freedoms
ECOSOC	Economic and Social Council
ECR	Court of Justice of the European Communities; Reports of cases before the Court of Justice and the Court of First Instance
ECtHR	European Court of Human Rights
EDNY	US District Court for the Eastern District of New York
EJIL	European Journal of International Law
EPIL	Encyclopedia of Public International Law (R. Bernhardt (ed.))

ETS	European Treaty Series
EU	European Union
EuGRZ	Europäische Grundrechte-Zeitschrift
GATT	General Agreement on Tariffs and Trade
GDR	German Democratic Republic
GYIL	German Yearbook of International Law
HCHR	United Nations High Commissioner for Human Rights
HRCee	Human Rights Committee
HRCion	Commission on Human Rights
HRLJ	Human Rights Law Journal
HRQ	Human Rights Quarterly
IACionHR	Inter-American Commission on Human Rights
IACtHR	Inter-American Court of Human Rights
ICC	International Criminal Court
ICJ	International Court of Justice
ICJ Reports	Reports of Judgments, Advisory Opinions and Orders of the International Court of Justice
ICLQ	International and Comparative Law Quarterly
ICRC Commentary	Commentary on the Additional Protocols of 8 June 1977 to the Geneva Conventions of 12 August 1949 (Y. Sandoz, C. Swinarski, and B. Zimmermann (eds.))
ICSID Convention	Convention on the Settlement of Investment Disputes Between States and Nationals of Other States
ICTR	International Criminal Tribunal for Rwanda
ICTY	International Criminal Tribunal for the Former Yugoslavia
ILM	International Legal Materials
ILO	International Labour Organization
ILR	International Law Reports
IRRC	International Review of the Red Cross
Max Planck UNYB	Max Planck Yearbook of United Nations Law
NATO	North Atlantic Treaty Organisation
NGO	Non-Governmental Organization
OAS	Organization of American States
OAU	Organization of African Unity
OECD	Organisation of Economic Cooperation and Development
OP-CCPR	[First] Optional Protocol to the International Covenant on Civil and Political Rights
OP-CEDAW	Optional Protocol to the Convention on the Elimination of Discrimination Against Women
OSCE	Organization for Security and Co-operation in Europe

PCIJ	Permanent Court of International Justice
PECHR	Publications of the European Court of Human Rights
Revista IIDH	Revista of the Inter-American Institute of Human Rights
RGDIP	Revue générale de droit international public
RIAA	Reports of International Arbitral Awards
TVPA	Torture Victim Protection Act
UDHR	Universal Declaration of Human Rights
UK	United Kingdom
UN	United Nations
UN Yearbook	United Nations Yearbook
UNCh	Charter of the United Nations
UNDP	United Nations Development Programme
UNESCO	United Nations Educational, Scientific and Cultural Organization
UNTS	United Nations Treaty Series
US	United States
US FSIA	United States Foreign Sovereign Immunities Act
WCAR	World Conference against Racism, Racial Discrimination, Xenophobia and Related Intolerance
WTO	World Trade Organization
YbECHR	Yearbook of the European Convention on Human Rights
ZaöRV	Zeitschrift für ausländisches öffentliches Recht und Völkerrecht (Heidelberg Journal of International Law)

1

Introduction

Human rights is a concept easily used not only by lawyers, but also by politicians and, more generally, the public at large. Claims are presented, criticisms are formulated by invoking human rights. More often than not, however, it remains rather unclear what connotation is attached to that concept. Indeed, depending on the speaker concerned, views may vary considerably as to what is understood by human rights. A theologian member of a Christian denomination will take as his/her starting point the Bible, even though he/she may be aware of the possibility to focus on human rights from a different viewpoint. A philosopher may establish his/her own system that will permit him/her to classify certain claims as human rights. A lawyer, too, will base his/her evaluation on specific methodological premises: he/she will quite naturally be led to describe human rights as part and parcel of a legal system. For him/her, to label a given wish or aspiration a 'right' makes sense only if a connection can be established with such a system.

On its part also, the concept of 'legal system' requires a definition. It is characterized by two criteria. In the first place, it is an intersubjective system, designed to apply to all the members of a given human community. Secondly, it generally encompasses mechanisms of enforcement. Legal rules, unlike rules of morality or ethics, are not addressed solely to human conscience. Since they are committed to the care of the public authorities of the community concerned, they are—or should be—vigorously defended, and sanctions should be imposed on anyone committing a breach. Law is the instrument by which a modern society regulates the processes of interaction among its members, the expectation being that its normative claims be translated into actual practice. Propositions confined to a mere existence 'on the books' would not qualify as legal rules.

This is also the perspective chosen for these lectures, which will primarily focus on human rights as part of domestic legal systems and the international legal order. To be sure, any legal regime has its intellectual and ideological foundations. Human rights, in particular, do not come out of the blue.[1] But ideas and concepts have to materialize as elements of a legal system, according to the applicable secondary rules, before being capable of being recognized as human rights. There is no denying the simple truth that the relationship between political ideas and their translation into legal substance is a very close one. And in fact, in former times the separation between the different disciplines which deal with standards for human conduct was not as clear as it is today in a time when, notwithstanding the manifold bridges between law, ethics and morality, law is considered as an autonomous branch of such rules in human society. Therefore, the philosophical ought must be distinguished from the legal ought. Maybe this distinction is nowhere as necessary as in the field of human rights where, on the most respectable and idealistic grounds, wishful thinking may be presented as the law in force.[2] Such overzealous pressing ahead, however, may have devastating consequences in undermining human rights as a branch of the law that must be taken seriously. Not everything that may serve to improve the wellbeing of individuals can or should be accepted as a human right. In that sense, even well-established international treaties may have to be scrutinized with a watchful eye. The International Covenant on Economic, Social and Cultural Rights (CESCR), in particular, has in some provisions gone to extremes which clearly exceed the capacity of governments to comply with the substance of the relevant guarantee. Thus, Article 11 enunciates a 'right of everyone . . . to the continuous improvement of living conditions'. This 'right' is more a reflection of the optimism which obtained in the industrialized world in the 1960s than a legal proposition suitable for implementation according to mechanisms and processes as they are at the disposal of governments wielding public power.

However, this does not mean that the ideological foundations of human rights should be lost sight of. The very idea of human rights presupposes a certain concept of the human being. By recognizing legal entitlements to every person, to men and women, to children and elderly persons, to business managers and to members of tribal communities alike, the international community has acknowledged that indeed all human beings have something in common. They are all recognized as persons whose dignity must be respected, no matter whether the individual concerned can take his/her own decisions on his/her life.[3] This is said implicitly in the preamble of the

---

[1] For a concise historical overview see Gerhard Oestreich, *Geschichte der Menschenrechte und Grundfreiheiten im Umriß* (2nd edn, Berlin, Duncker & Humblot, 1978). Recently, Shestack, 'The Philosophic Foundations of Human Rights', 20 *HRQ* (1998) 201, has provided an overview of the underlying moral and philosophical concepts.

[2] See the example given by Alston, 'Conjuring Up New Human Rights: A Proposal for Quality Control', 78 *AJIL* (1984) 607.

[3] See, for instance, Jack Donnelly, *Universal Human Rights in Theory and Practice* (Ithaca and London, Cornell University Press, 1989), at 17, 24. For an inquiry into this concept

Universal Declaration of Human Rights (UDHR),[4] which starts out with the words:

Whereas recognition of the inherent dignity and of the equal and inalienable rights of all members of the human family is the foundation of freedom, justice and peace in the world. . . .

Human dignity attaches also to the weak members of society, to the infant and to persons having lost the full use of their mental capacities at old age or on whatever other grounds. Nobody is rejected *a limine* from the community of human beings. Human rights are rights which a person enjoys by virtue of being human, without any supplementary condition being required.[5]

Three steps have to be taken on the road from Utopia—in the positive sense—to legal positivism: first of all, candidates for human rights must be identified. Those who have the power to initiate a process of norm creation at the international level must agree which wishes and desires are capable of being translated into legal substance. There have never been great difficulties in acknowledging that, first and foremost, human life belongs to the goods which should be protected through the procedures and mechanisms which are set into motion if something is identified as a human right. But there are many other items which raise delicate questions. The 'right to the continuous improvement of living conditions' was already mentioned—what about a 'right to tourism'? And going one step further: would a constitutional instrument at national or international level be able to set forth a 'right to happiness'? Even more clearly than in the preceding instances, this suggested 'right' draws the attention of the student to the inherent limitations of state power. States are entities set up with a certain mandate, namely to shield the human being from dangers surrounding him/her in the daily existence. But the state is not an almighty machine which totally controls everyone under its jurisdiction. As a matter of principle, the state has to stop its action at the gates of the intimacy of the individual. Happiness depends on many external factors which a state apparatus can influence, but it cannot be brought about

primarily from the viewpoint of German constitutional law see Starck, 'Menschenwürde als Verfassungsgarantie im modernen Staat', *Juristenzeitung* (1981) 457; for an assessment of human dignity within the framework of the European Convention on Human Rights (ECHR) see Clapham, 'The "Drittwirkung" of the Convention', in Ronald. St. J. MacDonald et al. (eds), *The European System for the Protection of Human Rights* (Dordrecht, Martinus Nijhoff, 1993), 163, at 203–206. For a comprehensive study of the concept see now David Kretzmer and Eckart Klein (eds), *The Concept of Human Dignity in Human Rights Discourse* (The Hague, Kluwer Law International, 2002).

[4] Adopted and proclaimed by GA Res. 217-A (III), 10 December 1948.
[5] Maurice Cranston, *What are Human Rights* (London, Bodley Head, 1973), at 36; Donnelly, 'Human Rights, Democracy, and Development', 21 *HRQ* (1999) 608, at 612: 'Human rights are . . . the rights that one has simply as a human being'; Shestack, *supra* n. 1, at 203.

by governmental efforts or orders. Therefore, the United States Declaration of Independence of 4 July 1776 recognized a right to the pursuit of happiness—and not a right to happiness as such. A more modern example is the right to a clean or healthful environment. Such a right of macrocosmic dimensions cannot be realized by governmental authorities alone, but presupposes cooperation not only by society at large, but also by other actors outside the national boundaries, more often than not at the universal level. It stands to reason that such a right is different in nature from, for instance, the right to free speech which is intimately linked to the individuality of the person concerned.

After identification, the second step consists of making the rights thus outlined binding in the sense of a juridical commitment. While at worldwide level the first step was achieved through the adoption of the UDHR in 1948, the second step commenced in 1966 with the adoption of the two treaty instruments for the protection of human rights, the International Covenant on Civil and Political Rights (CCPR) and the CESCR. Since these two treaties are by now widely accepted,[6] they constitute a framework which might even be said to have become binding on non-signatory states, in any event as far as their substantive content is concerned. The world is now endowed with a Bill of Human Rights by which the legitimacy of any government will be measured.

The binding character of a Bill of Human Rights can operate in two ways. It can either be conceived of as a set of rules engendering no more than duties, in particular for governments, and possibly even for private individuals, or it may be construed as a set of rules bringing into being true rights which may be invoked by their holders before any bodies vested with decision-making authority. It is well known that this choice seems to have been made for good in favour of rights within the meaning of the second alternative, to the extent possible, not excluding other alternatives. The mechanism by which protection of the wellbeing of human societies is sought to be ensured is the specific process of vindication of rights, and not a process of enforcement of duties alone. Consequently, the individual who may have been aggrieved by a governmental act has a much greater role to play than if the codification aimed at protecting human beings against arbitrariness and abuse had confined itself to setting forth duties to be observed by their addressees.

Lastly, and almost as a necessary consequence of the determination in favour of rights, the question arises whether human rights, in addition to being binding in substantive terms on governments, should also be enforceable. Here, the answer is not difficult. Once agreement has been reached on setting forth true rights, the necessary consequence is that such rights must indeed be incorporated into a system which secures their effectiveness

---

[6] As of 9 December 2002, the CCPR had 149 and the CESCR 146 states parties.

through appropriate procedures and mechanisms. In domestic systems, the interrelationship between substantive rights and their enforceability is a matter permitting of no doubt. According to an old English adage, where there is a remedy, there is a right. This proposition can also be turned around. Where there is a right, there is a remedy. In other words, for English lawyers, who have always been practice-minded, to speak of a right without being able to point to a remedy for the enforcement of that right, makes little sense. In international law, however, the connection is not as tight as in domestic law, and even almost non-existent. International law is handled by states themselves which more often than not prefer to settle their disputes via diplomatic channels, avoiding formalized procedures before international tribunals or other bodies.[7] Thus, it is—or was—a great step forward when in the field of human rights it was decided to depart from the usual model of international dispute settlement by creating procedures which the individual can initiate, obviously in most cases against his/her own state. One of the most successful institutions in this regard is the application which individuals under the jurisdiction of any of the 44 states parties to the European Convention on Human Rights (ECHR) can bring to the European Court of Human Rights (ECtHR). Its American counterpart is lagging far behind because in the Western Hemisphere the individual has no right of direct access to the Inter-American Court of Human Rights (IACtHR), being confined to submitting his/her complaints to the Inter-American Commission on Human Rights. Until 1998, the European system for the protection of human rights had a similar two-tier structure. The European Commission of Human Rights screened the incoming applications and ruled on their admissibility. Since the 11th Protocol to the ECHR came into force, however (1 November 1998), even the common man has a right of direct access to the Strasbourg Court of Human Rights.

To sum up the preceding observations, it can be said that human rights is not, and should not be used as, a term which comprises the most diverse factual situations. In the following discourse, in any event, human rights will be relied upon as a term of art. It will be particularly the mechanisms designed to translate human rights as legal propositions into a living reality which will capture our attention. We will not so much comment upon human rights as a branch of substantive entitlements, but rather on its procedural aspects, which indeed distinguish it from human rights in political discourse. Here, too, our main task will consist in carefully weighing the pros and cons of any device. The Olympic motto—'higher, faster, stronger'—cannot be the leading maxim by which to measure the desirability of a development under review.

[7] For this reason, H. L. A. Hart, *The Concept of Law* (2nd edn, Oxford, Clarendon Press, 1994), at 214–237, had great difficulties in recognizing international law as law proper.

2
History of Human Rights

Whenever the student probes into the history of human communities, he/she will find certain mechanisms designed to protect individual members of the community against violations of their rights. Systems of governance are generally based on reciprocity of protection and loyalty. Human beings, aware of the necessity to maintain and defend themselves in inimical surroundings, have invariably established structures of governance in the expectation that those entrusted with a leadership role will protect those under their command. This has also been one of the constant themes of state philosophy. How can the function of a ruler be justified, and why is a ruler entitled to require compliance with his orders? Ethnological studies progressively reveal that humankind has created the most diverse systems of governance since it developed the capacity to organize large collective entities with a separation of functions among its members.

I HUMAN RIGHTS AND THE RISE OF THE STATE IN EUROPE

Of course, the present lectures cannot go into such colourful—and often quite remarkable—details. By necessity, we must confine ourselves to those intellectual currents and factual developments which have helped shape the world as it exists today. The starting point should therefore be the period in European history which paved the way for the emergence of the modern state. It is this entity which has also brought into being human rights in the sense described above. Claiming that it is the supreme power in a given territory, not being subordinate to any other human system of governance, the modern state has at the same time elicited a response. Sovereignty may be acceptable as a legal instrument of defence against outside powers. But to apply the same philosophy of omnipotence internally vis-à-vis the ruled would have been a denial of a long history of constraints on the power of monarchs and princes.[1] Thus, the challenge of human rights is inextricably bound up with the history of the modern state: on the one hand, the state has been accepted as an organization well-suited to promote the interests of its members in the never-ending fight for resources among different communities; on the other hand, it has also been identified as a lethal threat to the life and wellbeing of its members.[2] Human rights have a dialectical function in overcoming that tension. They are designed to reconcile the effectiveness of state power with the protection against that same state power. On the one hand, the state is the guarantor of human rights, the institutional framework called upon to safeguard the existence, the freedom, and the property of the individual citizen; at the same time, however, historical experience tells the observer that time and again persons or authorities vested with sovereign powers have infringed the rights of the citizen.

II INTERNATIONAL PROTECTION OF HUMAN RIGHTS: A LATECOMER IN HISTORY

International protection of human rights is a chapter of legal history that has begun at a relatively late stage in the history of humankind. This late-coming has reasons which can easily be explained.

For centuries, it was considered as a self-evident truth that any ruler would take care in the most appropriate fashion of the fate of his subjects. In Europe, all the kings and other princes understood themselves as being committed to the values of the Christian faith. Thus, in general, no need was perceived by them to take action with a view to protecting the rights of people in another state. No reasons existed which would have made it plausible that outside intervention could remedy any perceived deficiencies in the performance of a system of governance. Power struggles were largely seen as a fact of life, regrettable but unavoidable. On the other hand, unfortunately, the common value bases did not generate a climate of tolerance that would also have manifested itself vis-à-vis people embracing a faith different from the prevailing state-authorized creed. In the religious wars of the sixteenth and seventeenth centuries, religious dissidents suffered brutal persecution. In the middle of the Thirty-Years War (1630), Sweden sent a military expedition force to save the Protestant movement in Germany from being overwhelmed

---

[1] For the earlier epochs see, e.g., van Gelderen, 'Vitoria, Grotius and Human Rights: the Early Experience of Colonialism in Spanish and Dutch Political Thought', in Wolfgang Schmale (ed.), *Human Rights and Cultural Diversity* (Goldbach, Keip Publishing, 1993), 215; Hersch Lauterpacht, *International Law and Human Rights* (London, Stevens, 1950), at 73–126.

[2] On the slow emergence of human rights in the modern state see Wolfgang Reinhard, *Geschichte der Staatsgewalt* (München, Beck, 1999), at 410–426.

by the Catholic counter-reaction (although it pursued also more self-interested goals). In a certain way, this early example of outside intervention repeated itself in the nineteenth century when Western powers several times undertook military actions in order to protect the Christian communities in certain parts of the Ottoman Empire. Such 'humanitarian interventions' occurred at random, without being guided by any predetermined criteria. They, therefore, more often than not smacked more of imperialism than of altruistic assistance to religious communities in an emergency situation.[3] Otherwise, however, governments refrained from concerning themselves with the fate of human beings under foreign rule. Neighbours of a country where injustice and violence reigned knew that they would have to face up to the consequences of such occurrences. But it was considered neither appropriate nor promising to make representations with a view to alleviating the fate of the victims. The revocation of the Edict of Nantes in 1685 was generally seen in Europe as a blow against the idea of religious tolerance. But the other European powers saw this as a French policy decision that could not be challenged from outside. Instead, they offered their help to the Huguenots who fled France, providing them hospitality in their countries.

Secondly, up to the twentieth century, there existed simply no international institutions capable of exercising a monitoring function. As long as the Holy Roman Empire of the Germanic Nation existed (it collapsed in 1806) the German Emperor discharged a certain role as a guarantor of law and order within the territory of that Empire. But there was no authority over and above the heads of independent kingdoms like England, France, Russia or Sweden. During the nineteenth century the so-called 'Holy Alliance' (Austria, France, Great Britain, Prussia, Russia), which emerged from the Vienna Peace Conference of 1815, sought to exercise a function of arbiter in the relationships among European states.[4] But this loose alliance disintegrated progressively with the rise of imperialist nationalism all over Europe. Furthermore, the Holy Alliance had seen it as one of its main objectives to shield monarchical legitimacy against any challenges by democratic forces. It was far from conceiving of its role as that of an institution entrusted with taking care of the concerns of the individual citizen. Since the democratic idea gained strength step by step during the nineteenth century, it could not survive for long. After Prussia and Austria had fought a war in 1866, it was definitively dead. The second half of the nineteenth century just saw a juxtaposition of sovereign nations, vying with each other for supremacy in Europe. In the

---

[3] For an extensive historical account see Fonteyne, 'The Customary International Law Doctrine of Humanitarian Intervention: Its Current Validity under the U.N. Charter', 4 *California Western International Law Journal* (1974) 203.

[4] Verosta, 'Holy Alliance', 2 *EPIL* (1995) 861.

circumstances, the idea of monitoring the conduct of governments vis-à-vis their own citizens lacked any real basis.

Lastly, it is clear that international protection of human rights cannot be dissociated from national protection of human rights. Human rights evolved as countervailing forces against state power. It is only at a second stage that the idea emerged to establish mechanisms at the international level in order to accommodate instances where a national system has broken down under the iron grip of a dictatorship or the assault of irrational forces of anarchy. First of all, human rights had to be accepted as an indispensable element of any constitutional order at the national level. In this regard, it may be noted that neither the German Empire under the Constitution of 1871 nor France's Third Republic of 1871 had in their constitutional instruments any section dealing with fundamental rights of the citizen. It is only after the First World War, after 1918, that generally the need was perceived to define the role of governments more accurately by assigning to them the task of respecting and ensuring certain basic rights of the individual. On that foundation, at a later stage, human rights could make their way to the international level.

III FROM THE SIXTEENTH CENTURY TO 1776

In the early centuries of the development of the doctrines that have shaped our contemporary understanding of the state and its legitimate mandate, two currents can be distinguished.

Protection of Human Beings by Denial of Human Rights

The older doctrine seeks to bring about peace and thereby to protect the citizen—without employing modern human rights terminology—by denying him/her the benefit of any rights vis-à-vis the ruler, whose task was seen as preventing armed conflicts between different societal groups. At first glance, the concept of protection of human rights by denial of human rights may seem fairly odd. But the logic of that approach can hardly be dismissed. It reflects the general conception of a well-ordered state of the *res publica* if everyone faithfully discharges his/her duties. However, that conception places great—and one may safely say: excessive—trust in the person of the ruler. The good king will always do the best for the wellbeing of his subjects. But if a morally corrupt person ascends to the throne, or if a group of criminals initially disguised as *Biedermänner* gets hold of power, the construction collapses. The citizen finds no institutional support within the state apparatus. He/she then can only claim a right of resistance against oppressive state power.

The first influential figure who defended that doctrinal position was the French author Jean Bodin (1530–1596). Faced with the challenge to the power of the French Kings by the Pope and by religious strife between Catholics and Protestants, he sought to confirm the royal authority. In his masterly work *Les Six livres de la République* (1576) he posited that the prince, the King of France, enjoyed a right of sovereignty which no one was entitled to call into question. Neither could this be done by any religious community in the name of allegedly eternal truths, nor by any external power, be it a spiritual or a secular authority like the German Emperor. There was no right of resistance which individuals could invoke.[5] The sovereign was not even bound to heed his own laws. He was only obligated to respect God's commands, natural law, and general principles of law, the 'loix humaines communes à tous peuples'.[6]

Whereas Bodin primarily emphasized the independence of the Kings of France vis-à-vis any outside powers, the English author Thomas Hobbes (1588–1679) stressed the rights of the sovereign power of the state over all the members of the common polity. Having been affected in his personal existence by the religious wars ravaging England, he thought to free state power, which he called 'Leviathan', from any constraints which could possibly justify a right of resistance. His perception of society, which provides the bases of his doctrinal edifice, is a pessimistic one. As he explains in the 'Dedicatory Epistle' of his work *De cive* (1642) to the Earle of Devonshire, man, following his instincts, would attack his neighbours if not restrained by public authority. In an anarchic society, the guiding maxim would be: *homo homini lupus*.[7] Only the superior might of the Leviathan can establish peace and mutual tolerance. In order effectively to discharge his mandate, the Leviathan must be exempted from all kinds of legal ties. Although it is incumbent upon him to secure the life and the property of his subjects, he is not bound by law to do so. The only obligations to which he is subject are the commands of God and the laws of nature. These rules, however, cannot be invoked vis-à-vis the sovereign power of the state. Only if the state fails in providing protection as agreed upon in establishing the sovereign authority, do the rights of the citizens come back to life.

---

[5] Gérard Mairet (ed.) (Paris, Librairie Générale Française, 1993), bk. I, ch. VIII: 'le sujet, qui est exempté de la puissance des lois, demeure toujours en la sujétion et obéissance de ceux qui ont la souveraineté' (119–120); 'Mais il n'est pas licite au sujet de contrevenir aux lois de son Prince, sous voile d'honneur, ou de justice...il n'est pas licite au sujet de contrevenir à l'édit de son Prince' (131).

[6] Ibid. at 121–122: 'Mais quant aux lois divines et naturelles, tous les Princes de la terre y sont sujets...la puissance absolue des Princes et seigneuries ne s'étend aucunement aux lois de Dieu et de nature.'

[7] Thomas Hobbes, *Man and Citizen* (English edn., Bernard Gert (ed.), Indianapolis and Cambridge, Hacket, 1991), at 89: 'Man to man is an arrant wolf.'

It goes without saying that this doctrine was born at a time when experiences with somewhat complex models of separation of powers within constitutional systems were still entirely lacking. At the heyday of absolutism in the world of European states, only fairly simple solutions could be imagined. Carried by the most noble intentions and wishing to put an end to any ideological justification of civil war, Hobbes saw no other way out than to plead for the right of authoritative decision of the sovereign power of the state. It needs no long explanation to demonstrate that his suggestions fitted well into a world dominated by monarchs and princes, but could hardly be amalgamated with the emerging democratic doctrines.

Protection of Human Beings by Grant of Human Rights

John Locke (1632–1704) is the author who took positions diametrically opposed to the recipes advocated by Thomas Hobbes. In his *Two Treatises of Civil Government* (1690), he proceeded from the premise that men were 'by nature all free, equal, and independent'.[8] Pursuing this proposition, he resolutely denied that a human being is able to divest himself of all natural rights, which he enjoys as a gift of nature. Although he shared the basic idea that the polity is founded by consent among its members, he rejected the suggestion by Hobbes that in establishing a 'body politic' man foregoes all of his natural rights. In a central passage, he writes:

nobody can transfer to another more power than he has in himself, and nobody has an absolute arbitrary power over himself, or over any other, to destroy his own life, or take away the life or property of another. A man ... cannot subject himself to the arbitrary power of another. ...[9]

This amounts to saying that everyone retains his natural freedoms even vis-à-vis the machinery of the state: the conclusion of the social compact founding the body politic is no unconditional surrender. Consequently, the way is open for fundamental rights which the individual can oppose to illegitimate requests of the state. In a famous passage, Eméric de Vattel follows this line of reasoning, postulating a right of resistance of citizens if a ruler commits 'clear and glaring wrongs', in particular by attempting to take away life without any justification.[10] Many decades earlier, Hugo Grotius had also expressed similar ideas in a summary reflection on the limits of sovereign power, but without elaborating a similarly impressive intellectual edifice as John Locke.[11]

---

[8] John Locke, *Two Treatises of Civil Government* (orig. edn 1690; W. S. Carpenter (ed.), London/New York, Dent, Everyman's Library, 1966), bk. II, ch. VIII, para. 95.

[9] Ibid. at bk. II, ch. XI, para. 135.

[10] *The Law of Nations or the Principles of Natural Law* (trans. from the 1758 edn. by Charles G. Fenwick, Washington, Carnegie Institution, 1916), bk. I, ch. IV, para. 54.

[11] *De Jure Belli ac Pacis Libri Tres* (orig. edn 1625; Francis W. Kelsey et al. trans., New York and London, Oceana and Wildy, 1964), bk. I, ch. IV, VIII.

It is interesting to note that Montesquieu (1689–1755), the author of the famous work *De l'esprit des lois* (1748), turned totally away from the somewhat artificial concept of a social compact concluded by the members of a given human community, developing instead a constitutional theory centring on the different functions that fall to be exercised within a polity. Although pursuing the same objective as John Locke, namely to secure the freedom of the citizen, he saw as the most appropriate means to reach this aim a strategy of strict separation of powers. In his view, the citizen will receive sufficient protection from the mechanisms of a well-ordered system of governance where the legislative function, the judicial function and the executive function are clearly separated from one another.[12] Within this conceptual framework, there is no room—and perhaps no need—for fundamental rights of the individual. Montesquieu concludes therefore:

la liberté politique ne consiste point à faire ce que l'on veut. Dans un Etat, c'est-à-dire dans une société où il y a des lois, la liberté ne peut consister qu'à pouvoir faire ce que l'on doit vouloir.... [13]

Freedom according to the yardstick of the law, and not independently of the law, is a dangerous proposition, even in a democratic system of government.

IV FROM 1776 TO 1914

Human Rights in National Constitutional Texts

In the Virginia Declaration of Rights of 12 June 1776, the first document of constitutional policy that came about on the North American continent, the ideas propagated by John Locke found an almost textual reflection. Section 1 of that instrument reads like an excerpt from the central passages of Locke's 'Two Treatises of Civil Government'. It provides:

That all men are by nature equally free and independent and have certain inherent rights, of which, when they enter into a state of society, they cannot, by any compact, deprive or divest their posterity; namely, the enjoyment of life and liberty with the means of acquiring and possessing property, and pursuing and obtaining happiness and safety.

It is this philosophy, which has prevailed in the more than two centuries since the adoption of that remarkable instrument, which a few days later, on 4 July 1776, found a reflection also in the American Declaration of Independence with the following words: .

---

[12] *De l'esprit des lois* (orig. edn 1748; Ganzague Truc (ed.), Paris, Garnier, 1956), vol. 1, bk. XI, ch. VI: 'De la Constitution d'Angleterre.'
[13] Ibid. at bk. XI, ch. III.

We hold these truths to be self-evident, that all men are created equal, that they are endowed by their Creator with certain unalienable rights, that among these are Life, Liberty and the pursuit of Happiness.

Likewise, the French Déclaration des Droits de l'Homme et du Citoyen of 26 August 1789 contains no trace of Hobbesian thinking. It also emphasizes the rights of the human person as being natural and inalienable (Article 2: 'Le but de toute association politique est la conservation des droits naturels et imprescriptibles de l'homme...'). Being the product of a revolution against the absolutist power of the French monarchy, the Declaration of 1789 obviously could not give back to the state what had just been conquered from it. Although it was a few years later submerged by the establishment of a French Empire under Napoleon I, the French Declaration set the tone for Europe at large. After the fall of the Napoleonic Empire in 1815, a consti-tutional movement commenced in all of the neighbouring states. In Germany, which after 1815 remained a fairly loose Confederation ('Deutscher Bund') until 1866, the first new Constitutions in the component states of the Confederation set forth fundamental rights as a matter of necessity. In Prussia, the largest German state, it took until 1850 before the Government agreed to accept a new Constitution with a lengthy section 'On the Rights of the Prussians' (Articles 3–42).

Abolition of the Slave Trade

All this needed to be consolidated at national level before a concept of international protection of human rights could emerge. Yet, already during the nineteenth century the first cautious steps towards an international regime can be observed. One of the decisions of the European powers to which rightly attention is invariably drawn is the 1815 Declaration on the Abolition of the Slave Trade, adopted during the Peace Conference in Vienna on 8 February 1815.[14] It is true that a big question mark can be put after that Declaration. First of all, the reader will not fail to note that is was not slavery as such that was forbidden, but the slave trade. It is a matter of common knowledge that in the United States slavery continued until the Civil War from 1861 to 1865. Secondly, it has been contended that essentially the ban served the economic interests of England. Wilhelm G. Grewe writes that to permit the continuation of the slave trade would have favoured the colonies of the enemy states of England.[15] Still, measured in objective terms, the

[14] Reprinted in Wilhelm G. Grewe (ed.), *Fontes Historiae Iuris Gentium* (Berlin/New York, Walter de Gruyter, 1992), vol. 3(1), at 376.

[15] *The Epochs of International Law* (Berlin/New York, Walter de Gruyter, 2000), at 557. For a different assessment see Onuma, 'When was the Law of International Society Born? An Inquiry of the History of International Law from an Intercivilizational Perspective', 2 *Journal of the History of International Law* (2000) 1, at 43.

adoption of the Declaration was a decisive step forward. The Declaration constituted a first international instrument prohibiting a practice which was profoundly at variance with the concept of human dignity. It may be viewed as the first stage of a long journey towards the development of a full-fledged principle of equality, coupled with the prohibition of discrimination on racial grounds.

Humanitarian Law

A further development with far-reaching consequences had its origins in the middle of the nineteenth century. Notwithstanding its almost uninterrupted history of wars, Europe, a continent that officially declared its attachment to Christian values, had not been able to establish a system designed to take care of the wounded in armed conflict.[16] Some rules had developed on the conduct of hostilities, although opinions differ largely as to their real impact on warring parties.[17] Grotius devoted large sections of his masterwork *De Jure Belli ac Pacis*[18] to the laws of war. But it had not been realized that some system had to be put in place to accommodate the vital needs of the victims on the battlefield. It was a citizen of Geneva, Jean Henri Dunant, who, having witnessed the battle of Solferino during the Italian War of National Unification, took the initiative to convene an international conference in Geneva in 1863. At Solferino, many thousands of wounded soldiers died who, under more favourable circumstances, could have been saved. After the successful conclusion of the first conference, a second 'Congress' took place in Geneva in 1864, which adopted the Convention for the Amelioration of the Condition of the Wounded in Armies in the Field.[19] As from that time, it was generally recognized that it was advisable to codify the laws of war in international treaties. As far as terminology is concerned, a distinction was introduced between 'Geneva law', the rules dealing with the victims of war, and the 'Hague law', the rules governing the conduct of hostilities, which many decades later were reunified in the two Additional Protocols of 1977 to the four Geneva Red Cross Conventions of 1949.

---

[16] For a summary account of the development of humanitarian law from ancient times to the contemporary epoch see Herczegh, 'Some Thoughts on Ideas that Gave Rise to International Humanitarian Law', in Michael N. Schmitt and Leslie C. Green (eds), *The Law of Armed Conflict: Into the Next Millennium* (Newport, Rhode Island, Naval War College, 1998), 292.

[17] See on the one hand Greenwood, 'Historical Development and Legal Basis', in Dieter Fleck (ed.), *The Handbook of Humanitarian Law in Armed Conflicts* (Oxford, Oxford University Press, 1995), 12; Adam Robert and Richard Guelff, *Documents on the Laws of War* (3rd edn, Oxford, Oxford University Press, 2000), at 3; on the other hand, Fritz Münch, 'War, Laws of, History', 4 *EPIL* (2000) 1386.

[18] (Paris, 1625).

[19] Reprinted in Grewe, *supra* n. 14, at 551.

From the instruments adopted by the two Hague Peace Conferences of 1899 and 1907, the most important one was Convention (IV) Respecting the Laws and Customs of War on Land with its Annex, the Regulations Respecting the Laws and Customs of War on Land. It codified all the rules which until that time had led a somewhat uncertain existence as rules of customary law.

No General Guarantees of Human Rights

Outside the sphere of humanitarian law, during the nineteenth century human rights does not yet exist as a separate chapter of international law. In some treaties concluded after the liberation of the Balkans from Turkish domination, religious freedom and the principle of non-discrimination on religious grounds were explicitly guaranteed.[20] But a look into the indexes of leading textbooks yields meagre, even totally negative results. Johann Caspar Bluntschli, one of the most famous authors of the second half of the nineteenth century, lists 'Menschenrechte' (human rights) in the index of his ground-breaking treatise of international law,[21] but he refers that concept exclusively to the laws of war.[22] Other textbooks completely ignore the word[23]—which is quite understandable given the absence of any practice to substantiate the concept.

Summing up the situation as it existed until the outbreak of the First World War, one may say that during the nineteenth century the first treaties came into being which directly took care of the individual. But none of these treaties addressed the relationship between a state and its citizens. The instruments setting forth norms of humanitarian law, in particular, dealt with situations which, by their very nature, had a transnational character. Human rights in general were considered as falling within the domestic jurisdiction of states. Protective mechanisms were not lacking altogether. Vis-à-vis other states, governments safeguarded the rights and interests of their citizens through the traditional procedure of diplomatic protection, which entitles the state indirectly injured in the person of its citizens to make

[20] See, for instance, Peace Treaty Concerning the Settlement of the Oriental Question (Act of the Congress of Berlin), 13 July 1878, reprinted in Grewe, *supra* n. 14, at 38: Articles V (Bulgaria), XXVII (Montenegro), LXII (Ottoman Empire).

[21] *Das moderne Völkerrecht der civilisirten Staten als Rechtsbuch dargestellt* (Beck, Nördlingen, 1868), at 514.

[22] Ibid. at 529, para. 529; 298, para. 533. Although in his epoch Bluntschli was a progressive spirit, he also fell prey to racial prejudices, see Martti Koskenniemi, *The Gentle Civilizer of Nations: The Rise and Fall of International Law 1870–1960* (Cambridge, Cambridge University Press, 2001), at 42–47, 77, 103–104.

[23] See, for instance, August Wilhelm Heffter and F. Heinrich Geffcken, *Das Europäische Völkerrecht der Gegenwart* (8th edn., Berlin, H. W. Müller, 1888); Henry Wheaton, *Elements of International Law* (Philadelphia, Carey, Lea & Blanchard, 1836).

representations and, as a last resort, to take reprisals to enforce the violated rights.[24] Internally, protection was progressively ensured by conferring on citizens fundamental rights by virtue of constitutional instruments and opening up access to judicial bodies. This construction, with its two windows of external and internal protection, seemed to add up to a consistent whole, not requiring any further complements. But the fact was that under the available international instruments individuals had no standing. They were unable to take steps for the protection of the rights enshrined in those instruments on their own initiative. Internally, on the other hand, legal remedies frequently did not lie with regard to sovereign decisions with political overtones. Furthermore, no defence was available against legislative acts. Even laws embodying grave injustices could not be attacked before a competent judicial body.

V BETWEEN THE TWO WORLD WARS

After the First World War the situation changed dramatically. The experience had been gained that even in an age which considered itself civilized and enlightened, states were able to abuse their powers. While during the nineteenth century Hegel had still concluded that the state embodied all the positive values of a nation, stating that it is 'the realized ethical idea',[25] this proposition now became untenable. It had to be realized that, ineluctably, governments are made up of human beings with all their virtues, but also their defects. Notwithstanding this recognition, the first steps taken on the international level were timid and cautious.

Mandate System of the League of Nations

The League of Nations was established as the first organization entrusted with ensuring international peace and security and thereby preventing war as the greatest threat to human life and physical as well as spiritual integrity. The preamble of its Covenant explicitly enunciated this task. On the other hand, the Covenant remained silent regarding human rights. Only in respect of mandated territories did it provide that 'freedom of conscience and religion' must be guaranteed and that 'abuses such as the slave trade, the arms traffic and the liquor traffic'—three entirely different items intimately coupled with one another!—had to be prohibited (Article 22(5)). In addition, Article 23(a)

---

[24] See also *infra* p. 218.
[25] *Grundlinien der Philosophie des Rechts* (Berlin, 1821), at para. 257: 'Der Staat ist die Wirklichkeit der sittlichen Idee'; English trans. by S. W. Dyde, *Philosophy of Right* (Amherst, New York, Prometheus Books, 1996), at 240.

provided that the administering powers (mandatories) would 'endeavour to secure and maintain fair and humane conditions of labour for men, women, and children'. In fact, it was a matter of public knowledge that the colonial powers did not treat the inhabitants of their colonial territories fairly, according to the same standards as the inhabitants of the metropolitan areas. Since the development of the peoples to be placed under the new mandate regime, who were formerly subject to the Ottoman Empire and the German Empire, was emphatically phrased a 'sacred trust of civilisation' (Article 22(1)), the international community could not leave these peoples entirely to the discretion of the administering states. Some minimum guarantees had to be established. It is noteworthy, though, that there was no mention of any political freedom. The Covenant confined itself to stating that the wishes of the communities concerned must be a principal consideration in the selection of the Mandatory (Article 22(4)).

However, there was an important novelty in that a mechanism of control evolved not on the basis of the Covenant, but under the pressure of events. Although neither the Covenant itself nor the terms of the mandates provided for petitions to be submitted to the League, petitions did arrive and hence had to be dealt with in one way or another.[26] The League then established rules of procedure. According to these rules, petitions had to be sent to the Secretariat of the League through the mandatory government. A Mandates Commission then processed the petitions, but few were passed on to the Council. All in all, the procedure was extremely deficient. Petitioners were never heard. No inspection visits took place to the mandated areas. Yet, as a matter of principle, an international control mechanism had been established which later could serve as a model under the trusteeship system of the United Nations.

International Protection of Minorities

Another new development was the establishment of a system for the protection of minorities. Although the Paris Peace Conference of 1919 had endeavoured to reshuffle the European map pursuant to the principle of self-determination of peoples, the disintegration of the Austro-Hungarian Empire as well as the extensive cessions of territory to which Germany had had to consent by virtue of the Versailles Peace Treaty, created new states which were in no way ethnically homogeneous. Concerning in particular the successor states of the Austro-Hungarian Empire, the persisting ethnic diversity was even worse than before under Hapsburg rule because the new states conceived of themselves as nation-states with one lead-nation, to whose language and culture the remaining minorities should adapt. Thus, many

[26] See Rauschning, entry 'Mandates', 3 *EPIL* (1997) 280, at 285.

ethnic Hungarians found themselves all of a sudden in Romania or Czecho-slovakia, ethnic Germans became Polish citizens, and, on the other hand, ethnic Poles continued to live in Germany, etc.

The Peace Conference realized that the new configuration of the map of Europe could lead to dangerous tensions. It feared that the new nations, which after centuries of foreign domination wished to assert their specific identity, would not be prepared to treat their minorities fairly. Therefore, it demanded that the status of these minorities be specifically regulated by treaty. A complex system emerged. Five states, in accordance with the Peace Treaties, concluded specific agreements with the Principal Allied Powers: Greece, Czechoslovakia, Poland, Romania, and Yugoslavia. Regarding a number of other states, the relevant provisions were included in the Peace Treaties (Austria, Bulgaria, Hungary, Turkey). Special regimes were laid down for the Memel district and for Danzig. Lastly, Germany and Poland con-cluded a Convention relating to Upper Silesia. In all of these instruments, special guarantees were laid down for the benefit of the minorities concerned. It may seem strange that such guarantees of an international character were stipulated just for smaller groups of the population, while the main part of the population was not deemed worthy of such protection. But it was felt that the majority group was in no need of outside assistance for the promotion and protection of its rights.

Generally, the relevant clauses were relatively brief. Thus, for instance, the Treaty Concerning the Protection of Minorities concluded between the Allied and Associated Powers and Poland of 28 June 1919,[27] enjoined Poland to practice non-discrimination and set forth that in educational institutions of the primary level instruction must be given to children through the medium of their own language. Additionally, it stressed that all inhabitants of Poland 'shall be entitled to the free exercise ... of any creed, religion or belief' (Article 2(2)). These central elements could be found in other similar instruments as well. It is vital for a minority not to suffer any discrimination. Additionally, however, it needs some special guarantees in order to maintain its cultural identity. If its language is not taught to its children, it will simply disappear through a process of gradual integration of its descendants in the mainstream of the majority group of the population. Thus, a guarantee of special educational institutions does not constitute a privilege, but rather a defence against forced assimilation.

Apart from these substantive guarantees, the system of minority protection involved a couple of innovative procedural arrangements. Thus, first of all the Treaty with Poland of 28 June 1919, which was already mentioned, provided that the stipulations on minority protection were to be recognized as 'funda-mental laws' of the country that could not be set aside by any official act, not

---

[27] Reprinted in Grewe, *supra* n. 14, vol. 3(2), at 921.

even by a parliamentary statute. It is well known that normally international treaties leave the method of implementation to the discretion of the state party concerned. States may choose either to make the treaty part and parcel of their domestic legal order or keep it as an international instrument which deploys its binding force only between the participating states. In the former case, states may also determine at what level a treaty is classified within the national legal order, at the level of the constitution or at the level of ordinary laws. Here, the intention was to guarantee maximum reliability to the minorities living in Polish territory. The Treaty on Minority Protection was defined as taking precedence over any statute or regulation. One may see it as a precursor of the stringent rules of precedence applied by the Court of Justice of the European Communities (CJEC).

Secondly, the minority treaties were placed under the guarantee of the League of Nations. In order to make this guarantee operational, the treaties permitted any member of the Council of the League of Nations to bring any violation or threat of violation of the relevant obligations to the attention of the Council. Lastly, if the Council was unable to settle such disagreement, the Member State concerned had a right to seize the Permanent Court of International Justice (PCIJ). It was clear from the very outset that this procedure would certainly not be used just by 'any' member of the Council, but essentially by members who had ethnic ties with the affected minority. Strangely enough, this opportunity was put into practice in three cases only, two of which were dropped, so that the PCIJ rendered judgment in no more than one case.[28] But it gave advisory opinions in another six cases.

Petitions from the minorities concerned were admitted as from 1920. Such petitions could emanate either from individuals or from associations acting on behalf of a minority group. Each case was examined by a Committee made up of three Council members. If a petition was considered admissible, the procedure thus initiated could lead either to informal negotiations between the Committee and the state concerned or to a referral to the Council, which had the power to make recommendations. Details are not relevant in the present connection. What matters, though, is the fact that individuals could play an active role before an international body. It is true that the procedure for the treatment of such petitions was extremely unsatisfactory for their authors. They could set a proceeding in motion, but they had no right to influence its further course, which was committed entirely to the discretion of the competent Committee. Yet the model thus established has left its marks on the regime for the protection of human rights as it prevails today.

On the whole, ex post appraisal of the system of minority protection under the authority of the League of Nations leads to rather negative results as far as

[28] *Rights of Minorities in Upper Silesia (Minority Schools)*, 1928 PCIJ Series A, No. 15, 26 April 1928.

the factual side is concerned. The system had no teeth. Abuses could not be prevented. Another flaw was the fact that no Western state had submitted to similar obligations. Thus the nations bound by specific obligations vis-à-vis their minorities felt that the regime as a whole was based on discrimination, a feeling which did not increase their willingness to abide by the commitments they had undertaken. It therefore fell into disrepute and was not revitalized under the auspices of the United Nations.

Objectives of the International Labour Organization

A cursory glance should also be directed towards the International Labour Organization (ILO). Created in 1919 as part of the peace settlement following the First World War (its Constitution formed Part XIII of the Treaty of Versailles), it was assigned the task of improving the condition of workers everywhere in the world. The preamble proclaimed the following:

> Whereas universal and lasting peace can be established only if it is based upon social justice;
> And whereas conditions of labour exist involving such injustice, hardship and privation to large numbers of people as to produce unrest so great that the peace and harmony of the world are imperilled; and an improvement of those conditions is urgently required.

This mandate was to be discharged primarily by the conclusion of treaties and the adoption of recommendations. Additionally, the ILO engaged in certain activities of supervision.[29] Although the individual was not directly addressed by its Constitution, the mandate entrusted to it made clear that it is a legitimate concern of an international organization to strive for the betterment of the living conditions of human beings who remain essentially subject to the sovereign powers of a nation-state. The former principle of exclusiveness of the jurisdiction of the state of nationality suffered thus another derogation.

Legal Doctrine

At the level of concept-building, the epoch between the two World Wars was still rather trapped in traditional thinking. It had not yet dawned on legal writers that the international community had a legitimate general mandate in seeking to uphold and enforce standards of civilized conduct in the relationship between governments and their citizens.[30] Although the

---

[29] For an assessment of the work of ILO from today's viewpoint see Leary, 'Lessons from the Experience of the International Labour Organisation', in Philip Alston (ed.), *The United Nations and Human Rights* (Oxford, Clarendon Press, 1992), 580.

[30] See Franz von Liszt and Max Fleischmann, *Das Völkerrecht* (12th edn, Berlin, Springer, 1925), who offer a blank space in the index. The word '*Menschenrechte*' (human rights) does not appear (751).

First World War had brought untold suffering on millions of people, it was not realized that, in principle, all the defences of the rule of law may break down in a given historical situation and that then the only conceivable remedy may be recourse to appropriate mechanisms of the international community.

One of the few exceptions to the intellectual aridity of the 20 years between the end of the First World War and the outbreak of the Second World War was the 'Déclaration des droits internationaux de l'homme', adopted by the Institute of International Law[31] at its New York session on 12 October 1929. This Declaration marked a resolute departure from the traditional stance according to which the relationship between a state and its citizens was a matter of domestic law, not to be interfered with from outside, neither by third states nor by institutions of the international community. Yet its preamble is more courageous than its operative part. Starting off with the words:

que la conscience juridique du monde civilisé exige la reconnaissance à l'individu de droits soustraits à toute atteinte de la part de l'Etat,

it first of all pays a tribute to the constitutional developments in France and in the United States where human rights were for the first time listed in comprehensive catalogues of rights, also as a gesture of courtesy towards the country the hospitality of which the members of the Institute enjoyed. The last paragraph of the preamble, too, makes the reader anxious to learn more about the transposition of human rights to the international level, inasmuch as it emphasizes that it is important to extend to the entire world the international recognition of human rights. However, the operative part is characterized by deep-going ambiguity in stating (Article 1):

Il est du devoir de tout Etat de reconnaître à tout individu le droit égal à la vie, à la liberté, et à la propriété, et d'accorder à tous, sur son territoire, pleine et entière protection de ce droit, sans distinction de nationalité, de sexe, de race, de langue ou de religion.

The following provisions, Articles 2 and 3, also start out with the words: 'Il est du devoir de tout Etat . . .'. This insistence on the duty of states raises doubts as to whether the Institute really wished to suggest individual entitlements, enforceable at the initiative of the person concerned, or whether it remained stuck within the traditional model of public duties. Nothing is said about remedies. The Institute just emphasizes with regard to equality that it should not be nominal, but must be effective (Article 5). Essentially, however, it seems that it views the state as the true and only guardian of human rights,

---

[31] For a cursory overview see Münch, 'Institut de droit international', 2 *EPIL* (1995) 997.

remaining silent as to the ways and means to enforce the rights committed to the care of the state.[32]

VI THE GREAT LEAP FORWARD: 1945

It was the atrocities committed by the criminal Nazi dictatorship all over Europe which definitively paved the way for a new understanding of the relationships between the individual, the state and the international community. Never again could it be maintained that human beings were placed, by law, under the exclusive jurisdiction of their home state. It had been learned during the horrendous years from 1933 to 1945 that a state apparatus can turn into a killing machine, disregarding its basic function to uphold and defend the human dignity of every member of the community under its power. The President of the United States and the British Prime Minister, Franklin D. Roosevelt and Winston S. Churchill, expressed this in very simple words in the Atlantic Declaration of 14 August 1941.[33] They wished to bring about a world where 'the men in all the lands may live out their lives in freedom from fear and want'.[34] It is true that in formulating this noble proposition, they thought more of their own peoples than of the colonial peoples over which European powers still held sway. Different standards were applied to those peoples in Africa and Asia. It proved immensely difficult, given the opposition of Britain and the United States, to insert a ban on discrimination on account of race in the UN Charter (Article 1(3)).[35] Yet, compared to the Hitlerian barbarism, all these differences had little significance and were bound to disappear soon. The goal was now clearly defined. 'Men' everywhere in the world were to enjoy a life in human dignity. Diplomatic dealings had ceased to centre exclusively on states as collective entities. The fate of the individual had definitively become a matter of international concern.

The Charter of the United Nations did not yet fulfil all the hopes for a new world at the centre of which the human being would be placed. During the founding conference in San Francisco, a number of countries wished to establish a complete list of human rights for inclusion in the pending draft.[36] But time was lacking. Even those pressing for such a revolutionary

---

[32] For a lucid comment see Mosler, 'Das Institut de Droit International und die völkerrechtliche Stellung der menschlichen Person', in Wilhelm Wengler (ed.), *Justitia et Pace. Festschrift zum 100jährigen Bestehen des Institut de Droit International* (Berlin, Duncker & Humblot, 1974), 77.

[33] 35 *AJIL* (1941), Supplement, 191.

[34] Atlantic Declaration, principle six.

[35] See von Senger, 'From the Limited to the Universal Concept of Human Rights: Two Periods of Human Rights', in Schmale, *supra* n. 1, 47, at 80–87.

[36] In particular, a number of Latin American countries made that request: Chile, UNCIO III, 294; Panama, UNCIO I, 560; Uruguay, UNCIO VI, 628.

change had to realize that drawing up a human rights Bill required great care and circumspection. Only the principle was established that to promote and encourage respect for human rights and fundamental freedoms belonged to the core purposes of the World Organization (Article 1(3)). As a consequence of that determination, the newly established Commission on Human Rights (HRCion) was entrusted with elaborating a suitable draft.[37] While it was engaged in the difficult process of study and drafting, the American Anthropological Association adopted in December 1947 a remarkable 'Statement on Human Rights' in which a vigourous plea was made for true universalism of the envisioned instrument.[38] Unfortunately, little is known about the impact which this declaration had on the work of the HRCion. In any event, the Commission discharged that task in the most effective manner. Already at its third session from 24 May to 18 June 1948, it was able to adopt the requested draft Declaration. Via the Economic and Social Council, that draft was passed on to the General Assembly, which adopted it on 10 December 1948 by a vote of 48 to none, with eight abstentions (Byelorussia, Czechoslovakia, Poland, Saudi Arabia, Ukraine, South Africa, USSR, Yugoslavia). For the first time in the history of mankind, a document had come into being which defined the rights of every human being, independently of his/her race, colour, sex, language or other condition. A new chapter of human history began on that day.[39]

[37] For the drafting history see the account in *Yearbook of the United Nations 1948–49*, at 524–535.

[38] 49 *American Anthropologist* (1947) 539, at 543. In other respects, however, that Statement is controversial, see Engle, 'From Skepticism to Embrace: Human Rights and the American Anthropological Association from 1947–1999', 23 *HRQ* (2001) 536.

[39] See Eide, 'The Universal Declaration in Space and Time', in Jan Berting et al. (eds), *Human Rights in a Pluralist World: Individuals and Collectivities* (Westport and London, Meckler, 1990), 15.

3

The Different 'Generations' of Human Rights: From Human Rights to Good Governance

I TERMINOLOGY

It has become routine to speak of different 'generations' of human rights.[1] According to the current terminology, human rights of the first generation are 'negative' human rights, or civil liberties, which enjoin states to abstain from interfering with personal freedom. Freedom and security of person or freedom of speech are paradigmatic examples of this class of rights. When referring to human rights of the second generation (or 'positive' rights), the speaker has in mind economic or social rights such as the right to work or the right to social security, which entitle individuals or collectivities to the provision of certain goods or social services. Lastly, human rights of the third generation are highly complex composite rights like the right to development, the right to peace and the right to a clean environment. Whereas the rights of the first two generations have found their reflection in numerous conventional instruments which are truly binding under international law, it is by no means certain that rights of the third generation do exist as legal propositions and not only as political manifestos. They have been affirmed in resolutions of the General Assembly and of state conferences, but have never been included in an international treaty. This lack of reliable legal bases does not, of course, detract from the fascination which they exert on everyone under their influence.

The classification scheme the parameters of which are 'generations' has more than once come under criticism.[2] Indeed, the imagery of generations can lead to erroneous conclusions. In human life, generations follow one

---

[1] Following French lawyer Vasak, 'A 30-Year Struggle', *The UNESCO Courier* (November 1977), 29.

[2] See, for instance, Carl Wellman, 'Solidarity, the Individual and Human Rights', 22 *HRQ* (2000) 639, at 641.

another. The generation of grandparents reaches the end of its life span when the grandchildren have left childhood behind and begin to frame their own lives as self-reliant adults. They are then doomed to passing away in the not too distant future. Drawing a parallel, one might believe that the new generations of human rights make the older generations obsolete. But this is not the case. Between the three generations of rights, a relationship of coexistence and mutual support exists. The rights of the first generation have kept—and will keep—their freshness as long as human beings live in community with others under a superior authority, that of the state or other entity that wields public power. The right to life, the guarantee of physical integrity, epitomized by the ban on torture, freedom of speech and other similar rights, reflect needs the fulfilment of which directly touches upon human existence. Without enjoying the rights of the first generation, the human being would remain subject to the whims and fancies of the rulers by whom he/she is confronted. Likewise, rights of the second generation, such as the right to social security, do not become superfluous on account of the emergence of rights of the third generation. On the contrary, it may be said from the very outset that step by step, the next generation leaves the path of legal entitlement by becoming heavily enriched with political elements.

It is because of this terminological inadequacy that proposals have been made to introduce different concepts. Some of these proposals sound perfectly reasonable. Thus, Eibe Riedel suggests we speak of different 'dimensions' of human rights.[3] Although noting that certain linguistic improvements could be made, we shall nonetheless stick to the traditional term of 'generations' since no one will draw any mistaken conclusions after the debate has served to warn of the pitfalls hidden in the choice of language.

II DEVELOPMENT OF FIRST GENERATION AND SECOND GENERATION RIGHTS AT NATIONAL LEVEL

As already pointed out, international human rights must be considered an offspring of the human rights that were originally codified at national level. The substance of what was first guaranteed by procedures and mechanisms within a national framework was later strengthened by a complementary international set of rules. Because of this dependency, it is again indispensable to glance at the instruments which evolved as from the end of the eighteenth century.

---

[3] 'Menschenrechte der dritten Dimension', 16 *EuGRZ* (1989) 9.

First Generation Rights

It can easily be perceived that the eighteenth as well as the nineteenth century, to the extent that living instruments of positive law and not purely utopian concepts are concerned, acknowledged only one category of human rights, namely rights of the first generation. The Virginia Declaration of Rights of 1776 contained clauses dealing with free elections, trial by jury, respect for property, and freedom of the press, but failed to mention any rights related to a social welfare function of the state. Likewise, the first 12 amendments to the Constitution of the United States, characterized by succinct language, refrained from going beyond minima. Amendment I, in pretorian style, guarantees freedom of religion, of speech, freedom of the press, and the rights of the people to peaceful assembly. Again, no trace can be found of any obligation incumbent upon the state to provide to its citizens other service than physical security and a functioning judicial system. Across the Atlantic in France, the same ideas prevailed. The Déclaration des Droits de l'Homme et du Citoyen of 1789[4] proclaims the freedom of man,[5] but does not burden the state with far-reaching demands. Its main task is to create a functioning system of governance with the three branches identified by Montesquieu. Beyond that, a bourgeois society did not feel any need for state intervention.

During all of the nineteenth century, national constitutions did not depart from that line. Invariably the catalogues of human rights, which were progressively deemed to constitute a necessary component of a modern constitutional text, were confined to classical freedoms. In that sense, the Belgian Constitution of 1831, which had a considerable influence on constitutional developments all over Europe, lists the well-known freedoms in Articles 4 to 23, without embarking on new paths. Prussia largely adopted that model in enacting its Constitution in 1850.

Since the beginning of the twentieth century only, civil liberties lost their monopoly as constituting the only class of fundamental rights acknowledged at a constitutional level. The Soviet Constitution of 1917 paved the way by setting forth a number of social and economic rights, and the German Weimar Constitution of 1919, which epitomized the resurgence of the German state from the ashes of the First World War, engaged in an ambitious programme of norm-setting by entrenching in that text not only the classical freedoms, but furthermore numerous rights of the new type. An interesting new accent was added to this development by the Irish Constitution of 1937 which, instead of employing the 'rights' terminology, included in Article 45 a

---

[4] Reprinted in Maurice Duverger, *Constitutions et documents politiques* (9th edn., Paris, Presses universitaires de France, 1981), at 9.

[5] The word 'homme' was taken literally, French women were not recognized as holders of the rights proclaimed by the Declaration, see Lenoir, 'The Representation of Women in Politics: From Quotas to Parity in Elections', 50 *ICLQ* (2001) 217, at 221.

provision on 'Directive principles of social policy'. Of course, up to the present time, and in spite of these variations, first generation rights have never been omitted from a constitutional text. They are rightly considered the core of the defence strategy against arbitrary use of power by governments.

Second Generation Rights

As just mentioned, second generation rights appeared fairly late on the stage of constitutional developments. They are a child of the twentieth century, when societies assumed their responsibility for the 'social question'. As a novelty, they both fascinated and frightened constitution-making bodies. Ireland's reluctance to commit itself to social welfare benefits at a constitutional level was mirrored after the end of the Second World War in the caution shown by France in dealing with the topic of human rights in general. Instead of incorporating them in the body of the Constitution of the IVth Republic, they were relegated to the preamble of that Constitution, being introduced by a clause which characterized them as political, economic and social principles 'particulièrement nécessaires à notre temps'.[6] The Federal Republic of Germany, having experienced great difficulties under the Weimar Constitution to handle in an effective manner the economic and social rights of that Constitution, decided to restrict the text of its post-war Constitution, the Basic Law, to a general clause setting forth that Germany was a 'social state'. A few decades later, such doubts as to the usefulness of economic and social rights were overcome. After having both lived under long-lasting dictatorships, Portugal and Spain proclaimed extensive lists of human rights, including rights of the second generation, when they eventually were able to reconvert themselves into democratic regimes (Portugal: Constitution of 1976; Spain: Constitution of 1978). A careful balance between classical rights and 'new' rights has been established in the Charter of Fundamental Rights of the European Union, adopted by the European Council at its summit meeting in Nice on 7 December 2000[7] provisionally as a non-binding instrument which may be included, at a later stage, in a European Constitution.[8]

In sum, there is a growing awareness in the constitutional systems almost everywhere in the world that it is not enough for a state to abstain from

[6] It took decades before the status of these principles was definitively clarified. Eventually, the French Conseil constitutionnel decided that the preamble of the Constitution of 1946, to which the preamble of the Constitution of 1958 referred, had the value of a true constitutional norm: judgment of 16 July 1971, *Liberté d'association*, reprinted in Louis Favoreu and Loic Philip, *Les grandes décisions du Conseil constitutionnel* (10th edn, Paris, Dalloz, 1999), at 252.

[7] *Official Journal of the European Communities*, 18 December 2000, C 364/1.

[8] See Guy Braibant, *La Charte des droits fondamentaux de l'Union européenne* (Paris, Editions du Seuil, 2001), at 44–46.

interfering with individual entitlements. Given their large increase in factual power over the lives of societies, governments have been burdened to an ever-growing extent with ensuring the wellbeing of their citizens. Legally, this tendency is reflected in the doctrine of equal importance of civil and political rights, on the one hand, and economic, social, and cultural rights, on the other.[9] No agreement, however, exists as to the ways and means suited to ensure economic and social rights. Nobody can contest that they are far more context-dependent than the traditional rights of the first generation. For that reason, some states refrain from guaranteeing them at a constitutional level. The United States is perhaps the country which most resolutely rejects economic and social benefits as constitutional entitlements while providing such benefits without any hesitation at the level of ordinary legislation.

III DEVELOPMENT OF THE CURRENT SYSTEM OF INTERNATIONAL PROTECTION OF HUMAN RIGHTS

It stands to reason that these constitutional developments, to the extent that they occurred before 1948 or 1966, could not but leave their hallmark on the deliberative processes when the competent bodies of the United Nations embarked upon drafting the so-called International Bill of Human Rights, i.e. the UDHR and the two International Covenants. Given the fact that during the period immediately following the Second World War the United Nations was essentially a joint undertaking run by Western states, on the one hand, and socialist states, on the other, the result of that drafting effort had to be a compromise. While the USSR and its allies favoured the inclusion of economic and social rights in the text of the Declaration and the drafts for the later treaty instrument(s), regarding civil liberties with a considerable degree of mistrust, Western states wished to remain faithful to their own consti-tutional traditions by injecting into these instruments the rights which they had learned to appreciate, while not being able to overcome their emotional distance from second generation rights. With a view to ensuring the success of the drafting exercise, however, both sides had to make some concessions. This compromise solution was much less damaging for the Western side than for the socialist states. By accepting freedom of speech and non-discrimination on political grounds, the East undermined the bases of the communist dictatorships. For the West, the ensuing burden was much lighter. Almost nobody in Western societies was against providing economic

---

[9] Epitomized by the UDHR and proclaimed by many UN General Assembly resolutions, in particular GA Res. 32/130, 16 December 1977, op. para. 1(a), and also by the Vienna World Conference on Human Rights of June 1993, Declaration, 32 *ILM* (1993) 1663, at 1665, op. para. 5: 'All human rights are universal, indivisible and interdependent and interrelated.'

and social services to citizens.[10] What was objected to was essentially the legal method of regulation. Even today, the majority of Western states are convinced that financial benefits should not be guaranteed as a constitutional right, but are a matter to be determined by ordinary legislation.

Universal Declaration of Human Rights

The UDHR constitutes in fact a unique mixture of rights of the most diverse nature. It starts out in Article 1 with a programmatic proclamation revealing the ideological bases of the instrument:

All human beings are born free and equal in dignity and rights. They are endowed with reason and conscience and should act towards one another in a spirit of brotherhood.

After having set forth in Article 2 the general principle of equality and non-discrimination, it first lists the traditional rights and freedoms in a fairly complete form (Articles 3 to 20), resuming the domestic experiences of the countries of the world which at that time were considered to be the intellectual and moral leaders.[11] Thereafter, it devotes one provision to the right of everyone to political participation in running the public affairs of 'his' country (Article 21). The remainder of the Declaration deals with economic, social, and cultural rights (Articles 22 to 27) in a way which still today sounds fresh and stimulating. Utopia of a heaven-like quality is finally reached in Article 28 where the Declaration states that:

everyone is entitled to a social and international order in which the rights and freedoms set forth in this Declaration can be fully realized.

As a lawyer, one cannot appreciate such a provision which promises just anything without indicating how that goal might possibly be reached. Before blaming the drafters, however, one should remind oneself of the political character of the UDHR. It was enacted as a resolution of the General Assembly. Being thus legally classifiable as a recommendation, it originally lacked any binding force and could therefore transcend boundary lines which a true legal instrument could not have crossed.

---

[10] It is a widely held erroneous assumption that Western countries reject social and economic rights. Their resistance relates to form, not to substance, see cogent observations by Freeman, 'Human Rights: Asia and the West', in James T. H. Tang (ed.), *Human Rights and International Relations in the Asia Pacific* (London and New York, Pinter, 1995), 13, at 14.

[11] In December 1948, when the UDHR was adopted, the United Nations counted no more than 58 Member States. Most of today's members had not yet gained or recovered their independence and, therefore, could not take part in the drafting of the Declaration. However, two persons from the Third World played a decisive role in that process, Mrs Mehta from India and Charles Malik from Lebanon.

In the years following the adoption of the UDHR it was attempted to translate its contents into hard legal substance. This was done at two levels, at the European level within the framework of the Council of Europe as well as in the fora of the United Nations.

European Convention on Human Rights and the European Social Charter

In Europe, Hitler's barbarism had caused the most horrendous wounds to peoples. After the end of the Second World War, therefore, it was felt particularly necessary to reaffirm the worth and dignity of the human person. The establishment of the Council of Europe was seen as one of the devices which could in the future prevent the recurrence of similar tragedies. Explicitly, the preamble of the Statute of the organization stated:

Reaffirming their devotion to the spiritual and moral values which are the common heritage of their peoples and the true source of individual freedom, political liberty and the rule of law, principles which form the basis of all genuine democracy.

It was therefore but natural that the newly established organs of the Council of Europe started immediately work on a conventional instrument designed to provide effective protection to human rights by mechanisms of collective enforcement. The Statute had come into force on 3 August 1949. The first session of the Consultative Assembly opened on 10 August 1949. Already on 4 November 1950 the text of the ECHR could be signed. In less than 15 months, the work had been completed.[12] Using the materials produced by the HRCion was one of the techniques providing the explanation how such remarkable speed could be achieved. The similarity of formulations encountered in the ECHR on the one hand and the CCPR on the other hand might lead to the erroneous conclusion that the United Nations relied largely on the European model when formulating its instrument. In reality, although the chronology gives priority to the ECHR, the sequence of events is a different one. The text of the CCPR had already been finalized by the HRCion when the Council of Europe started its work.[13]

Many years after the adoption of the ECHR, the nations which had brought that instrument into being realized that Europe would fall behind in the race for the leading position in the field of human rights if it continued to treat economic and social rights light-handedly as rights of lesser importance. It progressively emerged that, at the universal level, the instrument for

---

[12] See the account given by Teitgen, 'Introduction to the European Convention on Human Rights', in Ronald St. J. MacDonald et al. (ed.), *The European System for the Protection of Human Rights* (Dordrecht, Martinus Nijhoff, 1993), 3.

[13] The draft Covenant on Human Rights was adopted at the fifth session of the HRCion in June 1949, see *Yearbook of the United Nations 1948–49*, at 538.

the protection of civil and political rights would be accompanied by a parallel instrument for the protection of economic, social, and cultural rights. For that reason, it was decided within the Council of Europe to establish a regime that would place economic and social rights, too, under European supervision. These efforts took shape in the European Social Charter, signed on 18 October 1961 in Turin. Although the Social Charter was meant to carry Europe a big step forward, it visibly reflects all the reluctance of its authors towards a firm guarantee of rights of that specific type. States parties did not have to commit themselves with regard to all the rights enunciated in the Charter, but just had to choose from a menu which was offered to them in Article 20 (now Article A of Part Three). Furthermore, in order to make it absolutely clear that the Charter did not contain any true individual entitlements, the drafters stated in Part III of the Appendix that the Charter 'contains legal obligations of an international character, the application of which is submitted solely to the supervision procedure provided for in Part IV thereof'—a reporting procedure entrusted in the first place to a Committee of Experts. A Protocol amending the Charter was signed in 1991.[14] It seeks to strengthen this rather weak supervisory machinery, but has not yet (December 2002) obtained the necessary approval by all states parties to the Charter. As far as the substance of the Charter is concerned, major changes have been introduced by the revised Charter, a text signed in 1996[15] but which seems to be viewed by numerous governments with some reluctance. Among the absentees are, for instance, Germany, Spain, and the United Kingdom. To date, no more than 15 instruments of ratification have been received.[16]

The Two UN Covenants on Human Rights

At the universal level, the HRCion had decided to move ahead in three stages. After the identification of the rights to be taken into account by the UDHR, the second step consisted of producing a binding legal instrument, i.e. an international treaty. The first question which arose in this connection was whether the future Covenant should at all contain economic and social rights. What had been done in drawing up the UDHR could not necessarily serve as a blueprint since the Declaration was a political instrument, while the task was now to frame hard and fast law. By GA Res. 421E (V), 4 December 1950, however, the General Assembly determined that indeed the link between the

---

[14] Of 21 September 1991, *ETS* No. 142.

[15] Of 3 May 1996, *ETS* No. 163.

[16] Attention is also drawn to an Additional Protocol, *ETS* No. 158, of 1995, introducing a system of collective complaints according to which international organizations of employers and trade unions as well as other international non-governmental organizations which have consultative status with the Council of Europe may lodge complaints alleging unsatisfactory application of the Charter (for details see *infra* p. 238).

two sets of rights should be maintained since they were 'interconnected and interdependent'. The next question was whether the unity between first generation and second generation rights should also be formally maintained or whether the package should be split up into two or more separate pieces. GA Res. 421E (V) had spoken of one covenant, 'the' Covenant, while progressively awareness grew that different methods of implementation were needed for different groups of rights. Called upon by the Economic and Social Council (ECOSOC) to revise its determination in favour of one single instrument,[17] the General Assembly responded positively to that request and eventually decided that there should be two Covenants.[18]

This decision, in political rhetoric often criticized as one of the major pitfalls of the drafting process but in reality no obstacle to the full recognition of economic and social rights, remained unchanged on the long road until the definitive adoption of the two Covenants. The HRCion completed its work in 1954. The drafts prepared by it were then sent to the General Assembly. In a time of rising tensions between East and West, no chance seemed to exist for a successful outcome of the exercise. It was eventually pressure brought to bear upon the two antagonistic blocs which secured the approval by the General Assembly on 16 December 1966. By contrast to what had happened 18 years earlier when the UDHR had been adopted, this time the vote was not affected by any abstentions.[19]

Besides the International Bill of Human Rights, which is made up of the UDHR and the two Covenants, a multitude of other treaties and non-binding instruments exist. In the first place, the conventions combating discrimination must be mentioned, the International Convention on the Elimination of All Forms of Racial Discrimination (CERD, 1965) and the Convention on the Elimination of All Forms of Discrimination against Women (CEDAW, 1979). Other treaty instruments of paramount importance are the Convention against Torture and Other Cruel, Inhuman or Degrading Treatment or Punishment (CAT, 1984) and the Convention on the Rights of the Child (CRC, 1989). Additionally, the conventions seeking to outlaw and abolish slavery and similar practices deserve being counted as pertaining to the inner circle of human rights instruments.[20] Together with the two Covenants, these conventions form the core element of the legal tool kit for the protection of human rights at world level.[21]

---

[17] GA Res. 384 (XIII), 29 August 1951.

[18] GA Res. 543 (VI), 4 February 1952.

[19] GA Res. 2200A (XXI), 16 December 1966.

[20] See Dottridge and Weissbrodt, 'Review of the Implementation of and Follow-up to the Convention on Slavery', 42 *GYIL* (1999) 242.

[21] For a complete overview of all the existing treaties see Office of the High Commissioner for Human Rights, International Human Rights Instruments, http://www.unhchr.ch/html/intlinst.htm (visited December 2002).

American Convention on Human Rights

On the American continent, pride of place is given to the American Declaration of the Rights and Duties of Man, which was adopted at the Ninth International Conference of American States in Bogotá a few months before the UDHR in April/May 1948. A binding legal instrument for the protection of human rights, the American Convention on Human Rights (ACHR), came about many years later in 1969. This regional treaty is remarkable in its similarity with the ECHR and the CCPR. No specific political philosophy of Latin America can be gleaned from its text. However, the ACHR seeks to protect human life 'from the moment of conception' (Article 4(1)). Additionally, in a general clause (Article 26) all states parties pledge themselves to take measures for the full realization 'of the rights implicit in the economic, social, educational, scientific, and cultural standards set forth in the Charter of the Organization of American States'. Notwithstanding the existence of this sweeping clause, the Member States of the OAS decided that more specific detail was needed for the effective protection of such rights. For that reason, in 1988 they adopted a protocol[22] which complements the ACHR by a second pillar, following in that regard the existing models at world level and within the European context.

African Charter of Human and Peoples' Rights

Lastly, the African Charter of Human and Peoples' Rights of 1981 (the so-called Banjul Charter, AfCHPR) should be mentioned. Its originality resides in the fact that it deals at the same time with individual human rights and collective rights of peoples. Concerning human rights proper, it sets forth not only classical liberal rights, but also a limited number of economic and social rights such as the right to work, the right to health, and the right to education.[23] A few years ago, the commitment of the African states to human rights was solemnly renewed in the Grand Bay Declaration, a resolution adopted at a summit meeting of the OAU in April 1999.[24]

No Regional Instrument in Asia

Concerning Asia, to date no regional instrument has come into being. This failure is due not only to political difficulties, but also to the fact

[22] Additional Protocol to the American Convention on Human Rights in the Area of Economic, Social and Cultural Rights, 14 November 1988, 28 *ILM* (1989) 161.
[23] See Anselm Odinkalu, 'Analysis of Paralysis or Paralysis by Analysis? Implementing Economic, Social, and Cultural Rights Under the African Charter on Human and Peoples' Rights', 23 *HRQ* (2001) 327.
[24] http://ncb.intnet.mu/mfa/oau/decpl.htm (visited December 2002).

that Asia is a continent which lacks cultural homogeneity.[25] The Arab countries are a world apart, and although their endeavours to produce a human rights instrument came to fruition in 1994, the Arab Charter of Human Rights,[26] the outcome of their joint efforts has not attracted any ratifications to date.[27] India views itself almost as a continent with a rich intellectual heritage, and China, the Middle Kingdom, has always considered that it is the true centre of the world.[28] Japan, too, has a distinct cultural identity which can by no means be equated with Chinese culture. Not only do historical and ethnic traditions compete with one another, Asia is also divided by the different religions of its peoples. Given such divergencies, there is not the slightest prospect that one day an Asian convention on human rights reflecting a specific Asian civilization might see the light of the day.

Customary Law

The classical doctrine of customary law, as it is reflected in the *North Sea Continental Shelf* judgment of the ICJ,[29] does not easily lend itself to identifying rules in the field of human rights. Whereas relations between states can be observed by empirical means, the way in which states behave in their dealings with individual citizens escapes such methods. On the global plane, every second millions of contacts occur. Not even the most sophisticated electronic mechanism would be able to capture and register the human rights-specific features of all of these relationships. Therefore, emphasis must be placed on official acts and statements. In particular, in order to get hold of the relevant practice and *opinio juris*, the observer, following in that regard the methodology relied upon by the ICJ in its *Nicaragua* judgment,[30] must closely verify to what extent states present their practices as fully corresponding to the international rule of law or whether they simply deny charges brought against them. Even massive abuses do not militate against assuming a customary rule as long as the responsible author state seeks to hide and conceal its objectionable conduct instead of justifying it by invoking legal

[25] Thakur, 'Global Norms and International Humanitarian Law: An Asian Perspective', 83 (841) *IRRC* (2001) 19, at 20.

[26] Text: 18 *HRLJ* (1997) 151; for a comment see Mahiou, 'La Charte arabe des droits de l'homme', in *Mélanges offerts à Hubert Thierry. L'évolution du droit international* (Paris, Pedone, 1998), 305.

[27] An-Na'im, 'Human Rights in the Arab World: A Regional Perspective', 23 *HRQ* (2001) 701, at 714.

[28] See Onuma, 'Towards an Intercivilizational Approach to Human Rights', 7 *Asian Yearbook of International Law* (1997) 21, at 31.

[29] ICJ Reports (1969) 3, at 43–44.

[30] *Military and Paramilitary Activities in and against Nicaragua (Nicaragua v United States of America), Merits*, ICJ Reports (1986) 14, at 106–109.

reasons. According to this method, there exists today broad agreement to the effect that many of the rules enunciated in the UDHR have crystallized as customary law, in particular the right to life, the prohibition of torture, which is the reverse side of a right to physical integrity, the protection of personal freedom, and the prohibition of discrimination on racial grounds.[31] This list of rights and/or forbidden acts and activities is not so much based on actual stocktaking of the relevant state practice but rather on deductive reasoning: if human life and physical integrity were not protected, the entire idea of a legal order would collapse.[32] In searching for customary norms, additional clues can be gained, for instance, from a comparison between the UDHR and the CCPR: rights set forth in the first one of these instruments but omitted from the latter—such as the right to asylum, the right to a nationality as well as the right of ownership—do not easily qualify as having acquired a customary foundation. Over the years, the circle of custom-based rights may increase mainly through discourse in the relevant monitoring bodies, much less through real deeds supported by *opinio juris*. As pointed out above, the student finds himself here in an area where the orthodox rules on the formation of customary rules cannot be usefully resorted to.[33]

It is generally assumed to date that the core rights, which are directly related to human existence, are to be classified as *jus cogens*, i.e. as rules from which no derogation is permitted. An unchallengeable candidate for inclusion in this category is the ban on torture. It might appear at first glance that the right to life, too, must be accounted as *jus cogens*, since life conditions the enjoyment of all other rights. But life may lawfully be taken under certain factual circumstances, for example with a view to carrying out of a lawfully imposed death sentence or during armed conflict. Thus, only specific forms of interference with human life fall within the scope of *jus cogens*, like the prohibition of genocide, which consists of killing members of a given group of the population with intent to destroy that group. In its judgment

---

[31] See *Barcelona Traction, Light and Power Company*, ICJ Reports (1970) 3, at 32, para. 34, which mentions the prohibition of genocide as well as the basic rights of the human person, including protection from slavery and racial discrimination. The American Law Institute, *Restatement of the Law Third. The Foreign Relations Law of the United States* (St. Paul, Minn., American Law Institute, 1987), vol. 2, 161, para. 702, mentions as rules of customary law the prohibitions of genocide, slavery or slave trade, the murder or causing the disappearance of individuals, torture, prolonged arbitrary detention, systematic racial discrimination, or a consistent pattern of gross violations of internationally recognized human rights.

[32] See also Beyani, 'The Legal Premises for the International Protection of Human Rights', in *The Reality of International Law: Essays in Honour of Ian Brownlie* (Oxford, Clarendon Press, 1999), 21, at 31–34.

[33] For an attempt to take account of present-day developments by a 'reflective interpretive approach' see Roberts, 'Traditional and Modern Approaches to Customary International Law: A Reconciliation', 95 *AJIL* (2001) 757.

in the *Barcelona Traction* case, the ICJ indicated that certain particular serious forms of violation of human rights infringe obligations *erga omnes*,[34] a type of obligation which may *grosso modo* be equated with rules of *jus cogens*.[35]

Soft Law

The six instruments in treaty form referred to above have been supplemented at world level by a multitude of non-binding recommendations in the form of resolutions. The HRCion as well as the General Assembly have been particularly active in producing new sets of rules. Most of these instruments, however, do not deal with the human being as such, but purport to establish rules for specific areas or specific groups of persons, e.g. prison inmates, members of minorities, etc. All of these efforts to elevate the level of protection in situations where, according to practical experience, violations of human rights standards are likely to occur, have not only their legitimacy but also their usefulness. But they lack the paradigmatic significance in particular of the UDHR and the two Covenants, which have established the very simple—but also very demanding—proposition that every human being, just because he/she pertains to the human race, has a claim to certain basic rights permitting him/her to lead a life in dignity.

Despite their lack of bindingness proper, the many resolutions seeking to particularize specific human rights guarantees have a tremendous influence on the development of the law. Generally and almost ineluctably, domestic and international practice will adopt such resolutions as parameters guiding its actions. Progressively, then, a process of hardening into law can take place which one may either interpret as authentic interpretation of the relevant written rules or as the emergence of new rules of customary law. In any event, a lawyer acting in a dispute before an international body of adjudication would fail in his/her duties if he/she did not refer, in support of his/her arguments, to the existing soft law propositions, among which the general comments and recommendations of the monitoring bodies acquire an ever-growing weight.[36]

---

[34] ICJ Reports (1970) 3, at 32, paras 33, 34.

[35] See *infra* p. 196. Lists of human rights with *jus cogens* character have been established by Lauri Hannikainen, *Peremptory Norms (Jus Cogens) in International Law* (Helsinki, Finnish Lawyers' Publishing Company, 1988), at 425–520; Stefan Kadelbach, *Zwingendes Völkerrecht* (Berlin, Duncker & Humblot, 1992), at 284–315.

[36] See *infra* p. 156–158.

IV CONTENTS OF THE INTERNATIONAL BILL OF HUMAN RIGHTS

Substantive Provisions

It is not the aim of this book to comment in detail on the individual rights listed in the conventional instruments at universal or regional level. Therefore, only a few words will be devoted to this issue. The content of the CCPR offers no great surprise to a reader who is familiar with the UDHR and the traditions of national constitutions which have embraced the classical liberal model. To a large extent, it resembles also the ECHR. Later, the ACHR followed the same path. One finds in these instruments all of the guarantees shielding the human person from governmental interference and additionally a number of political rights of participation in public affairs. In one important respect the CCPR surpasses its regional predecessor at the European level. It sets forth a right of minority protection (Article 27) which is unknown to the ECHR as well as to the ACHR. At the European level, the ECHR originally contained no more than a modest non-discrimination clause in Article 14 where it forbade discrimination on ground of 'association with a national minority'. Only in recent years has this backlog been overcome by the adoption of two courageous instruments, the European Charter for Regional or Minority Languages[37] and the Framework Convention for the Protection of National Minorities.[38]

The CESCR essentially repeats the provisions already enunciated in the UDHR, but adapts them to the needs of application by public authorities. No new rights were added. Obviously, there is much room for development if policy determinations are made to extend the protection afforded to the weaker classes of the population. In that regard, the revised European Social Charter[39] holds a pioneering position. Other social rights are included in instruments such as the CEDAW or the CRC.

Rights and Obligations under Human Rights Treaties

There can be no doubt that human rights treaties like all other international treaties are binding on states parties. But the degree of bindingness may be different. This difference reflects on the position of the individual. Only if clearly definable duties are imposed on states can subjective rights of the human beings concerned arise. In that regard, the classical human rights of the first generation bear all the characteristics of hard and fast law. Under the

[37] Of 5 November 1992, *ETS* No. 148. [38] Of 1 February 1995, *ETS* No. 157.
[39] *Supra* n. 15.

ECHR and the ACHR, in particular, states are required to ensure specific results. By contrast, human rights of the second generation are generally framed in much softer terms.

Regarding the degree of bindingness of the two International Covenants, the difference between them is considerable. As far as the CCPR is concerned, the rights it encompasses are conceived of as strict obligations which states parties simply must abide by. In unambiguous language, Article 2(1) provides that states parties undertake to respect and to ensure to all individuals within their territory and subject to their jurisdiction the rights recognized in the instrument. This does not mean that the CCPR lacks any kind of flexibility. Almost all of the rights it sets forth are accompanied by limitation clauses which permit reduction in their scope depending on the existing social needs. However, all of these clauses must be construed under a strict requirement of proportionality. Some of these clauses specify explicitly that any restriction must be necessary (for instance: Articles 12(3); 18(3); 19(3); 21; 22(2)), some add that the yardstick of necessity must be gauged within the context of a 'democratic society' (Articles 14(1); 21; 22(2)), in a number of provisions reference is made to 'arbitrary' restrictions (Articles 9(1); 12(4); 17(1)), and Article 25 speaks of 'unreasonable restrictions'. In other instances, it may be doubtful, given the absence of a limitation clause, whether any restrictions are admissible. In any event, whatever the formulations, the HRCee has taken the view that any legitimate restriction must be in accordance with the requirements warranted in a democratic society.[40] Many decisions have touched upon borderline situations in this regard. Generally, the HRCee has proved to be a staunch supporter of political freedoms.[41] It is understandable, on the other hand, that the HRCee could not keep its unity on such delicate issues as the criminalization of speech denying the holocaust as a historical fact.[42]

A comparison with the CESCR demonstrates the wide conceptual divergence between the two instruments. The introductory clause of Article 2(1) is quite telling. It reads:

Each state party to the present Covenant undertakes to take steps, individually and through international assistance and co-operation, especially economic and technical, to the maximum of its available resources, with a view to achieving progressively the full realization of the rights recognized in the present Covenant by all appropriate means, including particularly the adoption of legislative measures.

[40] See General Comment No. 29: States of Emergency (Article 4), 24 July 2001, UN doc. CCPR/C/21/Rev.1/Add.11, 31 August 2001: 'the principle of proportionality which is common to derogation and limitation powers.'

[41] See from the recent case law final views in *Kim v Republic of Korea*, 3 November 1998, [1999] II Report of the HRCee, UN doc. A/54/40, 1; *Tae Hoon Park v Republic of Korea*, 20 October 1998, ibid. at 85 (in both cases illegitimate interference with freedom of expression).

[42] See final views in *Faurisson v France*, 8 November 1996, [1997] II Report of the HRCee, UN doc. A/52/40, 84.

Whereas the CCPR requires strict compliance with its stipulations, essentially its sister instrument boils down to a promotional obligation which, furthermore, is not owed to the individuals concerned. In fact, a close reading of the 'rights' listed in the CESCR reveals that it deliberately refrains from establishing true individual rights. Regarding the right to work, for instance, which is 'recognized' in Article 6(1), the obligations to be shouldered by states parties are specified in the second paragraph of the same provision. They are described as comprising steps for the full realization of this right, but do not refer to any individual person. What states have to do is stimulate economic activities in such a way that generally opportunities of full employment increase.

The term 'promotional obligation' should not be misunderstood, however. It connotes a genuine legal obligation.[43] But the drafters of the ESCR were aware of the factual elements conditioning performance of the commitments undertaken by states. Economic and social rights are to a large degree context-dependent, more than civil liberties. They have as their backdrop a concept of the state as a potent provider, but with the proviso that the duties owed to citizens can never be set out in absolute terms, but must take into account the scarcity of resources which any human community has to reckon with.

What is true in general, does not provide the full picture, however. Some of the provisions of the CESCR permit a different reading. Article 8 recognizes trade union rights, which are also set forth in the CCPR. No plausible reason exists which could explain why under the CESCR freedom to form and join trade unions should not be a right susceptible of immediate application. Other rights listed in the CESCR are more in the nature of classical liberal freedoms, in particular Article 13(3) and (4), which guarantees certain rights regarding the choice of schools, and Article 15(3), a provision setting forth freedom for scientific research and creative activity.[44] These rights belong to the classical liberal heritage. It is significant, in this regard, that the text of these provisions does not refer to national measures of implementation which, indeed, are not necessary to the extent that governments are simply enjoined to respect individual freedom.[45]

Additionally, some of the rights which are usually called economic or social rights imply a duty of the state to respect the individual's own efforts.

[43] See CESCRCee, General Comment No. 3 (1990), 'The Nature of States Parties' Obligations', in *Compilation of General Comments and General Recommendations Adopted by the Human Rights Treaty Bodies*, UN doc. HR/GEN/1/Rev. 5, 26 April 2001, 18, paras 1, 2, 19.

[44] Rightly stressed by the CESCRCee, ibid. at para. 5.

[45] See the list of provisions which, according to the view of the ESCRCee, are capable of being directly applied. The following Articles are mentioned: 3, 7(a)(i), 8, 10(3), 13(2)(a), (3) and (4), 15(3), see General Comment No. 3, adopted at 5th session (1990), para. 5, in *Compilation, supra* n. 43, at 18.

Regarding the right to work, in particular, the most important facet may be the obligation of the state not to interfere with the professional activity deployed by persons desirous of earning their own living.[46] Such prohibitions were a weapon in current use in socialist countries. Since the state was in control of the entire economy, it was easy for the governmental power apparatus to persecute dissidents by pushing them down to the lowest levels of the national workforce.[47] The 'duty to respect' is all the more important since it constitutes a liberal element suited to remove the suspicion that social and economic rights lead to huge bureaucracies which eventually end up suppressing the freedom of the individual by their sheer factual weight.[48]

Lastly, some of the rights which normally require just general efforts of governments to bring about a state of affairs in which the relevant rights can be realized, may be considered to contain minimum entitlements ('minimal core content') which may be asserted by individuals as true subjective rights.[49] Thus, the right to life (Article 6 CCPR) in conjunction with the right to an adequate standard of living (Article 11 CESCR) should protect everyone against starvation. Proceeding from this premise, the AfHPRCion established in *Union Interafricaine des Droits de l'Homme v Zaire* a violation of the right to health since the state failed to provide safe drinking water, electricity and medicines.[50] It is certainly true that Article 11 constitutes one of the least felicitous provisions of the CESR. No government is in a position to secure a 'continuous improvement of living conditions'. One may even go so far as to say that Article 11 is predicated on a basic misunderstanding of the relationship between the human being and its natural environment.

---

[46] See the case of *Annette Pagnoulle (on behalf of Abdoulaye Mazou) v Cameroon*, decided by the AfHPRCion, where a magistrate who had been imprisoned without trial failed to be reinstated while others were, referred to by Naldi, 'The OAU's Grand Bay Declaration on Human Rights in Africa in Light of the Practice of the AfHPRCion', 60 *ZaöRV* (2000) 715, at 720.

[47] For the persecution of the members of 'Charter 77' in Czechoslovakia see *infra* p. 233.

[48] Eide, 'Economic and Social Rights', in Janusz Symonides (ed.), *Human Rights: Concept and Standards* (Aldershot and Burlington/Paris, Ashgate and UNESCO, 2000), 109, at 126–128.

[49] See the ground-breaking article by Philip Alston, 'Out of the Abyss: The Challenges Confronting the New UN Committee on Economic, Social and Cultural Rights', 9 *HRQ* (1987) 332, which was essentially based on para. 25 of the 'Limburg Principles', 37 *Review of the International Commission of Jurists* (1986) 43, adopted by an expert meeting convened by the International Commission of Jurists in 1986: 'States parties are obligated, regardless of the level of economic development, to ensure respect for minimum subsistence rights for all.' This doctrine is now reflected in General Comment No. 3 of the CESCRCee, *supra* n. 43, at para. 10. See now also the 'Maastricht Guidelines on Violations of Economic, Social and Cultural Rights', 20 *HRQ* (1998) 691. For a general assessment see Jörg Künzli, *Zwischen Rigidität und Flexibilität: Der Verpflichtungsgrad internationaler Menschenrechte* (Berlin, Duncker & Humblot, 2001), at 283–287.

[50] Referred to by Naldi, *supra* n. 46, at 720.

However, every government, except in circumstances of a national calamity of wide dimensions, should be able to provide a minimum of food to its citizens in order to avoid death by famine.

A few other rights are so essential for a human life in dignity that they should also be acknowledged as true individual rights. Among them figures certainly the right to elementary education, to which priority is given by Article 13(2)(a) CESCR.[51] A child or adolescent who is denied even the ability to read and to write will be handicapped during all his/her life. In industrialized societies of today, it is almost impossible for a human being to attain an adequate position in society as an illiterate person. Again, this is a service which any organization claiming to be a state must be able to discharge for the benefit of its citizens.[52] By contrast, other services, which may have a similarly vital importance for everyone, are of a more sophisticated nature and require the putting into place of complex administrative structures, a challenge which may simply exceed the management capabilities of a developing nation. Thus, the right to social security (Article 9 CESCR) constitutes a pivotal element in any society since it ensures the dignity of the aging generation. But systems of social security must be operated for decades in different political and economic circumstances. In particular, they are based on an expectation of monetary stability over long periods. People who pay their first contributions at a young age must have the confidence that the system will still work when they go into retirement many decades later. In any event, a judge could never enforce a retirement pension if no system exists to which such a claim could be related. To date, many countries still lack such systems not because of any bad will of their governments, but because the launching of social security, albeit on a small scale, has proved too complex and onerous for the available resources. Asbjörn Eide has suggested, though, that even in developing countries based on a subsistence economy alternative strategies may be available.[53]

Equality and Non-discrimination

Background

Equality does not fit into the classification scheme which distinguishes between first generation and second generation rights. But it provides a legal standard which is intimately related to the very concept of human rights. If human rights accrue to every human being, without any additional requirements, discrimination and exclusion cannot be tolerated. And yet

---

[51] See Eide, *supra* n. 48, at 122.
[52] See also General Comment No. 13 of the ESCRCee (1999), in *Compilation*, *supra* n. 43, at 74.
[53] Eide, *supra* n. 48, at 149.

human history is characterized by a continuous fight against negative differentiations. Even after the First World War 'enlightened' European nations were not prepared to grant the same rights as in the metropolitain areas to the inhabitants of their colonies. Racial discrimination was rampant. It required great efforts to abolish the discriminatory system of voting rights based on wealth as it existed, e.g., until 1918 in England (no general parliamentary franchise for males and no right of vote at all for women) and Prussia (distribution of the electorate in three classes according to their tax contributions, each class having the same balloting power). When in 1933 Hitler came into power in Germany, the evil Nazi Empire persecuted the Jewish people by a criminal policy of genocide. Notwithstanding the horrors of the Second World War, racial discrimination continued to be practised in a number of countries. Racial segregation existed in the United States to the detriment of black Americans until the mid-1960s, and the Apartheid regime in South Africa, which was institutionalized in 1948, came to its end only after the fall of the white minority regime in 1993–1994. Likewise, until gaining independence, people in colonial territories lived under a trauma of inequality, compared to the status of their colonizers. At the same time, all of the socialist regimes in central and eastern Europe were openly based on political discrimination. And there remained still another major group of human beings suffering a denial of rights in many fields of life: women.[54] In France, women received full voting rights only in 1944.[55] Not without justification has it been contended that human rights, as they were proclaimed by the first classical human rights instruments, were rights of white adult males only.[56]

All these instances of disregard for the rights of certain groups explain the emphasis placed by their members on the principle of equality and non-discrimination. It is no wonder, in particular, that for Third World countries the fight against racial discrimination and Apartheid became one of their primary goals as soon as they had found access to the United Nations as newly independent states. Today it can be said that this battle has been won, although it requires renewed efforts at any moment.[57] On the other hand,

[54] See Fraser, 'Becoming Human: The Origins and Development of Women's Human Rights', 21 *HRQ* (1999) 853; von Senger, 'From the Limited to the Universal Concept of Human Rights: Two Periods of Human Rights', in Wolfgang Schmale (ed.), *Human Rights and Cultural Diversity* (Goldbach, Keip Publishing, 1993), 47, at 52–55.

[55] See Lenoir, 'The Representation of Women in Politics: From Quotas to Parity in Elections', 50 *ICLQ* (2001) 217.

[56] See, for instance, von Senger, 'Chinese Culture and Human Rights', in Schmale, *supra* n. 54, at 285, 315.

[57] van Boven, 'Discrimination and Human Rights Law: Combating Racism', in Sandra Fredman (ed.), *Discrimination and Human Rights: The Case of Racism* (Oxford, Oxford University Press, 2001), 111, points to other groups victims of deep-seated discrimination: Sinti and Roma, Dalits, indigenous peoples, and uprooted people, held under practices similar to slavery.

the quest for equality has not prevented a number of African nations from making explicit reservation for discrimination that exists under customary (tribal) law.[58] Likewise, women's fight for full equality with men has not yet reached its ultimate goal. Although most states subscribe to the postulate of gender equality, to date most Muslim nations do not share this philosophy. They have either avoided ratifying the relevant international instruments, or they have sought to keep their sovereign freedom in that regard by entering far-reaching reservations regarding the clauses that provide for equality between men and women.

Legal Instruments Banning Discrimination

Where equality and non-discrimination have been introduced in domestic contexts, these precepts apply pursuant to the relevant legal texts mostly across the board whenever state authorities act vis-à-vis the citizen. No differentiation takes place according to the subject matter concerned. Of course, the legal position is not necessarily reflected in hard facts. Under international treaty regimes, however, equality and non-discrimination are normally confined to a specific field of application. Two techniques are in current use.

On the one hand, discrimination on account of specifically identified grounds may be prohibited in all fields of life. Under the CERD[59] any kind of racial discrimination is forbidden (Article 2(1)(a)). Furthermore, states parties pledge to 'bring to an end, by all appropriate means, including legislation as required by circumstances, racial discrimination by any persons, group or organization' (Article 2(1)(d)). Similarly, the CEDAW condemns discrimination against women and additionally enjoins states parties to take affirmative action with a view to eliminating patterns of discrimination in society, in particular in the fields of education and employment (Articles 10, 11). It is significant, on the other hand, that discrimination based on religious grounds, though being addressed by a General Assembly resolution,[60] has not been translated into an international treaty. This lack of conventional consolidation demonstrates the lack of agreement which in this regard obtains in the international community.

On the other hand, a treaty for the protection of human rights may be confined to regulating a specific area of societal activity and may prohibit within that area any unreasonable distinction. Thus, the UNESCO Convention against Discrimination in Education[61] pronounces a ban on any

---

[58] See Ibhawoh, 'Between Culture and Constitution: Evaluating the Cultural Legitimacy of Human Rights in the African State', 22 *HRQ* (2000) 838, at 844, 851.

[59] Adopted by GA Res. 2106 (XX), 21 December 1965.

[60] Declaration on the Elimination of All Forms of Intolerance and of Discrimination Based on Religion or Belief, proclaimed by GA Res. 36/55, 25 November 1981.

[61] Adopted on 14 December 1960 by the General Conference of UNESCO.

discrimination based on race, colour, sex, language, religion, political or other opinion, national or social origin, economic condition or birth in the field of education. ILO Convention No. 111 concerning Discrimination in Respect of Employment and Occupation[62] pursues a similar objective. Concerning the two International Covenants of 1966, Article 2(2) CESCR provides that 'the rights enunciated in the present Covenant' may be exercised without discrimination of any kind. Reference is made by that clause to race, colour, sex, language, religion, political or other opinion, national or social origin, property, birth or other status. It is clearly discernible, therefore, that this clause has no autonomous role to play. It applies only in conjunction with one of the other rights guaranteed by the CESCR.

Article 2(2) CESCR provides a vast potential for dynamic development of the CESCR. Notwithstanding the fact that many of the rights enunciated by the CESCR do not bring into being individual entitlements, the non-discrimination clause permits everyone to invoke for his/her benefit parallel entitlements that have been set forth at national level but from which he/she has been excluded. To a very wide extent, the CESCR leaves it to states parties to decide how they wish to implement the obligations they have undertaken in the field of economic and social rights. Once, however, a legal regime is established it is subject to the principles of equality and non-discrimination. As from that moment, no state can argue that it was only bound to effectuate the relevant rights progressively. It loses the protection of Article 2(2) CESCR against individual claims.

The ECHR, too, contains no more than an auxiliary clause on equality and non-discrimination, which applies to 'the rights and freedoms set forth in this Convention' (Article 14). According to Protocol No. 12 to the ECHR,[63] the prohibition of non-discrimination would by extension apply generally in an autonomous fashion. However, although the Member States of the Council of Europe drew up this Protocol, they have shown great caution in entering into binding commitments. To date (September 2003), only five instruments of ratification have been deposited. Consequently, the Protocol is not yet in force.

Regarding the CCPR, the legal position raises more delicate issues. The CCPR contains two non-discrimination clauses, the first one worded exactly like the clause of the CESCR just referred to (Article 2(1)), the second one, however (Article 26), lacking any literal connection with the other rights set forth by the CCPR. According to its text, it establishes equality and non-discrimination as general principles.

It was a big challenge for the HRCee under the CCPR to construe this dichotomy in a way that would make sense of both clauses. Obviously,

---

[62] Adopted on 25 June 1958 by the General Conference of ILO.
[63] *ETS* No. 177, 4 November 2000.

the two propositions are contradictory if Article 26 is indeed understood as a general principle commanding equality and non-discrimination in all fields of life. With a view to resolving the issue, the Committee could have concluded that Article 26 goes beyond the scope *ratione materiae* of the CCPR in requiring that any law or regulation in force must be applied to all who are addressed by it without any unreasonable distinctions. However, it rejected that construction. In three famous views in the cases of *Broeks, Danning,* and *Zwaan-de Vries* it opined that Article 26 had to be taken literally.[64] Disregarding aspects of systematic interpretation which suggest that its function is generally confined to that of a body called upon to defend and protect civil and political rights, it held that it was authorized to measure the lawfulness of state conduct also in respect of economic and social rights and anywhere else, without any limitation *ratione materiae.* In a first reaction, the Dutch Government found those views so shocking that it seriously considered denouncing the OP-CCPR in order to ratify it again with a reservation excluding Article 26 from its acceptance.[65]

Its bold jurisprudence has led the HRCee into many difficulties. To date, the biggest number of cases complaining of a violation of Article 26 CCPR has reached the HRCee from the Netherlands. In many instances, the Committee has examined whether under Dutch legislation social benefits or the pensions of widows/widowers had been fairly calculated in comparison with the benefits or pensions of other persons with a slightly different curriculum vitae. There can be no doubt that by embarking on this road the Committee has not only construed the CCPR in the widest possible sense, but has also placed its working capacity under heavy strain. Should lawyers in more countries become aware of the opportunities provided by this expansive jurisprudence, the Committee would soon become a body for the settlement of tax disputes, the highest tax court at universal level. Indeed, in every country tax law is founded on a myriad of distinctions. Obviously, such a development would have disastrous consequences for the Committee. It should therefore critically review its jurisprudence, realizing, in particular, that if it sticks to the course it has now been steering for 15 years, it must as a minimum return to the text of Article 26, which does not prohibit just any distinction, but refers to discrimination based on criteria of 'status'.[66]

---

[64] Final views of 9 April 1987, II *Yearbook of the HRCee* (1987) 293, at 297 and 300.
[65] See Manfred Nowak, *UN Covenant on Civil and Political Rights: CCPR Commentary* (Kehl et al., Engel, 1993), at 461, para. 7.
[66] See 'The Human Rights Committee's Jurisprudence on Article 26—A Pyrrhic Victory?', in *The Human Rights Committee after 25 Years* (forthcoming, 2003).

The Unity, and the Difference in Character, of First Generation and Second Generation Rights

There can be no doubt that all three sets of rights are necessary for a life in full dignity. A person close to starvation is not satisfied by the right he/she has to mourn his/her fate in public speech. It is clear also that youths who are denied any education and who do not learn how to write and to read will almost certainly end up at the bottom of society. Liberal rights alone do not ensure the development of the personality of the individual. And yet, substantive differences do exist between first generation and second generation rights.

As a matter of principle, these differences can easily be identified. Essentially, civil and political rights demand of the state no more than to abstain from conduct violating these rights (duty to respect). Religious service must not be disturbed, state agents must abstain from mistreating and torturing prisoners in their custody, critical articles in the media may not be pleasant for a government, but it is not allowed to take any sanctions against a newspaper or a TV station which disseminates such criticism.

It has rightly been observed, however, that such examples do not exhaust the full meaning of obligations deriving for states from civil liberties. Already in the classical texts from the end of the eighteenth century, claims for judicial protection formed a key element. Judicial protection presupposes the existence of judicial machinery. A judicial system must be organized, judges must be appointed, and all of this must be financed. An attitude of passivity would not comply with the exigencies as they are today laid down in Article 6 ECHR or in Article 14 CCPR. Additionally, the jurisprudence of all the bodies called upon to monitor compliance with human rights has established duties of protection. Concerning the right to life, for instance, this duty is hinted in the text of Article 6(1) CCPR by the words: 'This right shall be protected by law.' It is not enough for a state, however, to enact laws which make homicide and murder a punishable offence. Over and beyond such legislative measures, it is required to take actual steps of enforcement with a view to preventing violations of the right to life or, if a violation could not be averted, to punishing the perpetrator(s). Similar comments can be made regarding torture. To be sure, the obligation incumbent on states (Article 7 CCPR; Article 3 ECHR) is framed in terms of a duty of abstention. But governments must take active steps that are suitable to ensure that indeed their obligation is effectively complied with by all their authorities. This comprehensive duty of protection extends also to other rights, for instance, the right to freedom of assembly[67] or the rights to one's private and home

---

[67] ECtHR, *Plattform 'Ärzte für das Leben'*, 21 June 1988, A 139, 12, para. 32.

life.[68] Particular emphasis is also placed by international humanitarian law on the duty of states to respect and ensure the applicable rules.[69]

According to the jurisprudence of the ECtHR, another consequence of the duty of protection incumbent upon states is the need to carry out an investigation if core human rights (in particular: right to life and physical integrity) have been allegedly violated by state agents.[70] Such procedural consequences constitute an essential component of the duty of protection. It may be said, therefore, that the gap existing between civil and political rights, on the one hand, and economic, social and cultural rights, on the other, has to some extent been closed. Still, the fact that many paths cross the demarcation line between the two classes of rights should not obscure the realization that the bulk of the obligations incumbent upon a state under the heading of civil and political rights can be discharged just by adopting an attitude of passivity.

The difference in substance between first generation and second generation rights has deep-going repercussions for the relevant procedures of implementation. It is obvious that judicial or quasi-judicial procedures are not well suited for the vindication of economic, social, and cultural rights. Since under the CESCR these rights are to be realized progressively, and since in general the CESCR refrains from setting forth true individual entitlements, it is hard to see how a judicial body could adjudicate claims for the grant of social benefits on the sole basis of that instrument, without having to rely on complementary domestic legislation. However, the distinctions already referred to must be borne in mind. There exists a 'duty to respect' even with regard to economic and social rights. As far as minimum core obligations are concerned, any community claiming to be a state must be able to provide them. To that extent, a complaint procedure would be perfectly viable. Most social benefits, however, must be organized and managed at domestic level. They can become operative only after states have enacted implementing legislation. Additionally, their effectiveness depends on the availability of a sufficient amount of public funds. Freedom of speech has no such factual preconditions. There will always be enough air for a person to express his/her views irrespective of the state of the economy of the country concerned. In sum, some of the social rights guaranteed in the CSECR, in particular the right to work, remain essentially (binding) guidelines for implementation at national level rather than genuine individual entitlements.

[68] ECtHR, *Hatton*, 2 October 2001, paras 95–107 (protection against aircraft noise), with comment by Smith, 96 *AJIL* (2002) 696.

[69] See Boisson de Chazournes and Condorelli, 'Common Article 1 of the Geneva Conventions Revisited: Protecting Collective Interests', 82 (837) *IRRC* (2000) 67.

[70] See below, chapter 12.

V THIRD GENERATION RIGHTS

Human rights of the third generation are sometimes also called 'solidarity rights'. The most prominent examples of such alleged rights are the right to peace, the right to development and the right to a clean (healthful) environment. None of these rights has solid legal foundations in a legal instrument of worldwide applicability. At the regional level, however, the AfCHPR has proclaimed the right to development (Article 22), the right to peace and security (Article 23) as well as the right to a 'general satisfactory environment' (Article 24).

The Three Rights

Right to Development

The right to development, the intellectual authorship of which is attributed to the Senegalese lawyer Kéba Mbaye,[71] was first affirmed in a number of resolutions of the HRCion. In Res. 5 (XXXV) of 2 March 1979 the Commission 'reiterated' that the right to development was a human right. A more stringent note was struck by the General Assembly, which, by GA Res. 36/133 of 14 December 1981, characterized the right to development as an 'inalienable' human right. Eventually, the General Assembly adopted a Declaration on the Right to Development by GA Res. 41/128 of 4 December 1986. Article 1 of that Declaration provides:

The right to development is an inalienable human right by virtue of which every human person and all peoples are entitled to participate in, contribute to, and enjoy economic, social, cultural and political development, in which all human rights and fundamental freedoms can be fully realized.

Clearly, this text mirrors the earlier text of Article 28 of the Universal Declaration.

As it is defined in GA Res. 41/128, the right to development appears as an aggregate right which draws its substance from the other instruments which set forth human rights and fundamental freedoms with binding effect.[72]

---

[71] 'Le droit au développement comme un droit de l'homme', 2–3 *Revue des droits de l'homme* (1972) 503. African authors have contributed a great deal to clarifying the meaning and scope of the right to development, see in particular Abi-Saab, 'The Legal Formulation of a Right to Development', in René-Jean Dupuy (ed.), *The Right to Development at the International Level* (Alphen aan den Rijn, Sijthoff & Noordhoff, 1980), 159; Bedjaoui, 'The Right to Development', in id. (ed.), *International Law: Achievements and Prospects* (Paris and Dordrecht et al., UNESCO and Martinus Nijhoff, 1991), 1177.

[72] For a recent appraisal see Baxi, 'The Development of the Right to Development', in Janusz Symonides (ed.), *Human Rights: New Dimensions and Challenges* (Aldershot et al. and Paris, Ashgate and UNESCO, 1998), 99.

Because of its extremely wide scope, it met with a large amount of scepticism on the part of Western states in particular. At the Vienna World Conference on Human Rights in 1993, the United States for the first time accepted the concept of a right to development. Thereafter, for many years working groups established by the HRCion have attempted to clarify in more detail its legal connotation. To date, all these efforts have proved of no avail. The latest resolution of the HRCion on the issue, dated 25 April 2002, again extends the mandate of a working group. Probably the time-honoured French adage applies here as well: *Qui trop embrasse, mal étreint*, which is tantamount to saying that whoever pursues too ambitious goals will eventually end up with empty hands.[73]

Right to Peace

The right to peace is the second candidate for a human right of the third generation. It also grew up within the HRCion, where it was first proclaimed in 1976. A next stage was reached when the General Assembly in 1978 adopted the Declaration on the Preparation of Societies for Life in Peace,[74] which affirmed that 'every nation and every human being... has the inherent right to life in peace'. The process of standard-setting came to its culmination in 1984 with the adoption of the Declaration on the Right of Peoples to Peace.[75] In the vote, not less than 34 states abstained even though the resolution solemnly proclaims 'that the peoples of our planet have a sacred right to peace'. After the demise of the communist regimes in central and eastern Europe, interest for this 'right' has faded away.[76] In recent years, resolutions of the General Assembly have abstained from referring to it.[77]

Right to a Clean Environment

The right to a clean or healthful environment, by contrast, has lost nothing of its original attractiveness. It was mentioned for the first time in the concluding Declaration adopted by the UN Conference on the Human

---

[73] For an optimistic assessment see, however, Udombana, 'The Third World and the Right to Development: Agenda for the Next Millennium', 22 *HRQ* (2000) 753.

[74] GA Res. 33/73, 15 December 1978.

[75] GA Res. 39/11, 12 November 1984.

[76] In praise of this right see Nastase, 'The Right to Peace', in Bedjaoui, *supra* n. 71, at 1219–1231.

[77] Cohen-Jonathan, 'De l'universalité des droits de l'homme', in *Ouvertures en droit international. Hommage à René-Jean Dupuy* (Paris, Pedone, 1998), 23, at 28, calls it an 'alibi' relied upon by states that wished to evade accountability concerning their human rights practices *stricto sensu*. Dimitrijevic, 'Human Rights and Peace', in Symonides, *supra* n. 72, 47, at 64, concludes that 'subsuming human rights under peace, or peace under human rights, is methodologically wrong and does not serve any meaningful educational or political purpose'. Recently, however, a revival has occurred, see GA Res. 57/216, 18 December 2002, which was adopted with 116 votes in favour to 53 against, with 14 abstentions.

Environment, held in June 1972 in Stockholm. Principle 1 of that Declaration starts out—in a politically incorrect fashion—with the words:

Man has the fundamental right to freedom, equality and adequate conditions of life, in an environment of a quality that permits a life of dignity and well-being.[78]

The Rio Declaration on Environment and Development of 14 June 1992[79] takes a more cautious approach in qualifying the relationship between humankind and its environment by stating that 'human beings... are entitled to a healthy and productive life in harmony with nature'. The Declaration refrains from speaking of a 'right' to a clean environment; rather, the duties of states to protect the natural environment are stressed. A total departure from an anthropocentric approach can be found in the World Charter for Nature, adopted by the General Assembly on 28 October 1982 (GA Res. 37/7), which asserts that nature—and with it humankind as a part of nature—'shall be respected'.

Uncertainties Surrounding Third Generation Rights

All human rights of the third generation are surrounded by deep-going uncertainties regarding their holders, the duty-bearers, and their substance.[80]

Holders of the Rights

According to the Declaration on the Right to Development, for instance, the right is vested in human beings and peoples alike, whereas the African Charter assigns it to peoples alone. As far as the right to peace is concerned, a glaring divergence springs to the eyes. Whereas the Declaration on the Preparation of Societies for a Life in Peace mentions nations and human beings side by side, the Declaration on the Right of Peoples to Peace confines itself to acknowledging a right of peoples to peace. As already pointed out, the right to a satisfactory environment is mentioned as a right of peoples only by the African Charter. Thus, the relevant instruments do not maintain a line of consistency. Generally, no great care is taken to specify to whom the benefits connected with the rights concerned should accrue. The arbitrariness with which these rights are bestowed upon individuals or collective entities amply demonstrates that the actual effects expected of them are not connected with their specific characteristics as rights under positive international law.

---

[78] See also GA Res. 45/94, 14 December 1990.

[79] 31 *ILM* (1992) 876.

[80] See Tomuschat, 'Human Rights in a World-Wide Framework', 45 *ZaöRV* (1985) 547, at 568–572; id., 'Rights of Peoples, Human Rights and their Relationship Within the Context of Western Europe' in Georges B. Kutukdjian and Antonio Papisca (eds), *Rights of Peoples— Droits des Peuples* (Padua, CEDAM, 1991), 61; id., 'Solidarity Rights (Development, Peace, Environment, Humanitarian Assistance)', 4 *EPIL* (2000) 460.

Duty Bearers

According to the ordinary understanding of the essence of a right, there must exist a duty as its corollary. Rights embody claims which another person is legally required to fulfil. Right and duty are just two sides of one and the same coin. In this regard, third generation rights have great weaknesses. Pursuant to the Declaration on the Right to Development, it is in particular states that have to strive for development by taking the steps necessary for that purpose. Translated into concrete terms this means that peoples are pitted against states, a dichotomy the legal implications of which are difficult to grasp. On the one hand, the relevant propositions could mean that peoples have rights against their own governments, which is in fact the tendency pursued by the Declaration of Algiers, a legal text drawn up by a private group of legal scholars in 1978;[81] or they could be interpreted to express the idea that poorer states have entitlements vis-à-vis other states, i.e. the international community. All this, however, does not fit easily into the traditional concept of international law where the international community as such has yet to find its proper place.

Contents

It is even more difficult to gain a clear picture of the content of third generation rights. Generally, all of the rights under discussion are extremely wide in scope. They do not set out specific measures and steps to be taken by states or governments, but enunciate comprehensive goals. As indicated by the Declaration on the Right to Development, development means a state of affairs permitting everyone to enjoy to their full extent 'all' rights and freedoms. Thus, development has a variety of components and constitutes an ideal situation that rests on a multitude of factual and legal elements many of which are not under the control of governments alone. Similar considerations apply to peace. Peace in the world depends on a wide array of factors, and it can be said that the entire system of the United Nations was established to ensure, in the first place, international peace and security. The effectiveness of the international mechanisms geared to ensure peaceful settlement of international disputes and to prevent wars from occurring is not enhanced by the creation or the recognition of a right of individuals or peoples to peace. The right to a clean and healthful environment, too, belongs to the same category of broadly framed rights, the content of which encompasses almost anything that has some bearing on the state of the environment. Agenda 21, the plan of action adopted by the Rio Conference in June 1992, constitutes in its printed version a book of not less than 400 pages.[82] It is in this plan of

---

[81] See Antonio Cassese (ed.), *Pour un droit des peuples. Essais sur la déclaration d'Alger* (Paris, Berger-Levrault, 1978).

[82] UN doc. A/CONF.151/26/Rev.1, vol. I, 14 June 1992.

action that the requirements of a healthy environment are spelled out in detail. However, it appears that no one has a legal right to demand that the many steps described therein be taken, since there exists no corresponding legal obligations, Agenda 21 having been conceived of as a political commitment only.

It is highly significant that not a single one of the rights of the third generation has to date received a clear profile. The fact that neither the holders of these rights, nor the corresponding duty bearers, nor the substance of the rights, have been unequivocally identified cannot simply be explained as accidental shortcomings which could without any difficulty be remedied by investing more of lawyers' skills and intelligence. The inference that must be drawn is obvious. It would be more correct to define third generation rights not as true rights, but rather as agreed objectives which the international community has pledged to pursue. Even so, they do not lose their juridical significance. They remain important signposts which mark the paths the international community should embark upon in conceiving and carrying out policies for the welfare of humankind as a whole. Indeed, individual human rights need a general framework of favourable conditions within which they can prosper. Any war threatens to lead to a total denial of individual rights by death and destruction. Although a state of affairs where everyone enjoys all the rights guaranteed by the UDHR and the two Covenants certainly guarantees peace, and in most instances also development, it has emerged that these macroconditions cannot be ensured from the microperspective of individual human rights. There is a clear necessity to work on both levels, establishing mechanisms for the vindication of individual rights, but attempting at the same time to ensure peace, development, and a clean and healthful environment on a global level where the issues related to these fields of action are tackled directly in all their complexity.

It is the recognition that human rights need a friendly and favourable environment which may also explain other initiatives which have sprung up in recent years. They are not placed under a heading of human rights, but they all are designed to build up that framework of security which is essential for individual rights to take their full effect.

VI DEMOCRACY

Democracy may not be a panacea to cure all ills, but it has its origins in the political rights of the individual as they are laid down in all conventional instruments, and on its part it also contributes to stabilizing and strengthening human rights. Article 21 UDHR contains everything that is conceivable in terms of political rights of the citizen in a democratic polity.

However, the word 'democracy' itself was carefully avoided. Concerning Article 25 CCPR, which reflects almost textually the earlier provision, the same observation can be made. Although the rights of democratic participation are fully covered, one vainly looks for the word 'democracy'. In some other places, though, in a somewhat hidden fashion, democratic standards are referred to. In the limitation clauses complementing the rights set forth in Articles 14(1), 21, and 22 CCPR, the requirements of a democratic society are mentioned as the criteria for the degree to which governmental interference may affect the substance of the rights concerned. Strangely enough, this yardstick makes no appearance in Article 19 CCPR, the guarantee of freedom of speech, which constitutes the paradigm of a democratic right. On this point, Article 10(2) ECHR is more consistent. Whatever the reasons for the apparent lack of logic in the CCPR may be, it makes clear that in 1966 the United Nations had not yet evolved a coherent concept of democratic governance.[83]

In recent years, this state of affairs has changed dramatically. Democracy is now explicitly acknowledged as the only legitimate form of governance. The origins of this development go once again back to the HRCion. At its spring session in 1999, the Commission adopted a resolution which affirmed in a fairly succinct way the basic principles of a democratic polity,[84] stressing in particular the interconnection between the democratic form of government and human rights by stating that 'democracy fosters the full realization of all human rights, and vice versa' (op. para. 1). One year later, the HRCion expanded the text considerably and included almost all the rights which are granted to citizens in a liberal state.[85] It is remarkable that the journey of this text did not end in the HRCion, which in spite of its expertise is a subordinate body within the World Organization, but found its way to the General Assembly where it was reviewed and eventually approved with only minor modifications.[86] A large majority supported this historic decision. A considerable number of states, however, abstained. The list of these abstentionists is highly revealing. It includes the following countries: Bahrain, Bhutan, Brunei Darussalam, China, Cuba, Democratic Republic of the Congo, Honduras, Laos, Libya, Maldives, Myanmar, Oman, Qatar, Saudi Arabia, Swaziland, Vietnam. Traditional monarchies march hand-in-hand with communist

[83] But see the article—written in 1992—by Franck, 'The Emerging Right to Democratic Governance', 86 *AJIL* (1992) 46. See further Gregory H. Fox and Brad R. Roth (eds), *Democratic Governance and International Law* (Cambridge, Cambridge University Press, 2000); Linos-Alexandre Sicilianos, *L'ONU et la démocratisation de l'Etat* (Paris, Pedone, 2000); Wheatley, 'Democracy in International Law: A European Perspective', 51 *ICLQ* (2002) 225.

[84] Res. 1999/57, 27 April 1999, Promoting and Consolidating Democracy.

[85] Res. 2000/47, 25 April 2000, Promoting and Consolidating Democracy.

[86] GA Res. 55/96, 4 December 2000, Promoting and Consolidating Democracy.

dictatorships and one or the other country which may have received wrong instructions from its capital.[87]

Given the weight of these 16 countries, it would be difficult to contend that democracy has become a binding standard under international customary law. China, in particular, cannot be brushed aside in the same way as an isolated vote of the Maldives would be ignored. Nonetheless, the posture taken by a large and almost overwhelming group of nations is a clear indication of the importance the international community attaches to the necessary environment of human rights. Human rights are part of a system of mutually supportive elements. To rely on them alone does not suffice to protect the human being from encroachments on his/her rights. A proper constitutional structure must provide the foundations of a polity where a life in dignity and self-fulfilment becomes an actual opportunity for everyone.[88]

At the European level, too, it was recognized that the complex mechanisms of the ECHR needed to be complemented by political monitoring efforts and expert advisory services in order to ensure the general framework within which human rights are located. For this purpose, in 1990 the Venice European Commission for Democracy was founded. It has assisted in particular the new Member States of the Council of Europe in building institutions that are permeated by a new spirit of democratic openness. Within the narrower context of the European Union, democracy figures prominently in the clause providing for structural homogeneity (Article 6(1) TEU).

VII GOOD GOVERNANCE

The considerations set out above are also the background of two more recent developments which seek to build up a framework for securing full enjoyment of human rights. It has been realized that a 'good life' depends not only on the basic principles upon which a system of government is predicated, but that the conduct of governmental elites and bureaucrats is a decisive factor in bringing the prevailing societal climate in a given state up to the level of the expectations raised by those principles. In this regard, international organizations and, in particular, the financial agencies of the international community have rightly started playing a role as defenders of public interest. Since 1989, the World Bank has evolved a doctrine of 'good governance', which it has described in the following terms:

[87] For comments on this progressive development see Sicilianos, 'Les Nations Unies et la démocratisation de l'Etat—nouvelles tendances', in Rostane Mehdi (ed.), *La contribution des Nations Unies à la démocratisation de l'Etat* (Paris, Pedone, 2002), 13; Tomuschat, 'L'intervention structurelle des Nations Unies', in ibid., 101.

[88] See Donnelly, 'Human Rights, Democracy, and Development', 21 *HRQ* (1999) 608, at 619–622.

Good governance is epitomized by predictable, open, and enlightened policy-making (that is, transparent processes); a bureaucracy imbued with a professional ethos; an executive arm of government accountable for its actions; and a strong civil society participating in public affairs; and all behaving under the rule of law.[89]

Other institutions have followed suit. For the International Monetary Fund, it was an almost natural move to adopt similar strategies. It uses negotiations for orderly exchange arrangements according to Article IV of its Statute to prevail upon Member States to adjust their policies to the requirements of good governance. The African Development Bank has recently adopted a 'Policy on Good Governance' which lists exactly the same headings, namely accountability, transparency, combating corruption, political participation of citizens, as well as legal and judicial reforms. This was done in response to the Grand Bay Declaration, adopted on 16 April 1999 by a summit meeting of the OAU,[90] which affirms the interdependence of the principles of good governance, the rule of law, democracy, and development (para. 3). Likewise, the European Community has included a clause to that effect in its latest agreement with the ACP (Africa, the Caribbean and the Pacific region) States (Article 9(3)).[91] Recently, the doctrine of good governance received its definitive benediction by its inclusion in the United Nations Millennium Declaration.[92] It is clear that a framework of good governance, if actually established, leads to a significantly increased effectiveness of human rights.

VIII HUMAN SECURITY

Almost at the same time when the World Bank evolved the concept of good governance, the United Nations Development Programme (UNDP) framed the doctrine of 'human security'.[93] For many decades, the concept of security was understood exclusively in a military sense. For the first time, the concept of human security made its appearance in the report of the Independent Commission on Disarmament and Security Issues (Palme Commission), issued in 1982.[94] After more than a decade, UNDP took up the ideas contained therein. In its 1993 Report it stressed that 'the individual must

---

[89] World Bank, *Governance: The World Bank's Experience* (Washington, 1994), at vii.
[90] http://ncb.intnet.mu/mfa/oau/decpl.htm (visited December 2002).
[91] Cotonou Agreement, 23 June 2000, OJ 2000, L 317/3, 15 December 2000.
[92] GA Res. 55/2, 8 September 2000.
[93] For more ample references see Bruderlein, 'People's Security as a New Measure of Global Stability', 83(842) *IRRC* (2001) 353; Zambelli, 'Putting People at the Centre of the International Agenda: The Human Security Approach', 77 *Die Friedens-Warte* (2002) 173.
[94] *Common Security: A Blueprint for Survival* (New York, 1982).

be placed at the centre of international affairs'.[95] Expanding the new concept, it attempted to give it a more fully substantiated content in its 1994 Report, where, criticizing again the exclusive military use of the term in the past, it mentions seven aspects of what it understands by human security. Starting out with economic security (freedom from poverty), it refers additionally to food security (access to food), health security (access to healthcare and protection from diseases), environmental security (protection from pollution), personal security (physical protection against torture, war, criminal attacks), community security (survival of traditional cultures), and political security (freedom from political oppression).[96]

It would appear that this new approach is largely the result of bureaucratic overzeal which has lost sight of the existing achievements in the field of human rights. Almost all of the security items mentioned in these reports are nothing else than a reflection of the rights enunciated in the two International Covenants of 1966. Obviously, what human rights seek to achieve is freedom from want and from fear—the classical formulation laid down in the Atlantic Charter of 1941. There is no real need to coin new concepts. Instead, what seems to be necessary is to relate the activities undertaken by international organizations like UNDP to the foundations as they were laid down many decades earlier in the treaties which, still today, constitute the groundwork of the entire gamut of international action in the field of human rights.

Nonetheless, the concept of human security should not be totally rejected. It highlights the function which institutions of the international community can discharge for the promotion and defence of human rights. Whoever speaks of human rights, has primarily in mind the bilateral relationship between the state and its inhabitants, in particular its citizens. It is not clear, at first sight, who else can make a contribution with a view to making these rights a living reality. The jargon of 'human security' changes the perspective in a constructive way. What is referred to is not a situation of rights, which seems to be a priori a positive achievement, but a public interest task. Security is never an existing state of affairs, it is an objective which requires continuous efforts for its attainment. In this sense also, a number of states, among them Canada[97] and Norway, have adopted the doctrine of human security as a *leitmotiv* for their foreign policy. Although the new motto does not usher in new contents, it makes clear that full enjoyment of human rights can only be achieved by structured efforts which view the looming

[95] *Human Development Report* (1993), at 2.
[96] *Human Development Report* (1994), 'New Dimensions of Human Security', at 22 et seq.; *Human Development Report* (1999), at 36 et seq.
[97] The Canadian Ministry of Foreign Affairs defines on its homepage human security as 'a people-centered approach to foreign policy which recognizes that lasting stability cannot be achieved until people are protected from violent threats to their rights, safety or lives', see http://www.humansecurity.gc.ca/menu-e.asp (visited December 2002).

challenge as a complex whole and not as a sequence of separate steps that can be taken independently from one another.

The term 'human security' highlights at the same time the factual conditions upon which real enjoyment of human rights is contingent. To establish a human rights-friendly environment is much easier in a wealthy than in a poor nation. Rightly, therefore, the fight against poverty has in recent years become one of the central themes of discourse on human rights. Thus, in the Millennium Declaration of the United Nations[98] a large section is devoted to this issue. While there is broad agreement as to the aim to be achieved, opinions differ as to the most suitable avenue that should be followed. Under the impression of—perfectly legitimate—ideas about social justice, great emphasis has been placed on the action to be taken by governments. There is no denying the fact that public authorities must provide an essential contribution in the development process of any nation. But it should also be recognized that under conditions of freedom societies themselves can do a lot to improve their living conditions.[99] Paternalism should not overshadow or eclipse private initiatives. It is a matter of political determination to find the appropriate balance between these two driving forces.

IX CONCLUSION

Concluding this chapter, we may say that the human rights idea has lost nothing of its original impetus. Nobody wishes humankind to return to a situation where the individual would have to endure impotently the decisions of his/her government, unable to invoke any legal title to found his/her legitimate claims. But there is a growing awareness that human rights must be seen within the context of appropriate institutions. Human rights alone do not ensure the survival of human rights. They must be included in a network of institutions which are guided by the same philosophy. In that regard, the human rights movement returns to its sources. Jean Bodin and Thomas Hobbes placed their trust primarily in a government of unlimited authority. Today, the very idea of human rights contradicts such extremist solutions. But it is clear again that human rights cannot be seen in isolation.

[98] GA Res. 55/2, 8 September 2000, section III.
[99] Rightly stated in the Millennium Declaration, ibid., where in the list of fundamental values freedom occupies the first place (para. 6).

4

Universality of Human Rights

I INTRODUCTORY CONSIDERATIONS

Emphatically, the UDHR proclaims the unity of the human race and the equality of all of its members by stating in Article 1:

All human beings are born free and equal in dignity and rights.

Following this premise, the ensuing articles all proclaim that either 'everyone' shall have certain rights or that 'no one' shall be subjected to a specific treatment considered to be incompatible with the philosophy underlying the Declaration. Equality and non-discrimination are again expressed in Article 2(1), where a long list of forbidden grounds of distinction is enunciated. Any kind of differentiation on grounds of 'race, colour, sex, language, religion, political or other opinion, national or social origin, property, birth or other status' is rejected as inadmissible. The Declaration does not openly address the issue of regional affiliation, but it is implicit in its line of thought that this issue is deemed to lack any relevance. Thus, the UDHR constitutes a manifesto advocating the universality of human rights.[1] Everyone everywhere is considered to be holder of the rights solemnly proclaimed on 10 December 1948. It is the quality of human being, without any additional qualification, which provides everyone with the rights considered to constitute the preconditions of a life in dignity.[2]

All of the later instruments for the protection of human rights have followed the same approach. The two International Covenants of 1966,

---

[1] See Bielefeldt, 'Muslim Voices in the Human Rights Debate', 17 *HRQ* (1995) 587, at 589; Higgins, 'The Continuing Universality of the Universal Declaration', in Peter Baehr et al. (eds), *Innovation and Inspiration: Fifty Years of the Universal Declaration of Human Rights* (Amsterdam, Royal Netherlands Academy of Arts and Sciences, 1999), 17.

[2] We do not go into the special problematique of group rights, see, with ample references, Jones, 'Human Rights, Group Rights, and Peoples' Rights', 21 *HRQ* (1999) 80.

too, adopted the linguistic mould used by the UDHR. The CCPR speaks of 'every human being' (Article 6), 'everyone' (Articles 9(1), 12(1), (2), 14(2), (3), (5), 16, 17(2), 18(1), 19, 22), 'all persons' (Article 10(1), 14(1), 26), 'anyone' (Article 6(4), 9(2–5)) or 'no one' (Articles 6, 7, 11, 15, 17(1)), and where it leaves the tracks of that scheme, it does so for reasons related to the substance of the rights concerned: due process of law in instances of expulsion proceedings is necessary only for aliens (Article 13), and political rights of participation in public affairs accrue only to the citizens of the country concerned (Article 25). The only major departure from the 'everyone philosophy' is constituted by the International Convention on the Protection of the Rights of All Migrant Workers and Members of Their Families,[3] which confines itself to protecting a narrow—but particularly vulnerable—group of people. It is self-evident, on the other hand, that treaties concluded within the framework of the specialized organizations of the United Nations, in particular within ILO, almost invariably seek to enforce the rights of specific groups of the population only.

Questions do, however, arise. Can there really be a common standard for mankind as a whole? Were the drafters of the UDHR and of the later instruments, which followed the same approach, blinded by their own ambitions so that they did not realize that the existing cultural differences between the many nations and other ethnic as well as linguistic communities of this globe simply could not be reconciled with the kind of uniformity which the establishment of universal principles carries with it as a logical corollary? A few years ago, there was a broad stream of voices which indeed called into question the concept of establishing human rights on a worldwide scale.[4] It was the view of these critics that the variety in religious and cultural values upheld by human communities was such that no truly common denominator could be found. Along similar lines, a prominent spokesman for the Third World, Mohammed Bedjaoui, who later was elected judge of the ICJ (11 November 1987) and even discharged the office of President from 1994 to 1997, diagnosed remnants of 'cultural imperialism' in present-day international law.[5] But precisely in the Third World voices can be heard which vigorously emphasize the universality of human rights. Thus, the well-known Senegalese jurist Kéba Mbaye, former judge of the International

---

[3] Adopted by GA Res. 45/158, 18 December 1990 (not yet in force on 9 December 2002, although, given the existence of 19 ratifications, only one more was necessary for its entry into force).

[4] For an outstanding representative of that current see Ruggie, 'Human Rights and the Future International Community', *Daedalus* (Fall 1983) 93, at 98–100.

[5] Statement, in René-Jean Dupuy (ed.), *The Future of International Law in a Multicultural World*. Workshop, The Hague, 17–19 November 1983 (The Hague, Nijhoff, 1984), 192, at 193.

Court of Justice, has stated that human rights was not an alien notion in Africa.[6] Likewise, Indian writer H. O. Agarwal states:

neither human rights can be different for eastern countries to western countries nor they can [*sic*] be different for developed countries and for the Third World countries. Human rights are colour blind and direction blind. They know neither right nor left, but only the human.[7]

It is a matter of common knowledge that one of the main schools denying the universality of human rights, the Marxist theory of the law and the state,[8] disappeared from the stage of world politics as an 'official' doctrine when the socialist system under Soviet domination fell apart in 1989 to 1990. To be sure, Marxism as a method for the analysis of society has by no means become obsolete. But the intellectual premise according to which human rights cannot be conceived of without and outside the state seems to have lost ground. In any event, the former socialist world has officially embraced the 'Western' concept of human rights first by subscribing to the Document of the 1990 Copenhagen Meeting of the Conference on the Human Dimension of the CSCE[9] and later to the Charter of Paris for a New Europe.[10] Currently, apart from Cuba, where socialism serves more as a pretext for justifying the dictatorship of a small power elite than as a doctrine permeating and guiding the conduct of the state, and North Korea with its irrational power games, the socialist concept of human rights has become obsolete, having lost all of its former advocates. It may survive in isolated intellectual circles, but has definitely had to abandon the key position which it occupied in the USSR and the countries of central and eastern Europe under Soviet domination.

This victory of the 'Western' concept of human rights over its most potent adversary does not put an end to legitimate questioning, however. Since human rights are intimately connected with the value system of a given community, it can and must be asked whether 'Western' values can be amalgamated with African and in particular Asian values to produce a blend which is still capable of providing support to a layer of legal rights.

---

[6] 'Human Rights in Africa', in Karel Vasak (ed.), *The International Dimensions of Human Rights* (Westport, Connecticut, and Paris, Greenwood Press and UNESCO, 1982), vol. 1, 583, at 599.

[7] *Implementation of Human Rights Covenants with Special Reference to India* (Allahabad, Kitab Mahal, 1983), at 17.

[8] See Grigorii I. Tunkin, *Theory of International Law* (Cambridge, Massachusetts, Harvard University Press, 1974), at 82: 'The extent and character of human rights within a specific state (they do not exist outside a state) are defined in the final analysis by the nature of the state, and this nature is itself a product of the economic system of a given society.' This basic proposition was particularized by Vladimir Kartashkin, 'The Socialist Countries and Human Rights', in Vasek, *supra* n. 6, at 631–650.

[9] Of 29 June 1990, 29 *ILM* (1990) 1306.

[10] Of 21 November 1990, 30 *ILM* (1991) 193.

Law does indeed need firm foundations within deeper strata of societal rules of conduct. Law which is superimposed on a society just by bureaucratic processes will always appear as a kind of artificial veneer that can fall off at any moment.

In order to analyse this problem, three methodological levels should be used. The first level, which is by no means negligible, is the juridical level. It permits the identification of the positions which the responsible organs of government have officially adopted. It does matter if and when a government formally pledges itself vis-à-vis the international community to respect certain rights of its citizens, not only to protect their lives and physical integrity but also to grant them rights of political participation and to take care of the family, etc. And yet, an analysis carried out at this level cannot reach definitive results. Regarding many countries, the objection may be raised that commitments entered into and declarations made in the course of conducting foreign affairs do not reflect realities. It is in fact true that in many parts of the world the governmental apparatus constitutes but a thin layer over societal processes driven by actors the interaction among whom is subject to totally different rules. Not infrequently, in order to gain internal as well as international legitimacy, governments simply bow to external pressures, following verbally a strong current which they feel they cannot resist. In this way, a kind of two-stage political culture may develop. On the one hand, there can be, for instance, policy statements, formalized through legislative enactments, which closely resemble the international texts which are binding on the state concerned, while, on the other hand, in the country-side life goes on as it had evolved over centuries, in no way or only very slightly affected by a modernized structure of government which is essentially confined to the urban centres. Recent empirical studies even seem to have proved that the general performance of states regarding their human rights obligations declines after the ratification of key human rights instruments.[11] Through ratification of such instruments, governments show to the outside world that they belong to the group of 'good countries', a gesture which removes them for a while from the sharp focus of international attention.

These criticisms, on their part, may miss the point, however. Normally, there will be a sincere will on the part of public authorities to be guided, in dealings with their citizens, by the standards enshrined in the existing international instruments. One may even venture to say that some critics at least display a neo-colonialist kind of patronizing paternalism in stating that Third World governments declaring their attachment to human rights do not really mean what they say, just paying lip service to some political necessities.

---

[11] Hathaway, 'Do Human Rights Treaties Make a Difference?', 111 *Yale Law Journal* (2002) 1935.

Such verbalism does exist. There are indeed instances of sheer hypocrisy. But such a faked attitude of law-compliance is certainly not the norm and should therefore not be depicted as such.

These considerations necessarily lead to a second level of investigation where the objective must be to find out whether there exists harmony or discrepancy between the normative layer and value concepts that lack any formalization.[12] Here, the methodological difficulties are much greater than in the field of normative analysis. While relatively precise findings can be made on whether a legal proposition is or is not in force, measured according to the secondary rules of the legal system concerned, hardly anything is more difficult than to determine whether a given society embraces a set of given values or not. Values resist any attempt at an accurate definition as to their scope *ratione materiae*, and additionally they cannot be considered as static units which continue in history while the human beings influenced by them come and go.[13] Whoever would be guided by such a prejudice would not only negate the freedom of humankind to take its fate into its own hands and to shape the course of history, but would also contradict the empirical lesson that any society changes during its existence in time and space. The industrialized environment of the human being of our time entails similar needs anywhere in the world.[14] On the other hand, it would seem to be one of the basic data of sociological knowledge that societies generally react inertly to external influences. They resemble convoys which quietly move through the waters because they must take account of the slowest among them.

As a third level of research, societal practice can be explored. A government may have committed itself more than once to respect and observe human rights, it may have become routine for it to express its attachment to certain societal values, and yet its actual conduct may contradict all these pledges. This field of empirical data cannot be excluded either, inasmuch as it reveals whether the many proclamations of faith are more than rhetoric, a façade behind which other considerations dominate, in particular the desire to stay in power.

[12] It is precisely on this level that Adamantia Pollis and Peter Schwab, *Toward a Human Rights Framework* (New York, Praeger, 1982), have challenged the concept of universality of human rights. Along those lines see also Pollis, 'Cultural Relativism: Through a State Prism', 18 *HRQ* (1996) 316.

[13] Rightly emphasized by Freeman, 'Human Rights: Asia and the West', in James T. H. Tang (ed.), *Human Rights and International Relations in the Asia-Pacific Region* (London and New York, Pinter, 1995), 13, at 15; Onuma, 'Towards an Intercivilizational Approach to Human Rights', 7 *Asian Yearbook of International Law* (1997) 21, at 61, 68, 80.

[14] See Cohen-Jonathan, 'De l'universalité des droits de l'homme', in Société française pour le droit international (ed.), *Ouvertures en droit international. Hommage à René-Jean Dupuy* (Paris, Pedone, 1998), 23, at 32.

II THE LEGAL DIMENSION

Notwithstanding its—relative—insufficiency as an indicator of the overall picture, the legal dimension should be analysed in the first place. Here the most visible developments have taken place. What has come into existence as part of the international legal order, constitutes the object which at a later stage will be examined as to its consistency with social value concepts and societal practice.

UDHR

First of all, the UDHR must be brought back into focus. As already pointed out, it was designed to become a standard of worldwide application. It cannot be denied, though, that it suffers from a sort of birth defect in that it was drawn up in a World Organization of 56 states, while today (August 2003) the United Nations counts 191 Member States.[15] The participation of Africa, in particular, was minimal. In 1948 the United Nations had only three African members (Egypt, Ethiopia, Liberia), while Asia was represented by 11 states (Afghanistan, Burma, China, India, Iran, Iraq, Lebanon, Pakistan, Philippines, Syria, Thailand). On account of this, there can be no doubt that Africa and Asia were not sufficiently involved in the elaboration of the UDHR. Although this conclusion must be modified to some extent because of the active role played by Mrs Mehta from India and Charles Malik from Lebanon, it remains true that the composition of the bodies which drafted the text did not mirror in an accurate fashion the population of the world.

To emphasize this 'birth defect' is not tantamount to saying that under the prevailing conditions it was totally impossible to establish a legal document reflecting the basic needs of all human beings. In 1948 the aim was not to create a charter for 'Western man'. Obviously, because of the strong presence of socialist states, the HRCion and the General Assembly were not and could not be guided by an exclusively 'Western' understanding of human rights. The motto was, as expressed in the Atlantic Charter, freedom from fear and want. And yet, those who could not participate in the drafting process might be reluctant to accept the UDHR as the authoritative constitutional document of the international community. Contradicting this assumption is the fact, on the other hand, that the UDHR has time and again been recalled in resolutions of international conferences at world level and in resolutions of

---

[15] During the 57th session of the General Assembly, East Timor and Switzerland became the 190th and 191st members of the World Organization. After the Security Council had recommended the admission of the two states by SC Res. 1414 (2002), 23 May 2002, and 1426 (2002), 24 July 2002, the General Assembly made the definitive determination by GA Res. 57/1, 10 September 2002 (Switzerland) and 57/3, 27 September 2002 (Timor-Leste).

the General Assembly. Suffice it to refer to the Vienna Declaration and Programme of Action, adopted by the World Conference on Human Rights on 25 June 1993,[16] which re-emphasized the importance of the UDHR as a 'common standard of achievement for all peoples and nations' (preamble, para. 8), and to the UN Millennium Declaration of the General Assembly,[17] wherein the Heads of State and Government present in New York on 8 September 2000 solemnly 'resolve(d)' to 'respect fully and uphold' the UDHR (para. 25). This shows that the UDHR has entered the body of common legal principles which are no longer challenged because of their origins.

The Two International Covenants

It has already been pointed out that it took a long time before the two Covenants, which the Commission on Human Rights had prepared almost concomitantly with the UDHR, could eventually be adopted. This long delay of 18 years had a great advantage, however. In 1966 the United Nations already had 122 members. France and the United Kingdom had by then given up their colonial empires, so that from 1960 to 1966 large numbers of Third World countries were able to join the World Organization. While originally dominated by the West, the United Nations had now a clear majority from the new countries in the South. And it was precisely this new majority which put the two antagonistic blocs under pressure to end their doctrinal fighting and to consent to the adoption of the two draft International Covenants. Eventually, all 106 delegations present in the Assembly hall voted in favour of the two instruments, thus approving at the same time the principle of freedom (freedom from fear) and the principle of responsibility of governments for the material wellbeing of all human beings under their jurisdiction (freedom from want). The charge that can be brought against the UDHR that it constitutes a Western product can no longer apply to the two Covenants, as the result of negotiations and processes in which all the countries of the world could participate.

　　It would be erroneous to contend that the representatives acting for their governments in New York were not aware of the importance of their actions and that they fell victim to an ephemeral spirit of euphoria. The subsequent practice of ratification brushed all such negative assumptions and preoccupations aside. Even after the Covenants had been weighed and measured at home by national parliaments, little resistance emerged. Today (December 2002), the CCPR has 149 states parties, while the CESCR is just behind with 146 states parties. Not only have European countries in large numbers adhered to the two Covenants, as well as Latin America and Africa, but

---

[16] 32 *ILM* (1993) 1663.　　　　[17] GA Res. 55/2, 8 September 2000.

also numerous Asian states. Egypt, Iran, and Iraq are among the states parties, as well as India and Japan. Only two poles of stubborn and tenacious resistance can be identified. On the one hand, one finds the states of the Arabian peninsula (Bahrain, Oman, Qatar, Saudi Arabia, United Arab Emirates), of whom not a single one has submitted to the obligations of the two Covenants; on the other hand, there is a small group headed by China which comprises China and some nations linked to it by close ties of friendship (Laos, Singapore): China ratified the CESCR on 27 March 2001, but concerning the CCPR is has confined itself to signing the instrument (5 October 1998). This signing is not an insignificant gesture. By so doing, China has manifested its will seriously to consider becoming a party. In other words, China does not categorically reject the CCPR although its current system of governance makes it hard for the leadership actually to take that step.

One of the most interesting facts is the continued membership of Iran. In first declarations after the 1980 revolution representatives of the new regime had stated that the signature of the earlier Government of the Shah had not been able to establish binding obligations for the Iranian nation and that vis-à-vis the Sharia the CCPR had no relevance at all.[18] Yet Iran has not attempted formally to shed that international commitment. For a number of years at least it continued to comply with the duties established in the CCPR, submitting the required reports, appearing before the HRCee and even listening to extremely critical observations by the Committee.[19] On the other hand, the latest available data from the HRCee indicate that Iran has not yet submitted its third periodic report, which was due on 31 December 1994.[20] Thus, for the last eight years it appears to have halted implementation of the CCPR.

Other Treaties

In later treaties, the reservations of the countries reluctant to commit themselves have crystallized in a more visible fashion. In 1979 the CEDAW was adopted, and 1989 saw the emergence of the CRC. Considering international

[18] See statement of the Iranian representative Khosroshahi, 15 July 1982, *Yearbook of the HRCee (1981–1982)*, vol. I, 345, para. 4: 'although many articles of the Covenant were in conformity with the teachings of Islam, there could be no doubt that the tenets of Islam would prevail whenever the two sets of laws were in conflict'; see also statement of 19 July 1982, ibid., 363, para. 12. Going even further, on the occasion of the examination of the second periodic report the representative stated that 'there had never been an instance in which a provision of domestic law had been found to be in conflict with the principles set out in the Covenant', see *Official Records of the HRCee* (1992/93), 411, para. 197.

[19] See comments of 29 July 1993, *Official Records of the HRCee*, 1992/93, 418–419, paras. 249–270.

[20] [2002] *Report of the HRCee*, UN doc. A/57/40, vol. I, 159.

public opinion, it was almost impossible for a government aspiring to be recognized as heading a modern state to reject either one of these two instruments. Vis-à-vis the more enlightened part of their own population, it would also have been extremely difficult not to be seen as a vigorous defender of the rights of the child. Yet many governments were not prepared unreservedly to venture their way into a new and unknown social environment. Regarding the CEDAW, in particular, many states, among them mostly Muslim states, found themselves in a clear dilemma. Towards the outside world, the power-wielders wished to portray their state as an enlightened polity, following current trends, while internally the conservative forces could not be openly snubbed. Thus, as a compromise, in many instances a Janus-faced solution was found. On the one hand, the treaties were ratified, on the other hand, an attempt was made to undermine their binding force through far-reaching reservations. The most well-known are the reservations of Egypt and Bangladesh concerning the key provision of Article 2 of the CEDAW. While Bangladesh openly states that it 'does not consider as binding upon itself the provisions of Articles 2 . . . as they conflict with Sharia law based on Holy Quran and Sunna', Egypt in a more subtle way declares that it would comply with the article 'provided that such compliance does not run counter to the Islamic Sharia'. Recently, to the amazement of many observers, even Saudi Arabia ratified the CEDAW (8 September 2000), but limited the gist of that ratification by a reservation which follows the direction indicated by Bangladesh and Egypt in the following terms:

In case of contradiction between any term of the Covenant and the norms of Islamic law, the Kingdom is not under obligation to observe the contradictory terms of the Covenant.

Pakistan attempted to reach the same result in a somewhat veiled fashion. It appended to its instrument of ratification the following reservation:

The accession by [the] Government of the Islamic Republic of Pakistan to the [said Convention] is subject to the provisions of the Constitution of the Islamic Republic of Pakistan.

Thus, Egypt, Saudi Arabia, and Pakistan have made it abundantly clear that they do not wish to depart from the Islamic traditions governing the status of women. Moreover, regarding Bangladesh, since Article 2 epitomizes the general thrust of the CEDAW, little is left of its substance if that provision is excluded from the scope of the acceptance of the instrument. On this issue, a definite divergence of opinions does exist. Although ratifying the instrument which seeks to implement in detail the principle of gender equality, the Islamic states have made clear that they do not wish to abandon their traditional patterns of relations between men and women in society. Under the terms of Article 19(c) of the Vienna Convention on the Law of Treaties, reservations of such calibre as to destroy the object and purpose of a treaty are clearly inadmissible.[21] Indeed, many objections have been raised, mainly by Western states, without any apparent effect on the legal position, however.[22]

Similar excesses in formulating reservations can be observed with regard to the CRC. Djibouti reserved 'its religion and its traditional values',[23] and Iran referred to the precedence given to 'Islamic Laws'.[24] Indonesia underlined that its ratification of the Convention did not 'imply the acceptance of obligations beyond the Constitutional limits'. Again, the Convention finds itself emasculated by such general reservations which reflect a deliberate intent not to bring about any changes that might be necessary in view of its substantive requirements.[25]

Vienna World Conference on Human Rights

Another remarkable event in the development of the concept of universality was the adoption of the Declaration of Bangkok, adopted by the Ministers and representatives of the Asian states in April 1993 on the occasion of a preparatory meeting on the eve of the Vienna World Conference on Human Rights. In a number of such preparatory meetings the organizers of the World Conference had planned to reap the fruits of regional experiences for the establishment of a balance sheet 45 years after the adoption of the UDHR. Whereas the Declaration of Tunis and the Declaration of San José do not display any weighty specificities, the Declaration of Bangkok accentuates a divergent position in one of its key paragraphs. In a few words, this paragraph says that states:

recognize that while human rights are universal in nature, they must be considered in the context of a dynamic and evolving process of international norm-setting, bearing

[21] For a general assessment of the reservations to the CEDAW see the report of the UN Secretariat *Reservations to the Convention on the Elimination of All Forms of Discrimination against Women*, UN doc. CEDAW/C/1997/4, 12 November 1996.

[22] In two general recommendations, the Committee on the Elimination of Discrimination against Women has addressed the issue of excessive reservations, without, however, being able to express more than its concern: Recommendation No. 4, adopted at its sixth session (1987), *Compilation of General Comments and General Recommendations by Human Rights Treaty Bodies*, UN doc. HRI/GEN/1/Rev. 5, 26 April 2001, 203; Recommendation No. 20, ibid., 222. See also its General Recommendation No. 21 on *Equality in Marriage and Family Relations*, UN doc. A/47/38, wherein the Committee noted 'with alarm' the number of states parties which have entered reservations to the whole or part of Article 16.

[23] The Committee on the Rights of the Child adopted extremely cautious language when formulating, on 2 June 2000, its Concluding Observations after the examination of the initial report of Djibouti, see UN doc. CRC/C/15/Add.131, para. 8.

[24] The same 'soft' language as in the case of Djibouti was used by the Committee on the Rights of the Child in its Concluding Observations on Iran, adopted on the same day (2 June 2000), see UN doc. CRC/C/15/Add.123, para. 6.

[25] Again, many objections were raised against these reservations.

in mind the significance of national and regional particularities and various historical, cultural and religious backgrounds.[26]

At first glance, this proposition does not seem to be dramatic. In principle,
it is trivial to note that human rights are invariably enmeshed in a specific
political context. But the Declaration intends to convey something more,
namely that within such a context human rights may take a special connotation[27] which—what no one wishes to say openly—would leave little of the
originally intended effect. 'Situational uniqueness', a concept coined by some
Asian leaders, may not only lead to 'sequential ordering of rights',[28] but may
easily be converted into a blanket power for disregarding basic human rights.

At the Vienna World Conference on Human Rights the topic of universality found itself indeed at the centre of heated debates. One has to read the
Declaration very carefully in order to understand its complexity. On the one
hand, the first introductory paragraph states unequivocally that 'the universal
nature of these rights and freedoms is beyond question', but, on the other
hand, attentive observers of the Conference have put a big question mark
behind that statement.[29] Embracing universality should at the same time
amount to embracing the UDHR as well as the two International Covenants.
However, as already noted, while the UDHR is referred to in the preamble
(paras. 3, 8) and in the operative part of the Declaration (para. 33), and while
the CESCR appears likewise in the preamble (para. 8) and in the operative
part (para. 33), the CCPR is mentioned solely in the preamble. Deliberately,
it was kept separate from the operative part of the Declaration. As it has been
reported, this is not an accident, but constitutes the fruit of tough negotiations for a compromise. According to these voices, it was in particular Asian
states which, following the lines of the Bangkok Declaration, wished to
distance themselves to some extent from the CCPR.

Regional Instruments

Regarding the regional instruments for the protection of human rights, the
ECHR does not significantly differ from the CCPR in respect of its guiding
principles. Feeling ashamed that the ECHR contains solely classical liberal

---

[26] Reprinted in Richard Reoch (ed.), *Human Rights: The New Consensus* (London, Regency
Press, 1994), 283, and 14 *HRLJ* (1993) 370.
[27] Openly explained by Kausikan, 'Asia's Different Standard', 92 *Foreign Policy* (1993) 24,
at 32: 'The myth of universality of all human rights is harmful if it masks the real gap that
exists between Asian and Western perceptions of human rights.' For a critical assessment of the
Bangkok Declaration see Freeman, 'Human Rights: Asia and the West', in Tang, *supra* n. 13, at
22–23.
[28] See Caballero-Anthony, 'Human Rights, Economic Change and Political Development:
A Southeast Asian Perspective', in Tang, *supra* n. 13, at 41.
[29] See Kausikan, *supra* n. 27; Pollis, *supra* n. 12, at 330–331.

rights, the states members of the Council of Europe decided in 1965 to complement that instrument by the European Social Charter, which in a fairly loose manner codifies a number of economic and social rights.[30] The same can be said of the American continent. The American Convention on Human Rights (ACHR) was opened for signature on 22 November 1969. *Grosso modo*, it constitutes a replica of the ECHR and the CCPR although from the very outset it contained a general clause on economic, social, and cultural rights (Article 26). By framing at a later stage a specific complementary instrument for the protection of such rights;[31] the Member States of the OAS remained in the mainstream authoritatively indicated by the CESCR. A new accent was introduced only by the African Charter of Human and Peoples' Rights[32] through the juxtaposition of individual rights of human beings and collective rights of peoples. However, on the individual side, the African Charter has few, if any, revolutionary aspects. It even remains more visibly attached to classical principles than the CCPR by explicitly safeguarding the right to property (Article 14). For the common citizen, a guarantee of property was deemed to be more reassuring than any promise of sweeping reforms of the existing social structures.

III THE VALUE DIMENSION

It had been recognized already at the time of the drafting of the UDHR that a set of rules which is not supported by broad political acceptance cannot reach true effectiveness. UNESCO therefore determined to consult eminent thinkers from all over the world in order to discover whether the Declaration reflects only the European heritage or whether, by contrast, it embodies values which enjoy worldwide acceptance. Although this sample test essentially elicited affirmative answers, there were also sceptical voices which were somewhat reluctant to welcome the idea of a worldwide codification of human rights. Thus, for instance, Mahatma Gandhi wrote in a short letter to Julian Huxley, at that time Director-General of UNESCO, that he had learned from his illiterate but wise mother 'that all rights to be deserved and preserved came from duty well done'.[33] Without explaining the philosophy behind this statement, he obviously was of the view that it was more important to have a doctrine of duties than a catalogue or a list of rights. Similar ideas were expressed by the Chinese Chung-Shu Lo, who observed:

The basic ethical concept of Chinese social political relations is the fulfilment of the duty to one's neighbour, rather than the claiming of rights.[34]

---

[30] See *supra* p. 31.   [31] See *supra* p. 33.   [32] 21 *ILM* (1982) 58.
[33] Reprinted in IV *Human Rights Teaching* (1985) 4.   [34] Ibid. at 17.

Without directly commenting on the Declaration, an Islamic thinker (Humayun Kabir)[35] and an expert on the Hindu concept of human rights (S. V. Puntambekar)[36] said that in any event they would put the emphasis in a different place. Summarizing these approaches, a Chinese author has recently defined Asian values as putting emphasis on a quest for consensual solutions, communitarianism rather than individualism, social order and harmony, respect for elders, discipline, a paternalistic state, and the primary role of government in economic development.[37]

In trying to present some of the key concepts of the great religious and cultural systems, one finds in fact that there can be no question of perfect harmony with the UDHR. On the other hand, the divergences do not rise to such heights that one would have to speak of a cacophony. We will confine ourselves to focusing on the so-called 'West' and on Asia, Africa being too difficult a continent for someone who is not an expert in ethnology.[38]

Western Values

Many writers handle the concept of 'Western civilization' without any precaution as if this concept had clear-cut contours. Normally, reference is made to the heritage of Christendom and to the thought of Greek and Roman antiquity. It is certainly true that Western Europe and North America are founded on these traditions. Samuel Huntington, for instance, describes 'the West' as one of the groups of civilization which he identifies.[39] But the barbarism of Nazi dictatorship reminded humankind only a few decades ago how fragile a community of values held together by the common Christian belief may be. Concerning the contemporary epoch, for instance, one cannot fail to note that the common recognition of the dignity of the human being does not exclude deep-going divergences in one of the core areas of human rights, the protection of human life.

There is no transatlantic consensus concerning the death penalty. In 38 states of the United States, this incorrigible form of penal sanction is stub-

---

[35] Reprinted in IV *Human Rights Teaching* 18–19.

[36] Ibid. at 19–20.

[37] Han Sung-Joo (1999), referred to by Boll, 'The Asian Values Debate and its Relevance to International Humanitarian Law', 83(841) *IRRC* (2001) 45, at 47.

[38] See the thoughtful study by Ibhawoh, 'Between Culture and Constitution: Evaluating the Cultural Legitimacy of Human Rights in the African State', 22 *HRQ* (2000) 838, which rightly discards many myths about a traditional culture of human rights; see also Tomuschat, 'Is Universality of Human Rights Standards an Outdated and Utopian Concept?', in *Das Europa der zweiten Generation. Gedächtnisschrift für Christoph Sasse* (Kehl and Strasbourg, Engel, 1981), vol. 2, 585, at 594–595.

[39] *The Clash of Civlizations and the Remaking of World Order* (London, Touchstone Books, 1998), at 46–47.

bornly maintained.[40] Only recently some movement towards restricting capital punishment can be observed. Thus, in *Atkins v Virginia*,[41] the US Supreme Court ruled that the execution of a mentally retarded person would amount to unlawful 'cruel and unusual punishment' as prohibited by the Eighth Amendment of the US Constitution. In Europe, by contrast, most states have abolished the death penalty. In this regard, one writer has explicitly spoken of a 'breakdown of the shared values and common alliance that have historically characterized EU–U.S. relations'.[42] The Sixth Protocol to the ECHR[43] provides that the death penalty shall be abolished, except in time of war or imminent threat of war, and the Thirteenth Protocol to the Convention will establish a complete ban.[44] Likewise, in the European Charter of Fundamental Rights (Article 2), the prohibition of the death penalty constitutes one of the central pillars of the planned system of protection. In recent years, the Albanian as well as the Lithuanian Constitutional Court have derived the prohibition of capital punishment from the guarantee of the right of life enshrined in the relevant constitutional texts.

Discrepancies can also be observed regarding abortion. The case law of the US Supreme Court, which in 1973 seemed to favour total freedom of a pregnant woman to decide on abortion,[45] seems to have distanced itself to some extent from that approach.[46] In Germany, the Federal Constitutional Court has never been won over to a position of freedom of abortion. In a constant line of decisions, it has maintained that growing human life partakes of the guarantee of human life as laid down in Article 2(2) of the Basic Law. It has softened its attitude only with regard to the means which according to its view the state must employ to enforce the untouchable character of such incipient life. If one takes additionally into account the case law of the constitutional courts of France, Ireland, Italy, and Spain,[47] the observer

[40] See, the Report by the International Commission of Jurists, 'Administration of the Death Penalty in the United States', 19 *HRQ* (1997) 165.

[41] Judgment of 20 June 2002, 536 U.S. 304 (2002).

[42] Dennis, 'The 57th Session of the UN Commission on Human Rights', 96 *AJIL* (2002) 181, at 184.

[43] Protocol No. 6 to the ECHR concerning the Abolition of the Death Penalty, 28 April 1983, *ETS* No. 114.

[44] Protocol No. 13 to the ECHR concerning the Abolition of the Death Penalty in All Circumstances, 3 May 2002, *ETS* No. 187 (not yet in force).

[45] *Roe v Wade*, 410 U.S. 113 (1973); *Planned Parenthood v Casey*, 505 U.S. 833 (1992) (a five to four decision).

[46] *Harris v McRae*, 448 U.S. 297 (1980); for a lengthy discussion of the pros and cons see Lawrence H. Tribe, *American Constitutional Law* (2nd edn, Mineola, New York, The Foundation Press, 1988), at 1341–1362.

[47] For a summary overview see Tomuschat, 'Das Bundesverfassungsgericht im Kreise anderer nationaler Verfassungsgerichte', in *Festschrift 50 Jahre Bundesverfassungsgericht* (Tübingen, Mohr Siebeck, 2001), vol. 1, 245, at 276–280.

finds himself in an imbroglio of diverging legal rules which again defy the easy assumption of a community of values.

Perhaps the worst divergence in value judgements concerning human life has arisen with regard to 'targeted killings'. What had been practised only by Israel for many years, namely the killing of suspected terrorists in surprise attacks mostly from the air, was adopted by the United States as an official policy in December 2002. As has been reported, the American intelligence services have established a list with roughly 500 names, everyone figuring on that list becoming subject to extra-legal execution if found by security forces and capture being 'impractical'.[48] Thus, the United States arrogates to itself the right to put to death persons whose guilt is by no means established and whose conviction and sentence is mainly based on evidence provided by intelligence services. These persons are denied any fair trial. They cannot call any witnesses for their defence. The presumption of innocence, a central element of any system predicated on the rule of law, is brushed aside. This policy can hardly be reconciled with the international commitments which the United States has undertaken. To date, no one can say whether its domestic legal order is defective in permitting the state to ride roughshod over generally accepted human rights standards: the US Supreme Court has not yet had the opportunity to pronounce on the issue. It is certain, however, that the new so-called anti-terrorism strategy is inconsistent with the rights set forth by the CCPR.

Two conclusions may be drawn from the preceding observations. First, Western civilization does not constitute a homogeneous whole. Secondly, it is certainly true that 'the West' invented the legal techniques which today are commonly considered to characterize human rights. However, to infer from that premise that human rights is part of the Western heritage only and cannot be traced back to other cultures[49] would seem to be a shortsighted intellectual step to take.

Latin America

Latin America is caught between different civilizations. Because of the layer of Spanish and Portuguese civilization imposed on the indigenous peoples by the Conquista, the countries from Mexico to the southern tip of the continent are generally considered as belonging to the West. In their official presentations, they portray themselves indeed as Hispanic countries, largely ignoring the indigenous element which in some of them (Bolivia, Peru,

---

[48] See report 'Bush Has Widened Authority of C.I.A. to Kill Terrorists' in *New York Times*, 15 December 2002.

[49] See Jack Donnelly, *Universal Human Rights in Theory and Practice* (Ithaca and London, Cornell University Press, 1989), at 49 et seq.

Guatemala) is even numerically superior to the population of Spanish origin. In a strange way, two civilizations exist side by side without really mixing, as happened by contrast in Mexico. At the official level, for centuries the indigenous civilizations did not exist. Progressively, however, the countries concerned are now finding the courage to identify themselves as multi-ethnic nations. It remains to be seen whether this new approach to identity will also stamp its hallmark on the general understanding of human rights.

Islamic Countries

Like the West, Islamic countries do not constitute a monolithic bloc. Given the large extension of Islam from Morocco to Indonesia across two continents with a vast array of different ethnic communities, uniformity could hardly be expected.[50] Notwithstanding their colourful diversity, all Islamic countries differ on two issues, in particular, from other systems of civilization, departing also from the standards of the UDHR.[51]

On the one hand, the Islamic faith does not accept individual freedom of religion.[52] A member of an Islamic denomination is not allowed to embrace another religion. In the UDHR, the right to change one's religion is explicitly laid down (Article 18). Of course a controversy on this issue had raged before the adoption of the Declaration. Amazingly, however, the provision was approved in 1948 by all governments of Islamic states members of the United Nations, with the exception of the Government of Saudi Arabia, which abstained in the final vote. This landmark decision did not put an end to the debate, however. Article 18 CCPR distances itself from the UDHR by introducing ambiguous language. It provides that the right to freedom of thought, conscience, and religion 'shall include freedom to have or to adopt a religion or belief of his choice'. This phrase can be interpreted in different ways and has in fact been subjected to such divergent interpretations. An even more restrictive formulation can be found in the Declaration on the Elimination of All Forms of Intolerance and of Discrimination Based on Religion or Belief of 1981.[53] Article 1 of that Declaration specifies that freedom of religion 'shall include freedom to have a religion or whatever belief of his choice'. The representatives from Islamic states made it unequivocally clear in the debate preceding the vote that this provision was by no means intended to

---

[50] Ann Elizabeth Mayer, *Islam and Human Rights* (2nd edn, Boulder and San Francisco/London, Westview Press, 1995), generally cautions against assessing Islam as a coherent whole. For an insightful discussion see also Bielefeldt, *supra* n. 1.

[51] Christopher G. Weeramantry, *Islamic Jurisprudence: An International Perspective* (Basingstoke, Macmillan, 1988), at 113–127, confines himself to studying the sources in the holy scriptures of Koran, without taking into account contemporary writings or practice.

[52] See, for instance, Bielefeldt, *supra* n. 1, at 597–600.

[53] Adopted by GA Res. 36/55, 25 November 1981.

confer a right to change one's religion. What found its expression at the intergovernmental level in the fora of the United Nations as wrestling with textual nuances, corresponds to deep-seated religious positions. Whoever belongs to the Islamic faith is deemed not to be authorized to sever this link. He/she must stick to this faith and is prevented from following the voice of his/her conscience which may suggest that another religious denomination satisfies his/her religious needs to a greater extent. Islamic clergy and state authorities following their teachings consider it a particularly grave sin—and crime at the same time—to leave the Islamic faith or to found a new religious movement of a sectarian character.[54] This explains the persecution of the Baha'is who, in Iran, up to this date have to endure a situation of complete lawlessness.

The second main divergence is constituted by equality—or inequality—between men and women.[55] In their majority, Islamic writers argue that there can be no schematic equality between the two sexes. Equality, they say, is not lacking, but it exists in a qualitative sense. Men and women have different rights and duties, but a comprehensive balance sheet shows that there is indeed a perfect equilibrium.[56] One may legitimately doubt whether this assertion is well-founded. In the first place, the right of men to marry up to four women constitutes a blatant encroachment on the principle of gender equality. The rules on divorce, too, are much more favourable to men than to women; by obtaining a claim to the restitution of her dowry, a divorced woman receives only a modest compensation for the regime of discrimination to which she is subject.[57] Some Islamic states have attempted to emancipate themselves from the cage of traditionalism with its male domination. Tunisian civil law, in particular, proceeds from the premise that precisely according to the Sharia polygamous marriages must be deemed to be excluded since under the conditions of modern life a man can love only one wife. The extreme contrast was the situation in Afghanistan under the Taliban regime where women had been relegated to the status of objects without any rights. This kind of blind fundamentalism went to such lengths that the General Assembly felt impelled to censure the Taliban regime for the 'continuing and substantiated reports of human rights violations against women and girls, including all forms of discrimination against them'.[58] Whatever

[54] See Mahiou, 'La Charte arabe des droits de l'homme', in *Mélanges offerts à Hubert Thierrry* (Paris, Pedone, 1998), 305, at 315, commenting on Article 27 of the Arab Charter of Human Rights, 18 *HRLJ* (1997) 151, which omits from its body most of the guarantees contained in Article 18 CCPR.

[55] For a brief survey see Bielefeldt, *supra* n. 1, at 596–597.

[56] See, for instance, Sami A. Aldeeb Abu-Shlieh, *Les Musulmans face aux droits de l'homme* (Bochum, Dieter Winkler, 1994), at 160.

[57] See Aldeeb Abu-Sahlieh, ibid. at 178–181.

[58] GA Res. 55/19, 4 December 2000, adopted without a vote.

may be said about the illegitimate excesses of the Taliban regime, it is a fact that the legislation of most Islamic countries is permeated by the belief that equality between men and women cannot be a schematic concept, contrary to the prevailing and otherwise universally accepted doctrine of human rights.

East Asia

In trying to assess the influence of traditions in the modern societies of East Asia, the student is first of all confronted with the difficulty of having to find out where at all such customary concepts have survived as elements capable of impacting societal patterns of thought and practices. A brochure of the State Council of the People's Republic of China from 1991 does not disclose any traces of such rootedness in the past. It states:

Under long years of oppression by the 'three big mountains'—imperialism, feudalism and bureaucrat-capitalism—people in old China did not have any human rights to speak of. Suffering bitterly from this, the Chinese people fought for more than a century, defying death and personal sacrifices and advancing wave upon wave, in an arduous struggle to overthrow the 'three big mountains' and gain their human rights.[59]

Freedom of religion is mentioned somewhere in the brochure, but rather lightly, obviously with a certain degree of window-dressing. It is presented as a kind of private pleasure of citizens, but not as one of the ideological foundations from which the nation could derive its force and vitality. Religious matters are subject to strict control by the state, while the ruling elites base themselves on Marxist ideology. Thus, China finds itself in an antagonistic tension between inherited traditions, which by now may have largely dried up, and an imported Western ideology. Consequently, the country must experience great difficulties in taking a clear stand with regard to the established set of universal human rights.[60] This is not only a problem for China, but affects all Asian countries—in the same way as any country in the world. Through the permanent processes of interaction between the different regions of the world, philosophies and concepts have also travelled and shaped the value systems of human communities. Today, almost no one lives insulated from the outside world. In most instances, it is not even possible any more to identify the 'new' elements of civilization.[61]

---

[59] Information Office of the State Council, *Human Rights in China* (Beijing, Foreign Languages Press, 1991), at 1.

[60] For a lucid analysis see von Senger, 'Chinese Culture and Human Rights', in Wolfgang Schmale (ed.), *Human Rights and Cultural Diversity* (Goldbach, Keip Publishing, 1993), 281.

[61] Onuma, *supra* n. 13, at 30, openly acknowledges that the contemporary Japanese culture has grown out of different roots, comprising also 'Westcentric modern, mass-culture oriented twentieth century American . . . civilizations'.

The American author Neil A. Englehart recently presented an interesting case study concerning Singapore.[62] This study has disclosed that the argument of 'Asian values' can be arbitrarily used by political leaders in order to shield their domination from any kind of challenge. Lee Kuan Yew, Prime Minister of Singapore for more than 30 years from 1959 to 1990, frequently made statements to the effect that the first priority was to build up the country and to develop it, while all the rest, in particular the rights and freedoms of citizens, were a matter of secondary importance.[63] In order to give this approach an ideological foundation, Confucianism was relied upon. The leadership assumed that Confucianism with its basic values, in particular respect for authorities, emphasis on the strong links tying the individual to his/her community of origin, and his/her consequential absorption by that community,[64] was ideal for proving that democracy and human rights could not be reconciled with Asian values. After a while, however, it turned out that Confucianism had no genuine roots in Singapore. Consequently, it was difficult to continue to maintain that the authoritarian style of government was a legitimate offspring of the ideological heritage of that religion. For that reason, in 1991 a new course was embarked upon. A doctrine of 'shared values' was constructed with propositions to the effect that the nation takes precedence over the community and society over the individual, that the family is the basic unit of society, and that instead of conflict consensus should reign.[65] The author of the case study does not hesitate to characterize the public discourse on Asian values as no more than rhetoric, a political device of the kind that has come into current use since the end of the Cold War in order to justify authoritarian structures of governance.[66]

Buddhism as it has materialized in Japan does not oppose conferral of rights on individuals.[67] The Japanese author Yasuaki Onuma[68] doubts whether the 'duties' doctrine should be given as much weight as is attributed to it by many Asian authors. But he emphasizes other aspects which have

---

[62] 'Rights and Culture in the Asian Values Argument: The Rise and Fall of Confucian Ethics in Singapore', 22 *HRQ* (2000) 548.

[63] Similar statements have been reported from Malaysia's Prime Minister Mahathir, see Davis, 'The Price of Rights: Constitutionalism and East Asian Economic Development', 20 *HRQ* (1998) 303, at 309.

[64] See Weeramantry, 'Cultural and Ideological Pluralism in Public International Law', in *Liber Amicorum Judge Shigeru Oda* (The Hague, Kluwer Law International, 2002), vol. 2, 1491, at 1508–1510.

[65] For a critical assessment of the doctrine of shared values see also Ghai, 'Asian Perspectives on Human Rights', in Tang, *supra* n. 13, at 59–60.

[66] Indeed, Kausikan, *supra* n. 27, at 38, seeks to justify 'detention without trial' and 'curbs on press freedom' in the name of Asian values. For a forceful rebuttal of his views see Neier, 'Asia's Unacceptable Standard', 92 *Foreign Policy* (1993) 42.

[67] See Weeramantry, *supra* n. 51, at 1506–1508.

[68] *Supra* n. 13, at 21–81.

more to do with the modalities of enforcement of rights. Referring to his home country, he notes that modesty is highly appreciated. Self-assertive posturing and propagation of one's own ideas is viewed as arrogant, uncivilized, and therefore, in the last analysis, counter-productive. Anyone wishing to reach certain goals must patiently seek to convince his/her partners through talks and negotiation, possibly also mediation and other appropriate procedures for the settlement of disputes. In contrast, trying to enforce a claim by resorting to judicial remedies is seen as violating norms of proper social behaviour. In fact, the number of legal proceedings is minimal in Japan in comparison with Germany or the United States. Even in big cities like Tokyo, violent street crime is practically unknown. Notwithstanding these features of seeming stability and harmony, during the Second World War Japan brutally oppressed the neighbouring countries which it had invaded and occupied, and one may be inclined to draw a parallel to Germany: even the Christian belief as the basic foundation of societal values did not prevent the merciless persecution and extermination of the Jewish population in the whole of Europe.[69]

More important than reliance on traditional values seems to be the emphasis which many Asian countries place on economic development. Being proud of the strides they have made in advancing the wellbeing of their peoples, their leaders tend to give absolute priority to the requirements of economic progress.[70] The famous dictum of the Singaporean leader Lee Kuan Yew that economic and social rights must take precedence over civil and political rights is still well-remembered. A similar statement was made by the Chinese Vice-Foreign Minister at the Vienna World Conference on Human Rights.[71] Clearly, this confrontation has no real philosophical background, but is rooted in day-to-day political considerations of wise statesmanship which are not specifically related to an Asian value system.

Despite the cursory character of the preceding reflections on the value systems of some Asian societies, which have disclosed many contradictions and inconsistencies, one may generally conclude that a central thesis can be identified in Asian thought, namely that societies cannot gain their stability solely from the rights of individuals. It is assumed that good order in the polity materializes almost automatically if everyone—including

---

[69] For an attempt at assessing the current situation of human rights in Japan see Roger Goodman and Ian Neary (eds.), *Case Studies on Human Rights in Japan* (Richmond, Japan Library, 1996).

[70] See Caballero-Anthony, *supra* n. 28, at 43–47.

[71] 'For the vast number of developing countries, to respect and protect human rights is first and foremost to ensure the full realization of the rights to subsistence and development. When poverty and lack of adequate food and clothing are common-place . . . priority should be given to economic development', see *Beijing Review* (28 June–4 July 1993), 9.

governmental institutions—discharges his/her duties in good faith.[72] The legitimacy of such ideas can hardly be contested. Regarding such comprehensive third generation rights as the right to a clean or healthful environment, the duty of everyone to contribute to maintaining the natural environment should be stressed in the Western area of civilization as well.

IV THE EMPIRICAL DIMENSION

Empirical practice was identified as the third test for evaluating the concept of universality of human rights. Although measurable in hard facts and figures, practice is perhaps even more difficult to grasp because of the dimensions of the phenomena to be taken into account. Who could ever say that he is well-informed about human rights practices in the 191 states of the globe? Again, generalizations must be made which risk distorting realities.

The 'West' is proud of its achievements in the field of human rights, and rightly so. Protection against arbitrary use of powers by the state has reached a high degree of perfection. Under the ECHR, everyone can eventually take an alleged infringement of his/her rights to the ECtHR. This great achievement of a liberal concept of state and society has not remedied, however, all the ills which continue to exist in society. The vulnerable groups of the population—mentally ill patients, homeless people, prisoners, to name but a few—are not forgotten, but they live at the margins of society. One of the most worrying features of the status of society in the United States is the fact that almost 0.7 per cent of the population consists of prison inmates,[73] which shows that society has not been able to master the task of socialization of marginal, underprivileged groups. However, one may venture to say that these deficits do not call into question the concept of universality. Human rights connote primarily claims against the state and its institutions. They do not contain a blueprint for social life as a whole. Although the state has a large burden to shoulder in complying with economic, social, and cultural rights, it is not able to bring about a state of affairs which is satisfactory to all groups of the population. Society, too, with is manifold organizations, must cooperate in taking care of those who fall behind in the eternal race for happiness and success in a competitive society. In particular, the necesssary spirit of tolerance and human empathy cannot be generated by juridical processes. A society where human rights are fully guaranteed may still remain essentially

---

[72] Onuma, *supra* n. 13, at 78, thinks that the idea of duty in ancient Asian cultures is generally overstated today.

[73] See statistics provided by US Department of Justice, Bureau of Justice Statistics, http://www.ojp.usdoj.gov/bjs/prisons.htm (figures relating to 31 December 2001).

dominated by egoism. Human rights cannot be equated with happiness 'all over the place'. Enjoyment of human rights creates the basis upon which humane relations among all members of society *can* be established. They are a necessary, but not sufficient condition for personal happiness.

In Asia, Japan has taken the most remarkable steps forward, not only providing to its citizens a high degree of material wellbeing, but also ensuring an enviable degree of legal certainty and political freedom.[74] All this has been achieved in the sense contemplated by Yasuaki Onuma largely without any formalized procedures for the protection of human rights. Constitutional review of the legality of parliamentary statutes does exist, but this procedure has largely remained a dead letter since it is not resorted to in practice. In Japan, to institute judicial proceedings resembles a last act of despair, the plaintiff risking discrediting him/herself by setting in motion the judicial machinery which the state puts at the disposal of everyone for the settlement of emerging disputes. Japan derives its stability from the forces of societal cohesion. In other words, a state of social wellbeing is not brought about by the specific device of human rights, but by other, more complex mechanisms.[75]

Precisely for this reason it is eminently difficult in Japan to remedy social diseases which do not have their roots in governmental acts, but in 'simple' societal prejudices. There is a group of persons in Japan, the Burakumin, who suffer from gross discrimination.[76] Externally they do not differ in the least from other Japanese, but they are the descendants of parents and ancestors who in the past had professions which were considered 'impure'. Belonging to this unfortunate group is a mark of stigma. No Japanese will easily marry a member of the Buraku community; almost any family will try to prevent such a marriage. Similarly, foreigners in Japan do not always live in happy circumstances. In particular, the descendants of Koreans who were deported to Japan before and during the Second World War were for many years subjected to a harsh regime of discrimination. Apart from these negative features, however, Japan has been able to reach a level of far-reaching societal harmony.

It is, of course, difficult to evaluate in general the situation of human rights in Islamic countries. None of them has been able to reach the same or a similar situation of political freedom as in Western Europe, the United States,

[74] See Yūyi Iwasawa, *International Law, Human Rights Law and Japanese Law: The Impact of International Law on Japanese Law* (Oxford, Clarendon Press, 1998) passim; Alston, 'Transplanting Foreign Norms: Human Rights and Other International Legal Norms in Japan', 10 *EJIL* (1999) 625; Pollis, *supra* n. 12, at 333–334.

[75] Onuma calls this the 'intercivilizational approach' to human rights, *supra* n. 13, passim.

[76] See Neary, 'In Search of Human Rights in Japan', in Goodman and Neary, *supra* n. 69, at 12–14.

or Japan. Nowhere has a true democratic system of political participation of citizens in the conduct of public affairs taken shape. The worst degenerations of a political system took place until recently in Afghanistan. The neighbouring countries, Iran and Pakistan, also live under conditions which, given their features of authoritarian arbitrariness, certainly do not qualify as models of the rule of law. The crimes committed by Iraqi dictator Saddam Hussein are a matter of public knowledge, and Syria is still being ruled with an iron fist. It would be easy to extend this list. Necessarily, therefore, the question arises whether there exists an intimate connection between Islam and the countries in which it holds a dominant position. The available evidence does not permit us to answer this question by a clear-cut yes or no. All of the countries mentioned are confronted with serious conditions of poverty, which generally promote tendencies to resolve problems using violent means. Consequently, to govern in a civilized form heeding the rule of law is not facilitated under such circumstances. But it can certainly be said that the authoritarian practices in almost all Islamic states provide little evidence for the thesis that Islam is a religion imbued by tolerance. Its advocates rightly refer to the fact that in the Balkans Christian communities were tolerated for centuries and were not compelled to embrace the Islamic faith. But modern times do not provide many images of a tolerant Islam which has accepted pluralism as a regulatory principle for society.

The most ambiguous impressions can be gained from casting a glance at the situation in China. Daily life in China seems to progress in great freedom. Commerce and industry flourish. The upsurge of capitalism does not seem to be constrained by any limits. But the political rights of citizens are subject to intrusive limitations. The big political decisions continue to be made by a small elite of political leaders. It may well be true that the views of citizens are taken into account via discrete political opinion polls. But true democratic processes of decision-making do not exist. It is not difficult to guess what is hidden behind the repressive policy. On the one hand, China's political leadership seeks to maintain the unity of the Empire which is by no means as stable as portrayed in official speeches. Additionally, quite naturally, the socialist leadership is afraid of losing its positions of power which are tied to the Communist Party of China. On the other hand, no traditional links can be perceived that would tie this policy to the sources of the historical identity of the country. Given this complex situation, the West is prepared to recognize that a disintegration of China in a gradual process of secession would be an evil which, with its inevitable concomitant phenomena of death and destruction, would entail immense losses of human rights substance. Hence, there exists a certain indulgence vis-à-vis China and its government—an attitude which cannot be explained solely by the competition among influential Western countries for big commercial orders from Beijing.

V CONCLUSION

Many arguments have been found which support the conclusion that the reliance on specific national or regional values has served more as a political weapon than having been prompted by a preoccupation over the loss of national identity under the pressure of 'stateless' international values. In this regard, a statement by UN Secretary-General Kofi Annan is instructive. He said:

It was never the people who complained of the universality of human rights, nor did the people consider human rights as a Western or Northern imposition. It was often their leaders who did so.[77]

This is also the lesson to be drawn from the Bangkok meeting in preparation for the Vienna World Conference on Human Rights in 1993. While during the official negotiations the political leaders of Asian states battled for formulations which were to give some room for the specificities of Asian thought on human rights, the human rights organizations of these countries requested nothing else than full and integral respect for, and observance of, the individual rights laid down in the universal instruments for the protection of human rights.[78] And yet, the divergences just identified are not that easily overcome.

How should these divergences be evaluated? Should one speak of a lack of a genuine universal civilization of human rights, or should one, on the contrary, speak of a broad consensus on fundamental issues which dissolves only in some marginal areas? Neither of these two inferences may hit the nail on the head. The American political scientist and social philosopher Michael Walzer rightly speaks of a 'minimal and universal moral code' which is accepted on a worldwide level without any objections. This minimal code comprises, in his view, the prohibition of murder, of slavery, torture, and genocide.[79] In fact, in no country of the world do public authorities claim to be allowed to deal with the life, the freedom, and the physical integrity of citizens according to their arbitrary pleasure. Although this happens time and again, such practices are not recognized as guiding maxims of a right policy. No serious thinker puts in doubt the proposition that the power of state

[77] See Lindgren, 'The Declaration of Human Rights in Postmodernity', 22 *HRQ* (2000) 478, at 498.

[78] See Bangkok NGO Declaration on Human Rights, UN doc. A/CONF.157/ASRM/8, 27 March 1993.

[79] *Interpretation and Social Criticism* (Cambridge, Massachusetts, Harvard University Press, 1987), at 24. For a similar assessment see Chan, 'The Asian Challenge to Universal Human Rights: A Philosophical Appraisal', in Tang, *supra* n. 13, at 29–30. Donnelly, *supra* n. 49, at 26, while recognizing that human rights have evolved over time, is of the view that the rights enshrined in the relevant UN instruments constitute precisely the adequate responses to the needs of our time for all societies.

authorities must be limited by firm constraints. All in all, it seems to be legitimate to go even further than Michael Walzer. Our examination of the main religious and political systems has yielded almost nothing that would militate against the rights enshrined in the CCPR—except the fact that they are formulated as individual rights. Nowhere has a doctrine emerged which would permit the state to curtail freedom of speech, of assembly, and association according to its whims and fancies. Such limitations do constitute empirical facts of life, but they are generally justified on account of prevailing exceptional situations; they have not brought into being a doctrine of individuals as subjects only, deprived of any rights of active participation. Widespread agreement exists as to the aims of governmental policies, namely to ensure to citizens a life in dignity. It is only the means which give rise to controversies: should the individual be endowed with enforceable rights or should one place all the trust in the automatic operation of a system of comprehensive duties?

The CESCR requires a different assessment. Although this Covenant, which has been conceived of as an instrument for the establishment of social justice, generally enjoys large sympathy, it has only weak ideological foundations. When the strong religious and ethical currents determining the world of today came into being, the state as provider of public goods and services to individual persons was more or less unknown. In today's world, not only failing or failed states experience great difficulties in bringing about the kind of social redistribution which the CESCR requires. Lastly, the consensus on human rights issues meets its boundaries where commands for interference with existing societal structures are imparted. In this regard, marriage and family constitute a true minefield. A human rights concept confined to constraints limiting governmental action has much better chances of universal recognition than a more comprehensive concept which considers human rights as public order elements for state and society alike.

In conclusion, we may refer to a famous dissenting opinion of the Japanese judge Tanaka, which is appended to the judgment by which the ICJ in 1966 rejected the application by Ethiopia and Liberia denouncing the treatment of the inhabitants of the former German colony of South-West Africa. Tanaka pointed out:

The principle of the protection of human rights is derived from the concept of man as a *person* and his relationship with society which cannot be separated from universal human nature. The existence of human rights does not depend on the will of a State; neither internally on its law or any other legislative measure, nor internationally on treaty or custom, in which the express or tacit will of a state constitutes the essential element.[80]

---

[80] ICJ Reports (1966) 250, at 297.

A stronger proclamation of faith in the universality of human rights is hardly possible. If human rights are to be derived from the nature of the human being, any possible societal divergences will appear as secondary and insignificant.

A last observation should be devoted to the effects of globalization. In the modern world of electronic media with unbridled international communication, no system of civilization remains unaffected by influences which it receives from outside. One should not overlook, in particular, the impact which the UDHR has had on national constitutional systems. It is true that words must not be taken for hard facts. On the other hand, however, normative propositions which in official and high-ranking documents are repeated time and again, will progressively shape the ways in which human beings think and argue. They may fail to be implemented for some time, they may be openly violated, but in the long run they will shape the ideological environment within which state power has to legitimate itself.

5

Implementation at National Level

I DUTY BEARERS

States

The term 'international protection of human rights' could lead an ill-informed observer to erroneous conclusions. He/she might assume that human rights operate on an international level, where the individual is exposed to threats caused by some 'international' entity. In fact, however, 'international' protection of human rights denotes an ensemble of procedures and mechanisms which, although they have their roots in strata of inter-national law, are primarily designed to protect human beings against their own state. Protection is generally needed at home. Human rights have been brought into being as a supplementary line of defence in case national systems should prove to be of no avail. Although the state is on the one hand reckoned with as the indispensable guarantor of human rights, historical experience has also made clear that the state—or more precisely, the governments acting on its behalf—may use the sovereign powers at its disposal to commit violations of human rights, even crimes that would under normal circumstances be recognized as punishable offences. One should always remember the devasta-tion caused by the Nazi dictatorship in Germany. The regime had been able to bring the entire administrative and judicial apparatus of the state under its control, and of course legislation was also a tool adroitly used by the Nazi leadership. Thus, what remained of the rule of law was no more than a formal principle, devoid of any substantive content, since the law had been reduced to a name that could cover arbitrariness of the most horrendous nature.

What has been said about human rights in general, applies also to economic, social, and cultural rights. Rights of this specific class embody calls on the state to improve the living conditions of its citizens. Again, no one else than the state is the main addressee. To be sure, there are occasions in the life of a nation when the international community intervenes to make available goods and services which the state is unable to provide. This happens normally in situations of natural disasters, when for reasons beyond their control public authorities are unable to satisfy the demands of their citizens. When an earthquake strikes, when floods submerge large parts of a country, or when famine cripples a nation, the international community may feel—and should feel—compelled to take action in order to accommodate the basic needs of the victims. Under conditions of normalcy, however, the international community takes the view that a state should assume full responsibility for the human beings in its territory. Sovereignty comprises first of all territorial jurisdiction, and territorial jurisdiction can be equated with territorial responsibility.

International Organizations

European Communities

In few instances only will it be necessary to secure protection against acts of governmental power issued by organs of international organizations. Two examples may be referred to in this connection. On the one hand, it is a well-known fact today that the European Communities have been endowed with far-reaching powers over the whole breadth of the tasks they are mandated to perform. According to Article 249 EC Treaty, the European Community can make regulations, issue directives, and take decisions. All of these acts produce binding effects for their addressees. Consequently, it was necessary to establish a system of judicial protection which grants European Union citizens a degree of protection which is by and large equivalent to the kind of protection a person enjoys in his/her national environment. Notwithstanding some criticism, the system ushered in by the EC Treaty essentially lives up to this assignment. Someone who feels that his/her rights have been breached by an act of Community power can either challenge that act directly by instituting proceedings before the CJEC (Article 230(4) EC), or he/she can contest national acts taken on the basis of European legislation before national tribunals which, should they share the view that inconsistency does in fact exist between the relevant act of secondary legislation and any higher ranking treaty provision or principle, must then refer the case to the CJEC. In such instances, human rights can play a decisive role. According to Article 6(1) Treaty on European Union (TEU), the European Union is founded on the principles of liberty, democracy, respect for human rights and fundamental freedoms, and the rule of law. Para. 2 of that provision additionally specifies that the Union shall respect:

fundamental rights, as guaranteed by the European Convention for the Protection of Human Rights and Fundamental Freedoms signed in Rome on 4 November 1950, and as they result from the constitutional traditions common to the Member States, as general principles of community law.

   The provisions of the EC Treaty on remedies lying to the CJEC implement this act of faith in the traditional heritage of the nations that have joined under the roof of the European Union.

   Unfortunately, there are some small lacunae in the system of judicial protection. As a matter of principle, individuals may not contest acts which, although producing direct effects for them, do not concern them 'individually' (Article 230(4) EC). In such instances, the general assumption is that the relevant Community acts will be implemented by national authorities in the form of national decisions and that any addressee will then have the opportunity to file a remedy with the competent domestic courts which, on their part, may seek a preliminary ruling by the CJEC. This concept does not work out, however, if no enforcement by national administrative or other authorities is necessary because of the self-executing character of the act in issue. This can happen especially in regard to regulations. In 2002 the question of what to do in such circumstances came before the CJEC and its Court of First Instance. While in the case before the CJEC Advocate General Jacobs argued that an action should be considered admissible if the challenged measure 'has, or is liable to have, a substantial adverse effect' on the interests of the applicant,[1] the CJEC found that such a construction of Article 230(4) EC would amount to a true amendment of the EC Treaty and had therefore to be dismissed. It stated—somewhat lightly—that it was the responsibility of Member States to establish within their domestic legal orders a system of legal remedies and procedures which ensure respect for the right to effective judicial protection.[2] In the meantime, the Court of First Instance had already endorsed in another dispute the view expressed by the Advocate-General.[3] This judgment will certainly be set aside on appeal. For the time being, therefore, there may be cases where notwithstanding the high degree of sophistication of the Community legal order, alleged violations of human rights may not be brought before a competent judicial body.

United Nations

Under the legal regime established by the Charter of the United Nations (UNCh) and the statutes of the specialized agencies, the need for substantive human rights protection, to be implemented through some judicial mechanism, is far less evident. Generally, the United Nations lacks the power to take binding decisions, and even less a power of enforcement. Only the Security Council holds authority under Chapter VII of the Charter to take measures with a view to combating threats against international peace and security.

---

[1] Opinion in *Unión de Pequeños Agricultores v Council*, 21 March 2002, 23 *HRLJ* (2002) 88, at 101, para. 102(4).
[2] Judgment of 25 July 2002, ibid., 101, at 105, paras 41–46.
[3] Judgment of 3 May 2002, *Jégo-Quéré*, ibid., 106, at 109, paras 49–54.

Generally, however, the Security Council refrains from directly addressing individuals. Its embargo resolutions, in particular, are invariably directed to states which are enjoined to take the necessary measures of implementation by first enacting the requisite legal rules, and secondly enforcing these rules against those active in international business transactions.[4] Therefore, no need was originally perceived to grant judicial remedies to those whose interests may be affected by measures under Chapter VII.

Yet, with the emergence of peacekeeping, the screen which originally separated the United Nations from the man on the street disappeared.[5] It is obvious, too, that resolutions which do not directly hit individuals may hit them by ricochet in such a way that the Security Council cannot deny its responsibility, to the extent that they produce binding effects which the UN Member States must comply with.[6] Therefore, the Security Council must take into account the repercussions on the affected population.[7] In this connection, it has been contended time and again that the comprehensive economic embargo still imposed on Iraq after its abortive attempt to annex Kuwait by force has driven up infant mortality rates to frightening heights.[8] The Oil for Food Programme established by SC Res. 986 (1995)[9] did not seem to have alleviated appreciably the plight of the Iraqi population. Eventually, after the successful US–British invasion of Iraq in March/April 2003, the Security Council lifted the embargo by SC Res. 1483 (22 May 2003). Although every nation is to some extent responsible for the political

[4] See, for instance, the famous SC Res. 661 (1990), 6 August 1990, imposing an embargo on all states regarding commercial activities with Iraq.
[5] For a general overview see August Reinisch, 'Governance Without Accountability?', 44 *GYIL* (2001) 270, at 279–286.
[6] Even the UN Secretary-General acknowledged the negative effects of sanctions on vulnerable groups in the targeted countries, see *Supplement to an Agenda for Peace*, UN doc. A/50/60–S/1995/1 (1995), para. 70.
[7] See strong criticism of the Security Council's practices by Graf Sponeck, 'Sanctions and Humanitarian Exemptions: A Practitioner's Commentary', 13 *EJIL* (2002) 81. For ample references to critical voices see Bennoune, ' "Sovereignty vs. Suffering"? Re-examining Sovereignty and Human Rights through the Lens of Iraq', ibid. at 252–254, and Dorothee Starck, *Die Rechtmäßigkeit von UNO-Wirtschaftssanktionen in Anbetracht ihrer Auswirkungen auf die Zivilbevölkerung* (Berlin, Duncker & Humblot, 2000). The CESCRCee has devoted one of its general comments to this issue: General Comment No. 8 (1997), 'The Relationship Between Economic Sanctions and Respect for Economic, Social and Cultural Rights', in *Compilation of General Comments and General Recommendations Adopted by the Human Rights Treaty Bodies*, UN doc. HRI/GEN/1/Rev. 5 (26 April 2001), 54.
[8] As it appears, the charge was brought for the first time by the New York-based Center for Economic and Social Rights, *Unsanctioned Suffering: A Human Rights Assessment of UN Sanctions on Iraq* (May 1996), http://www.cesr.org (visited December 2002). Now the Center has published a second report (6 August 2002): *Iraq Sanctions: Humanitarian Implications and Options for the Future*.
[9] See Oette, 'Die Entwicklung des Oil for Food-Programme und die gegenwärtige humanitäre Lage im Irak', 59 *ZaöRV* (1999) 839.

regime under which it lives, the international community cannot simply equate a people with its leaders. To be sure, sanctions are designed to strike home, but there must be certain limits, to be derived from human rights law or humanitarian law or both regimes.[10] No people may be pushed into starvation, a principle which is a traditional element of humanitarian law.[11] It is for this reason that in the recent past sanctions have been 'smartened' or better targeted. General sanctions mostly affect the lower classes of the population of a given country in the hardest way.

In recent years, the general picture has changed dramatically. On the one hand, the Security Council has established two International Criminal Tribunals. Mandated with prosecuting those who have committed grave crimes in the former Yugoslavia and in Rwanda, these Tribunals have to deal directly with all those who take part in the proceedings which take place before them: arrest warrants must be issued against persons under indictment, witnesses may have to be fined because they refuse to testify,[12] lawyers may have to be refused audience because of incorrect behaviour.[13] In all of these instances, a direct relationship between the two Tribunals and the addressees of their decisions comes into being. Generally, decisions susceptible of injuring individual rights may be appealed. When such an appeal is deemed admissible by the Tribunal concerned, it will have to evaluate it in light of the applicable rules, including general human rights standards. Recently, the question has been raised whether acts taken by the ICC might conflict with guarantees set forth by the ECHR.[14] Indeed, pretrial detention was rather problematic in the early practice of the ICTY and could again become a problem for the ICC,[15] and in the Rome Statute the lack of clearly defined penalties could be attacked from the viewpoint of the proposition *nulla poena sine lege*.[16]

An even more complex situation has arisen in territories where the United Nations has assumed tutorial functions of a trustee. The prime example today is Kosovo, where in accordance with SC Res. 1244 (1999)[17] an international civil presence and an international security presence cooperate with a view to

[10] For a well-pondered view see Reinisch, 'Developing Human Rights and Humanitarian Law Accountability of the Security Council for the Imposition of Economic Sanctions', 95 *AJIL* (2001) 851.

[11] Article 54(1) AP I, Article 14 AP II. For an extensive discussion see Conlon, 'The Humanitarian Mitigation of UN Sanctions', 39 *GYIL* (1996) 249; Craven, 'Humanitarianism and the Quest for Smarter Sanctions', 13 *EJIL* (2002) 43; Gasser, 'Collective Economic Sanctions and International Humanitarian Law', 56 *ZaöRV* (1996) 870; Mary Ellen O'Connell, 'Debating the Law of Sanctions', ibid. at 69–79 (advocating to apply, by analogy, the law on counter-measures). The prohibition on starvation is also stressed by Reinisch, *supra* n. 10, at 861.

[12] ICTY, Rules of Procedure and Evidence, Rule 77(A).

[13] ICTY, Rules of Procedure and Evidence, Rule 46(A).

[14] Caflisch, 'The Rome Statute and the ECHR', 23 *HRLJ* (2002) 1.

[15] Ibid. at 3.   [16] Ibid. at 8.   [17] Of 10 June 1999.

pacifying the situation and securing 'substantial autonomy and meaningful self-administration' to the inhabitants of the province. Originally, it was by no means clear whether any remedy could lie against the decisions of the UN administration. The question becomes more urgent as time goes by and as it emerges that the special status of Kosovo will not last for just a short period of time, but will continue for years to come. It stands to reason that the population of a territory that has been removed from Yugoslav jurisdiction precisely on the ground that Yugoslavia grossly violated generally accepted human rights standards cannot remain deprived of enjoyment of human rights because it has been placed under some kind of trusteeship authority.[18] Inasmuch as the United Nations continues to assume similar tasks, it will have to elaborate general rules for dealing with such situations. It will have to specify, in particular, whether it will respect and observe the legal instruments which were elaborated under its auspices within its norm-setting bodies.[19]

While the situation in Kosovo may be viewed as transitional in nature, some procedural mechanism should be put into place for the ever-growing number of instances where the Security Council does not confine itself to issuing orders addressed to states, but identifies itself—through a subordinated committee[20]—the persons which it wishes to target. The most salient examples have emerged in connection with the fight against terrorism. In fact, SC Res. 1390 (2002) enjoins states to freeze the assets of 'individuals, groups, undertakings and entities' suspected of being related to Al-Qaeda or the Taliban. It is not known from which sources the Committee gathered the list of names which were transmitted to the Member States as supporting these criminal organizations. According to all probability, intelligence services were the main providers of information. In any event, the Member States, for which in Western Europe the European Community had to act because of the transfers of powers that have taken place on the basis of the Community treaties, had no choice but to adopt appropriate internal acts suited to effect

---

[18] For details see Frowein, 'Die Notstandsverwaltung von Gebieten durch die Vereinten Nationen', in *Völkerrecht und deutsches Recht: Festschrift für Walter Rudolf* (München, Beck, 2001), 43; Irmscher, 'The Legal Framework for the Activities of the United Nations Interim Administration Mission in Kosovo: The Charter, Human Rights, and the Law of Occupation', 44 *GYIL* (2001) 353; Stahn, 'The United Nations Transitional Administrations in Kosovo and East Timor: A First Analysis', 5 *Max Planck UNYB* (2001) 105, at 148 et seq.; id., 'International Territorial Administration in the Former Yugoslavia: Origins, Development and Challenges Ahead', 61 *ZaöRV* (2001) 107; Stahn and Zimmermann, 'Yugoslav Territory, United Nations Trusteeship or Sovereign State? Reflections on the Current and Future Legal Status of Kosovo', 70 *Nordic Journal of International Law* (2001) 423, at 429–451; Wilde, 'From Danzig to East Timor and Beyond: The Role of International Territorial Administration', 95 *AJIL* (2001) 583.
[19] Matheson, 'United Nations Governance of Postconflict Societies', 95 *AJIL* (2001) 76, at 85, goes much too far in defining the powers of the United Nations as a 'new' trustee.
[20] Established according to SC Res. 1267 (1999), 15 October 1999.

the required freeze. No opportunity is provided to the victims to challenge their listing. The Committee of the Security Council does not grant them a hearing. Nor can they effectively challenge their being mentioned on the lists annexed to the internal acts concerned because domestic legislative bodies are bound to heed the orders of the Security Council.[21] In the long run, such a denial of legal remedies is untenable. To be sure, no one wishes to protect Al-Qaeda or the Taliban. But the freezing of assets is directed against persons alleged to have close ties with these two organizations. Everyone must be free to show that he/she has been unjustifiably placed under suspicion and that therefore the freezing of his/her assets has no valid foundation.[22]

World Trade Organization

Under the regime of the treaties covered by the WTO, the legal problematique is of a different nature. The WTO has not been entrusted with enforcing its own law. States parties which feel adversely affected by practices of another state party that are contrary to its obligations, may turn to the WTO to request a ruling on their grievances. In such proceedings, the question arises whether non-compliant states may invoke their human rights commitments to justify their conduct. Generally, the doctrine applies that each state has to take care of the compatibility of the obligations which it has entered into. Inconsistencies do not normally lead to unlawfulness of one of the conflicting obligations. Only norms of *jus cogens* prevail in all circumstances. But it is highly improbable that *jus cogens* might impede implementation of duties arising from one of the treaties placed under the authority of the WTO.[23]

Transnational Corporations

There is currently a certain tendency among human rights lawyers to claim that transnational corporations should also be subject to human rights obligations. In fact, many stimulating articles have been written to propound that alleged need.[24] It is true that, particularly in developing countries,

[21] For the EC see Council Regulation 881/2002, 27 May 2002, OJ 2002 L 139/9, 29 May 2002.

[22] Conclusion also reached by Marc Bossuyt, Special Rapporteur of the Sub-Commission on the Promotion and Protection of Human Rights, in his working paper *The Adverse Consequences of Economic Sanctions on the Enjoyment of Human Rights*, UN doc. E/CN.4/Sub.2/2000/33, para. 107.

[23] For a comprehensive discussion see Marceau, 'WTO Dispute Settlement and Human Rights', 13 *EJIL* (2002) 753.

[24] See Menno T. Kamminga and S. Zia-Zarifi, *Liability of Multinational Corporations under International Law* (The Hague, Kluwer, 2000); Paust, 'Human Rights Responsibilities of Private Corporations', 35 *Vanderbilt Journal of Transnational Law* (2002) 801; Ratner, 'Corporations and Human Rights: A Theory of Legal Responsibility', 111 *Yale Law Journal* (2001)

transnational corporations bear a heavy moral responsibility because of their economic power, which may occasionally exceed that of the host state. But on the level of positive law, little if anything has materialized. The OECD, which has elaborated Guidelines for Multinational Enterprises, has consistently emphasized that compliance with these Guidelines, which constitute no more than recommendations, is voluntary.

II RELATIONSHIP BETWEEN INTERNATIONAL LAW AND DOMESTIC LAW IN THE FIELD OF HUMAN RIGHTS

One of the major issues lawyers are discussing with regard to human rights is the relationship between international and domestic law. Proceeding from the premiss that protection against encroachments on the rights of individuals is necessary at home, it would of course seem to matter whether the rights which may serve as defence against such infringements are part and parcel of the domestic legal order concerned. Closer examination shows, however, that some distinctions are necessary. Whether a given right may be able to operate also at national level does not have the same relevance for all classes of human rights.

Third Generation Rights

As far as third generation rights are concerned, it matters little how one identifies their location. As was pointed out, human rights of the third generation have to be understood essentially as political objectives the realization of which requires concerted efforts not only on the part of states, but also of societies. Thus, they permeate the international legal order as well as domestic legal systems, operating as guidelines and policy benchmarks, but cannot be described as individual legal entitlements. Thus, the implementation of third generation rights defies identification in terms of hard and fast law. Third generation rights cut across all fields of public life. Whenever action is taken, it must be asked whether such action is suitable to reach the relevant goals or rather contradicts efforts to reach them. Generally, such possible inconsistencies do not rise to the level of justiciable disputes. Where divergences of opinion arise, such divergences are fought out and possibly settled in political debates. No third generation right possesses the accuracy which would be necessary to legitimate adjudication by judicial bodies.

443; Stephens, 'Expanding Remedies for Human Rights Abuses: Civil Litigation in Domestic Courts', 40 *GYIL* (1997) 117; id., 'Translating Filártiga: A Comparative and International Law Analysis of Domestic Remedies for International Human Rights Violations', 27 *Yale Journal of International Law* (2002) 1; Tomuschat, 'Grundpflichten des Individuums nach Völkerrecht', 21 *Archiv des Völkerrechts* (1983) 289.

Second Generation Rights

Much the same is true of second generation rights. Since rights of this class are generally not directly invokable, their precise location has little relevance under normal circumstances. However, it was explained that second generation rights encompass different legal aspects. Generally, they do not embody individual legal entitlements to specific performance on the part of the state. To the extent, however, that they are suited to protect the individual against state interference or that they are relied upon in connection with the relevant clauses on equality and non-discrimination, they may serve as causes of action.[25] Under such circumstances, obviously, clarity needs to exist as to their existence as integral components of a national legal system. In 1998 the Committee on Economic, Social and Cultural Rights devoted a long General Comment to 'The Domestic Application of the Covenant'.[26] It recognizes that the CESCR does not require any specific means of implementation. This General Comment says:

> 5. The Covenant does not stipulate the specific means by which it is to be implemented in the national legal order. And there is no provision obligating its comprehensive incorporation or requiring it to be accorded any specific type of status in national law. Although the precise method by which Covenant rights are given effect in national law is a matter for each State party to decide, the means used should be appropriate in the sense of producing results which are consistent with the full discharge of its obligations by the State party.

The weakness of this General Comment, however, cannot be overlooked. The Committee is not prepared to acknowledge that, in general, the 'rights' under the CSECR are different in nature from those enunciated in the CCPR. Therefore, it is largely exaggerated to place as much emphasis on individual remedies as the Committee does throughout the General Comment. Where legal rules like the rules setting forth the right to work or the right to the 'highest attainable standard of physical and mental health' (Article 12(1)) boil down to nothing more than an objective of social policy, there is simply no individual entitlement and, hence, individual remedies are inconceivable: where there is no right, there can be no remedy.

First Generation Rights

Concerning first generation rights, the issue of the proper place of the rights within the domestic legal order has high priority. All of the rights pertaining to this class are not only suitable, but also designed to be directly invoked by

---

[25] See *supra* p. 44.
[26] General Comment No. 9, adopted at 19th session (1998), in *Compilation, supra* n. 7, at 58.

individuals who feel that they have become victims of unlawful governmental interference. Hence, if the numerous rights listed in the treaties for the protection of human rights are excluded from the domestic legal order concerned, they cannot produce their intended legal effect.

According to a general rule of international law, states are free to decide how they discharge the international obligations they have entered into. International law does not prescribe a specific method of implementation. What matters is the result. It is self-evident that the choice of the method of implementation must not affect the basic principle of *pacta sunt servanda*. States must abide by their duties. They are not authorized to restrict the substance and scope of their commitments by opting for methods of implementation which seem to be less onerous than others. Only occasionally does a treaty provide that a specific method of implementation is obligatory. This is true, in particular, of the treaties on European integration and the secondary law issued by the institutions of the two Communities. In all 15 Member States, Community law must be applied as such. It cannot be effectuated by processes of indirect application through national acts of legislation that would reproduce the text of the original provisions. The highly sophisticated system of the Communities could not function properly if national sovereignty acted as a screen between the two legal orders. In particular, the procedure of preliminary rulings (Article 234 EC) would be greatly hampered or would completely grind to a halt.

Notwithstanding this fundamental proposition, states have always tried to evade their responsibilities by choosing methods which deprive an unpleasant treaty of its full effectiveness. In the field of human rights, much depends on that initial choice. It stands to reason that a human rights treaty is more effective if it permits a potential victim directly to claim the benefits of a provision which has allegedly been infringed, than if a legal configuration exists under which the state, the guarantor and potential violator of human rights, bears overall and exclusive responsibility and where the citizen is relegated to the role of an object of paternalistic protection. On the other hand, in states close to the brink of collapse, or where the modern concept of the rule of law has not yet been able to establish itself, compliance with human rights treaties is as aleatory as compliance with national law.[27]

Essentially, two methods can be relied upon in implementing an international treaty in the domestic sphere. On the one hand, a treaty can as such be transposed from the international level into the domestic legal order so

---

[27] In an ethnological study, G. Elwert, 'The Command State in Africa: State Deficiency, Clientelism and Power-Locked Economies', in Steffen Wippel and Inse Cornelssen (eds), *Entwicklungspolitische Perspektiven im Kontext wachsender Komplexität. Festschrift für Dieter Weiss* (München, Weltforum-Verlag, 2001), 419, at 427, writes: 'The only problem is that laws are there without consequence. Parliaments may invent legal texts as they wish. But it is open whether administration and the police intend to respect them.'

that its rules form part of that legal order to the same degree as any other legal rule of genuine national origin. Normally, this transposition or transformation, or whatever name one may give to that process, occurs by virtue of a national act, in case of important international treaties by way of a parliamentary statute. Traditionally, Western Europe adheres to this practice. National parliaments have a say in treaty-making. After they have given their approval, the treaty concerned must be directly applied by the competent administrative agencies and judicial bodies. However, a treaty remains a treaty even after incorporation into a domestic legal system. Its interpretation remains subject to the relevant rules of international law, and its entry into force and its possible termination are also governed by international law.

The second method emphasizes the dualist understanding of the relationship between international and domestic law even to a greater extent. According to this method, which is in current use in the United Kingdom, international treaties are regarded as acts of the executive power ('the Crown') which bind the United Kingdom vis-à-vis the other states parties, but do not count as elements of the domestic legal order. Consequently, the citizen is not directly affected; he/she neither enjoys any rights, nor is burdened by any obligations. In order to implement a treaty, the United Kingdom normally enacts a statute or other convenient act of secondary legislation which sets forth in terms of British law the consequences deriving from that treaty.

The question is whether freedom of choice exists also with regard to treaties for the protection of human rights. None of these treaties contains a specific clause making a determination on the issue.

European Convention on Human Rights

The ECHR confines itself to stating that the states parties 'shall secure to everyone within their jurisdiction the rights and freedoms defined in Section I of this Convention'. In its case law, the ECtHR has been confronted with the general obligation of implementation a couple of times. Although many arguments could be adduced to argue that human rights treaties should not follow the general pattern as it has evolved in international law, the ECtHR has consistently held that states parties could indeed decide at their discretion how they wished to discharge their duties. It explicitly said that states are not obligated to transpose the ECHR directly into their national legal system. What appeared for the first time in the reasoning of the *Swedish Engine Drivers* case,[28] was later (in 1991) repeated in the *Sunday Times* (II) case[29] and the case of *The Observer and Guardian*.[30] No change of the case law has

---

[28] Judgment of 6 February 1976, *Swedish Engine Drivers' Union* case, *Publications of the European Court of Human Rights, Series A: Judgments and Decisions*, A 20, 18, para. 50.
[29] Judgment of 26 November 1991, A 217, 32, para. 61.
[30] Judgment of 26 November 1991, A 216, 36, para. 76.

occurred since then.[31] One may assume that the Court felt compelled to take this position since the United Kingdom, which had actively participated in drafting the instrument, was a member state of the first hour. In the early 1950s no one would have thought that international law might one day go beyond the traditional role, requiring that an international treaty must be made self-executing within the borders of the state concerned.

In spite of the lenient attitude of the ECtHR, the United Kingdom has recently decided to make the ECHR internally applicable to some extent at least. In fact, the belief that the chosen method of implementation was faultless because the relevant domestic law was an inexhaustible source of individual rights, surpassing by far the requirements of the ECHR, had proved to be a complete misconception. This was particularly evident in *Malone*, a case concerning telephone tapping, where such practices had been carried out without any legal basis, notwithstanding the clear proposition enunciated by Article 8 ECHR that any interference with one's home and correspondence requires a legal basis. When the case came before the competent British courts during the first stage of the proceedings, the judges perspicaciously recognized that the operations under review could not be reconciled with the ECHR. But, since the ECHR was not part of the domestic law of the United Kingdom, nothing could be done to make a finding declaring the unlawfulness of the conduct of the public authorities involved. Consequently, the case went on to Strasbourg where, inevitably, the United Kingdom lost.[32] After many years, the government felt that it was time to remedy this situation, and Parliament followed its lead. The Human Rights Act 1998[33] did not directly incorporate the ECHR into the domestic legal order of the United Kingdom, but essentially enjoined UK authorities to take into account the ECHR and the judgments of the ECtHR. At the same time, however, through a sophisticated system, care was taken to ensure that parliamentary sovereignty was not impaired. Judges are allowed to bring to the attention of the government any inconsistency found to exist between British law and the requirements of the ECHR, but they have not received authority to strike down statutes which they consider to be incompatible with Convention rights. Generally, the ECHR serves as a guideline to interpret the law of the United Kingdom.

Sweden, which originally followed the British model, incorporated the ECHR with effect as from 1 January 1995.[34] But—like the United

---

[31] See judgments in *Smith and Grady v UK*, 27 September 1999, *Reports of Judgments and Decisions* (1999–VI), 45, at 94, para. 135; *Khan v UK*, 12 May 2000, para. 44; *P. G. and J. H. v. UK*, 25 September 2001, para. 85.

[32] Judgment of 2 August 1984, A 82.

[33] 38 *ILM* (1999) 466.

[34] See Cameron, 'The Swedish Experience of the ECHR since Incorporation', 48 *ICLQ* (1999) 20.

Kingdom—it did not grant the same place to the CCPR. Thus, the rights under the ECHR can be invoked directly before Swedish administrative authorities and courts, while the rights under the CCPR are ensured through acts emanating from Swedish law-making sources. This difference in legal technique should not diminish the real impact of the CCPR in any significant manner.

International Covenant on Civil and Political Rights

The case of the CCPR is more complex. The general clause on the duty of states parties to discharge the commitments arising under the Covenant (Article 2(1)) does not differ significantly from the corresponding clause under the ECHR, although it disjoins the verb 'secure' into the two elements of 'respect' and 'ensure', thereby emphasizing the fact that apart from duties of non-interference, the Covenant carries with it also duties of protection. But the CCPR gives much more room to the requirements of an effective remedy where an individual has suffered an infringement of his/her rights (Article 2(3)). To be sure, Article 13 ECHR also uses textually the term 'effective remedy'. On the whole, however, Article 2(3) CCPR is a much more elaborate provision than Article 13 ECHR. Therefore, the question could not but arise whether the insistence on remedies permitting the individual to defend his/her rights does not presuppose that those rights must be present within every domestic legal order of states parties to the CCPR. Furthermore, the CCPR explicitly directs states parties to take the necessary steps 'to give effect to the rights recognized in the present Covenant', if necessary even by adopting legislative measures (Article 2(2)).

During its early years, the HRCee, the body entrusted with monitoring compliance by states with their obligations under the CCPR, adopted a General Comment in which it expressed its view that 'article 2 of the Covenant generally leaves it to the States parties concerned to choose their method of implementation in their territories'.[35] At that time, which was still dominated by strong tensions between East and West, all of the socialist states had opted for non-introduction of the CCPR into their domestic legal orders. Consequently, no one could invoke the CCPR before internal bodies. Neither the executive branch nor judicial bodies were authorized to apply the guarantees laid down therein. In Czechoslovakia, the members of 'Charter 77' were subjected to brutal oppression.[36] This was clearly an insupportable situation: clearly, socialist states had refrained from incorporating the CCPR into their

[35] General Comment 3 (13), 28 July 1981, *Yearbook of the HRCee (1981–1982)*, vol. II, 299. This conclusion was recently confirmed in para. 11 of a General Comment on Article 2 CCPR: The Nature of the General Legal Obligation Imposed on States Parties to the Covenant, UN doc. CCPR/C/74/CRP.4/Rev.3, 5 May 2003.
[36] See *infra* p. 233.

legal systems because they wanted to deny their citizens the benefits deriving therefrom.

Inevitably, the question arose whether freedom of choice is really granted under the CCPR.[37] The question has received renewed relevance in view of the United States' ratification on 8 June 1992, which was accompanied by a series of far-reaching reservations, declarations, and understandings.[38] The first one of the 'declarations' specifies that 'the provisions of Articles 1 through 27 of the covenant are not self-executing', which means that judges are directed not to apply them. By and large, hence, the United States has followed the example of socialist states which wished to achieve that the citizens of their countries had no direct contact with the rights established under the CCPR. Additionally, on a number of issues the United States has made clear by a formal reservation that it accepts the obligations under the Covenant to the extent only that these obligations do not go beyond the corresponding obligations deriving from the US Constitution (reservation concerning Article 7). Observers assessing the bundle of reservations, declarations, and understandings, focusing in particular on the denial of a need for implementing legislation and the additional denial of direct applicability of the CCPR to private citizens, have concluded that these restrictions leave the CCPR 'without any life in United States law'.[39] The author of this sentence, Louis Henkin, until 2002 a member of the HRCee, has even ventured to speak of an 'anticonstitutional practice of declaring human rights conventions non-self-executing'.[40] No matter how well-founded this criticism may be, it cannot be denied that to declare an international treaty domestically non-self-executing is an option states may legitimately choose without violating their international obligations. Such a declaration does not constitute a reservation.[41]

---

[37] See discussion by Harland, 'The Status of the ICPPR in the Domestic Law of State Parties: An Initial Global Survey Through UN HRCee Documents', 22 *HRQ* (2000) 187 (with statistical overview); Tomuschat, 'National Implementation of International Standards on Human Rights', *Canadian Human Rights Yearbook (1984–85)*, 31, at 39–52.

[38] Reprinted in Hurst Hannum and Dana Fischer (eds), *U.S. Ratification of the International Covenants on Human Rights* (Irvington-on-Hudson, New York, Transnational Publishers, 1993), 327. For the report of the US Senate Committee on Foreign Relations see 31 *ILM* (1992) 648.

[39] Henkin, 'U.S. Ratification of Human Rights Conventions: The Ghost of Senator Bricker', 89 *AJIL* (1995) 341, at 349.

[40] Ibid.; see also Seibert-Fohr, 'Domestic Implementation of the International Covenant on Civil and Political Rights Pursuant to its Article 2 para. 2', 5 *Max Planck UNYB* (2001) 399, at 451. See further critical comments by van Genugten, 'The United States' Reservations to the CCPR; International Law *versus* God's Own Constitution', in *The Role of the Nation-State in the 21st Century: Human Rights, International Organisations and Foreign Policy: Essays in Honour of Peter Baehr* (The Hague, Kluwer Law International, 1998), 35; Shelton, 'Issues Raised by the United States Reservations, Understandings, and Declarations', in Hannum and Fischer, *supra* n. 38, at 269–277.

[41] Flawed discussion by Francisco Forrest Martin, *Challenging Human Rights Violations* (Ardsley, New York, Transnational Publishers, 2001), at 17–30.

Although such an assessment under the US Constitution must be distinguished from an assessment under general international law and, in particular, under the CCPR, it is remarkable that the HRCee has gone many steps forward in defining more accurately the duties of states regarding the implementation process. It has abstained from reviewing and strengthening its former General Comment on the issue. In final views on individual communications, it has clarified that it sticks to what it said in 1981. Thus, in *Araujo-Jongen v The Netherlands* it held—and implicitly approved—'that the method of incorporation of the Covenant in national legislation and practice varies among different legal systems'.[42] One of the lawful methods can be to abstain from introducing the Covenant itself into the domestic legal order, provided that its effectiveness does not suffer therefrom. Indeed, in *Roberts v Barbados*, the HRCee pointed out that, 'although the Covenant is not part of the domestic law of Barbados which can be applied directly by the courts, the State party has nevertheless accepted the legal obligation to make the provisions of the Covenant effective'.[43]

It is the substantive criterion of effectiveness which the HRCee has employed as the guiding principle for its assessment of the different methods of implementation, rather than the formal criterion of incorporation of the CCPR into the domestic legal order. In that regard, it considers as equivalent the direct method or an indirect method which consists of enacting national legislation reflecting the substance of the Covenant. A recent article by Anja Seibert-Fohr has demonstrated that as from 1993 the Committee has asked all states appearing before it in connection with the examination of their reports under Article 40 CCPR, to codify all Covenant rights domestically. Concerning the United Kingdom, the Committee observed in July 1995:

> The Committee is concerned by the extent to which implementation of the Covenant is impeded by the combined effects of the non-incorporation of the Covenant into domestic law, the failure to accede to the first Optional Protocol and the absence of a constitutional bill of rights.[44]

Along similar lines the HRCee more recently criticized the legal position in Guyana, stressing that 'not all Covenant rights have been included in the current Constitution and therefore cannot be directly enforced'.[45] Substantially the same criticism was directed at the Czech Republic. The Committee observed that, although the Covenant formally had a status superior to domestic legislation, not all of its rights were incorporated in the Czech Charter of Fundamental Rights and Freedoms, 'which leads to confusion as

---

[42] Final views, 22 October 1993, [1994] *Report of the HRCee*, vol. II, UN doc. A/49/40, 114, at 118, para. 7.5.
[43] Final views of 19 July 1994, [1994] *Report of the HRCee*, vol. II, 322, at 325, para. 6.3.
[44] [1995] *Report of the HRCee*, vol. I, UN doc. A/50/40, 68, para. 416.
[45] [2000] *Report of the HRCee*, vol. I, UN doc. A/55/40, 53, para. 351.

to the full protection of all Covenant rights'.[46] Apparently, the Committee opines that protection afforded on the basis of a national instrument of constitutional value is even more effective than protection on the basis of the Covenant itself.

Given this line of reasoning, we do not concur with Anja Seibert-Fohr who thinks that the HRCee has moved an important step further by requiring direct applicability of the CCPR.[47] She relies on the Committee's concluding observations on Israel in 1998, where it was noted:

with regret that, although some rights provided for in the Covenant are legally protected and promoted through the Basic Laws, municipal laws, and the jurisprudence of the courts, the Covenant has not been incorporated in Israeli law and cannot be directly invoked in the courts.[48]

Similarly, in formulating its concluding observations on Tanzania, the Committee expressed the following:

While the Committee is encouraged to hear that the courts are beginning to refer to the Covenant in judgments, it recommends that the Covenant be given formal recognition and applicability in domestic law (art. 2).[49]

These observations should not be overrated. They show that the HRCee is seeking to increase the effectiveness of the Covenant, which in fact will result from direct applicability of its provisions. But the two sentences just quoted are too weak a basis for the suggestion that the basic parameters of the traditional system of implementation have been overturned. Such a conclusion is even less warranted inasmuch as the Committee, in its revised version of General Comment 3(13) of 1981 (General Comment of 5 May 2003), has confirmed its original assessment of the issue. Furthermore, it emerges clearly from recent observations concluding the examination of state reports that incorporation of the CCPR into a domestic legal order is viewed not as obligatory, but as the method which is preferable since it increases the effectiveness of the rights guaranteed by the CCPR.[50]

In sum, our conclusion is that for the HRCee the decisive issue is that of effectiveness. A person who feels aggrieved by a governmental act affecting any of his/her rights under the CCPR should be able to confine him/herself

---

[46] [2001] *Report of the HRCee*, vol. I, UN doc. A/56/40, 84, para. 5.

[47] *Supra* n. 40, at 436: 'States parties need to ensure that the Covenant itself can be applied directly by domestic courts. The Covenant needs its own formal place in the domestic legal system so that the Covenant provisions themselves become enforceable by domestic courts.'

[48] [1998] *Report of the HRCee*, vol. I, UN doc. A/53/40, para. 305.

[49] Ibid., at para. 394.

[50] See concluding observations on the United Kingdom, [2002] *Report of the HRCee*, vol. I, UN doc. A/57/40, 38, para. 7; Sweden, ibid., 58, para. 6. The renewed effort of Seibert-Fohr, 'Neue internationale Anforderungen an die Überführung von Menschenrechtsabkommen in nationales Recht', 62 *ZaöRV* (2002) 391, at 401–404, is not persuasive.

to invoking that right without having laboriously to search for the corresponding guarantees of national origin. In such instances, the state should not be able to respond that the CCPR itself is not part and parcel of the domestic legal order. The author, when he was a member of the HRCee in the early years of its existence, observed in commenting on the Swedish report on 18 January 1978:

the rights accorded by the Covenant to the individual could not be dependent upon the way in which they were incorporated in the legislation of various countries. Consequently, even in a country which had not made the Covenant part of its domestic law, an individual should have the right directly to invoke its provisions before domestic courts.[51]

In fact, the weakness of the CCPR in socialist countries resulted from the fact that it was considered as officially non-existent. Not even the name of the CCPR could be referred to before official bodies. That was a clear violation of Article 2(2).

A number of consequences flow from that insistence on effectiveness. The HRCee has openly manifested its mistrust vis-à-vis unwritten guarantees, although they may be an integral element of a national tradition. According to this approach, it criticized the United Kingdom,[52] Ireland,[53] and Iceland.[54] In that latter case, the Committee seems to have exceeded the bounds of legitimate criticism[55] by stating that, 'no matter how effective the Icelandic constitutional tradition of relying on unwritten fundamental rules and principles may be, codification of the rules governing the protection of human rights is an important element of protection'. Yet codification cannot be an objective by and for itself. Effectiveness is the only acceptable yardstick.

In general, it can be said that effectiveness is best ensured if a human rights treaty is made part of national law.[56] Only if human rights guarantees can be relied upon by the parties concerned, if the judicial body called upon to adjudicate an ensuing dispute must take account of and apply such guarantees, and if as a consequence progressively a body of national decisions builds up, will the relevant provisions shape the public conscience of the country concerned. If, on the other hand, the relevant human rights treaties remain outside the domestic legal order, little interest in clarifying their scope and meaning will emerge. Indeed, in the United States the CCPR is viewed as marginal and almost irrelevant. The author is not aware that in the

---

[51] *Yearbook of the HRCee (1977–1978)*, vol. I, 183, para. 38.
[52] [1995] *Report, supra* n. 44, at 68, para. 416; 69, 427.
[53] [2000] *Report of the HRCee*, vol. I, UN doc. A/55/40, 62–63, paras. 432–433.
[54] [1994] *Report of the HRCee*, vol. I, UN doc. A/49/40, 20, para. 74.
[55] See Seibert-Fohr, *supra* n. 40, at 432.
[56] This is also the conclusion drawn by Heyns and Viljoen, 'The Impact of the United Nations Human Rights Treaties on the Domestic Level', 23 *HRQ* (2001) 483, at 527.

competent American fora burning issues of human rights policies are discussed or decided with reference to the CCPR, notwithstanding the fact that the United States is a party fully subject to the obligations deriving therefrom.

III PLACE OF HUMAN RIGHTS INSTRUMENTS IN THE DOMESTIC LEGAL ORDER

Proceeding from our assumption that the HRCee has to date refrained from requiring that the CCPR be introduced into the domestic legal order of every state party, the question of what place must be given to it in the hierarchy of domestic legal sources is moot. Contrary to our view, Anja Seibert-Fohr believes that the Covenant must receive constitutional rank so that it prevails over any inconsistent legislation.[57] Yet nothing the HRCee has said in its concluding observations after the examination of state reports goes beyond the simple assertion that in case of conflict the Covenant must prevail. This is a simple consequence of the maxim *pacta sunt servanda*. It is left to states to ensure that precedence of the Covenant is in fact ensured through effective mechanisms.

Clearly, the ECHR and the CCPR raise more problems in this connection than any other international treaty. They differ from the usual type of treaty which governs a transaction between two or several states. Conceived as instruments that should remain in force forever, while extending their reach to all sectors of state activity, they risk conflicting with numerous earlier and later legislative enactments, and to do so many times over. Regarding the bulk of international treaties of the normal type, issues of possible conflict with the national constitution are mostly artificial figments of juristic fantasy. The CCPR, on the other hand, because of its ambition *ratione materiae* and *ratione territorii*, cannot avoid getting into conflicts on a daily basis. Such battles must be fought by the HRCee as its guarantor. Therefore, the maxim *pacta sunt servanda*, notwithstanding its naive simplicity, raises problems of a complexity hitherto unheard of. The need to secure the pre-eminence of the CCPR over any kind of conflicting normative rules requires an elaborate system of remedies. In the last analysis, the CCPR would have to be given precedence even over any constitutional provisions. Such a requirement might give rise to a conflict of legitimacy. In almost all countries, the CCPR was adopted like an ordinary international treaty on the basis of the normal majorities prescribed for that purpose. Now it seems, as everyone could easily have guessed, that its aspiration is to be a super-constitution, binding on any subsequent parliamentary assembly.

---

[57] *Supra* n. 40, at 439–443.

Most international treaties contain denunciation clauses, designed to resolve conflicts for which no other solution can be found. The CCPR, however, lacks any denunciation clause, contrary to its first Optional Protocol (Article 12(1)). Legally, therefore, states are not able to rid themselves of the obligations which a former government may have accepted in pursuing political objectives totally different from the objectives of the current government.

For the first time in the history of the CCPR, such denunciation occurred in 1997. On 27 August of that year the Democratic People's Republic of Korea by a formal declaration communicated its intention to withdraw from the commitment it had entered into by its act of accession. In a General Comment,[58] the HRCee stressed that the CCPR was not subject to denunciation.[59] It pointed out that 'the rights enshrined in the Covenant belong to the people living in the territory of the State party':

> once the people are accorded the protection of the rights under the Covenant, such protection devolves with territory and continues to belong to them, notwithstanding change in government of the State party. . . .

However, the principle of absolute stability of CCPR obligations also has another side. In the future, careful consideration will have to be given to this conflict between the principle of *pacta sunt servanda* and the principle of democratic self-determination. As long as the two International Covenants remain the centrepiece of the human rights policy supported by the United Nations, they will probably resist any challenge and prevail over any arguments founded on the democratic principle.

In most countries where human rights treaties have been introduced into the national legal order, they have been given the rank of ordinary statutes. In some countries, however, international treaties generally receive higher rank than ordinary laws (but below the level of the Constitution itself), and other countries reserve such higher rank to human rights treaties. In the first group are France and the Benelux countries, while Peru belongs to the second group. By specific legislation, Austria raised the ECHR to the level of a constitutional statute while keeping the CCPR at the level of an ordinary law, a differentiation which raised some discontent with the members of the HRCee when the first Austrian report came to be considered in March 1983.[60] A study presented some years ago by Felix Ermacora, Manfred Nowak, and Hannes Tretter showed that this 'beatification' of the ECHR yielded almost no concrete effect. Generally, the Austrian courts

---

[58] General Comment No. 26, adopted on 29 October 1997, in *Compilation, supra* n. 7, at 162.

[59] See Frumer, 'Dénonciation des traités et remise en cause de la compétence par des organes de contrôle', 104 *RGDIP* (2000) 939, at 951.

[60] See *Yearbook of the HRCee (1983–1984)*, vol. II, 445, para. 182.

were much more cautious in interpreting the ECHR than the ECtHR.[61] No significant initiative on their part could be registered in the course of three decades. In France and the Netherlands, where judges are barred from examining parliamentary acts as to their conformity with the Constitution once they have entered into force, the result seems to be somewhat awkward, if considered from a national viewpoint. While, because of the precedence of the ECHR and the CCPR, judges may review national statutes regarding their compatibility with these two instruments, they are unable to enforce the human rights standards laid down in their own Constitutions.[62] While this may be quite desirable for an advocate of international human rights law, it distorts the general order of priorities. International human rights law should always operate as a device of last resort, when domestic mechanisms have failed to protect rights which allegedly have been infringed.

It emerges also from the practice of the HRCee in examining state reports that many countries have given the CCPR the rank of an enactment of constitutional value;[63] or else, they may instruct their judicial bodies to take the applicable international instruments into account when interpreting the Constitution and other municipal laws.[64] Whatever the technique chosen, it has emerged that such formalities alone do not bring about the desired results.[65] Much more is necessary for a legal enactment to be respected as the highest norm in the country concerned. Thus, in April 2001, the Committee noted with regard to the Dominican Republic that notwithstanding a generous provision in Article 3 of the current Constitution, which recognizes and applies the norms of international law accepted by the Republic, thus conferring constitutional standing on the CCPR,

---

[61] Nowak, 'Allgemeine Bemerkungen zur Europäischen Menschenrechtskonvention aus völkerrechtlicher und innerstaatlicher Sicht', in Felix Ermacora, Manfred Nowak, and Hannes Tretter (eds.), *Die Europäische Menschenrechtskonvention in der Rechtsprechung der österreichischen Höchstgerichte* (Wien, Braumüller, 1983), 37, at 48–49.

[62] In *Lorenzi*, 30 October 1998, 115 *Revue du droit public et de la science politique* (1999) 649, the French Conseil d'Etat declared a parliamentary statute that infringed the procedural guarantee of an oral hearing under Article 6 ECHR inapplicable.

[63] See Seibert-Fohr, *supra* n. 50, at 407–412; Tomuschat, 'National Implementation of International Standards on Human Rights', *Canadian Human Rights Yearbook (1984–85)*, 31, at 43.

[64] One of the early examples is Article 10 of the Spanish Constitution, which provides: '(1) The dignity of the person, the inviolable rights which are inherent, the free development of the personality, respect for the law and the rights of others, are the foundation of political order and social peace. (2) The norms relative to basic rights and liberties which are recognized by the Constitution shall be interpreted in conformity with the Universal Declaration of Human Rights and the international treaties and agreements on those matters ratified by Spain.'

[65] According to Article 10 of the 1992 Constitution of Burundi, the UDHR and the two Covenants were part of the Constitution itself. This programmatic statement could not prevent the well-known mass killings in the country.

a significant body of legislation was still incompatible with the CCPR, despite the latter's higher standing and the fact that more than 21 years had elapsed since the Republic acceded to it.[66] A similar criticism was addressed to Croatia, where international treaties generally have legal force superior to that of domestic legislation and where most of the rights of the CCPR have been specifically incorporated into the Constitution. And yet, the Committee noted, there was very little direct enforcement of Covenant rights since the judiciary lacked training in international human rights law.[67]

IV IMPLEMENTATION OF INTERNATIONAL HUMAN RIGHTS VIS-À-VIS THE INDIVIDUAL

All the legal techniques resorted to in order to give the CCPR and the ECHR an appropriate place within domestic legal systems just serve to prepare the ground for application of the rights which they stipulate. After all, the aim is actual enjoyment of human rights by individuals. The CCPR provides specifically that each state party 'undertakes to respect and to ensure to all individuals' the rights recognized by it (Article 2(1)). Similarly, the four Geneva Conventions of 1949 on humanitarian law set forth the obligation of the 'High Contracting Parties' 'to respect and to ensure respect for the present Convention in all circumstances'. These stipulations, which have become a standard formula in human rights treaties, are not necessary. The proposition that states are to respect and to ensure the individual rights which they have accepted by virtue of an international treaty is no more than a reflection of the basic rule of *pacta sunt servanda*. Nevertheless, it serves as a useful reminder that compliance with the commitments entered into not only presupposes (passive) respect for the rights concerned, but may also require proactive steps to protect these rights.

As the preceding observations have already shown, implementation is not a mechanical exercise. Even if a state has created all the necessary preconditions for giving full effect to the rights it has undertaken to comply with by making the treaty concerned part and parcel of its legal order, the persons active in its bureaucratic sector may be slow to react accordingly. This applies to administrators, judges, and lawyers alike. Manifold reasons explain the reluctance which one finds more often than not in the 'legal staff' of a given country. First of all, international treaties must be known to the persons of that group. Even if the CCPR, or another international instrument, like the ECHR, is

---

[66] Observations of 3 April 2001, [2001] *Report of the HRCee*, vol. I, UN doc. A/56/40, 55, para. 6.
[67] Observations of 4 April 2001, ibid., 66, para. 7.

referred to by someone, the text may not be available. And even if there exists a translation into the national language, the fact remains that the practice concerning the major human rights instruments is not easily accessible. The ECtHR renders its judgments in English and French, and even a successful applicant does not obtain 'his/her' judgment in his/her native language. At the level of the United Nations, the number of official languages is greater, but it certainly does not include all the languages which are spoken in the world. The difficulty in accessing the judgments and other acts of the competent bodies makes national judges extremely reluctant to make use of the materials which concretize and clarify the scope and meaning of the different instruments. Rightly, they fear that they may not be able to handle the materials stemming from an international background as easily as they handle the rules of their national system, which are the tool which they have to apply on a daily basis. Much could be done to publicize the work of the ECtHR and the HRCee. But it would be a Herculean—and almost impossible—task to produce translations into all of the major languages of the world.

Apart from these obstacles, which are of a technical nature, legal norms derive their efficacy from constituting a framework of reference in the human community concerned. General awareness is needed of the fact that the state has submitted to a set of rules and principles which are binding on all three branches of government.[68] A treaty which no one knows is unable to become a guideline for correct behaviour of state agents as a matter of fact. In this regard, societal forces ('domestic constituencies') can play an important role. They should insist that the governmental machinery abide by the obligations which it has undertaken of its own free will. A climate fostering compliance will not emerge overnight, but it can be created by steadfast endeavours by committed groups,[69] provided that in the country concerned freedom of communication is ensured as a minimum. Of course, in a dictatorship, where merely a word of dissent can mean persecution and even death, it would be vain to hope that the formal act of ratification might automatically, just by the normative effect inherent in any legal rule, produce the effects which should attach to an international human rights instrument. The example of 'Charter 77' has already been mentioned. For the communist regime in Czechoslovakia, participation in the treaty system was no more than window-dressing. No intention whatsoever existed to respect the principle of non-discrimination on political grounds.[70]

---

[68] In this regard, see cogent observations by An-Na-im, 'Human Rights in the Arab World: A Regional Perspective', 23 *HRQ* (2001) 701, at 706.

[69] See the study by Heyns and Viljoen, *supra* n. 56, at 488, 518 and passim.

[70] See *infra* p. 233.

V TERRITORIAL SCOPE OF APPLICATION OF
INTERNATIONAL HUMAN RIGHTS INSTRUMENTS

The scope of application of the ECHR is defined in Article 1 by a phrase indicating that states shall secure the rights and freedoms concerned to everyone 'within their jurisdiction'. Concerning the CCPR, the qualification clause contains two elements. Article 2(1) specifies that the duty of a state 'to respect and to ensure' extends to all individuals 'within its territory and subject to its jurisdiction'. In most instances, these phrases cause no great difficulties of interpretation. Within their territory, states generally enjoy full jurisdiction, except with regard to persons or entities which are placed under a special regime of immunity. Whenever a state takes action outside its territory, however, it would seem at first glance that it remains free from any constraints. Since in the world of today extraterritorial activities are constantly increasing, this restriction would open up a serious gap in the protection individuals enjoy. One may seriously question the wisdom of such a decision taken during the drafting process.

European Convention on Human Rights

The ECtHR was faced with the interpretation of Article 1 first in the *Stocké* case[71] and later in the *Loizidou* case.[72] In *Stocké*, it pointed out that, contrary to a literal interpretation of the provision, the obligations of states parties were not limited to their national territory, but extended to all persons under their actual authority and responsibility. This line of reasoning was continued in *Loizidou*. Mrs Loizidou was a Cypriot citizen of Greek ethnicity who lost access to a number of plots of land in the northern part of Cyprus near the city of Kyrenia when Turkish troops invaded the island in 1974. All her attempts to regain her property in that region were in vain. Since the invasion, the two parts of the country have been sealed off from one another. Turkey in conjunction with the authorities in the northern part, which has established itself as the 'Turkish Republic of Northern Cyprus (TRNC)' since November 1983, have constructed a wall of separation which is almost impenetrable. No Cypriot Greek citizen can travel to the north, even less claim the property he/she had to leave behind. Given this situation, Mrs Loizidou introduced an application with the Strasbourg Court, claiming that her rights under Article 8 ECHR (respect for her home) and her right to property under Article 1 Protocol No. 1 to the ECHR had been violated.

---

[71] Judgment of 19 March 1991, A 199, 24, para. 166.
[72] For an overall assessment see Lawson, 'The Concept of Jurisdiction and Extraterritorial Acts of State', in Gerard Kreijen (ed.), *State, Sovereignty, and International Governance* (Oxford, Oxford University Press, 2002), at 281–297.

Responding to this claim, Turkey argued that the Court was prevented from examining it as to its merits, given the fact that the presence of Turkish armed forces in northern Cyprus did not amount to 'jurisdiction' any more than was the case with the armed forces of other countries stationed abroad. Turkish armed forces had never exercised 'jurisdiction' over life and property in northern Cyprus.[73] The Court, however, was not impressed by this argument. It stated that the concept of 'jurisdiction' was not restricted to territorial jurisdiction. The responsibility of a state party could also arise when, as a consequence of military action, it exercises effective control outside its national territory. As to the factual aspects of the dispute, it affirmed that Turkish troops had indeed factual control over the northern part of Cyprus.[74] Consequently, it determined, after having rejected other preliminary objections as well, that the application was admissible.

One may wonder whether the Court has remained consistent in its case law when it ruled that the application in the case of *Bankovic and others* was inadmissible.[75] Proceedings in that case had been instituted by the surviving next of kin of four persons of Yugoslav nationality who were killed when, during the NATO air operation against Yugoslavia in the spring of 1999, a missile hit the building of the television station Radio Televizije Srbije ('RTS'). The applicants complained about the bombing of that building and contended that the following provisions of the ECHR had been violated: Article 2 (the right to life), Article 10 (freedom of expression), and Article 13 (the right to an effective remedy). The respondent governments—the governments of all the NATO states parties to the ECHR—argued that the attacks carried out against targets in Yugoslavia did not bring those targets under their jurisdiction.[76] They contended that the exercise of jurisdiction in the sense contemplated by Article 1 presupposes the assertion or exercise of legal authority, actual or purported, over persons owing some form of allegiance to that state or who have been brought within that state's control. They also suggested that the term 'jurisdiction' generally entails some form of structured relationship normally existing over a period of time.[77]

The Court confirmed that extraterritorial acts may fall within the scope of application of the ECHR. But it stated that essentially a state's jurisdiction is territorial, all other titles of jurisdiction being exceptional and requiring special justification. Rejecting the argument of the applicants that by firing

---

[73] Loizidou (Preliminary Objections). Judgment of 23 March 1995, A 310, 21, para. 56.
[74] Ibid., 23–24, paras 62–63.
[75] Decision of 12 December 2001 on Application 52207/99, not yet published.
[76] The Prosecutor of the ICTY established a special committee to investigate the incident and found that because of the military uses of the station the attack could not be deemed to breach rules of humanitarian law, see report of 2 June 2000, 21 *HRLJ* (2000) 257, at 269, para. 76.
[77] Ibid., at para. 36.

the lethal missile NATO states had established jurisdiction over the victims, the Court said that to construe the notion of jurisdiction in such a broad fashion would be tantamount to saying that any victim of an alleged violation was under the jurisdiction of the responsible state; thus, the criterion of jurisdiction would be eliminated for all practical purposes.[78] Additionally, the ECHR was a regional instrument and was not designed to be applied throughout the world.[79] To buttress its line of reasoning, the Court additionally invoked the *travaux préparatoires* of the Convention.[80]

The decision seems to be founded on valid grounds. There is no inconsistency between *Loizidou* and *Bankovic*. Turkish armed forces are permanently deployed in Cyprus, they constitute the backbone of the so-called Turkish Republic of Northern Cyprus. This entity would not be viable without the support which it receives from Turkey. Thus, responsibility for almost everything that occurs in the northern part of the island falls to Turkey or is shared by Turkey and the institutions of the Turkish Cypriot entity. On the other hand, NATO forces have never claimed that they hold any legal title authorizing them to control public life in the territory of Yugoslavia. Obviously, this does not mean that in their air operations NATO forces were free of any legal constraints. They had to comply with the standards laid down in the Hague Rules of 1907 and in particular with Additional Protocol I of 1977. These rules of humanitarian law, however, cannot be asserted in a proceeding under the ECHR.[81]

On one issue, however, the Court seems to have missed the point. While it is certainly true that armed conflict in far-away countries is not subject to the rules of the ECHR, the legal position changes as soon as the armed forces of a state party to the ECHR have made someone a prisoner. Persons in custody are under the jurisdiction of the custodial power. In such circumstances, the applicability of the ECHR cannot be denied. Although during the drafting process, awareness may have been lacking that the ECHR might become applicable under specific circumstances outside Europe, there is no reason to depart from the clear wording of Article 1. The only requirement which Article 1 establishes is the requirement of jurisdiction. Purely factual contacts do not establish jurisdiction. No justification could be found, however, for denying persons under the direct control of any one of the states parties the protection of the ECHR. This has obvious consequences for units of the armed forces of the European allies of the United States in their fight against any remaining

---

[78] See report of 2 June 2000, 21 *HRLJ* (2000) 257, at 269, at para. 75.
[79] Ibid. at para. 80.
[80] Ibid. at para. 63.
[81] Lawson, *supra* n. 72, at 294, would probably have reached a different conclusion since he insists that jurisdiction must be deemed to exist if there is a *direct and immediate link* between the extraterritorial conduct of a state and the alleged violation of an individual's rights.

fighters of Al-Qaeda in Afghanistan. As long as active combat continues, the only legal regime that applies is the regime of international humanitarian law. As soon, however, as fighters have surrendered and have fallen into the hands of their European adversaries, the protection of the ECHR sets in. Custody entails both jurisdiction and responsibility. It would profoundly contradict cultural traditions of civilized countries, which the European states claim to be, to try to deny responsibility for prisoners committed to their care.

International Covenant on Civil and Political Rights

Pursuant to the text of Article 2(2) CCPR, not only one, but two conditions must be fulfilled to make the CCPR applicable to a given situation. Early in its jurisprudence, the HRCee decided that Article 2(2) cannot be applied textually in all instances covered by the CCPR. The most blatant example of an obvious contradiction is provided by Article 12(4), according to which no one shall be arbitrarily deprived of the right to enter his own country. *Per definitionem*, a person suffering a violation of this right finds him/herself outside of his/her own country. Since, however, Article 12(4) does set forth a right, this right exists, although it does not correspond to the line drawn by Article 2(2). Consequently, the HRCee did not feel prevented from entertaining communications complaining that a person residing outside his country of nationality had been unlawfully denied a passport and thereby prevented from returning back home, or to leave his/her country of residence (Article 12(2)).[82] In later decisions, the Committee had to deal with cases where a dictatorial regime (Uruguay) had sent secret agents to a foreign country (Argentina) with the aim of kidnapping a dissident who lived there as an exile. The HRCee did affirm the applicability of the CCPR to that illegal arrest and detention, relying on Article 5, according to which the Covenant may not be invoked as justification for acts aimed at the destruction of any of the rights and freedoms recognized therein.[83] In an individual opinion, it was pointed out that the phrase 'within its territory' was intended to cover objective difficulties which might impede the implementation of the CCPR in specific situations, in particular regarding the obligation to 'ensure' the enjoyment of the rights guaranteed by it. This obligation indeed encounters serious difficulties concerning citizens living abroad, or in instances of occupation of foreign territory. It was never envisaged, however, to grant states unfettered discretionary power to carry out wilful

[82] See final views in *Vidal Martins v Uruguay*, 23 March 1982, HRCee, *Selected Decisions under the Optional Protocol*, UN doc. CCPR/C/OP/1 (New York, 1985), 122, at 123, para. 7; *Pereira Montero v Uruguay*, 29 August 1981, *Selected Decisions of the HRCee under the Optional Protocol*, vol. 2, UN doc. CCPR/C/OP/2 (New York, 1990), 136, at 137, para. 5.

[83] See final views in *López Burgos v Uruguay*, 29 July 1981, *Yearbook of the HRCee (1981–1982)*, vol. II, 324, at 326, para. 12.3.

and deliberate attacks against the freedom and personal integrity of their citizens living abroad.[84] Indeed, in its comments on the report of the United States (1995) the HRCee rejected the view expressed by the government that the CCPR lacked extraterritorial reach under all circumstances.[85]

Recently, the HRCee has expanded its jurisprudence to include also situations of military occupation of foreign territory. Regarding the obligations of Israel in the territories which came under its de facto control through the war of 1967, it said in its concluding observations on the Israeli report, adopted on 28 July 1998, that Israel was responsible for the implementation of the CCPR to the extent that it exercised 'effective control'.[86] It is true that this broad construction of Article 2(2) may give rise to serious doubts as to the proper role of the HRCee. Is it authorized to interpret the CCPR in an authentic fashion? The language of Article 2(2) is relatively clear. On the other hand, it cannot be prohibited from inquiring into the reasons underlying Article 2(2). Plausible grounds must be found to explain the restriction *ratione territorii* of the reach of the CCPR. Only one reason comes to mind. Normally, a state lacks consolidated institutions abroad that would be in a position to provide to an aggrieved individual all the guarantees which, in particular, Articles 9 and 14 CCPR require. If, however, a state holds possession over the territory concerned for many years and has established there an administrative structure, the grounds for the softening of the standards to be observed simply disappear. To that extent it would seem fully warranted to disregard a literal interpretation of Article 2(2) CCPR.

This conclusion can be directly applied to the prisoners of war captured by the United States and transported by them to their military base at Guantánamo in Cuba. It is no mystery that the choice of this rather strange place of detention was suggested by the case law of American tribunals according to which enjoyment of American civil liberties needs to be guaranteed to its full extent only on the soil of the United States, not abroad.[87] Additionally, the United States has become enthralled by its own case law concerning so-called 'unlawful combatants'.[88] But it seems to have totally lost sight of the obligations deriving for it from the CCPR (as well as from international humanitarian

---

[84] See final views in *López Burgos v Uruguay*, 29 July 1981, *Yearbook of the HRCee (1981–1982)*, vol. II, 324, at 326.

[85] [1995] *Report of the HRCee*, vol. I, UN doc. A/50/40, 49, para. 284.

[86] UN doc. CCPR/C/79/Add.93, 18 August 1998, para. 10.

[87] *Johnson v Eisentrager*, 339 U.S. 763 (1950); *United States v Verdugo Urquidez*, 494 U.S. 259 (1990); *Cuban American Bar Association v Christopher*, 43 F.3d 1412, 1430 (11th Cir. 1995).

[88] *Quirin*, 317 U.S. 1 (1942).

law).[89] Its authorities originally denied—on grounds which are hardly persuasive—the applicability of international humanitarian law, arguing that the persons arrested by them were not prisoners of war.[90] But even if this contention should be true, the CCPR applies in any event. The philosophy of the *López Burgos* decision of the HRCee can be resorted to without any difficulty since the United States does not find itself in a situation of emergency. The Al-Qaeda movement is defeated. Guantánamo was deliberately chosen as the place of detention in order to deprive the prisoners of the full protection of American law. Article 2(2) should not be misconstrued as a device designed to open up loopholes permitting manipulative curtailment of rights and freedoms under the CCPR.[91]

---

[89] See criticism by Gasser, 'Acts of Terror, "Terrorism" and International Humanitarian Law', 84(847) *IRRC* (2002) 547, at 567–568; Naqvi, 'Doubtful Prisoner-of-War Status', ibid. at 571–595; Weckel, 'Le statut incertain des détenus sur la base américaine de Guantánamo', 106 *RGDIP* (2002) 357.

[90] Documentary references: 92 *AJIL* (2002) 475. To equate all Taliban fighters with Al Qaeda, as attempted by Wedgwood, 'Al Qaeda, Terrorism, and Military Commissions', 96 *AJIL* (2002) 328, at 335, is hardly persuasive; for a rebuttal see Fitzpatrick, 'Jurisdiction of Military Commissions and the Ambiguous War on Terrorism', ibid. at 345–354, at 353.

[91] Mundis, 'The Use of Military Commissions to Prosecute Individuals Accused of Terrorist Acts', 96 *AJIL* (2002) 320, at 324–325, rightly acknowledges the applicability of Article 14 CCPR in Guantánamo; same view: Fitzpatrick, *supra* n. 90, at 350–352; Hongju Koh, 'The Case against Military Commissions', ibid. at 338–339.

6

The Work of Political Bodies of International Organizations

I UNITED NATIONS

Since it is one of the purposes of the United Nations to promote and encourage respect for human rights and fundamental freedoms (Article 1(3) UNCh), the organs of the World Organization should seek to achieve that goal, each one within the area of the competence assigned to it. Different functions can be distinguished in that connection. Standard-setting is the first step in promoting and protecting human rights. International protection requires international standards. Without such uniform standards, the United Nations would be criticized for acting inconsistently by applying different yardsticks. A second—and more decisive—step is taken by appraising the human rights situation in a given country or by reviewing individual cases. It does not need to be emphasized that the enactment of generally applicable rules is far less controversial than a practice which seeks to identify the weaknesses in the conduct of a given country. No government loves being exposed to criticism. However, situations which objectively deserve blame should indeed be blamed. Institutions not daring to speak openly would have no raison d'être.

It is of course possible to establish specific mechanisms and procedures by way of international agreement. Every state is free to accept such treaties and thereby to submit to modalities of control which are not available under general international law. In this chapter, we shall primarily deal with ways and means of international monitoring which have no specific legal foundation, but which have evolved on the basis of treaties—such as the UN Charter—confining themselves to imparting a general mandate to the institutions concerned to work for the protection of human rights, without, however, making determinations on the devices to be used in that endeavour. It will be interesting to see to what extent the actual connotation of the provisions setting forth the powers of the different bodies of the World

Organization depends on external circumstances which have nothing to do with the text of the Charter.

It is trivial to note that both the General Assembly and the HRCion are political bodies. While every state member of the United Nations has a seat in the General Assembly, the HRCion is a functional organ of ECOSOC with a limited membership of 53 states. Political bodies have great difficulties in satisfying the requirement to act in a fair and objective manner, above all when they are called upon to assess the situation in a given country. On the other hand, their voice carries much more weight than assessments by expert bodies. Consequently, they must by necessity be involved especially in the arduous task of supervision and monitoring. The machinery for the protection of human rights would lack real teeth if it consisted solely of expert bodies. Thus, a delicate course has to be steered between mustering sufficient political support and complying with the requisite standards of impartialiy and objectiveness. Time and again, political considerations take the upper hand in the proceedings under the auspices of the two bodies concerned. Occasionally, truly frustrating experiences occur. The selection of the members of the HRCion should be confined to states that do not have an outright black record in the field of human rights. In January 2003 great emotions were stirred up by the election of Libya, a country hardly known as an advocate of the rule of law, to the Presidency of the HRCion. Hopefully, this new responsibility will incite the country to adjust to the rules and principles which it will be called upon to defend in the exercise of its office.

Norm-setting

As already indicated in Chapter 3 above, the United Nations embarked on an ambitious programme of norm-setting since the inception of its work in 1945. Beginning with the UDHR, it has over the years established dozens of instruments designed to bring into being, consolidate, and strengthen human rights. Such activity can easily be understood as 'promotion' of human rights. Whenever an instrument is elaborated and adopted, the chances for the rights recognized therein to be observed increase, perhaps not significantly, but in any event to some extent.[1]

The General Assembly is the natural candidate for processes of codifying existing rules or progressively developing new rules, as explicitly stated in Article 13(1)(a) UNCh. On many occasions, the process of norm-setting started out with the adoption of a declaration on the topic chosen for legal regulation. The most prominent example is of course the UDHR,

---

[1] But see doubts raised by Hathaway, 'Do Human Rights Treaties Make a Difference?', 111 *Yale Law Journal* (2002) 1935.

the substance of which later found its reflection in the two International Covenants. A similar procedure was followed, e.g., regarding racial discrimination,[2] discrimination against women,[3] or the rights of the child.[4] In one instance, the process was blocked after the first stage: a ban on discrimination on religious grounds is set out only in the Declaration on the Elimination of All Forms of Intolerance and of Discrimination Based on Religion or Belief,[5] but has not advanced to the status of a binding conventional prohibition. Concerning protection of minorities, on the other hand, the conventional provision came first (Article 27 CCPR), and the later Declaration on the Rights of Persons Belonging to National or Ethnic, Religious and Linguistic Minorities of 1992[6] has attempted to substantiate the somewhat poor wording of Article 27. In the case of more recent declarations, such as the Declaration on the Rights and Responsibility of Individuals, Groups and Organs of Society to Promote and Protect Universally Recognized Human Rights and Fundamental Freedoms,[7] an instrument designed to afford protection to human rights defenders, it remains to be seen whether in the future steps can be taken to translate their substance into a binding international agreement.

A broad mandate of norm-setting has also been entrusted at the regional level to the Council of Europe. Inter alia, under Article 1 of its Statute the Council is called upon to promote the aims specified by the Statute through agreements and common action in economic, social, cultural, scientific, legal, and administrative matters and in the maintenance and further realization of human rights and fundamental freedoms. In other words, to draw up appropriate instruments for that purpose belongs to the core tasks of the Council of Europe.

Monitoring

Monitoring of the performance of states in discharging their human rights obligations is an infinitely more difficult task. Article 2(7) UNCh prohibits the World Organization from intervening 'in matters which are essentially within the domestic jurisdiction of any state'. According to the old doctrine,

---

[2] Declaration on the Elimination of All Forms of Racial Discrimination, proclaimed by GA Res. 1904 (XVIII), 20 November 1963; International Convention on the Elimination of All Forms of Racial Discrimination, adopted by GA Res. 2106 A (XX), 21 December 1965.

[3] Declaration on the Elimination of Discrimination against Women, proclaimed by GA Res. 2263 (XXII), 7 November 1967; Convention on the Elimination of All Forms of Discrimination against Women, adopted by GA Res. 34/180, 18 December 1979.

[4] Declaration of the Rights of the Child, proclaimed by GA Res. 1386 (XIV), 20 November 1959; Convention on the Rights of the Child, adopted by GA Res. 44/25, 20 November 1989.

[5] Proclaimed by GA Res. 36/55, 25 November 1981.

[6] Adopted by GA Res. 47/135, 18 December 1992.

[7] Adopted by GA Res. 53/144, 9 December 1998.

which prevailed before the Second World War, the relationship between a state and its citizens was indeed committed to the exclusive responsibility of the state concerned. Article 2(7) UNCh might therefore have served to fend off any attempt by the political organs, in particular the General Assembly and the HRCion, to concern themselves with human rights issues occurring in a domestic context.

The General Assembly and the HRCion

Indeed, during the first years after 1945 there was no room on the agenda of the General Assembly for allegations that a given state had breached obligations incumbent upon it to respect and observe human rights. The legal position was marked by uncertainty about the legal consequences deriving for states from the Charter. Since Article 1(3) UNCh confines itself to listing one of the purposes of the United Nations, it could be argued—and indeed was argued—that it established no more than a promotional obligation for the organization itself, while refraining from imposing a true legal commitment on Member States.[8] In their commentary on the Charter, Goodrich and Hambro did not feel it necessary to deal with this issue.[9] Eventually, the debate came to its end when in 1971 the ICJ ruled that South Africa had violated the obligations arising for it under the Charter to observe and respect 'human rights and fundamental freedoms for all without distinction as to race'.[10] As from that moment, it was clear that the references to human rights and fundamental freedoms in the text of the Charter were to be viewed not only as guidelines for the action of the UN, but also as determinations establishing firm legal commitments for states.[11]

It is hardly amazing that in a time when the legal position had not yet been clarified states were reluctant to be subjected to review by the General Assembly as to their human rights practices. It could still be argued that not much had changed in comparison with the pre-War period since human rights was still mainly a programme of action, which did not suffice to remove any relevant issues from the exclusive jurisdiction of states. Yet, some situations were of such gravity that even a world body largely dominated by the West felt that the voice of the international community could not remain silent. The treatment of persons of Indian origin in South Africa prompted the General Assembly for the first time to suggest practical steps for the solution of a human rights problem, although in very moderate terms by inviting the two litigant governments to report to the next session of the

[8] Hudson, 'Integrity of International Instruments', 42 *AJIL* (1948) 105.
[9] Lleland M. Goodrich and Edvard Hambro, *Charter of the United Nations: Commentary and Documents* (2nd edn, Boston, World Peace Foundation, 1949), at 96–97.
[10] *Legal Consequences for States of the Continued Presence of South Africa in Namibia (South West Africa) notwithstanding Security Council Resolution 276 (1970)*, Advisory Opinon, ICJ Reports (1971) 16, at 57, para. 131.
[11] See Schwelb, 'The International Court of Justice and the Human Rights Clauses of the Charter', 66 *AJIL* (1972) 337, at 348.

Assembly,[12] notwithstanding the argument put forward by the South African delegation that this was a matter within the domestic jurisdiction of the Union. A next controversy with a human rights dimension was raised by the Soviet refusal to let the Russian wives of citizens of other nationalities, in particular of foreign diplomats, leave the USSR together with their husbands, in the case of foreign diplomats after the termination of their mission in Moscow. In a strongly worded resolution, which referred to the rights enshrined in the UDHR to leave any country, including one's own, and the right freely to marry without any limitation due to race, nationality, or religion, it was recommended to the USSR to withdraw the constraining measures it had taken.[13] Almost at the same time, suppression of political freedoms in eastern European countries which had fallen under communist rule was stigmatized. For the first time, the General Assembly went as far as to express 'its deep concern' at the grave accusations made against the governments of Bulgaria and Hungary regarding the suppression of human rights and fundamental freedoms in those two countries.[14] As from 1952, the General Assembly concerned itself with the system of *Apartheid* which had emerged in South Africa in 1948.[15] These first steps were not generalized, however, to form a coherent system according to which the General Assembly and possibly the HRCion would intervene in all situations which seemed to reveal patterns of gross violations of human rights.

This became evident in particular with regard to petitions which the HRCion received immediately after its establishment from many parts of the world, in particular from eastern Europe.[16] These petitions were not welcomed by the Commission. Not only the USSR and its allies were afraid of being made accountable for their Stalinist practices, also Western states themselves did not have unchallengeable balance sheets. In the United States, racial discrimination was still rampant, and the principal European powers had not yet abandoned their large colonial possessions where on many occasions the rule of law was flouted. In ECOSOC Res. 75 (V), 1947, ECOSOC, the body to which the HRCion is hierarchically subordinated, declared that the Commission had 'no power to take any action in regard to any complaints concerning human rights'. Twelve years later, in 1959,

---

[12] GA Res. 44 (I), 8 December 1946. In subsequent resolutions until 1962, the tone was slightly raised. Still in 1954, South Africa enjoyed considerable sympathy for its standpoint that the General Assembly lacked competence in the matter, see *UN Yearbook (1954)*, at 86–88.

[13] GA Res. 285 (III), 25 April 1949.

[14] GA Res. 272 (III), 30 April 1949.

[15] GA Res. 616 A–B (VII), 5 December 1952.

[16] For full details see Alston, 'The HRCion', in id. (ed.), *The United Nations and Human Rights* (Oxford, Clarendon Press, 1992), 126, at 138–142; Carlos Villán Durán, *Curso de derecho internacional de los derechos humanos* (Madrid, Editorial Trotta, 2002), at 623–643.

ECOSOC adopted another resolution (728F (XXVIII), 30 July 1959) which consolidated the prior practice, although formally introducing some improvements by deciding that two lists had to be compiled of all incoming petitions, first a non-confidential list of all communications dealing with general human rights principles, and a separate confidential list giving brief indications of the substance of the other relevant communications. The latter list was transmitted to all members of the Commission in private meeting, and a copy of any communication referring to a particular state was sent to the government concerned which could, if it so wished, submit a reply to the Commission. But this was the end of a 'proceeding' which, in reality, was none: the Commission did not act upon the lists it received, and the author of a communication received no more than a letter confirming that his communication had been duly registered by the United Nations.

Rightly, this practice was severely criticized by leading international scholars. Sir Hersh Lauterpacht spoke of an 'extraordinary degree of... abdication' of the United Nations' proper functions,[17] and John Humphrey, former director of the human rights department in the UN Secretariat, called it 'the world's most elaborate waste-paper basket'.[18] It was clear that this state of affairs would heavily damage the reputation of the United Nations if no more generous attitude was taken in dealing with the thousands of letters which the United Nations continued to receive every year notwithstanding its refusal to take action.

Changes came about slowly and half-heartedly. On 27 May 1970, ECOSOC adopted Res. 1503 (XLVIII), which provided for action to be taken on the lists of confidential communications established by the Secretary-General. The Sub-Commission on Prevention of Discrimination and Protection of Minorities[19] was authorized to examine the communications contained in these lists with a view to finding out whether they 'appear to reveal a consistent pattern of gross and reliably attested violations of human rights and fundamental freedom'. A working group of the Sub-Commission was mandated to carry out the first screening, whereas the Sub-Commission itself was to be presented with a 'cleansed' list. Thereafter, the Sub-Commission could refer such communications to the HRCion which, on its part, was mandated to establish whether a 'consistent pattern' of gross violations might exist in the country concerned. Eventually, the HRCion could conduct a 'thorough study', which could lead to a report and recommendations thereon to ECOSOC, or establish an ad hoc committee to carry out an investigation.

Just the description of this cumbersome procedure shows that it could hardly be very effective. Difficulties were compounded by the fact that until

---

[17] *International Law and Human Rights* (London, Stevens, 1950), at 236.

[18] *Human Rights and the United Nations: A Great Adventure* (Dobbs Ferry, NY, Transnational Publishers, 1984), at 110.

[19] Its new name is Sub-Commission on the Promotion and Protection of Human Rights.

the very last moment all meetings were to be held in private. According to reliable (personal) information, in the working group of the Sub-Commission, a body of five persons, members more often than not acted on purely political grounds, seeking to fend off any attack against their country or any country of the 'camp' to which they belonged. Originally, it was not even allowed to publicize the names of the states under review in proceedings under ECOSOC Res. 1503 (XLVIII); only since 1978 has the chairperson of the HRCion announced the names of the countries concerned. These names were also mentioned in the report of the Commission, but in a way which made them almost irretrievable for someone not accustomed to such obfuscatory strategies. Just recently, more transparency has been offered. The Office of the High Commissioner for Human Rights has taken to publicizing on the Internet a list of states examined under the 1503 procedure (up until 2001), which now comprises 80 states. Unfortunately, the type of charge is not indicated. While the United States figures in this compilation, China and Russia do not. Political influences certainly are not absent from the proceedings. It is difficult to get information on whether the last stage has ever been reached.

Essentially, the merits of the procedure lie in the fact that a proceeding takes place and that at the level of the HRCion the diplomatic representatives of 53 countries look into the allegedly stained human rights record of the country concerned. Another advantage of the system is the character of automaticity which it can have if all the bodies in the complex hierarchical sequence act bona fide. If a certain number of communications reaches the UN, and if indeed these communications all complain of the same deficiencies, the procedure should start rolling. Hence, in principle no difficult choices are necessary.

Over the years, the 1503 procedure lost much of its importance because it had received a competitor in the 'open' procedure under ECOSOC Res. 1235 (XLII), 6 June 1967. This disaffection may have stimulated initiatives for reform. In fact, the procedure was recently amended by ECOSOC Res. 2000/3, 16 June 2000. While the original version of Res. 1503 said nothing about the way the situation in the country concerned was to be examined by the HRCion, leaving it in that regard complete discretion, the amended text has introduced principles of adversarial dispute settlement. At a first of two closed meetings, the country concerned will be invited to make an opening presentation, and thereafter a discussion is held by the members of the HRCion and the government concerned. When a draft resolution is considered during a second closed meeting, the representatives of the country concerned have the right to be present as well. Thus, the principle of due process has now been firmly established.

ECOSOC Res. 1235 (XLII) was adopted earlier in time than ECOSOC Res. 1503 (XLVIII). But the potentialities of the 'open' procedure it establishes had not immediately been recognized.[20] By adopting ECOSOC Res. 1235, the majority in the United Nations had wished to forge another instrument for combating the system of Apartheid in South Africa as well as remaining phenomena of colonialism and racial discrimination in Namibia and Southern Rhodesia (Zimbabwe). But the text of ECOSOC Res. 1235 is not confined to those territories. It focuses on grave violations of human rights anywhere in the world, again related to the formula: 'consistent pattern of violations of human rights.' The advantage of ECOSOC Res. 1235 is that it permits the HRCion and its Sub-Commission directly to deal with information it has received about such situations of grave violations, without having to go beforehand through an array of preliminary procedural steps. Thus, the two bodies do not depend on a specific number of communications having reached them, although originally the text of the resolution wished to tie them again to the lists of incoming petitions established in accordance with ECOSOC Res. 728F. They can rely on information from any reliable source. Delays can be avoided. Whenever an urgent situation arises, the HRCion may immediately proceed to examining the situation to which its attention has been drawn.

The major turnaround towards this new understanding of ECOSOC Res. 1235 came in 1974/1975 after the coup d'état against President Allende in Chile. The HRCion decided to set up a working group of five of its members to examine the situation that had arisen as a consequence of the coup.[21] For the development of the mechanisms for the protection of human rights, the conjunction of circumstances present on that occasion was extraordinarily propitious. On the one hand, Western states, posing as champions of the defence of human rights, could not raise objections against an objective inquiry to be carried out according to standards of fairness. On the other hand, socialist states were full of bitter resentment over the fall of a regime that had embraced ideals of socialism. Thus, they also gave their consent. Third World countries saw in the toppling of the Allende Government the hand of the US Central Intelligence Agency. For them, showing solidarity with the people of Chile was a natural gesture.

When the HRCion applied ECOSOC Res. 1235 to Chile, it had taken away from that resolution its contextual connotation as a tool for combating the evil practice of Apartheid. It was clear now that the resolution could be used also against the backdrop of other patterns of gross violations. But it took yet another four years until Res. 1235 became fully operative in this new perspective. Eventually, in 1979 the HRCion was prepared to follow the Chilean precedent by using the resolution generally for all kinds of serious

---

[20] For a detailed examination of the practice under that resolution see Alston, *supra* n. 16, at 155–181.

[21] GA Res. 8 (XXXI), 27 February 1975, adopted without a vote.

human rights violations. It may have been encouraged to embark on this new path as in the meanwhile the HRCee under the CCPR had taken up its work. Domestic situations and disturbances had thereby definitively lost their character as sacred zones not to be touched upon by international bodies. By Res. 14 (XXXV), 13 March 1979, the HRCion 'condemn[ed]s the violations of human rights and fundamental freedoms by the Nicaraguan authorities'. On the same day, by Res. 15 (XXXV), it decided to entrust a special rapporteur with the task of making a thorough study of the situation of human rights in Equatorial Guinea. Lastly, on 14 March 1979, one day later, it sent a telegram to the government of Guatemala, expressing its profound regret over the assassination of Alberto Fuentes Mohr, a former Minister of Foreign Affairs and Finance of Guatemala.[22] Through these actions, the entire system of human rights protection was freed of its one-sided orientation towards South Africa and the neighbouring countries in Southern Africa, Israel, and Chile. By its greater degree of objectiveness, it gained legitimacy and trustworthiness.

The very next year, new countries appeared on the list of those examined under ECOSOC Res. 1235. The Commission 'condemn[ed] all the gross and flagrant violations of human rights which have occurred in Kampuchea'.[23] Likewise, it expressed its 'profound concern at the situation of human rights and fundamental freedoms in Guatemala'.[24] Today, all inhibitions of a legal nature have evaporated. The HRCion feels entitled to inquire into any situation which it believes deserves to be examined. During the spring session of 2002, for instance, resolutions were adopted on the following countries: Burundi, Democratic Republic of the Congo, Iraq, Sudan, Cuba, Afghanistan, Sierra Leone. Nobody can deny that in fact in all of these countries the situation of human rights is far from meeting the standards required by the Charter or the conventional instruments which these countries have accepted. On the other hand, it has progressively emerged that the choice of the countries to be examined under the procedure of ECOSOC Res. 1235 goes through a preliminary phase of intense political haggling. Which country will eventually be put under scrutiny may depend more on its own might or the influence of its allies than its human rights record proper. It is remarkable, in this respect, that in 2001 Russia was for the second time in its history[25] made the target of severe criticism on account of its policies in Chechnya. In Res. 2001/24[26] (para. 3), the HRCion:

---

[22] Decision 12 (XXXV).
[23] Res. 29 (XXXVI), 11 March 1980.
[24] Res. 32 (XXXVI), 11 March 1980.
[25] The first resolution on Chechnya, Res. 2000/58, 25 April 2000, was worded in much softer terms.
[26] Of 20 April 2001.

strongly condemn[ed] the continued use of disproportionate and indiscriminate force by Russian military forces, federal servicemen and State agents, including attacks against civilians and other breaches of international law as well as serious violations of human rights, such as forced disappearances, extrajudicial, summary and arbitrary executions, torture, and other inhuman and degrading treatment.

This resolution clearly reflects the enormous loss of power which Russia has suffered since 1990. Yet, no matter how beneficial it may be that even a permanent member of the Security Council is called to account, it is clear that the will of the international community to respond to grave human rights violations should not depend on the factual weight of the nation concerned in the matrix of world power politics. For that reason, the automaticity inherent in the procedure under ECOSOC Res. 1503 may usefully compensate for the politicization to which ECOSOC Res. 1235 has been subjected. Human rights organizations, in any event, tend to become ever more critical of the performance of the HRCion. Thus, the International Commission of Jurists used such strong terms as 'shameful display of expediency' regarding the failure of the UN Commission to address serious human rights abuses in Zimbabwe, China, or Chechnya at its 2002 spring session.[27]

The developments in the HRCion were mirrored in the General Assembly. Like the Commission, before 1974 the General Assembly had focused its attention exclusively on South Africa and Israel. Still in 1973, the Third Committee, the body to which human rights questions are assigned, had on its agenda exclusively general questions of human rights policy which affect all countries alike. The Special Political Committee, on the other hand, dealt extensively with the report of the Special Committee to Investigate Israeli Practices Affecting the Human Rights of the Population of the Occupied Territories[28] and the Policies of Apartheid of the government of South Africa.[29] None of the criminal practices of other governments left any traces whatsoever in the register of the supreme body of the world community. This blindness, 28 years after the World Organization had been founded and entrusted with promoting and encouraging respect for human rights and fundamental freedoms, was truly disheartening.

It was a courageous step for the General Assembly to take when, on 6 November 1974, it adopted a resolution wherein it expressed its 'deepest concern' that constant flagrant violations of basic human rights and fundamental freedoms in Chile continue to be reported and 'reiterate[d] its repudiation of all forms of torture and other cruel, inhuman or degrading treatment or punishment'.[30] Obviously, the political configuration was the same as a few months later in the HRCion. The fact, however, that certain

[27] Press release, 26 April 2002.   [28] GA Res. 3092A, B (XXVII), 7 December 1973.
[29] GA Res. 3151A-G (XXVIII), 14 December 1973.   [30] GA Res. 3219 (XXIX).

political considerations stood behind this resolution does not detract from its great value as a general precedent for the development of enforcement mechanisms with regard to human rights. Many politicians and diplomats may not have noted in 1974 that a basic paradigm had changed, and it indeed took some years before the new orientation imposed itself on the practice of the General Assembly. While the HRCion had embarked on the course of country-specific implementation in the spring of 1979, the General Assembly followed in the autumn of 1980 with a resolution on human rights in Bolivia.[31] In 1982 attention was drawn on the situation of human rights and fundamental freedoms in Guatemala[32] and El Salvador.[33] With these two resolutions, the new course was definitively consolidated. Today, assessing the situation of human rights in a given country has become a matter of routine. At its 56th session in 2001 the General Assembly adopted resolutions on Cambodia,[34] Iran, 'parts of South-Eastern Europe', the Democratic Republic of the Congo, Iraq, the Sudan, Afghanistan,[35] and Myanmar.[36]

It is our conjecture that the new stance which the General Assembly took as an experiment in 1974 and generally six years later in 1980, can only be explained by the fresh approach to human rights ushered in by the HRCee. As before the Committee, an expert body of 18 persons, states had to answer searching questions concerning all aspects of their human rights policies, why should the General Assembly impose upon itself a discipline of complete silence even vis-à-vis the worst forms of lawlessness and arbitrariness in one or the other Member State? In strict juridical terms, the two settings could not be compared. The CCPR explicitly authorizes the HRCee to examine state reports. Politically, however, a comparison imposed itself. The main forum of the international community could not possibly appear to be much weaker than a body of 18 people chosen by the governments of the states parties to the CCPR.

It is obvious that the HRCion and the General Assembly need accurate and reliable information on a given country before they can proceed to pronouncing on the degree of compliance with the applicable human rights standards, or even stating that the country concerned disregards its obligations. In order to gain such knowledge, both bodies have developed a system of country rapporteurs. The official titles of these rapporteurs have been changed many times and are characterized by many nuances. Sometimes, even groups of independent persons were mandated to explore a given situation, as happened in the case of Chile. In general, the mandates of country rappor-

[31] GA Res. 35/185, 15 December 1980.
[32] GA Res. 37/184, 17 December 1982.
[33] GA Res. 37/185, 17 December 1982.
[34] GA Res. 56/169, 19 December 2001.
[35] GA Res. 56/171–176, 19 December 2001.
[36] GA Res. 56/231, 24 December 2001.

teurs do not vary a great deal. All of them are first of all entrusted with travelling to the country concerned to collect the requisite evidence. Evidently, a rapporteur must enjoy absolute freedom in the discharge of his/her functions. He/she must be free to see and to interview whoever he/she wishes to establish contact with. In no case may a government dictate to a rapporteur the choice of the evidence on which the report will be founded. In many cases, however, governments have refused to cooperate. After a first stay of the group of five in Chile, the Chilean government decided that some of the members of the group would no longer be allowed to visit the country. Therefore, a lot of the evidence had to be collected by interrogating witnesses in New York or in Geneva. Later, Cuba and Iran showed a similarly negative attitude. Concerning Iraq, the Special Rapporteur was allowed to visit the country for the first time after many years for five days in February 2002.[37] In such instances of denial of access, the report must be based on the sources available outside the country concerned or it cannot be drafted. Under the current system of international law, where states hold on to their territorial sovereignty, admission of a rapporteur for the discharge of a task mandated by the General Assembly is a decision which the state concerned may take at its discretion. It may be recalled that, unlike the Security Council, the General Assembly is not vested with powers of enforcement.

In the practice of the United Nations, it has also turned out that it is not enough to focus attention on individual states, since there existed—and still do exist—phenomena of non-respect of human rights which are not peculiar to one specific country, but cause havoc like an endemic disease across entire regions. After the HRCion and the General Assembly had acknowledged their full competence and hence their responsibility for the promotion and protection of human rights, they could no longer turn a blind eye to such practices occurring in countries for which no country rapporteur had been appointed. First of all, the HRCion, under the influence of an NGO campaign, established the Working Group on Enforced or Involuntary Disappearances, a decision designed to respond to developments in Latin America (Argentina, Chile, and Guatemala).[38] This new approach to securing human rights seemed originally more easily acceptable to the states under review because they were not individualized in the same fashion as in the case of appointment of a country rapporteur.[39] In fact, to date the resolutions addressing the issue studied by the special rapporteur do not even mention the names of the states where major departures from the path of correct law compliance were found. Additionally, the first mechanism of thematic

---

[37] See Report of the Special Rapporteur, Andreas Mavrommatis, on the situation of human rights in Iraq, UN doc. E/CN.4/2002/44, 15 March 2002.

[38] Res. 20 (XXXVI), 29 February 1980.

[39] See Villán Durán, *supra* n. 16, at 706.

reporting had essentially a humanitarian objective: the aim was to make disappeared persons reappear and not so much to expose the countries concerned to criticism. But the concept of thematic reporting soon developed a considerable dynamism. In 1982 a Special Rapporteur on Summary or Arbitrary Executions was appointed,[40] and 1985 saw the establishment of a Special Rapporteur on Torture.[41] Today, there exists a broad array of thematic procedures.[42] It would need a careful examination of the practice of the HRCion in order to be able to appraise accurately whether this bulk of information can really be adequately processed and serves a useful purpose. Instead of strengthening the procedure, the great number of rapporteurs rather seems to weaken it.

Just because of the scarcity of available resources and the limited working capacity of an individual, thematic rapporteurs cannot travel every year to any country that would deserve being scrutinized. They have to prioritize their work, trying to visit on a regular basis those countries where the worst deficiencies seem to exist. As individuals, they need no rigid rules of procedure.[43] In particular, they are in a position to receive individual communications without having to insist on prior exhaustion of local remedies. During their visits to a given country, they are able directly to contact responsible authorities in order to settle with them particularly urgent matters. Much depends on the courage of a rapporteur on such occasions. They must never be deterred from raising matters which the host government may utterly dislike being discussed. In their reports, they can formulate recommendations, and will normally do so.[44] But the formal conclusion of their work will be embodied in a resolution of the HRCion or the General Assembly.

Although resolutions of the HRCion and the General Assembly are important tools of a world policy for the protection of human rights, they are certainly no panacea to cure any conceivable ills. Their moral weight is considerable. No state likes being blamed by the world community for failure to heed generally recognized international standards. Therefore, if the spectre of a condemnation arises, governments normally work hard to avert such blame being addressed to their country. It is, in principle, the 'good' countries, which have an almost faultless record, that are most eager to keep the purity of that record. On the other hand, some 'loners' have become accustomed to living outside the mainstream. They have discovered that a state of

[40] ECOSOC Res. 1982/35, 7 May 1982.
[41] HRCion, Res. 1985/33, 13 March 1985.
[42] According to a report of the Secretary-General, *Effective Functioning of Human Rights Mechanisms: Human Rights and Thematic Procedures*, UN doc. E/CN.4/2002/112, 26 February 2002, the number of thematic procedures stood at 19.
[43] For a detailed study see Rudolf, 'The Thematic Rapporteurs and Working Groups of the United Nations HRCion', 4 *Max Planck UNYB* (2000) 289.
[44] For an overview see UN doc. E/CN.4/2002/112, *supra* n. 42.

harmonious coexistence with all the members of the international community is not a necessary condition for their survival. Cuba, for instance, takes pride in being the only country in the American hemisphere that dares to resist the United States—and has therefore the sympathies of many other states in Latin America which normally bow subserviently to American wishes.

The HRCion and the General Assembly have evolved a rich array of formulae to manifest in a nuanced way their views on the situation obtaining in a given country. At the lowest level, concern is expressed. Rising one step, 'grave concern' may be voiced. The gravity of this judgment may probably be equated with suggestions that certain occurrences must be 'deplored'. The intensity increases if one of the two bodies 'condemns' or 'strongly condemns' a development. Concerning Chile, the General Assembly expressed 'its profound distress' in GA Res. 3448 (XXX).[45] There are no limits to the imagination of the drafters of a resolution. In any event, as a rule the text reflects quite well the mood that prevailed in the body which authored it, making clear how serious the violation or the pattern of violations is judged to be. However, even if the disapproval of certain practices reaches its highest degree of intensity, this does not lead to any quantum leap that would empower the General Assembly to free itself from the constraints of its competences. Its judgment remains essentially a political one, having the legal character of a recommendation.

In sum, one may note that the two main bodies for the protection of human rights do not feel prevented in any way by Article 2(7) UNCh. With regard to human rights, this provision is not even invoked any more by the countries targeted by a resolution. This development needs to be explained.

Some authors attempt to argue that Article 2(7) UNCh has never been applicable to pure verbal utterances. Referring to classical statements about intervention, they have drawn attention to the features an act must have to be characterized as unlawful under the prohibition of that form of violation of national sovereignty. Indeed, according to a well-established definition given by Oppenheim and Lauterpacht, intervention is 'dictatorial interference by a State in the affairs of another State for the purpose of maintaining or altering the actual condition of things'.[46] This definition is in full agreement with the constitutive elements as they have been set out in the Friendly Relations Declaration of 1970,[47] where the verb 'coerce' stands at the centre of the rule enunciating unlawful intervention,[48] and the judgment of the ICJ in the

---

[45] Of 9 December 1975.

[46] L. Oppenheim and H. Lauterpacht, *International Law: A Treatise* (8th edn., London, Longmans, 1955), vol. 1, at 305.

[47] Annex to GA Res. 2625 (XXV), 24 October 1970.

[48] 'No State may use or encourage the use of economic, political or any other type of measures to coerce another State in order to obtain from it the subordination of the exercise of its sovereign rights.'

Nicaragua case, where coercion has also been highlighted as the criterion which marks the boundary line between lawful and unlawful political conduct in interstate relationships.[49]

This line of reasoning, however, is woefully flawed. The principle of non-intervention, as it applies in interstate relationships, and the principle laid down in Article 2(7) UNCh are not identical. Apart from the Security Council, which holds enforcement powers under Chapter VII of the Charter, no other UN organ has been vested with powers of 'coercion'. No sovereign entity can be deemed to suffer coercion just because its policies are censured by a resolution. Since, however, action taken by the Security Council on the basis of Chapter VII has been excluded from the scope of Article 2(7) UNCh, the rule laid down therein would have no field of application at all if, for its proper understanding, coercion were taken as the determining criterion as well. In other words, it follows by logical implication that intervention in the sense contemplated by Article 2(7) UNCh encompasses 'softer' forms of dealing with matters under domestic jurisdiction. Inasmuch as it is primarily aimed at the General Assembly, it certainly includes resolutions, i.e. pure verbal criticism, even without any threat of further action.[50]

Consequently, Article 2(7) UNCh would in principle apply if human rights issues had to be considered as 'matters essentially within the domestic jurisdiction' of the state concerned. After the rise of human rights in international law, this condition will rarely be met. According to the judgment of the PCIJ in the *Nationality Decrees in Tunisia and Morocco* case,[51] the question whether a matter is solely within the domestic jurisdiction of a state is a relative one, the answer to which depends on the development of international relations. To the extent, therefore, that a given issue is encompassed in the scope *ratione materiae* of a human rights guarantee, it can no longer be claimed by the state concerned as belonging to the area exclusively placed under its sovereignty. Since most states today have ratified the two International Covenants, and since additionally the body of customary international law of human rights is growing at an increasing pace, little, almost nothing is left that remains shielded from the reach of international normative standards. However, it must not be overlooked that Article 2(7)

---

[49] *Military and Paramilitary Activities in and against Nicaragua (Nicaragua v United States of America), Merits*, ICJ Reports (1986) 14, at 108.

[50] Completely self-contradictory were the observations by Felix Ermacora, comments on Article 2(7), in Bruno Simma (ed.), *The Charter of the United Nations* (Oxford, Oxford University Press, 1994), 150, para. 30; for a more accurate description of the legal position see now Georg Nolte in Bruno Simma (ed.), *The Charter of the United Nations* (2nd edn., Oxford, Oxford University Press, 2002), 152 at paras. 10–22. No definitive stance is taken by Gilbert Guillaume, comments on Article 2(7), in Jean-Pierre Cot and Alain Pellet (eds), *La Charte des Nations Unies* (2nd edn, Paris, Economica, 1991), 149.

[51] PCIJ, Judgment of 7 February 1923, Series B, No. 4, 24.

UNCh is generous in protecting national sovereignty by requiring less than full domestic jurisdiction. The boundary line runs where a given matter, even if touched upon by rules of international law, still lies with its main weight on the side of the state concerned.

The respect thus shown for national sovereignty is to be welcomed. Not any minor violation of a rule of international law should push a matter over the line and under the jurisdiction of the World Organization. Particularly in the field of human rights law, where every day thousands and maybe millions of cases fall to be handled in accordance with internationally based standards, it would be impossible if any small detail could immediately be put on the agenda of the HRCion or the General Assembly. Some degree of gravity, of increased relevance, must additionally characterize the situation under consideration. In this regard, as a rule of thumb one can certainly rely on the formula laid down by ECOSOC Res. 1235 and 1503: a consistent pattern of (gross and reliably attested) violations of human rights. This formula should not be treated as providing the only conceivable parameter. Thus, for instance, the assassination of a single person, a well-known human rights leader, or the house arrest to which the leader of the Burmese opposition, Aung San Suu Kyi, was subjected for years rise without any doubt to the level of gravity which is required. But the two main bodies of the World Organization dealing with human rights have absolutely no reason to go into tiny details. Whenever they decide to focus on a situation deemed by them not to be in conformity with the conduct required of a State by virtue of its human rights obligations, this shows in and by itself that the situation is of international concern. As far as we can evaluate their record of activity, they have never been discouraged from taking up allegations of serious human rights violations by the argument that this was a matter of domestic jurisdiction.

The line taken by the HRCion and by the General Assembly corresponds fully to the general and principled statements which the international community has in recent years rendered on its responsibility regarding human rights issues. The Declaration of the Vienna World Conference on Human Rights specifies that 'the promotion and protection of all human rights is a legitimate concern of the international community'.[52] A solemn commitment was also entered into by the heads of state and government present in New York to adopt the Millennium Declaration (paras. 24, 25),[53] which is not a document approved by the leaders of the world individually, but under the organizational cloak of the United Nations. Thus, this commitment stresses the responsibility of the international community organized in the United Nations.

Last not least, the United Nations High Commissioner for Human Rights (HCHR) should be mentioned among the institutional elements of the

---

[52] *ILM* 32 (1993) 1663, para. 4.   [53] GA Res. 55/2, 8 September 2000.

framework for the protection and promotion of human rights.[54] Established
by GA Res. 48/141, 20 December 1993, the HCHR enjoys an extremely
wide mandate. On the other hand, it is not easy for him/her to find an
appropriate place among the many bodies based either on the Charter or on
specialized treaties. On the one hand, it is incumbent upon him/her to
ensure, as part of the UN Secretariat, the implementation of the decisions
of the political bodies. The Office of the HCHR provides the material
resources for the different operational missions to be carried out in the field
of human rights. On the other hand, he/she has a wide margin of discretion
in defining concrete tasks. The greatest advantage of the Office is the
flexibility and swiftness with which the HCHR is able to act in situations
of emergency.[55] He/she can draw the attention of the international community to situations that require a rapid response.[56] On the whole, the office
holder can exert moral leadership in mobilizing and activating the international community. Success or failure in the discharge of this function
depend to a great extent on his/her personal stature. Unfortunately, as the
former Irish President, Mary Robinson, experienced during her time as
HCHR, the international community does not always appreciate a clear
stance and open words on situations and occurrences that imply grave
human rights deficiencies.

The Security Council

The Security Council has not been established as an organ for the protection
of human rights. As explicitly stated in Article 24 of the Charter, its mandate
is a different one. It bears primary responsibility for the maintenance of
international peace and security. At first glance, protection of human rights
and maintenance of international peace and security seem to have little,
if anything, in common. And yet, as the preamble to the Charter states, war
and armed conflict have been placed under the regime of the Charter because
they are susceptible of bringing 'untold sorrow to mankind'. This is tantamount to saying that prevention of war constitutes indirect protection of
human rights. In other words, there exists a clear connection between the task
of the Security Council and the task of the General Assembly to promote and
encourage respect for human rights and fundamental freedoms. In the practice
of the Security Council, this link has become visible time and again.[57]

---

[54] See Bertrand G. Ramcharan, *The United Nations High Commissioner for Human Rights*
(The Hague, Kluwer Law International, 2002); Villán Durán, *supra* n. 16, at 588–593.

[55] See, for instance, Howland, 'Mirage, Magic, or Mixed Bag? The UN High Commissioner for Human Rights' Field Operation in Rwanda', 21 *HRQ* (1999) 1.

[56] See, for instance, the latest *Report of the HCHR to the General Assembly*, UN doc.
A/57/36, 23 October 2002.

[57] See Bertrand G. Ramcharan, *The Security Council and the Protection of Human Rights*
(The Hague, Kluwer Law International, 2002).

Sydney S. Bailey has written a long chapter on the Security Council in the book *The United Nations and Human Rights*, edited by Philip Alston.[58] He distinguishes four sets of circumstances in which the Security Council has concerned itself with human rights. The first one of these four classes is the most interesting, being made up of instances where gross and persistent violations of human rights constitute a threat to international peace and security. It is clear that whenever a territorial situation is not definitively settled, the human rights situation in the disputed territory can serve as the litmus test for the existence of tensions coming within the purview of Article 39 UNCh. Consequently, the Security Council invariably takes into account the degree of compliance with the applicable human rights standards when assessing the overall situation. However, an even more pertinent question can be put: has the Security Council ever looked into a domestic situation when, in the absence of any territorial dispute, or dispute about the legitimacy of actually exercised territorial jurisdiction as in the case of Namibia, nothing else was at stake than the relationship between a state and one of its citizens or a group of its citizens? In such instances, human rights come into play not only as an appendix to a problem of peace and security, but as an autonomous issue.[59]

In one of its first resolutions after taking up its activity, the Security Council addressed the situation in Spain. The Security Council decided to make a study in order to determine whether the internal situation in the country—which had not yet been admitted to the UN—'has led to international friction and does endanger international peace and security'.[60] Although reference was thus explicitly made to 'international' peace and security, there can be no doubt that it was just the conditions of a dictatorship obtaining in the country which had aroused the anger of the Security Council. Furthermore, Spain was considered an outsider who had failed to support the efforts of the international community in bringing down the Nazi regime in Germany. Contrary to most other nations, Spain had remained neutral during the Second World War. One may therefore assume that a little element of ex post revenge underlay that resolution, the political orientation of which gave in the following years rise to vivid debates in the General Assembly, where progressively opposition to Spain became a predilection of socialist countries.[61] In hindsight, this first case serves as a perfect illustration how easily one may portray human rights concerns as matters

---

[58] 'The Security Council', in Alston, *supra* n. 16, at 304–336.

[59] See Aznar-Gómez, 'A Decade of Human Rights Protection by the Security Council: A Sketch of Deregulation?', 13 *EJIL* (2002) 223, at 225 et seq.

[60] GA Res. 4 (1946), 29 April 1946. Beforehand, by GA Res. 32 (I), 9 February 1946, the General Assembly had determined that Spain under the Franco dictatorship was ineligible for membership in the UN.

[61] See *UNYB (1948–49)*, 311–315; *UNYB (1950)*, 341–344.

coming within the scope of the Security Council as threats to international peace and security.

In the following years, one of the most significant determinations showing the concern of the Security Council for human rights was the adoption of SC Res. 554 (1984), 17 August 1984, declaring 'null and void' the new Constitution of South Africa (op. para. 2). For the first time, this Constitution had conferred some political rights on coloured people and people of Asian origin. Clearly, this constitutional reform was profoundly at variance with the principle of racial equality, one of the cornerstones of the legal framework of the United Nations. But it had nothing to do with international peace and security, except for the fact that the situation in South Africa as a whole was considered to constitute a threat to international peace and security.

The case which made abundantly clear that patterns of gross violations of human rights may be deemed to meet the requirements of Article 39 UNCh even outside a general framework of truly international tensions was SC Res. 794 (1992) on Somalia.[62] By that time, Somalia was already in complete disintegration. It did not threaten any of the neighbouring countries. On the contrary, it could be feared that perhaps one of its neighbours might avail itself of the weakness of the Somalian structures of governance to annex parts of Somalian territory. Given this situation, and without taking in any way into account the burden which the flow of refugees could entail for other countries, the Security Council determined 'that the magnitude of the human tragedy caused by the conflict in Somalia . . . constitutes a threat to international peace and security' (third preambular paragraph). This characterization was implicitly reaffirmed in SC Res. 814 (1993), 26 March 1993, where, after a detailed account of the situation prevailing in the territory of Somalia, the determination was made that that situation 'continues to threaten peace and security in the region' (last preambular paragraph), enabling the Security Council to take measures under Chapter VII. Although the Security Council avoided speaking of human rights, it stated that 'the re-establishment of local and regional administrative institutions is essential to the restoration of domestic tranquillity', thereby underlining the importance of a truly operative system of governance for the wellbeing of the population, i.e. enjoyment of human rights.

The Security Council dealt with the situation in Haiti along similar lines. After turmoil had disrupted the lawful exercise of governmental powers in the country, an attempt was made by the Council to restore the legitimate government of President Aristide. There could be no question of a threat to

---

[62] On the chain of resolutions starting out with SC Res. 794 (1992) see Lillich, 'The Role of the Security Council in Protecting Human Rights in Crisis Situations: UN Humanitarian Intervention in the Post-Cold War World', 3 *Tulane Journal of International and Comparative Law* (1994) 1.

international peace and security. Obviously, the United States had to shoulder a great part of the humanitarian burden resulting from an exodus of refugees, but such secondary consequences of internal instability remain largely below the threshold of a threat to international peace and security. Again, in a series of resolutions the Security Council deliberately avoids the word 'human rights', but speaks of 'humanitarian crisis' and a 'climate of fear of persecution'[63] and reaffirms the international community's commitment to 'a restoration of democracy'.[64] An objective assessment of these resolutions, however, permits the inference that the Security Council implicitly at least maintains that it is within its legitimate power to take measures for the protection of human rights if the situation concerned affects the whole population. This understanding also underlies SC Res. 929 (1994), 22 June 1994, on the situation in Rwanda, where the Security Council determined that 'the magnitude of the humanitarian crisis in Rwanda constitutes a threat to peace and security in the region'.[65]

In most situations dealt with by the Security Council, internal turmoil and violations of human rights go hand in hand with threats to neighbouring countries. By and large, the observer gains the impression that the Council has lost its fear of the word 'human rights'. Thus for instance, commenting on the situation in Sierra Leone, it referred to 'the continued violence and loss of life . . . following the military coup of 25 May 1997, the deteriorating humanitarian conditions in that country, and the consequences for neighbouring countries'.[66] Regarding Afghanistan, two years before the events of 11 September 2001, it 'reiterated its deep concern over the continuing violations of international humanitarian law and of human rights, particularly discrimination against women and girls',[67] and concerning the Democratic Republic of the Congo it expressed 'its deep concern at all violations of human rights and international humanitarian law, including atrocities against civilian populations'.[68] This broad vision of the concept of international peace and security is to be welcomed. It underlines the existence of peace as a precondition for the enjoyment of human rights. The Security Council thus has an active role to play in securing the general framework within which human rights become a tangible asset for human beings. It does not stand outside the framework for the enforcement of human rights.[69]

---

[63] SC Res. 841 (1993), 16 June 1993, preambular paras. 9, 11.
[64] SC Res. 862 (1993), 31 August 1993, preambular para. 5.
[65] Last preambular paragraph.
[66] SC Res. 1132 (1997), 8 October 1997.
[67] SC Res. 1267 (1999), 15 October 1999, preambular para. 3.
[68] SC Res. 1355 (2001), 15 June 2001, preambular para. 6.
[69] Obviously, however, it would hardly be helpful to engage the Security Council in the fight against HIV/AIDS, see David, 'Rubber Helmets: The Certain Pitfalls of Marshaling

II EUROPEAN UNION

In the European Union activities concerning the protection and promotion of human rights play an ever-increasing role. While for long decades the three European Communities lacked a text which formally established such activities as one of the goals of the common policies, this changed with the Treaty of Maastricht of 1992, which established (Article F(2)):

The Union shall respect fundamental rights, as guaranteed by the European Convention for the Protection of Human Rights and Fundamental Freedoms signed in Rome on 4 November 1950 and as they result from the constitutional traditions common to the Member States, as general principles of community law.

The Treaty of Amsterdam of 2 October 1997 expanded this formula by setting forth a new paragraph (Article 6(1)), worded as follows:

The Union is founded on the principles of liberty, democracy, respect for human rights and fundamental freedoms, and the rule of law, principles which are common to the Member States.

For the first time in the history of European integration, these principles were made operative. Article 7 TEU establishes a procedure under which the Council, acting by unanimity, may determine the existence of a serious and persistent breach by a Member State of the principles referred to in Article 6(1) EC. After that determination has been made—the vote of the state under review not being counted for the purposes of unanimity—the Council may then proceed to suspending certain of the rights of membership, including voting rights in the Council. To date, this procedure has never been set into motion. When in January 2000 a centre–right coalition seemed likely to come into power in Austria, after elections in October 1999 had resulted in a new majority with the rise of the Austrian Liberal Party, the European Union applied irregular methods to show its political disapproval of such a shift to the right. On 31 January 2000 the Portuguese EU Presidency notified the Austrian government that sanctions would be taken against Austria[70] if the Liberal Party were included in a new governmental coalition. Nobody could seriously contend that Austria had committed a 'serious and persistent' breach of its obligations under Article 6 TEU. Therefore, the lawfulness

Security Council Resources to Combat AIDS in Africa', 23 *HRQ* (2001) 560. In SC Res. 1308 (2000), 17 July 2000, the Security Council wisely restricts its attention to the danger which HIV/AIDS may pose to peacekeeping troops.

[70] Text of the note reproduced in 55 *Austrian Journal of Public and International Law* (2000) 237: 'Governments of XIV Member States will not promote or accept any bilateral official contacts at political level with an Austrian Government integrating the FPÖ; There will be no support in favour of Austrian candidates seeking positions in international organizations; Austrian Ambassadors in EU capitals will only be received at a technical level.'

of the strategy resorted to by the other 14 Member States depended on whether the procedure under Article 7 is meant to have an exclusive character or whether in cases of minor importance political discretion in responding to allegations of conduct incompatible with the commitment to respect human rights and fundamental freedoms is unlimited. It is understandable that a heated debate broke out on this issue.[71] At the end of the day, the stronger arguments were on the side of the defenders of the Austrian position. This was also the conclusion of the 'three wise men' mandated to assess the dispute.[72]

To comply with the requirements established by Article 6 TEU is also a requirement of membership. Any country wishing to join the European Union must live up to the standard set forth therein. Whereas for Member States a formal procedure exists which guarantees a fair hearing, candidates for membership lack such an opportunity to present their arguments if allegations of non-compliance are brought against them. Informally, of course, they are free to show that their record is faultless. But the necessity for any treaty of accession to be approved by all the existing members of the European Union constitutes a formidable procedural obstacle. This unanimity rule carries with it considerable political leverage, which could also be used for political manoeuvering. Currently, allegations are being raised against the Czech Republic that by endorsing and even praising to the present time the decision taken in 1945 to expel all the Sudeten Germans as well as the Hungarian minority of the population, the Czech Republic is not fit for membership in the European Union. Particularly worrying is a statute adopted on 8 May 1946, one year after the capitulation of Germany, still in force, which provides that all acts taken until October 1945 in a spirit of 'just retaliation' against the occupation forces 'and their accomplices' are not illegal—thus even murder and possibly also acts of genocide.[73] On the basis of three expert legal opinions,[74] however, the European Commission and Council have officially come to the conclusion that the shadows of the past do not impede the access of the Czech Republic to the European Union.

Instead of looking into its own affairs, the European Union has made it a habit to deal with the human rights situation in other countries, contrary to

[71] See, in particular, articles by Winkler, Hummer and Obwexer, Leidenmühler, Regan, and Weinberger, 55 *Austrian Journal of Public and International Law* (2000) 231 et seq.

[72] Martti Ahtisaari, former President of Finland, Jochen Frowein, former Vice-President of the European Commission of Human Rights, Marcelino Oreja, former Spanish Minister of Foreign Affairs. Report adopted on 8 September 2000, www.virtual-institute.de/en/Bericht-EU/report.pdf (visited December 2002); French version: 12 *RUDH* (2000) 154.

[73] See Tomuschat, 'Reckoning with the Past in the Czech Republic: A Test of the Homogeneity Clause Pursuant to Article 6 EC Treaty', in *European Integration and International Coordination: Studies in Transnational Economic Law in Honour of Claus-Dieter Ehlermann* (The Hague, Kluwer Law International, 2002), 451.

[74] Ulf Bernitz, Jochen Frowein, and Lord Kingsland.

what is happening at the United Nations. In 1983 the European Parliament began to publish reports on human rights in the world, following in that regard the documentation which is regularly published by the US Department of State.[75] Every year, it also adopts numerous resolutions on serious violations of human rights committed by governments anywhere in the world, depending on the gravity of the occurrences under review. It is hard to say whether these resolutions really impress their addressees or whether the routine character which they have taken on acts rather as an immunization, depriving them of any real effectiveness, all the more so since governments know that a parliamentary institution does not have at its disposal the necessary means of enforcement.

Since 1999 the European Council also publishes an Annual Report on Human Rights.[76] This report, departing from the model of the earlier reports of the European Parliament which were only outward-looking, focuses primarily on the 'domestic' situation in the European Union. But it refrains from examining the situation in individual Member States. Instead, it deals with certain topics of general importance for all of the members, such as racism and xenophobia, asylum and migration, and trafficking in human beings. Additionally, it gives an account of the practice of the European Union and its member countries in the bodies of the United Nations, the Council of Europe, and the OSCE. In this connection, the reader is informed about the steps taken by the European Union with regard to third states in Africa, Asia, Eastern Europe, the Middle East, and Asia.

The meetings of the European Council, where the Heads of State and Government of the Member States of the European Union meet, also produce regularly a series of formal statements about third countries whose human rights policies give rise to concern. Thus, at the Barcelona meeting of the European Council on 15 and 16 March 2002,[77] the Council addressed the situation in Zimbabwe,[78] in the Democratic Republic of Congo,[79] and in Nigeria.[80] Additionally, it published a 'Declaration of Barcelona on the Middle East', in which it admonished both parties to the Palestinian conflict to return to the path of strict observance of the law. After condemning the practice of suicide bombings, the European Council said that Israel must:

---

[75] Country Reports on Human Rights Practices; first report of 16 May 1983, *EuGRZ* (1983) 286.

[76] Latest report: http://europa.eu.int/comm/external_relations/human_rights/doc/report_01_en.pdf, 8 October 2001.

[77] Presidency Conclusions, Barcelona European Council, 15 and 16 March 2002.

[78] The Council expressed its 'concern about ongoing threats to the civil and political rights of senior members of the opposition party in Zimbabwe', ibid. at para. 66.

[79] 'Concern at the evolution', not substantiated, ibid. at para. 69.

[80] 'Deeply concerned by information . . . on the potential stoning of a woman in Nigeria', ibid. at para. 70.

immediately withdraw its military forces from areas placed under the control of the PA, stop extra-judicial executions, lift the closures and restrictions, freeze settlements and respect international law. Both parties must respect international human rights standards. The use of excessive force cannot be justified.

All this is certainly to be welcomed. But two caveats should be borne in mind. First of all, the European Union is a third party when it judges occurrences outside the Union itself—which it has never touched upon. Therefore, its declarations may from time to time appear as the expression of a patronizing attitude, rejected for no other reason than a feeling that the European Union continues a colonial tradition of domination, only with more sophisticated instruments than in earlier times. Secondly, if criticism is not supported by any real tools of enforcement, it is likely to be brushed aside, just as criticism expressed by the European Parliament will mostly be ignored. However, the European Council does have some means at its disposal. It can suspend preferential treatment under the new Cotonou Agreement with the ACP countries associated with the European Union. It can also stop any payments to a country committing grave breaches of its human rights obligations. Concerning Zimbabwe, the European Council hinted that it will consider possible 'targeted measures against its Government'.[81] In such a way, the more pastoral expressions of blame and reprobation may get real teeth.

III CONCLUSION

In conclusion, it can be said that political organs of international organizations play an important role in upholding human rights and fundamental freedoms. However, there is a great danger that statements of censure may wear out fairly quickly if and when the targeted states discover that such human rights activities have become a matter of routine for their authors and that no serious consequences will follow if no remedies are taken to introduce fundamental reforms.

---

[81] Ibid. at para. 66.

7

The Work of Expert Bodies: Examination of State Reports

I INTRODUCTORY CONSIDERATIONS

Today, the most current method of monitoring compliance by states with the obligations they have undertaken under a treaty for the protection of human rights consists of examining reports which states are required to submit at regular intervals.[1] In the ILO, this method has a long tradition. According to Article 22 of the Constitution of the ILO,[2] states parties to any of the agreements concluded under the auspices of the organization are subject to an obligation annually (in practice: periodically) to provide information on the ways and means by which they implement the commitments resulting from such agreements. Article 22 was already part and parcel of the original version of the Constitution, which came about as Part XIII (Articles 387–427) of the Treaty of Versailles (1919). Over the years, a sophisticated system of review took shape. The task of probing into the reports was entrusted to an expert committee (Committee of Experts on the Application of Conventions and Recommendations) comprising some 20 independent experts whose conclusions as to the degree of compliance with the commitments entered

---

[1] For a general assessment see Philip Alston and James Crawford (eds), *The Future of UN Human Rights Treaty Monitoring* (Cambridge, Cambridge University Press, 2000); Graefrath, 'Reporting and Complaint Systems in Universal Human Rights Treaties', in Allan Rosas and Jan Helgesen (eds), *Human Rights in a Changing East–West Perspective* (London and New York, Pinter, 1990), 290; Tomuschat, entry 'Human Rights, State Reports', in Rüdiger Wolfrum and Christiane Philipp (eds), *United Nations Law, Policies and Practice* (München and Dordrecht, Beck and Martinus Nijhoff, 1995), vol. 1, 628.

[2] 'Each of the Members agrees to make an annual report to the International Labour Office on the measures which it has taken to give effect to the provisions of Conventions to which it is a party. These reports shall be made in such form and shall contain such particulars as the Governing Body may request.'

into are submitted to the annual Labour Conference for further action. They are also widely publicized.

This system, which is still in operation today,[3] served as the blueprint when work started on the two human rights Covenants of the United Nations. Due to the long delays which the work on the Covenants suffered until its successful conclusion in 1966, it materialized for the first time in the CERD. According to Article 9(1) CERD, states parties undertake to submit for consideration by the CERDCee reports on the legislative, judicial, administrative, or other measures which they have adopted and which give effect to the provisions of the Convention. One year later only, the two Covenants came into being. Their primary modality of supervision follows indeed the ILO experience. States are required to report to the competent bodies on their practice, and these bodies then look into the information received (Article 40 CCPR, Article 16 CESCR). All later treaties adopted the same system, with slight variations of language only. Under all of these treaties, the reporting system constitutes the central pillar of the mechanism of control. Reporting is compulsory. Every state party must establish a balance sheet of its strengths and weaknesses. No reservation would be permissible regarding the duty to report. By contrast, all the other procedures are generally non-compulsory. They must be accepted specifically, requiring supplementary declarations which states parties are free to make or not to make.

In particular, for socialist states, which were extremely sovereignty-minded, the reporting procedure marked the outer limit of what they were prepared to agree to in terms of international supervision of their treaty compliance. According to their common position, any kind of complaint procedure went far beyond the realm of competence of the World Organization. Additionally, they were most critical vis-à-vis the methods evolved by some of the expert bodies, insisting that examination of state reports should not degenerate into some kind of investigation.[4] However, they could not stop the dynamic progress of the procedures which the members of the relevant bodies built up step by step with a view to making the conduct of proceedings a worthwhile exercise, one that would really contribute to enhancing the condition of the members of the national community concerned.

---

[3] These standards are subject to constant supervision by the ILO. Each member country agrees to present periodically to the International Labour Office a report on the measures taken to apply, in law and in practice, the Conventions which it has ratified. The government reports are examined by the Committee of Experts on the Application of Conventions and Recommendations, composed of some 20 independent, eminent figures in either the legal or social field and who are also specialists in labour matters. The Committee submits an annual report to the International Labour Conference, which is closely examined by a tripartite committee composed of government, employer, and worker members.

[4] See Graefrath, *supra* n. 1, at 300, 302, 306.

There is only one major human rights treaty which lacks a clearly defined reporting procedure, namely the Convention relating to the Status of Refugees.[5] To be sure, pursuant to Article 35(2) of the Convention states parties undertake to provide to the Office of the High Commissioner for Refugees information and statistical data concerning the condition of refugees, the implementation of the Convention and the text of laws, regulations, and decrees applicable to refugees. But there is no organ entrusted with examining that information. The High Commissioner him/herself, who is an international civil servant, cannot do so because he/she functionally depends on the states parties to the Convention. Thus, the information received, while being useful as a basis for carrying out assistance and rescue missions and generally reflecting the magnitude of the refugee population in the world, cannot be checked as to the compatibility of the reported facts with the legal regime introduced by the Convention. It has emerged that this lack of a genuine control procedure constitutes a major weakness of the Convention.[6]

II REPORTING SYSTEMS AT REGIONAL LEVEL

European Convention on Human Rights

At the regional level, reporting procedures also have some importance, although the relevant procedures have nowhere reached the degree of refinement which characterizes them within the UN system. Thus, according to Article 52 ECHR, the Secretary General of the Council of Europe may request from states parties explanations on the manner in which their internal law ensures the effective implementation of the provisions of the ECHR. But again, it is striking that the ECHR does not provide for a well-organized procedure to deal with the information furnished by the states concerned. In particular, the ECHR does not provide that reporting shall be done on a regular basis. Thus, requests may be made from time to time, when tangible clues suggest that a problem exists which requires particular attention. Originally, requests were only made to all states.[7] But Article 57 is by no means confined to that modality which, politically, does not presuppose any delicate choices inasmuch as by selecting a specific state the Secretary General would implicitly suggest that this state must be suspected of not living up to its commitments under the ECHR. Nothing, however, stands in the way of in fact making requests to individual

---

[5] Adopted on 28 July 1951 by the UN Conference on the Status of Refugees and Stateless Persons.

[6] On this gap in the protective system see Fitzpatrick, 'Refugee Protection in the Twenty-First Century', 43 *GYIL* (2000) 77, at 86–88.

[7] See Jochen Frowein and Joachim Peukert, *Europäische Menschenrechtskonvention. EMRK-Kommentar* (2nd edn, Kehl, Engel, 1996), at 735.

states only.[8] It is understandable, however, that given the procedure of individual applications, which since 1998 is compulsory for all states parties, the reporting procedure plays a marginal role only. Anyone who feels that his/her rights have been infringed may take his/her case to the Strasbourg Court of Human Rights. One can therefore assume that any major human rights problem will sooner or later end up before that Court, which is the most qualified body to assess a given situation as to its compatibility with the standards set by the ECHR.

African Charter of Human and Peoples' Rights

Under the African Charter of Human and Peoples' Rights (AfChHPR),[9] too, the reporting procedure constitutes the main modality of control regarding fulfilment by states of their obligations. According to Article 62 of the Charter, states must submit a report every two years. Examining such reports was not included in the original mandate of the African Commission on Human and Peoples' Rights (AfHPRCion) as set forth in the Charter. But the Commission sought permission to do so from the Assembly of Heads of State and Government, and it was authorized to proceed. Unfortunately, little is known about the real impact which the procedure may have had in the past. At the initial stage, observers had the impression that the 11 experts making up the African Commission on Human and Peoples' Rights were not able to act as independently as their colleagues at world level. Still today, the examination of reports seems to be characterized by a low-intensity approach. Thus, for instance, the Twelfth Annual Activity Report covering the years 1998 and 1999 devotes three small paragraphs to that exercise. Lumping together three countries, it states (para. 15):

The initial Periodic Reports of the Republic South Africa, Burkina Faso and Chad were presented at the 25th Ordinary Session. Expressing satisfaction at the quality of the Reports submitted and the dialogue thus established, the Commission thanked the Representatives of the States concerned for their services and encouraged the said States to continue their efforts, to make the fulfilment of their obligations stated in the Charter a tangible reality.[10]

---

[8] On 15 December 1999 the Secretary General of the Council of Europe requested from Russia 'explanations concerning the manner in which the Convention is currently being implemented in Chechnya, and the risk of violations which may result', see 20 *HRLJ* (1999) 454, footnote 73. As described by Rabiller, 'Le pouvoir d'enquête du Secrétaire général du Conseil de l'Europe', 104 *RGDIP* (2000) 965, at 979, this request elicited a response which essentially confined itself to portraying the Chechens as terrorists.

[9] Of 27 June 1981, 21 *ILM* (1982) 58.

[10] See critical comments on the lack of intensity of the examination process by Evans, Ige, and Murray, 'The Reporting Mechanism of the African Charter on Human and Peoples Rights', in Malcolm Evans and Rachel Murray, *The African Charter on Human and Peoples' Rights* (Cambridge, Cambridge University Press, 2002), 36, at 53–55.

The last available report, adopted in May 2002, reflects in similarly broad and unspecific terms the examination of the reports submitted by Cameroon, Lesotho, Mauritania, and Togo[11] (although it must be acknowledged that the annual reports may not always provide a true picture of the proceedings).[12] Additionally, few of the 51 states parties have submitted their initial reports as required.[13] Thus, the African system would have to make great strides ahead before being able to compete with the parent bodies, the work of which is described below.

III REPORTING SYSTEMS AT UN LEVEL

Monitoring Bodies

All of the bodies entrusted with examining the reports presented by states are made up of experts, i.e. persons discharging their mandate in full independence without being subject to instructions imparted to them by their governments. The CCPR, for which the HRCee exercises the monitoring function,[14] does not directly mention the word 'independence'. It provides that the members of the HRCee 'shall serve in their personal capacity' (Article 40(3)). Essentially, however, this formula means nothing else than independence and impartiality, as borne out by Article 38 CCPR, which requires newly elected members to make a solemn declaration according to which he/she 'will perform his [her] functions impartially and conscientiously'. Similar language can be found in the other treaties.

With regard to the CESCR, a different solution was provided for in the text of Article 16(2). The reports to be submitted on treaty compliance were to be transmitted to the Economic and Social Council (ECOSOC) for consideration. This proviso implied that the examination of reports in the field of economic, social, and cultural rights was regarded as a political task.

---

[11] http://www1.umn.edu/humanrts/achpr/activityreport15.html (visited December 2002).

[12] See the account given by Evelyn A. Ankumah, *The African Commission on Human and Peoples' Rights: Practice and Procedures* (The Hague, Martinus Nijhoff, 1996), at 99–107, and Murray, 'Report on the 1998 Sessions of the AfHPRCion', 21 *HRLJ* (2000) 374, at 380–384; ead., 'Report of the 1999 Sessions of the AHPRCion', 22 *HRLJ* (2001) 172, at 186–197.

[13] See Umozurike, 'Six Years of the African Commission on Human and Peoples' Rights', in *Recht zwischen Umbruch und Bewahrung: Festschrift für Rudolf Bernhardt* (Berlin, Springer, 1995), 635, at 638; Evans, Ige, and Murray, *supra* n. 10, at 41.

[14] On the HRCee see, for instance, Thomas Buergenthal, 'The U.N. Human Rights Committee', 5 *Max Planck UNYB* (2001) 341; Dominic McGoldrick, *The Human Rights Committee: Its Role in the Development of the International Covenant on Civil and Political Rights* (Oxford, Clarendon Press, 1991); Christoph Pappa, *Das Individualbeschwerdeverfahren des Fakultativprotokolls zum Internationalen Pakt über bürgerliche und politische Rechte* (Bern and Wien, Stämpfli and Manz, 1996), at 55–69.

ECOSOC is a political body, whose members are states, so that diplomats would have been in charge of assuming the workload resulting from that assignment. However, it is quite clear that in principle states are not willing to render such services to the international community through their delegates. Consequently, ECOSOC would have relied on preparatory work carried out by the UN Secretariat. For civil servants, on the other hand, it is highly delicate to suggest appraising the performance of states, which are after all the masters of the organization, in a specific—negative—way. In sum, it was discovered after a short while that upon closer reflection the mechanism had not been established with the necessary circumspection, and indeed the first experiences with ECOSOC as the monitoring body fully confirmed that negative prejudice.[15] In order to remedy this structural deficiency and to align the procedure under the CESCR with the procedures under the other treaty instruments, in particular the CCPR, ECOSOC adopted on 28 May 1985 Res. 1985/17 whereby it decided to establish an expert body of 18 members for the examination of reports submitted under the CESCR. After elections had taken place in May 1986, the newly constituted Committee on Economic, Social and Cultural Rights (CESCRCee) held its first session in March 1987, 10 years after the first session of the HRCee. The reform of the system was an unreserved recognition of the superiority of reliance on independent experts.

The question has arisen whether Article 40(3) CCPR implicitly establishes principles of incompatibility. Can an active minister, for instance, comply with the duty to act impartially? During its first term of office of four years from 1977 to 1980, the HRCee counted among its members the Minister of Education of the Imperial Government of Iran, Manouchehr Ganji, whose name was well known in the human rights community on account of two books containing a careful analysis of the human rights policies of the United Nations.[16] His membership, however, was not contested before the revolution in Iran. The new power-wielders attempted by every means to have Mr Ganji removed from office, but of course on account of his political orientation, not because of an alleged incompatibility of functions which came to an end the day the revolution was successful.[17] A minister is in a particularly delicate situation, having to promote the interests of his country at all times. It will be difficult for him to wear exclusively the hat of an

---

[15] Thus, in 1979, more than three years after the entry into force of the CESCR, the HRCion expressed 'the hope' that the consideration of reports submitted under that instrument 'will be undertaken by the Economic and Social Council', see Res. 6 (XXXV), 2 March 1979.

[16] *International Protection of Human Rights* (Genève, Droz, 1962); *The Realization of Economic, Social and Cultural Rights* (New York, United Nations, 1975).

[17] See hints at that attempt in the summary record of the 149th meeting of the HRCee, 26 April 1979, *Yearbook of the HRCee (1979–1980)*, vol. I, 115, paras 26–28.

independent member of the HRCee while being in session in Geneva or New York. For ambassadors, many of whom have been members of the HRCee, the dilemma does not reach the same degree of intensity although they, too, remain tied by the duties of their primary professional function. On balance, the requirements of impartiality and independence must be judged with a great deal of generous flexibility. No one is able to earn his/her living just by being a member of the HRCee or other expert body. In the past, members received a per diem and no more than modest honorarium, which was abolished (reduced to one symbolic dollar) with effect as from 1 January 2003. In other words, members of the expert bodies need a 'bread and butter' job to sustain their livelihood. That they should sever all links with their employers would therefore be an absolutely artificial request.

The second question in this connection is linked to the authority to make a determination on any issue of compatibility of functions. The HRCee or other expert body cannot expel any of its members. A replacement procedure is provided for in the CCPR only for instances where a member 'has ceased to carry out his functions' (Article 33(1)). Nonetheless, a decision of dismissal could *à la rigueur* be taken by the electoral body, according to the theory of *actus contrarius*: who elects the members of a human rights body may be able to put an end to their term of office. However, if and when the conference of states parties, which generally holds the power of appointment, makes clear by electing a certain person as member of the relevant expert body that it considers the requirements of membership to be fulfilled, this is a determination which cannot be challenged by anyone. Obviously, any appraisal of persons through elections is a highly sensitive process. Approval or disapproval of personal fitness for a post of public responsibility depends to a large extent on subjective judgement. Consequently, it is the governments assembled in the conference of states parties who bear the responsibility for ensuring a composition of the relevant bodies which corresponds to the specifications set out in the relevant texts.

Examining State Reports in Practice

The Early Stages

In hindsight, the development of the procedures applied today seems to flow automatically from the nature of the task to be performed. But it should be recalled that the period of the mid-1970s was still characterized by strong tensions between East and West. Socialist states, in particular, were extremely reluctant in framing the working details. When the CERDCee commenced its activities in 1970, it examined the reports it had received in the absence of anyone from the countries concerned. After a few years, however, it came to the conclusion that such endeavours were largely futile if there was no one to listen to the criticisms advanced by its members. For that reason, in 1972 the CERDCee adopted an amendment to its Rules of Procedure. Under the new Rule 64A, states parties were to be informed of the place and time for the consideration of their reports and thus be given the opportunity of being present.[18]

When the HRCee started considering the modalities of its work under Article 40, it also had to decide first whether representatives of states should be present at its deliberations. Broad consensus emerged as to the usefulness of such presence as it would make it possible to conduct a dialogue with the government whose report was under review. Article 40 lacks any clear indication in that respect. It confines itself to providing that the Committee 'shall study' the reports submitted by states parties. Constructive legal thinking was therefore necessary to devise an adequate procedural mechanism. Examination without a counterpart would have deprived the process of any effectiveness. Only if the arguments and counter-arguments are openly put forward can the ensuing debate on the substance of a report gain the necessary depth and intensity. Both sides benefit from an adversarial procedure. It is clear that on the one hand the HRCee—as any other expert body—is able to voice its concerns with more determination. If governmental representatives are present, it can be sure that its views will in fact arrive in the capital of the country concerned, reaching there the responsible ministerial departments. Commentaries in writing, by contrast, might have disappeared in the flood of paper produced every day by the huge administrative machine of the United Nations. On the other hand open oral proceedings can also be advantageous for states. If given the opportunity to participate in an oral exchange of views, a government can defend its policies by presenting the arguments supporting the decisions it has taken. It has an opportunity to reject criticisms that have been brought against it. These arguments were not fully discussed by the HRCee. The Secretariat had prepared a draft which, following the steps taken some years earlier within the framework of the CERD, provided for the presence of governmental representatives.[19] This prejudgment proved decisive. The members of the HRCee wrangled only about details of the role

---

[18] The current version of Rule 64 reads as follows: 'The Committee shall, through the Secretary-General, notify the States parties (as early as possible) of the opening date, duration and place of the session at which their respective reports will be examined. Representatives of the States parties may be present at the meetings of the Committee when their reports are examined. The Committee may also inform a State party from which it decides to seek further information that it may authorize its representative to be present at a specified meeting. Such a representative should be able to answer questions which may be put to him by the Committee and make statements on reports already submitted by his State, and may also submit additional information from his State.'

[19] Preliminary draft provisional Rules of Procedure submitted by the Secretary-General, *Yearbook of the HRCee (1977–1978)*, vol. II, 1, at 6: Rule 69.

to be played by such representatives. Eventually, it was decided to include in the Rules of Procedure the identical wording of Rule 64A of the Rules of Procedure of the CERDCee.[20]

Nothing was said in the Rules of Procedure on the way the questioning of the representatives present at the HRCee's deliberations would be conducted. The Committee discussed for several hours the method to be adopted for that purpose.[21] Since the power of examination is a power vested in the Committee and not in individual members, a formula could have been devised according to which members first had to agree on the questions to be posed, which would then have been put by the chairman. Such a cumbersome procedure, however, was not suggested by anyone. Even the member from the USSR, Mr Movchan, was of the view that every member should be free to put his questions as he saw fit.[22] In that regard, his proposals were generally supported. Eventually, therefore, it was decided that the state representative would introduce the report, that there would be an exchange of questions and answers, that the state representative would be given the opportunity to make a further statement to the Committee, and that lastly the Committee would express its thanks.[23]

This procedure proved effective, but it had certain limitations. For a couple of years, the second stage consisted of two totally separated parts. After the introduction of the report, the members of the HRCee one by one put their questions if they felt that the report was incomplete, contained inconsistencies, or needed to be clarified in light of factual data of which they had been apprised either by studying relevant materials on their own initiative or by information received from human rights groups, among whom Amnesty International demonstrated the highest degree of continuous perseverance. In such a way, hundreds of questions piled up. It was difficult for the delegations present, in particular if they lacked human rights specialists sent from their capitals to the meetings of the Committee, fully to understand all of these questions, to note them down, and eventually to reply to them after a period of two or three days. In that connection, it turned out that the quality of the dialogue depended largely on the quality of the persons sent to conduct the dialogue with the HRCee. The Committee therefore formulated the wish that the delegation present should comprise truly competent persons, rather than members of the diplomatic missions present in New York or Geneva.[24]

---

[20] Tenth meeting, 28 March 1977, *Yearbook of the HRCee (1977–1978)*, vol. I, 33, para. 29. It became Rule 68. For the current version of Rule 68 see [2001] *Report of the HRCee*, vol. I, UN doc. A/56/40, 180.

[21] 25th meeting, 16 August 1977, ibid. at 90–95.

[22] Ibid. at 91, para. 11.

[23] Ibid. at 95, para. 48.

[24] The guidelines for state reports in their current version, adopted in October 2000, [2001] *Report of the HRCee*, vol. I, UN doc A/56/40, Annex III, 162, at 166, specify in rule

For Committee members, too, it required a great deal of patience to listen to the answers given en bloc at one of the following meetings. Often, it could not be discovered whether an answer had been provided to a question or not. It was even more difficult to know whether the replies were true. After the Committee had for the first time examined the report of the People's Republic of Korea, lengthy explanations were given which apparently portrayed a country that was in full compliance with all the rights enshrined in the CCPR, a country which had little in common with the People's Republic.[25] And yet, it was impossible for the HRCee to react to the falsehoods with which it was provided since not even human rights organizations had reliable information on North Korea which they could have relayed to the members of the Committee.

On the other hand, the freedom enjoyed by members of the HRCee to put questions under their exclusive personal responsibility had many positive aspects. One country was particularly worried by the frankness with which they performed their functions—the USSR. Never before had the USSR in the long years of its membership in the World Organization been compelled to face up to really searching questions which it could not evade. Now a new tone was struck. Sir Vincent Evans (UK) requested information on a point which must have really shocked the representatives present. He said:

Reports had been published of healthy persons being interned in Soviet psychiatric institutions for political or punitive reasons, which would appear to be a clear violation of the terms of that Article [Article 7]. He asked whether those reports had been investigated and what precautions were being taken in the Soviet Union to ensure that such treatment did not occur.[26]

In its reply, the USSR tried to play down the political dimension of the question it had been asked. Its representative stated:

In the Soviet Union, persons suffering from illnesses that—for instance, venereal disease, leprosy, chronic alcoholism and drug addiction—constituted a danger to others could be made the subject of an order for compulsory medical treatment or hospitalization . . . There was, however, absolutely no question of any person in good health being interned. Indeed, such an occurrence was quite unthinkable.[27]

G.3: 'The State party's delegation should . . . include persons who, through their knowledge of and competence to explain the human rights situation in that State, are able to respond to the Committee's written and oral questions and comments concerning the whole range of Covenant rights.'

[25] 509th, 510th and 516th meeting, 9 and 12 April 1984, *Yearbook of the HRCee (1983–1984)*, vol. I, 439, paras. 2–9; 454–457, paras 3–34.

[26] 108th meeting, 24 October 1978, *Yearbook of the HRCee (1977–1978)*, vol. I, 378, para. 50.

[27] 112th meeting, 26 October 1978, ibid. at 399, para. 19.

It was clear to any observer that this response did not provide an answer to the real problem which at that time did exist in the USSR. Although from a formalistic viewpoint the examination had ended in a stalemate, since there were two statements which contradicted one another, it was a great victory in the interests of human rights that for the first time in history such issues could be openly addressed in an official body whose activities could not be dismissed as the expression of propaganda by foes of the USSR. It did not really matter that the discrepancy was not brought to a conclusion. It was a matter of common knowledge that internment of healthy persons allegedly on psychiatric grounds was one of the strategies pursued by the Soviet government to silence dissidents who could not be silenced by other methods.

Of course, at the centre of the procedure under Article 40 CCPR is the report submitted by the state concerned. It is understandable that states generally seek to describe the human rights situation within their territory in the rosiest colours. Contrary to the guideline established by Article 40(2), factors and difficulties affecting the implementation of the CCPR were rarely mentioned. The first few reports which the Committee received were highly unsatisfactory. Syria initially submitted a report of just one page, which indicated that the country was in full compliance with its obligations and that there existed no problems. This report, however, was immediately withdrawn after the attention of the country's representatives in Geneva had been drawn to the fact that such a report could not possibly meet the requirements of Article 40(1) CCPR.[28] Hardly any better was the initial report by Cyprus, which was also a document of great substantive modesty, covering in its printed version in the *Yearbook of the HRCee* less than half a page.[29] Very soon, therefore, the Committee adopted guidelines for states in order to inform them how they should deal correctly with their reporting obligation.[30] Nothing revolutionary was said in those guidelines. It was emphasized that reports should be in two parts. The first part was to set out the general legal framework of the country concerned. The second part, it was pointed out, should provide detailed information on each and every Article of the CCPR; sometimes even on a clause-by-clause basis, including factors and difficulties susceptible of hampering the full implementation of the CCPR.

As a consequence of these lessons, the general qualitative level of the reports soon rose quickly. But still, for many years and up to the present time, governments have a tendency to furnish the HRCee with all the bright

---

[28] For the report which replaced the original Syrian report see *Yearbook of the HRCee (1977–1978)*, vol. II, 16.

[29] Ibid. at 19.

[30] General Guidelines Regarding the Form and Contents of Reports from States Parties Under Article 40 of the Covenant, *Yearbook of the HRCee (1977–1978)*, vol. II, 248. Current version, as amended in October 2000: [2001] *Report of the HRCee*, vol. I, UN doc. A/56/40, 162.

sides of their legal system, demonstrating especially that their basic consti-tutional instruments contain all the guarantees enunciated by the CCPR. Rarely is a government prepared to admit that it experiences considerable difficulties in trying to translate the law on the books into living practice. Notwithstanding many obviously defective reports, the HRCee has only on a very few occasions made use of its power to request a new and better report (Article 40(1)(b) CCPR).[31]

For many years, the examination of a state report came to no real conclu-sion. After stage three, the response by the state representatives present at the meeting, the chairman thanked the delegation for its contribution, and that was the end of it. This unsatisfactory state of affairs was not only attributable to political tensions between members from the East, i.e. from socialist states, and members from the West, but resulted largely from the imprecise drafting of Article 40 CCPR. In the second clause of paragraph 4 of that provision, it is said that the HRCee 'shall transmit its reports, and such general comments as it may consider appropriate, to the States Parties'. But what are 'its reports'? and what are 'general comments'? This text not only raised problems of proper construction in a technical sense, but required answering the almost philosophical question what the essence of the reporting procedure was. While in particular Bernhard Graefrath, the member from the German Democratic Republic, suggested at one point that the role of the HRCee was confined to examining whether reports received were complete in pro-viding information on all the rights contained in the CCPR,[32] the majority of the members was of the view that a substantive review of the human rights practices of the country concerned was within the terms of reference of the Committee. In fact, the latter interpretation of Article 40 prevailed as soon as the oral encounters between the HRCee and the government authors of the reports under review began.

It would have been part of the logic of that approach to permit concluding observations by the HRCee after its 'study' of the report concerned. Without a summary of the main results, it was of course rather difficult to know what had really happened. Nonetheless, members from socialist states resisted any suggestions to formalize the conclusions to be drawn from the examination exercise.[33] Since the Committee had from its very inception decided to work

---

[31] This happened in the case of Chile on 26 April 1979, see *Yearbook of the HRCee (1979–1980)*, vol. II, 475, para. 108, and in the case of Guinea in November 1983, see *Yearbook of the HRCee (1983–1984)*, vol. II, 560, para. 156.

[32] However, in a later article he described the function of the HRCee as 'stimulating compliance, mutual understanding and the exchange of experiences in applying different means and procedures in the fulfilment of a common obligation' (*supra* n. 1, at 302). See also id., *Menschenrechte und internationale Kooperation: 10 Jahre Praxis des Internationalen Menschenrechtskomitees* (Berlin, Akademie-Verlag, 1988), at 136.

[33] For a precise reflection of those views see Graefrath, *supra* n. 1, at 305.

by consensus, a majority vote was ruled out. Instead, for the time being after lengthy debates in 1980 a compromise solution was found. In a statement on its duties under Article 40,[34] the HRCee decided to confine itself, during a first stage, to drawing up 'general comments' as mentioned in Article 40(4) CCPR. Such general comments were not addressed to individual states, but were designed to summarize the experience the Committee had gained generally in considering state reports. While immediately after issuing this statement the Committee indeed took as the basis for formulating general comments only the insights it had gained while examining reports, it later took to expressing in general comments its views on any difficulties it had had to tackle in discharging its mandate, also under the Optional Protocol.[35]

The compromise struck in 1980 did not resolve the issue of principle, namely what outcome a meeting with representatives of a state should eventually lead to. All the efforts to find a lawyers' solution by construction of the terms of Article 40 CCPR proved in vain. Since, as was clear from a careful perusal of the *travaux préparatoires*, the drafters had not had any clear ideas as to what 'its reports', i.e. the reports of the HRCee, were meant to be—its annual report to the General Assembly (Article 45) or special reports drawn up on the results of the examination of a country report[36]—a solution had to be evolved in the practice of the Committee.

Later Developments: The Current Situation

The lack of any formal conclusion of lengthy and intense meetings with state representatives was progressively felt to constitute a major weakness of the procedure under Article 40 CCPR. Such meetings could extend over several days, they could involve searching questions and carefully prepared answers on the entire constitutional system of the country concerned, but all that found no specific expression in a written opinion which everyone could rely upon. In that regard, a breakthrough came about when in July 1984 the second report of the German Democratic Republic (GDR) was examined. After the delegate from the GDR had finished answering the questions that had been put to him, a number of members asked for the floor and stated under their personal responsibility what had been, in their view, the main results of the dialogue which had gone on between the Committee and the delegation present before it. In that connection, they underlined that many questions had not been replied to and that, despite the answers furnished, some important problems of seeming inconsistency between the practice of the GDR and the requirements of the Covenant remained.[37] This practice

---

[34] Adopted on 30 October 1980, *Yearbook of the HRCee (1981–1982)*, vol. II, 296.
[35] See *infra* pp. 156–157.
[36] See on that issue McGoldrick, *supra* n. 14, at 89–96.
[37] 536th meeting, 20 July 1984, *Yearbook of the HRCee (1983–1984)*, vol. I, 541–543.

was soon generalized. In the summary records covering the discussion with the representatives of Chile in October 1984, this last phase of the proceedings was even placed under the heading 'General observations'.[38] In the following years, the annual reports regularly contained a section headed: 'Concluding observations by individual members.'

It is clear that such individual assessment by individual members did not have the quality of a collective assessment by the HRCee itself. However, if many members concurrently state that according to their view there exist major shortcomings in the practice of the state concerned, this carries considerable weight. In fact, for many years this new modality was accepted as a viable compromise while still a definitive answer as to how proceedings should be concluded failed to materialize. During the time of East–West antagonism, in any event, no solution was possible. A new system emerged only after the demise of the doctrine of socialism in central and eastern Europe.

It was during the examination of the Algerian report in March 1992 that the HRCee fundamentally changed its course. It decided that henceforth comments would be adopted reflecting the views of the Committee as a whole at the end of the consideration of each state report.[39] In fact, the Algerian report was the first one to be assessed collectively according to a scheme comprising the following sections: 1. Positive aspects; 2. Factors and difficulties impeding the application of the Covenant; 3. Principal subjects of concern; 4. Suggestions and recommendations.[40] All the other human rights bodies followed suit.[41] Before the decision of the HRCee, the CESCRCee, which had never drawn such a clear-cut distinction between concluding observations by individual members and a collective assessment by the Committee itself, defined at its sixth session in November/December 1991 its approach to the formulation of concluding observations.[42] No matter who can claim priority, the fact is that today not a single one of the human rights expert bodies refrains from pronouncing clearly on the facts and data as submitted by the government of the state under review. Interestingly enough, some states have begun to respond on their part to the concluding observations of the expert bodies. Sometimes, such a response may be highly constructive.[43] In other instances, the justifications put forward by the country

---

[38] 548th meeting, 24 October 1984, *Yearbook of the HRCee (1985–1986)*, vol. I, 17.
[39] *Official Records of the HRCee (1991/92)*, vol. II, 275, para. 45.
[40] Ibid. at 306.
[41] For the CERDCee see [1991] *Report*, UN doc. A/46/18, para. 31.
[42] CESCRCee, *Report on the Sixth Session* (25 November–13 December 1991), UN doc. E/1992/23, 99, para. 383.
[43] See, for instance, the Comments by the Government of the Dominican Republic on the Concluding Observations of the HRCee, UN doc. CCPR/CO/71/DOM/Add.1, 28 May 2002. It is doubtful whether the same can be said of the commentary by Syria, UN doc. CCPR/CO/71/SYR/Add.1, 28 May 2002.

concerned are poor.[44] In any event, the dialogue continues. If states act in good faith, the exchange of arguments may indeed lead to an improvement of the human rights situation to the benefit of the population concerned.

Over the years, the system has been further refined and amended. One of the characteristic features of the method in use today is the fact that regarding the examination of subsequent periodic reports—a new report is due every five years—states will receive a list of issues some months ahead, in order to be able to prepare themselves for the meeting with the HRCee.[45] Such periodic reports do not have to address each and every Article of the CCPR, but are required to respond to the concluding observations on the previous report as well as on the Articles in respect of which there have been significant developments since the submission of the previous report. Understandably, particular attention is given to the issues highlighted in the earlier concluding observations.[46] The Committee discusses the relevant issues one after another, expecting that a delegation present before it is in a position to provide immediate answers to most of the questions raised. In April 2002, in order to enhance the quality of the dialogue with the governmental delegations, the HRCee furthermore decided to establish 'country report task forces' consisting of no fewer than four and no more than six Committee members who are assigned the main responsibility for the conduct of the debate. In other words, these members are expected to be particularly well prepared. The formalism of the early years, where no additional questions were authorized after the governmental representative had made his/her point, is long gone. Interestingly enough, the reflection of the proceedings in the Annual Report of the HRCee to the General Assembly has been reduced to the reproduction of the concluding observations of the Committee. It would seem that such brevity does not do justice to the submissions of the governmental representatives, whose statements simply no longer appear in the Annual Report, not even in a summarized form.

Contribution of NGOs

Although members of human rights treaty bodies are elected as 'experts', this characterization should not be overrated. No one can have an intimate

---

[44] See Replies submitted by the Democratic People's Republic of Korea, UN doc. CCPR/CO/72/PRK/Add.1, 5 August 2002.

[45] This practice of establishing lists of issues to prepare the ground for a meaningful exchange of views was based on the Statement on the Duties of the HRCee Under Article 40 of the Covenant, adopted on 30 October 1980, *Yearbook of the HRCee (1981–1982)*, vol. II, 296, at 297 lit. (i). It actually commenced three years later, in October/November 1983, on the occasion of the examination of the Yugoslav report, see *Yearbook of the HRCee (1983–1984)*, 564–565, paras. 193–194. For a recent example of a list of issues see the document regarding Egypt, UN doc. CCR/C/76/L/EGY, 5 August 2002.

[46] For the revised consolidated guidelines for state reports under Article 40 CCPR see [2001] *Report of the HRCee*, vol. I, UN doc. A/56/40, Annex III A., 162.

knowledge of the human rights situation in all of the countries of the world. In order to discharge their functions meaningfully, members of such bodies therefore need outside support. Many non-governmental human rights organizations (NGOs) have perspicaciously seized the opportunity to inform them about the relevant problems.[47] Indeed, only if members are apprised of the actual situation obtaining in a given country can they put questions capable of remedying any possibly existing deficiencies. According to the HRCee's Rules of Procedure, NGOs have no official role to play. They are not allowed to intervene in debates where a state report is being examined. But of course they cannot be prohibited from seeking personal contacts with the members, furnishing them with information material which the members can then use at their discretion.[48] By resorting to such informal methods, however, NGOs have gained a considerable influence in the process. For the first time in 1981, a Dutch national NGO submitted a counter-report to the official national report.[49] When Japan's second report was examined in July 1988, several Japanese NGOs provided information to the members of the HRCee. It is common knowledge that on the occasion of the consideration of Japan's fourth report[50] this practice reached its peak: no less than 23 such 'shadow reports' were submitted.[51] Only the CESCRCee has granted official standing to NGOs. According to Article 69 of its Rules of Procedure, NGOs are free to make submissions to the Committee 'that might contribute to full and universal recognition and realization of the rights contained in the Covenant'.

Such response by national NGOs to the official report of their own government lacks all the overtones of Western cultural domination which similar information may have that is submitted by international NGOs. Amnesty International has always accompanied the work of the HRCee in a constant effort of sincere objectivity. Other international NGOs have their favourite themes or their favourite countries, and also their negative heroes. In any event, however, the international NGOs are one of the few sources of information on countries where political repression is so intense that no organization monitoring human rights compliance is tolerated. Thus, in

---

[47] General assessment by Clapham, 'UN Human Rights Reporting Procedures: An NGO Perspective', in *The Future of UN Human Rights Treaty Monitoring*, Alston and Crawford, *supra* n. 1, at 175–198.

[48] By Res. 1 (XL) of 1991, the CERDCee specified that members of the Committee may use all forms of information at their disposal, even materials provided by NGOs.

[49] 321st meeting, 21 October 1981, see *Yearbook of the HRCee (1981–1982)*, vol. I, 205, para. 11. Reference to that NGO document was criticized by the Soviet member, Mr Movchan, ibid. at 206, para. 21.

[50] On 28 and 29 October 1998, [1999] *Report of the HRCee*, vol. I, UN doc. A/54/40, 36, para. 143.

[51] Heyns and Viljoen, 'The Impact of the United Nations Human Rights Treaties on the Domestic Level', 23 *HRQ* (2001) 483, at 507.

the early years, not a single NGO could operate in any of the socialist countries. In the GDR, the symbol of the Peace Movement 'Swords into Plowshares' was considered a subversive symbol, and persons manifesting their adherence to that motto faced criminal prosecution. As already pointed out, the realities in the People's Republic of Korea totally escaped the Committee because it had no specific information to rely upon in its consideration of the report of that country. These occurrences show that the reporting procedure is not per se an effective tool for the protection of human rights. Where in a given country conditions of total repression and isolation obtain (which of course becomes somewhat rare in a globalized world), it does not have the potential to bring into the light the crucial issues affecting the legal system and the practice of that country. Ideally, any official report should be made public before submission to the HRCee or other body so as to enable citizens to inform themselves about the perception of their own government of the domestic human rights situation. Such publication would then provide NGOs with an opportunity to raise objections, possibly in the form of a counter-report with which they would furnish the members of the Committee. After the examination, the government should inform the public as to how the proceedings went. In particular, the government should publicize the concluding observations by the Committee.[52]

Delayed Reports

One of the major problems the HRCee has to face is failure by states parties to respect the deadlines for the submission of their reports. To some extent, those delays are understandable. Within the UN system, and in particular in the field of human rights, states are currently subject to a multitude of reporting obligations. For small states, this may sometimes be an almost unbearable burden, and even larger states do not feel comfortable in that respect, more often than not submitting their reports considerably late. Notwithstanding the sympathy which is due to weaker states, it is worrying to note that some of the delays incurred are enormous, to such an extent that the raison d'être of the reporting procedure would seem to be endangered. Thus, Gambia is the worst with a second report overdue for 17 years, with Suriname, Kenya, and Mali following closely behind with 16 years each.[53]

Under the CERD, some of the delays incurred by states are even more troubling. In 2002 Liberia, Guayana, and Suriname had not even submitted their initial reports. According to the 2001 Report of the CERDCee the delays amounted respectively to 24, 23, and 16 years.[54] But worst of all was

[52] The CERDCee makes this recommendation routinely in formulating its concluding observations.

[53] Ibid. at 29, para. 68.

[54] See [2001] *Report of the CERDCee*, UN doc. A/56/18, 92, 93, 98. The Committee also adopted a special decision on Liberia, decision 2 (59), ibid. at 107.

Sierra Leone, which after the submission of its third report in 1976 had stopped cooperating with the Committee.[55] Many other states have fallen behind for 15 to 19 years. Such obstruction by non-compliance with the time frame set by the CERDCee strikes at the heart of the idea of international monitoring. According to the classical rules, under such circumstances no examination can take place, since the report is the centrepiece of the process which is to take place before the Committee. Unfortunately, the consequences of such policies of neglect cannot be reduced to the simple proposition—no report, no examination of a non-existing report—but amount to non-examination of the situation in the country concerned, which may be disastrous for the population.

Therefore, with a view to discharging its responsibilities at least to a modest degree, the HRCee has recently decided to amend its Rules of Procedure in order to lay the foundations for an examination of the human rights situation in the country concerned even in the absence of a report—or in the absence of a delegation sent to introduce and defend a report that was actually submitted.[56] According to Rules 68 and 69A,[57] the state concerned will have to be notified of the intentions of the Committee. The Committee is also required to inform the state concerned of the materials chosen to form the basis for the examination where no report has been submitted. Ample precaution is taken not to affect the state's legitimate interests; such meetings will therefore be held in closed session. During the 75th session of the HRCee in July 2002, this new procedure was applied for the first time to Gambia, the second periodic report of which had been due since 1985. Very discretely, in full compliance with Rule 68(3) of its Rules of Procedure, the HRCee confines itself to stating that it adopted 'provisional concluding observations' which were transmitted to the Gambian government, not disclosing the contents of these observations. Another experiment was scheduled for October 2002 in the case of Suriname.[58] It remains to be seen how useful such proceedings *in absentia* of the respondent may prove to be.

On this issue, the CERDCee was ahead of the HRCee for many years. In 1991 it began a practice according to which compliance with the CERD can be reviewed in the case of states whose reports are overdue for more than five years. It is still hesitating to what extent under such circumstances it can base its findings on materials provided by NGOs.[59] In 2001 the situations in Gambia, Sierra Leone, Togo, and Liberia were examined. Only in the latter

[55] Ibid. at 97.

[56] As long ago as 1983, for the first time a report was examined in the absence of a representative from the country concerned (Guinea), see *Yearbook of the HRCee (1983–1984)*, vol. II, 558.

[57] [2001] *Report of the HRCee*, vol. I, UN doc. A/56/40, 181.

[58] See [2002] *Report of the HRCee*, vol. I, UN doc. A/57/40, para. 54.

[59] See *Report of the CERDCee, supra* n. 54, at 101, para. 467.

case, however, did the Committee adopt substantive observations.[60] Whatever the outcome of such proceedings where no interlocutor appears for the
state under examination, there is no doubt, in any event, that states which for
more than a decade are not able to furnish a report are on the brink of failing
as entities called upon to exercise governmental functions in a responsible
manner.

Consequences

Follow-up

In the early years of the HRCee, the notion of a follow-up procedure was
simply inconceivable. Since the examination of state reports did not lead to
a formal conclusion, there was nothing—no decision, no guideline,
no recommendation—the observance or implementation of which could
have been monitored. When in March 1992 the HRCee introduced its
practice of collective concluding observations, the foundations were laid for
a more proactive strategy. In its recently revised Rules of Procedure, the
HRCee has attempted to establish some kind of follow-up procedure. Rules
70(5) and 70A provide that a state may be requested to report back to
the Committee within a specified period, providing responses to the
Committee's recommendations. Such responses will be examined by a
working group and will result in the determination by the plenary of the
Committee of a definitive time limit for the submission of the next report.[61]
A decision adopted during the 2002 spring session[62] has further refined this
procedure. The Committee decided to appoint a Special Rapporteur for
Follow-up on Concluding Observations, who will first examine the information received from the state party concerned and transmit his/her findings
to the Committee. It appears that this new procedure is currently at its
experimental stage.

Effects of Concluding Observations

Quite naturally, the question arises what concrete effect the examination of a
report may have. It is clear that none of the human rights expert bodies has
the power to issue binding determinations. The 'concluding observations' are
no more than recommendations to the state concerned. But the lack of
juridical bindingness does not necessarily affect the effectiveness of such
observations. Countries that are eager to have a positive balance sheet in
the field of human rights, because in general they are committed to the rule of
law, will carefully evaluate any observations which have been addressed to

---

[60] See *Report of the CERDCee*, *supra* n. 54, at 74–76, paras. 429–443.
[61] [2001] *Report of the HRCee*, vol. I, UN doc. A/56/40, 25, para. 53.
[62] [2002] *Report of the HRCee*, vol. I, UN doc. A/57/40, Annex III, 153.

them, seeking to remedy any deficiencies to the greatest extent possible. Much depends also on the interest of the media. If the media of the country concerned consider the proceedings of human rights bodies as something not worthwhile to be reported, the government will feel less inclined to take the appropriate measures than if the media follow the consideration of their country's report with keen interest. Dictatorships may sometimes publicize their official report, or the statements of their representatives, but they generally abstain from providing access to the conclusions reached by the relevant human rights bodies. In the age of the Internet, such repressive strategies have lost much of their effectiveness, however. By accessing the website of the UN, everyone is in a position to inform him/herself independently, without needing the territorially available print or electronic media. Lastly, apart from the self-interest of the country concerned, it is pressure from outside which may induce it to change its human rights policies. In other words, the reporting procedure should be seen as a step in a process with several stages. The phase before the human rights bodies, where a critical assessment is made, is the phase where the international community takes cognizance of the relevant facts.[63] The last stage would have to be one of genuine enforcement. Entities and institutions of the most diverse nature should rely on the findings of the human rights bodies, demanding that the requests formulated by those bodies should be translated into reality. Understandably, third states will carefully weigh the pros and cons before taking any sanctions on their part. Thus, in the first place institutions of the international community should put their enforcement power at the service of the conclusions reached by the HRCee or other human rights bodies.

Expounding the weaknesses of the reporting procedure, Andrew Clapham has made far-reaching reform proposals. In a long-term perspective, he suggests that a permanent professional treaty body should be set up.[64] It is true that the burden on the members of human rights expert bodies is continuously increasing. For a person who is not a governmental civil servant, it has become almost impossible to serve on one of the relevant committees. Thus, there is a certain danger that almost the same people are to be found on both sides of the table. But the suggested concentration process would have a paralyzing effect on the monitoring system. The different treaty bodies have prospered in a certain climate of competition. Governmental delegations meet fresh faces and fresh ideas when they have to explain their country's

---

[63] See the vigorous defence of the reporting procedure by Alston, 'Beyond "Them" and "Us": Putting Treaty Body Reform into Perspective', in Alston and Crawford, *supra* n. 1, at 501–525, against criticism by Anne F. Bayefsky.

[64] *Supra* n. 47, at 197. He followed a call by Philip Alston to establish an expert group entrusted with studying the modalities for 'consolidating' the six treaty bodies, UN doc. E/CN.4/1997/74, 7 March 1997, para. 94.

performance within another field of human rights law. To destroy this pluralism would be fatal.[65]

General Comments and General Recommendations

General comments were already mentioned as the constructive outcome of a confrontation that took place in the HRCee about the correct interpretation of Article 40(4) CCPR. Seen originally as some kind of second-rate *Ersatz* for the absent assessment of state reports, general comments soon showed their usefulness in that the HRCee could explain to states parties how certain problems arising in the implementation of the CCPR should be dealt with. In the Introduction to a collection of the general comments hitherto adopted, the Committee stated in 1989:

The purpose of these general comments is to make this experience available for the benefit of all States parties in order to promote their further implementation of the Covenant; to draw their attention to insufficiencies disclosed by a large number of reports; to suggest improvements in the reporting procedure and to stimulate the activities of these States and international organizations in the promotion and protection of human rights. These comments should also be of interest to other States, especially those preparing to become parties to the Covenant and thus to strengthen the cooperation of all states in the universal promotion and protection of human rights.[66]

Although the examination of state reports was to be the main basis of general comments, the ensuing practice blurred this rigid demarcation. In the following years, the HRCee did not hesitate also to take into account its experiences from the consideration of individual communications under the OP-CCPR in framing general comments. Almost naturally, the first comments were devoted to the reporting obligations of states. Thereafter, the HRCee endeavoured mainly to comment on the scope and meaning of individual provisions of the CCPR. But it adopted also a number of comments on topics that cut across the entire Covenant, such as the position of aliens under the Covenant,[67] reservations to the CCPR,[68] or the continuity of obligations in instances of state succession.[69] It stands to reason that, in examining state reports or considering communications under the OP-CCPR,

[65] In a similar vein Scott, 'Bodies of Knowledge: A Diversity Promotion Role for the UN High Commissioner for Human Rights', in Alston and Crawford, *supra* n. 1, at 403–437.

[66] UN doc. CCPR/C/21/Rev. 1, 19 May 1989. See also Klein, 'General Comments— Zu einem eher unbekannten Instrument des Menschenrechtsschutzes', in *Recht—Staat—Gemeinwohl. Festschrift für Dietrich Rauschning* (Köln, Heymanns, 2001), 301.

[67] No. 15 (1986), *Compilation of General Comments and General Recommendations by Human Rights Treaty Bodies*, UN doc. HRI/GEN/1/Rev. 5, 26 April 2001, 127.

[68] No. 24 (1994), ibid. at 150.

[69] No. 26 (1997), ibid. at 162.

the HRCee will be guided by these interpretations. States parties, therefore, have the greatest interest in carefully reviewing the general comments, voicing their opposition in cases of disagreement about the proper understanding of the CCPR. In fact, it is above all the general comment on reservations (No. 24, 1994) which has elicited negative responses from the United Kingdom and the United States.[70]

Concerning the CESCR, the legal position was different. Part IV of the CESCR is rather vague and confines itself to prescribing that the reports received from states shall be submitted to ECOSOC 'for consideration'. But as far as the outcome of such consideration is concerned, the CESCR is more explicit than the CCPR in stating that the ECOSOC may submit from time to time to the General Assembly reports with recommendations of a general nature (Article 21). One may infer from this proviso, in particular, that one of the aims of the reporting procedure is to resolve practical problems of implementation. In any event, stimulated by the precedent set by the HRCee, the ECOSOC invited the CESCRCee in 1987 to begin the preparation of general comments,[71] and this invitation was endorsed by the General Assembly.[72] Thereupon, the CESCRCee adopted its first general comment in 1989. In general, the general comments particularizing the duties flowing from the CESCR are especially stimulating in that they make a tremendous effort to define the hard substance of economic and social rights. In that regard, general comment No. 3 on the nature of states parties' obligations set the tone.[73] After that statement of principle, the Committee moved forward step by step. It has issued general comments on the right to adequate housing (No. 4, 1991; No. 7, 1997),[74] on the right to adequate food (1999),[75] the right to education (1999),[76] and the right to the highest attainable standard of health (2000).[77] In order to establish a framework of objective criteria, it has attempted to lay down in all of these general comments specific benchmarks that are designed to permit measuring compliance by states in each one of the fields of action concerned. Although the Committee is prepared to take into account differences in development, it will not be easy for many states to live up to these standards.

In the case of the CERD, the legal position presented no difficulties since Article 9(2) clearly authorizes the CERDCee to 'make suggestions and general recommendation based on the examination of the reports and information

---

[70] [1995] *Report of the HRCee*, vol. I, UN doc. A/50/40, 126 and 130.
[71] ECOSOC Res. 1987/5, 26 May 1987.
[72] GA Res. 42/102, 7 December 1987, op. para. 5.
[73] *Compilation, supra* n. 67, at 18.
[74] Ibid. at 22 and 49.
[75] General comment No. 12, ibid. at 66.
[76] General comment No. 13, ibid. at 74.
[77] General comment No. 14, ibid. at 90.

received from the States Parties'. Most of these 'general recommendations' are of a summary nature. But some of them go far beyond devices for the resolution of technical problems. Thus, the Committee made pronouncements like the HRCee on state succession with regard to the CERD (general recommendation XII, 1993),[78] on the right of self-determination, denying a right of secession of groups within a state (general recommendation XXI, 1996),[79] on the rights of indigenous peoples (general recommendation XXIII, 1997),[80] and on discrimination against Roma (general recommendation XXVII, 2000).[81]

In the CEDAW, the formula contained in the CERD was copied identically (Article 21(1)). Therefore, the right of the CEDAWCee to formulate 'general recommendations' was firmly established from the very outset. Among the recommendations which it has drawn up over the years, some deserve special attention: its rejection of female circumcision (1990),[82] its condemnation of violence against women (1992),[83] its plea for real equality in marriage and family relations, which is a perfect elaboration of Article 16 CEDAW (1994),[84] and its insistence on equality in political and public life (1997).[85] By the choice of these topics, the Committee has shown that it understands the nature of the problems which afflict women in all or some parts of the world.

On the whole, the general comments and general recommendations have become a treasury of rules and principles which should guide every enlightened state party to the relevant human rights instruments in discharging its obligations. Unfortunately, their dissemination is not secured. Additionally, it cannot be overlooked that some of the statements of the monitoring bodies (e.g. violence against women) are directed against societal evils which even a well-intentioned state is not able easily to eradicate with the means it has at its disposal.

---

[78] General comment No. 14, *Compilation, supra* n. 67, at 182.
[79] Ibid. at 189.
[80] Ibid. at 192.
[81] Ibid. at 196.
[82] General recommendation No. 14, ibid. at 211.
[83] General recommendation No. 19, ibid. at 216.
[84] General recommendation No. 21, ibid. at 222.
[85] General recommendation No. 23, ibid. at 233.

8

The Work of Expert Bodies: Complaint Procedures and Fact-finding

I COMPLAINT PROCEDURES

Stocktaking

The international treaties for the protection of human rights have introduced two different complaint procedures: procedures open to states parties according to which one state charges another state with not fulfilling its duties under the treaties concerned (interstate complaints), and procedures permitting individuals believing themselves to be victims of a violation of their rights to bring a complaint to the attention of the competent review body (individual complaints). As far as terminology is concerned, at the UN level the practice has become firmly established to speak of 'communications' instead of complaints. In substance, there is no difference between a communication and a complaint, but the terminological downgrading of complaints to the level of mere communications has served to make acceptance of the relevant control mechanism easier for states. A communication, taken literally, is no more than a message, a piece of information, whereas a complaint carries the unpleasant connotation of a charge, an indictment against the respondent state. Thus, the word 'communication' is meant to portray a relationship of good understanding, where a constructive dialogue may remedy all the problems raised by its author. Communications suggest a friendly environment free of tensions that disrupt all bridges between the litigant parties.

Universal Level

Interstate Complaint Procedures

Interstate complaint procedures are provided for in many,[1] but not all[2] of the human rights treaties concluded under the auspices of the United Nations

---

[1] CAT, Article 21; CCPR, Article 41; CERD, Article 11; International Convention on the Protection of the Rights of All Migrant Workers and Members of Their Families, Article 76.
[2] CEDAW, CESCR, CRC.

since 1965. Except for the CERD (Article 11), interstate communications generally presuppose a special declaration to be made by the two states, the applicant as well as the respondent state. In practice, it has turned out that states have no great interest in resorting to formal international procedures when they are in disagreement with the human rights policies of another state. They generally prefer to make use of informal diplomatic methods, believing that such methods are more effective than formal procedures which invariably involve a third party. It is a fact, too, that to institute proceedings under a human rights instrument requires careful preparation, which is costly and may need a quantity of qualified manpower simply unavailable in the services of the ministries that would have to shoulder such a mission, the ministry of foreign affairs or the ministry of justice. In any event, none of the interstate procedures provided for in the relevant UN treaties has to date ever been activated. There are good reasons to believe that this state of affairs will not change in the near future, in any event not significantly.

Individual Communication Procedures

Individual communications constitute an important remedy which permits victims of human rights violations to vindicate their rights independently of any authorization by state agencies. Indeed, any such requirement would be absolutely contradictory since in the majority of cases it is the home state of the aggrieved individual which bears responsibility for the alleged interference. If and when private persons have thus been endowed with autonomous procedural rights operating at the international level, they may be called subjects of international law. In such instances, the state against which the complaint is directed is placed at the same level as the complainant, without being able to avail itself of its sovereign rights in order to extinguish the action brought against it. Even the enactment of a law would not produce the desired result. Only an act of denunciation in full conformity with the relevant denunciation clause, if any, can deploy an effect on the international plane. Thus, individual complaint procedures make human rights truly effective. In extreme terms, judge Cançado Trindade of the IACtHR observed in a concurring opinion in the case of *Castillo Petruzzi v Peru* that without the right of individual petition the ACHR 'would be reduced to a little more than dead letter'.[3]

The first of the UN treaties establishing an individual complaint procedure was the CERD. According to Article 14 CERD, states can, by virtue of a special declaration, recognize the competence of the CERDCee to receive and consider communications from individuals or groups of individuals. Only a few states have made that declaration. When the CERCee adopted

---

[3] 20 *HRLJ* (1999) 186, at 191.

its 2002 Report, the number of participating states stood at 41, which is hard to explain given the almost unanimous condemnation of racial discrimination in the international community. Quite surprisingly, furthermore, only a few persons have availed themselves of the opportunities provided by Article 14 CERD. In its latest annual report, the CERDCee was able to give a comprehensive account of its case law, covering slightly more than 20 concluded cases, in five small paragraphs on less than two pages.[4] Quite obviously, the individual complaint procedure is widely unknown to victims and to their lawyers.[5]

In the case of the CCPR, the complaint procedure has its legal basis in an additional instrument, the [First] Optional Protocol to the CCPR (OP-CCPR), which has accompanied the basic text since its very beginning. Consequently, a separate ratification according to the rules of the Vienna Convention on the Laws of Treaties is necessary. Currently (July 2003), the OP-CCPR has 104 states parties, which means that more than half of the members of the United Nations, two-thirds of the states parties to the CCPR, have accepted that their conduct may be scrutinized as to its compatibility with the standards established by the CCPR. No one could ever have hoped in 1966 that the OP-CCR would find such a positive echo in the international community.

Two states, however, have denounced the OP-CCPR—Jamaica and Trinidad and Tobago. Both countries were motivated to take that step after many clashes with the HRCee over persons awaiting execution in death row cells. In many instances, when persons sentenced to death filed individual communications, the HRCee requested by way of an interim ruling that no execution should take place until it had examined the case. However, the two countries were also under the supervision of the (British) Privy Council, the highest (constitutional) court for the British Commonwealth. According to the case law of the Privy Council, everyone who has waited for his/her execution for more than five years has suffered prohibited inhuman treatment and must therefore be released. It was the case that proceedings before the HRCee inevitably brought the length of proceedings close to the deadline of five years. Accordingly, the two governments felt that individual communications lodged by prison inmates sentenced to suffer capital punishment could be used as a means to obstruct the course of justice. The Government of Trinidad and Tobago therefore denounced the OP-CCPR on 26 May

---

[4] [2002] *Report of the CERDCee*, UN doc. A/57/18, 78–79, paras. 479–483. For a general assessment see Britz, 'Die Individualbeschwerde nach Art. 14 des Internationalen Übereinkommens zur Beseitigung jeder Form von Rassendiskriminierung', 29 *EuGRZ* (2002) 381–391; van Boven, 'The Petition System under the International Convention on the Elimination of All Forms of Racial Discrimination', 4 *Max Planck UNYB* (2000) 271.

[5] This is also the explanation provided by van Boven, ibid. at 285, for the 'dismal record' of Article 14.

1998, re-acceding to the instrument, however, on the same day with effect from 26 August 1998, subject to a reservation:

Trinidad and Tobago re-accedes to the Optional Protocol to the International Covenant on Civil and Political Rights with a Reservation to article 1 thereof to the effect that the Human Rights Committee shall not be competent to receive and consider communications relating to any prisoner who is under sentence of death in respect of any matter relating to his prosecution, his detention, his trial, his conviction, his sentence or the carrying out of the death sentence on him and any matter connected therewith.

In the case of *Kennedy v Trinidad and Tobago*, however, where the HRCee handed down its views on 2 November 1999,[6] it determined that the reservation was impermissible and therefore could not produce any legal effect. Consequently, it ruled that the communication brought by Kennedy was admissible and that the respondent government had to submit its observations on the merits of the case.[7] Understandably, Trinidad and Tobago did not accept this decision. It not only refused to cooperate any further in the case of *Kennedy*, but it then availed itself of the opportunity to denounce the OP-CCPR definitively on 27 March 2000.[8] It is clear that the overzealous attitude of the HRCee has done more harm than good to the cause of human rights.

Following chronological order, the next treaty is the 1984 Convention against Torture and Other Cruel, Inhuman or Degrading Treatment or Punishment (CAT). Article 22 CAT also provides for a procedure of individual communications, applicable to states making a special declaration to that effect. Few states have availed themselves of this opportunity (by May 2002: 49 states). Nonetheless, to date the CATCee has processed more than 140 communications. In 21 cases, violations by the respondent states were found.[9] Most of the communications concerned Article 3(1) CAT according to which no state party may expel, return, or extradite a person to another state 'where there are substantial grounds for believing that he would be in danger of being subjected to torture'.[10] It is interesting to note, in this regard, that almost all

[6] [2000] *Report of the HRCee*, vol. II, UN doc. A/55/40, 258.
[7] See dissenting opinion by Committee members Ando, Bhagwati, Klein, and Kretzmer, ibid. at 268. The confrontation between the HRCee and Trinidad and Tobago regarding the validity and effectiveness of its reservation has recently continued with the views expressed by the Committee in the case of Evans, 21 March 2003, UN doc. CCPR/C/T1/D/908/2000, with individual opinion Wedgwood.
[8] See [2002] *Report of the HRCee*, vol. I, UN doc. A/57/40, 146.
[9] For the statistical breakdown—which seems to be slightly inaccurate—see [2002] *Report of the CATCee*, UN doc. A/57/44, 73–5, paras 206–214.
[10] In order to apply this formula, the CATCee first asks whether in a given country there exists a consistent pattern of gross, flagrant, or massive violations of human rights. But this is not enough. The individual concerned must be personally at risk. He/she must face a foreseeable, real, and personal risk of being tortured.

states saw the procedure of interstate applications under Article 21 and the procedure of individual complaints under Article 22 as a unit, accepting them both, while Japan, Uganda, the United Kingdom, and the United States confined themselves to submitting to Article 21, with Azerbaijan, Mexico, and the Seychelles going in the opposite direction.[11]

In 1990 the International Convention on the Protection of the Rights of All Migrant Workers and Members of Their Families came into being. This Convention, too, provides for a procedure of individual communications (Article 77). Although it has not yet come into force, it will soon be removed from its unenforceable existence. The UN Secretary-General has now received 21 instruments of acceptance, and as Article 87 required acceptance by 20 states as the threshold for its entry into force, it will do so on 1 July 2003. However, even then the impact of the Convention will at best be modest. None of the major countries of immigration has chosen to become a party. Obviously, these countries are not interested in submitting to a tight discipline which considerably restricts their sovereign freedom to establish the kind of regime for aliens which they see fit.

Realizing that the real impact of an international human rights instrument is greatly enhanced by the availability of an individual communication procedure, many NGOs pushed for complementing the CEDAW by such a procedure. In fact, after many years of preparation an Optional Protocol providing for such communications to be filed with the CEDAWCee was adopted by GA Res. 54/4 on 6 October 1999. In contradistinction to the slow process of acceptance of the Migrant Workers Convention, this Protocol has been able to make rapid strides forward. It entered into force one year later, on 22 December 2000. To date (July 2003), it has been adhered to by 51 states. Since the CEDAW rapidly attracted an important number of ratifications, it can be expected that the OP-CEDAW, too, will continue to increase its membership fairly rapidly. To date, there exists no relevant practice of dealing with individual communications.

Lastly, mention must be made of two projects which might strengthen two more treaties for the protection of human rights.

In the CESCR, no provision is made for a procedure of individual communications. Obviously, this lack must be attributed to the nature of most of the rights under this Covenant, as explained above.[12] Again, however, efforts have been undertaken to bring the CESCR closer to the parallel instrument, the CCPR, by framing an optional protocol that would permit individuals to bring allegations of infringements of the rights enunciated in the CESCR to the attention of the CESCRCee. In 1996 the CESCRCee adopted a draft optional protocol for the consideration of communications

---

[11] See [2001] *Report of the CATCee*, UN doc. A/56/44, 80, Annex III.
[12] See Chapter 3 above.

concerning non-compliance with the CESCR.[13] As for the range of rights to be covered, the CESCRCee recommended that persons should have the right to raise complaints with regard to any of the rights enunciated in Articles 1 to 15 CESCR. This option may have rung a premature death bell for the project. It is of course extremely difficult to choose among the CESCR rights those which are suitable to be pursued under a complaint procedure. Any such choice risks antagonizing those favouring a 'holistic' approach. But to extend a future optional protocol to all of the rights, even those which unequivocally are confined to setting general goals for the policies of the country concerned, is unrealistically ambitious. Since the proposal was tabled by the CESCRCee, even 'progressive' countries such as Canada[14] and Sweden[15] have clearly expressed their misgivings. An independent expert was appointed to clarify the legal position, but his report[16] has not brought about the necessary elements of legal certainty since he felt committed to remain faithful to the intentions of the CESCRCee. Nor has a workshop held in Geneva in February 2001 been able to prepare the ground for a definitive determination on the issue. The HRCion, by its Res. 2002/24 of 22 April 2002, attempted to give the matter a new impetus by renewing the mandate of the independent expert for one year and committing itself to establishing, at its next session in 2003, an open-ended working-group to be entrusted with considering the various options. It cannot be expected that this brainstorming will yield the results wished by the CESCRCee, given the specific characteristics of economic and social rights.[17]

The CRC, too, lacks a complaint procedure. Compliance by states with their obligations under the Convention is monitored by examining reports. In legal doctrine, suggestions have been put forward to complement the Convention by providing for a system of individual communications.[18] To date, however, no initiative to that effect has been officially set in motion. Since the CRC contains a vast array of legal guarantees, reaching from civil and political rights to economic and social rights to provisions of a more philosophical nature, it would again constitute a major challenge for any

[13] [1996] *Report of the CESCRCee*, UN doc. E/1997/22, 91, Annex IV; UN doc. E/CN.4/1997/105, Annex.

[14] See UN doc. E/CN.4/1998/84/Add.1, 16 March 1998.

[15] See UN doc. E/CN.4/1999/112/Add.1, 4 March 1999; E/CN.4/2001/62/Add.1, 20 March 2001.

[16] E/CN.4/2002/57, 12 February 2002.

[17] For a short review of the confrontation which took place at the HRCion in 2001 see Dennis, 'The 57th Session of the UN Commission on Human Rights', 96 *AJIL* (2002) 181, at 188–189.

[18] Geißler, 'Die Rechte der Kinder durchsetzen: zur Frage der Schaffung einer Individual-beschwerde zum Übereinkommen über die Rechte des Kindes', 14 *Humanitäres Völkerrecht* (2001) 148; Weiß, 'Wäre ein Individualbeschwerdeverfahren auch im Rahmen der Kinderrechtskonvention sinnvoll?' 6 *Menschenrechtsmagazin* (2001) 85.

drafting body to select from the whole body of rules those which appear suited to be claimed in a complaint procedure. It can easily be predicted that this would be a Herculean task. It should not be overlooked, in this regard, that a child is a human being like any other human being so that it can avail itself of the opportunities provided by the existing complaint mechanisms. Real progress would be achieved if it proved feasible to identify those elements of the CRC which establish specific guarantees purporting to remedy the particular vulnerability of the child. A complaint mechanism linked to these elements would constitute a useful new piece in the toolkit of available mechanisms.

Regional Level

Interstate Complaint Procedures

Interstate complaints are provided for in Article 45 ACHR and in Article 47 AfChHPR. While in the former case a special declaration to be made by the respondent state conditions the admissibility of such a complaint, the AfChHPR does not establish a corresponding requirement. In Europe, the interstate complaint as set forth in Article 33 ECHR goes directly to the ECtHR.[19] In the Americas not a single such proceeding has been instituted so far, and regarding Africa just one case may be noted, the complaint brought by the *Democratic Republic of Congo v Burundi, Rwanda, and Uganda*,[20] which paralleled a proceeding that was pending for adjudication before the International Court of Justice.[21] The reasons for the modest role of the interstate complaint within a regional context are the same as those that have been shown to explain the lack of enthusiasm for recourse to the interstate complaint at the universal level.

Individual Complaint Procedures

Individual complaints have long since become a defining feature of the landscape of human rights protection mechanisms. In Europe, apart from the ECHR, which channels individual applications directly to the ECtHR,[22] a system of collective complaints has taken shape within the framework of the European Social Charter.[23] Precisely because the specific nature of economic and social rights makes it difficult to understand them as individual

---

[19] See Chapter 9 below.

[20] See Viljoen, 'Admissibility under the African Charter', in Malcolm Evans and Rachel Murray (eds), *The African Charter on Human and Peoples' Rights* (Cambridge, Cambridge University Press, 2002), 61, at 98.

[21] It is to be expected that this complaint will be withdrawn inasmuch as the three respondent countries pulled back their troops from Congolese territory in September 2002.

[22] See Chapter 9 below.

[23] Additional Protocol to the European Social Charter Providing for a System of Collective Complaints, 9 November 1995, *ETS* No. 158, in force since 1 July 1998.

entitlements, a number of carefully defined organizations have been given standing to raise claims alleging non-compliance with the commitments incumbent upon the state party concerned. These organizations are (Article 1) international organizations of employers and trade unions, other international non-governmental organizations having consultative status with the Council of Europe, and representative national organizations of employers and trade unions within the jurisdiction of the contracting party against which they wish to file a complaint. Any complaints actually lodged are examined by the Committee of Independent Experts. Although the circle of states parties is small, it comprises not less than nine states (December 2002). To date, the Committee of Experts has received 12 complaints, some of which are still pending before it. Essentially, the procedure under the Additional Protocol may be characterized as bearing the features of a class action.

In the Americas, the IACionHR existed more than a decade before the IACtHR. The latter came into being as a consequence of the entry into force of the ACHR on 22 November 1969, while the former was established by virtue of a resolution of the Fifth Consultative Meeting of the Foreign Ministers of the OAS in August 1959. Later, it received a formal legal basis in Article 112 of the Charter of the Organization of American States as amended in 1967.[24] Given the fact that the Commission predates the Court by a significant timespan, it has largely kept its former autonomous position without being reduced to an auxiliary body of the Court, only entrusted with screening communications as to their admissibility before they reach the Court. More often than not, the reports drawn up by the Commission remain the last word on the matter. Thus, the 2001 Report of the Commission[25] lists four cases in which a report on the merits was established, this being the last stage of the procedure.[26] The Commission does not feel obligated to submit any case or legal issue of defining importance to the Court. Again in its 2001 activity report, it boasts of more than 12,000 'pending or completed' cases.[27] One can even speak of an open rivalry between the two institutions which may not necessarily serve the cause of human rights.[28]

Since the IACionHR sees no need to submit all the cases it has received to the IACtHR, it must deal itself with all remaining cases. It does so in an

---

[24] Protocol of Buenos Aires, 27 February 1967, 21 UST 607.

[25] Doc. OEA/Ser./L/V/II.114, 16 April 2001.

[26] According to Article 51(3) ACHR not all reports are published. This is done only on the basis of a specific decision to that effect, in particular if the state concerned has not heeded the recommendations of the Commission.

[27] See *supra* n. 25.

[28] It is true, though, that to submit a case to a second examination as to its merits may lead to a harmful delay and to an unnecessary waste of intellectual and material resources in many instances.

impressive manner. Article 50 ACHR directs it to establish a report setting forth the facts and stating its conclusions after the examination of a case. This report may also be accompanied by appropriate proposals and recommendations. The state party then has a period of three months to react (Article 51). If the matter has not been settled by the expiry of that period, the IACionHR will, where appropriate, make pertinent recommendations and fix another period adapted to the circumstances of the matter. If that second deadline has also expired, the IACionHR 'shall decide...whether the State has taken adequate measures and whether to publish its report'. The number of such reports actually published is far greater than the number of judgments delivered by the IACtHR. To be sure, the reports do not contain any binding orders, but until recently the IACionHR proceeded from the assumption that a well-drafted report setting out the circumstances of the case at hand will carry such a high degree of authority that states will normally comply with its suggestions. This hope has evaporated on the basis of empirical data collected and reproduced in the IACionHR's 2001 report.[29] From the inquiries made concerning 17 recommendations, it has emerged that not a single case of complete compliance could be identified. Partial compliance was the diagnosis in two cases, while in 13 cases the response from the government concerned was entirely negative.

In Africa, too, the Commission established under the AfChHPR has been vested with power to receive and consider individual communications. Article 55 of the Charter explicitly states that communications may originate from other authors than states parties. In fact, a certain practice has evolved which seems to be improving over the years.[30] A new Protocol adopted in 1998[31] provides for the establishment of an African Court on Human and Peoples' Rights. According to the terms of this Protocol, the Court may be seized, on a regular basis, only by the Commission and the states affected by a case. But if a state makes a special declaration, the Court will be authorized to hear cases directly brought by NGOs and by individuals (Article 5(3), 34(6)). This Protocol, however, has not yet entered into force. By May 2002, it had received just five declarations of acceptance. For a long time, therefore, the communication to the AfHPRCion will remain the sole available remedy at the regional level in Africa. This remedy, though, has definite weaknesses. The Commission is not empowered to make binding decisions. Upon the consideration of a communication, it may submit its report to the Assembly

---

[29] OEA/Ser./L/V/II.114, doc. 5 rev., 16 April 2001, Chapter III.D: 'Follow-up on Compliance with Recommendations of the IACionHR.'

[30] See Murray, 'Decisions on Individual Communications by the African Commission for Human and Peoples' Rights', *ICLQ* 46 (1997) 412; Viljoen, 'Admissibility under the African Charter', in Evans and Murray, *supra* n 20, at 61–99.

[31] Reprinted in Ian Brownlie and Guy S. Goodwin-Gill, *Basic Documents on Human Rights* (4th edn, Oxford, Oxford University Press, 2002), at 741.

of the Heads of State and Government. Such a report may be published only upon a decision of the Assembly. In other words, no systematic collection of its case law exists. The fact that, starting in the mid-1990s, some indications were given about the facts and the recommendations adopted[32] in the annual reports was certainly not enough. Thus, the system looked doomed to failure as long as no general overhaul took place.[33] Such an overhaul seems, however, to have been carried out in practice.[34] Since its 1994 Annual Activity Report, the Commission reproduces views on cases submitted to it in their entirety as annexes, the publication of which must be authorized by the Assembly of Heads of State and Government of the OAU. But today, the Assembly no longer shies away from authorizing the publication even of opinions which are extremely unpleasant for the respondent state. Thus, in 2000 an opinion on discrimination against blacks in Mauritania was disclosed to the public.[35] The Fifteenth Annual Activity Report, adopted in May 2002,[36] reproduces the full text of the decision on a complaint brought against the Nigerian government on account of the treatment of the Ogoni people in connection with the exploitation of the oil resources in the Ogoni region. Without guarding its language, the Commission concludes that indeed massive violations have taken place. To publicize such a decision can be called true institutional progress—which certainly does not mean that in fact the victims will be granted effective relief.[37]

---

[32] See U. Oji Umozurike, *The African Charter on Human and Peoples' Rights* (The Hague, Martinus Nijhoff, 1997), at 79, referring to the Seventh Activity Report of 1994.

[33] See the criticism by Evelyn A. Ankumah, *The African Commission on Human and Peoples' Rights: Practice and Procedures* (The Hague, Martinus Nijhoff, 1996), at 74–77.

[34] See a well-balanced assessment by Anselm Odinkalu and Christensen, 'The African Commission on Human and Peoples' Rights: The Development of its Non-State Communication Procedures', 20 *HRQ* (1998) 235.

[35] Opinion of 11 May/12 July 2000, 21 *HRLJ* (2000) 413.

[36] http://www1.umn.edu/humanrts/achpr/activityreport15.html (visited December 2002).

[37] The essential conclusion reads as follows: 'Appeals to the government of the Federal Republic of Nigeria to ensure protection of the environment, health and livelihood of the people of Ogoniland by:
- Stopping all attacks on Ogoni communities and leaders by the Rivers State Internal Securities Task Force and permitting citizens and independent investigators free access to the territory;
- Conducting an investigation into the human rights violations described above and prosecuting officials of the security forces, NNPC and relevant agencies involved in human rights violations;
- Ensuring adequate compensation to victims of the human rights violations, including relief and resettlement assistance to victims of government sponsored raids, and undertaking a comprehensive cleanup of lands and rivers damaged by oil operations;
- Ensuring that appropriate environmental and social impact assessments are prepared for any future oil development and that the safe operation of any further oil development is guaranteed through effective and independent oversight bodies for the petroleum industry; and

Reservations

It is an issue of great importance whether states, when making a special declaration accepting a procedure providing for individual complaints, or when accepting an optional protocol for that same purpose, are free to enter reservations as they see fit. Of course, it would always be possible to insert a clause to that effect into the relevant conventional instruments. Nowhere, however, have such precautions been taken. It was therefore left to the interpretive efforts of the bodies concerned, in particular their case law, to settle the issue.

In one of its 'general comments' under Article 40(4) CCPR, the HRCee dealt comprehensively with the admissibility of reservations. This general comment No. 24 (52), adopted on 2 November 1994,[38] has become famous on account of its firm stand against the classical rules governing the issue. On the one hand, the Committee gave a very wide scope to the formula found in the Vienna Convention on the Law of Treaties according to which reservations incompatible with the object and purpose of a treaty may not be entered (Article 19(c)). On the other hand, it also said that such reservations must be deemed to be non-existent, meaning that a state having vainly attempted to limit the scope of its commitment under the CCPR will be bound over the whole breadth of the instrument, even with regard to the obligations it did not wish to accept. Quite naturally, this assessment of the legal position has elicited protests from a number of states, among them, most prominently, the United States and the United Kingdom.[39]

Drawing the logical consequences from the premise chosen, the HRCee argued in general comment 24 (52) that reservations to the OP-CCPR would be contrary to its object and purpose (paras. 13, 14). It said that the object and purpose of the OP-CCPR is 'to allow the rights obligatory for a State under the Covenant to be tested before the Committee'. The Committee 'must control its own procedures'. Generally, the Committee concluded, a reservation appended to the Optional Protocol would amount to a veiled attempt to make a reservation to the substantive provisions of the CCPR itself. Thus, according to the Committee, there exists a clear-cut alternative: a state can either refrain from submitting to international review, or it can accept that review, but intermediate formulae are not admissible. This rigid

---

- Providing information on health and environmental risks and meaningful access to regulatory and decision-making bodies to communities likely to be affected by oil operations.'

[38] [1995] *Report of the Human Rights Committee*, vol. I, UN doc. A/50/40, 119, Annex V; 34 *ILM* (1995) 840.

[39] United States: [1995] *Report of the HRCee*, vol. I, UN doc. A/50/40, 126, Annex VI, A.; United Kingdom: ibid. at 130, Annex VI, B.

position entailed as its first victim a reservation made by Trinidad and Tobago, as mentioned above.[40]

One of the most interesting reservations is the reservation by Germany. When it ratified the OP-CCPR (25 August 1993), it excluded from the scope of its instrument of acceptance communications 'by means of which a violation of article 26 of the [said Covenant] is reprimanded, if and insofar as the reprimanded violation refers to rights other than those guaranteed under the aforementioned Covenant'.[41] This reservation has to be seen against the backdrop of the jurisprudence of the HRCee in *Broeks, Danning,* and *Zwaan-de Vries,* where it held that by invoking Article 26 individuals are able to bring to the attention of the Committee any kind of unlawful discrimination, even instances of discrimination which relate to economic and social rights.[42] According to this viewpoint, there exists no limitation *ratione materiae* whatsoever for the Committee, provided that a complainant brings forward allegations of discrimination. Considering that the HRCee is a body specifically entrusted with protecting civil and political rights, that on the other hand is has little or no expertise in the field of economic and social rights, the German government sought to bar the Committee from extending its examination of cases to fields outside its mandate proper. To date, no case has arisen where a determination on the issue would have had to be made. It is fairly certain, though, that the HRCee would push the Article 26 reservation aside, following the precedent of the *Kennedy* case, but thereby risking that Germany might withdraw from the OP-CCPR altogether.

When the OP-CEDAW was drawn up, everyone involved in the drafting process was aware of the complex issue of reservations. The solution eventually found was simple. Article 17 simply forbids any reservation. Thus, states know beforehand that they cannot pick and choose from among the rights of the CEDAW those which they feel suited for being asserted in a complaint procedure, although such a choice may seem attractive specifically in the case of the CEDAW.

General Features of Individual Communication Procedures

Persons Entitled to File Communications

Generally, only *individuals* may file a communication. This results in the case of the CERD, the CAT, and the CEDAW from the logic inherent in these treaties. Only individuals, human beings, can suffer discrimination on racial

---

[40] See *supra* p. 162.

[41] A similar reservation was entered by Liechtenstein when it ratified the OP-CCPR on 10 December 1998.

[42] Final views of 9 April 1987, *Selected Decisions of the HRCee under the Optional Protocol* (hereinafter: *Selected Decisions*), vol. 2, UN doc. CCPR/C/OP/2 (New York, 1990), 196, 205, and 209; see *supra* p. 45.

grounds (Article 14(1) CERD). Likewise, only individuals, human beings of flesh and blood, can be victims of torture (Article 22(1) CAT). Lastly, since the CEDAW seeks to uphold the right of women to equality, it is women who can bring communications under the OP-CEDAW (Article 2). A question could arise, however, under the OP-CCPR. According to Articles 1 and 2 of that instrument, 'individuals' may bring communications to the attention of the HRCee. Since the CCPR is not confined to a specified category of persons, it could be asked in this connection whether corporate bodies or juristic persons are also placed under its protection. Under the ECHR, indeed, corporate bodies may invoke the rights guaranteed to 'everyone', as it results implicitly from Article 34 which grants the ECtHR authority to receive applications from 'any person, non-governmental organization or group of individuals'.[43] The HRCee has not adopted such a wide interpretation. Following a textual approach to the interpretation of the CCPR itself (Article 2 (1): 'to respect and to ensure to all individuals') it ruled in a number of cases that corporate bodies cannot rely on the provisions of the CCPR.[44] This inference is also buttressed by a number of teleological considerations. Within a European context it would seem almost natural to extend protection also to corporate bodies, since economic life takes place largely between and among actors who are organized as juristic persons. Protection of property, freedom of association, and freedom of entrepreneurial activity all concur to equate juristic persons with natural persons, human beings. At the universal level, however, the outlook is a different one. The HRCee was primarily set up for the protection of individual victims of human rights violations anywhere in the world. The opportunity to be listened to by the Committee is a scarce commodity. If corporate bodies were admitted as applicants, fierce competition for that scarce resource would ensue. Corporate bodies have other means at their disposal to secure their rights. Lastly, the CCPR is by no means 'economy-minded'. It neither guarantees the right to property, nor does it recognize a right to work or a right to professional activity. Therefore, the context is entirely different from the European context.

It is unclear what is meant by the formula that communication may be brought not only by individuals, but also by 'groups of individuals'. While

---

[43] Confirmed by the case law of the Court since its judgments in *National Union of Belgian Police*, 27 October 1975, *Publications of the European Court of Human Rights* (PECHR), Series A, vol. 19, and *Sunday Times*, 26 April 1979, PECHR, Series A, vol. 30 (hereinafter A 19 and A 30).

[44] See final views in *J. R. T. and W. G. Party*, 6 April 1983, 2 *Selected Decisions* (1990) 25, at 27, para. 8, and *Group of Associations*, 10 April 1984, ibid. at 48, para. 5. This jurisprudence has recently been confirmed by the General Comment of the HRCee on Article 2, The Nature of the General Legal Obligation Imposed on States Parties to the Covenant, UN doc. CCPR/C/74/CRP.4/Rev.3, 5 May 2003.

Article 14(1) CERD mentions 'groups of individuals' alongside individuals, Article 2 OP-CEDAW has set out a complex formula which should be quoted word for word:

Communications may be submitted by or on behalf of individuals or groups of individuals . . . claiming to be victims of a violation of any of the rights set forth in the Convention by that state party. Where a communication is submitted on behalf of individuals or groups of individuals, this shall be with their consent unless the author can justify acting on their behalf without such consent.

It is obvious that no special provision is needed for instances where a plurality of persons brings a claim before the CEDAWCee, each person acting, however, on her own behalf, so that the only link is of a temporal nature or consists of common representation by counsel. Therefore, it would appear that the specific mention of 'groups of persons' has a special meaning. It is certainly not too far-fetched to argue that, by explicitly referring to 'groups of persons', the drafters wished to indicate that in such instances the victim requirement—the requirement that a person bringing a communication claim that she has been the victim of a violation—should be softened. Whereas as an individual a woman would have to show that she personally was the target of an official act affecting her rights, in the case of groups it could be sufficient to show that by virtue of a legislative act or of a general administrative measure a given group was placed under some kind of general discrimination. Consequently, Article 2 OP-CEDAW would provide the basis for some kind of *'abstrakte Normenkontrolle'*, which under German constitutional law is a concept with well-defined contours.[45] Since the CERDCee has not yet had to address this problem of legal construction and since regarding the OP-CEDAW there exists no practice whatsoever as yet, no definitive answer can be given at this point in time.

At the regional level both in the Americas and in Africa, the criteria of admissibility *ratione personae* are more generous. Article 44 ACHR specifies explicitly that any group of persons or 'any non-governmental entity legally recognized in one or more member states of the Organization' may lodge petitions. In contrast, Article 56 AfChHPR does not set forth an explicit rule on who may legitimately assert his/her rights before the African Commission. This lacuna has been interpreted, however, to mean that NGOs are free to institute proceedings.[46]

---

[45] For a first attempt at clarification see Tomuschat, 'Learning from the Human Rights Committee's Experience: The Optional Protocol to the Convention Banning Discrimination Against Women', in *Recht—Staat—Gemeinwohl: Festschrift für Dietrich Rauschning* (Köln, Heymanns, 2001), 313.

[46] See Viljoen *supra* n. 20, at 76.

Rights that Can be Asserted

In most instances, it will not be difficult to identify the *rights* the violation of which an applicant will have to claim in order to meet the requirements of admissibility. Under the CCPR, in particular, all the Articles in Part III (Articles 6 to 27) set forth individual entitlements which everyone can assert through filing a communication with the HRCee. However, the CEDAWCee will have to face up to considerable difficulties when beginning its work under the OP-CEDAW. This prediction is first of all due to the fact that the CEDAW is not framed as a text which enunciates rights of women, but has been formulated according to the 'duties model': it generally enjoins states to 'take all appropriate measures to...' eliminate some of the inequalities which still exist. Although some of these duties can be conceived of as rights of women, which are perfectly susceptible of being claimed by way of individual communication, others are of such a general nature that it would certainly be hard to construe them at the same time as rights which individual women or groups of women could possibly vindicate under the OP-CEDAW. A good example is provided by Article 10(c) CEDAW according to which states parties are to ensure 'the elimination of any stereotyped concept of the roles of men and women at all levels and in all forms of education by encouraging coeducation and other types of education which will help to achieve this aim'. In order to prevent such difficulties, the drafters of the OP-CEDAW could have made an appropriate choice among the different provisions of the CEDAW, selecting those provisions suitable for direct application to the benefit of individuals and leaving aside those other provisions which require concretization by complementary acts of legislation. This option, however, was rejected, and admittedly to make that choice would have required a huge intellectual effort. Given this restraint on the part of the competent drafting bodies, it will now fall to the CEDAWCee to determine, in each case, whether a provision the violation of which the applicant relies upon does indeed enshrine an individual entitlement.

It would be even more difficult to carry out a similar exercise with regard to the CESCR. As described above, the future optional protocol recommended by the CESCRCee is meant to cover all the substantive rights set forth in the CESCR, including even Article 1, the right to self-determination, to the extent that 'economic, social and cultural rights dimensions of that right are concerned'. First of all, it should be noted that the right of self-determination is not an individual right, but a right of peoples. It would therefore be quite illogical to include Article 1 in the list of rights the violation of which could be invoked under an optional protocol providing for individual communications. Rightly, the HRCee has evolved a jurisprudence which excludes Article 1 CCPR from the scope of the OP-CCPR, given that that instrument is designed to assist individuals in their defence against unlawful governmental acts.[47] Secondly, the maximalist approach of the CESCRCee deliberately avoids taking note of the specific character of the rights laid down in the CESCR. It implicitly contends that all of the rights listed in Articles 2 to 15 CESCR provide individual entitlements, which visibly they do not. The majority of states have made their reluctance clear by simply not responding to the many calls of the UN Secretary-General and the HRCion to submit comments on the draft optional protocol.

According to the new Rules of Procedure of the IACionHR, adopted in 2001,[48] petitioners may now claim violation of any right contained in one of the many human rights instruments of the OAS, including the Additional Protocol in the Area of Economic, Social and Cultural Rights (Article 23). It is not yet certain how this experiment will work out. It would appear that to date the scarce available evidence does not even permit a provisional appraisal of this fairly bold step.

Standing

Obviously, the issue of standing must arise in this connection as well. It is an important question whether an individual or other entity authorized to file a communication may assert only his/her own rights or whether he/she may defend the rights of other persons or raise in general the issue of compatibility of the challenged act with the rights guaranteed under the instrument concerned. Given the fact that in many instances of criminal state conduct individuals are kept incommunicado, unable to establish contact with their families or a lawyer, the HRCee set forth from the inception of its work in Rule 90(b) of its Rules of Procedure that it may accept a communication submitted 'on behalf of the alleged victim' when it appears that the victim is unable to file the communication personally. This rule has met with widespread recognition. It can also be found in Rule 107(a) of the CAT Rules of Procedure, Rule 91(b) of the CERD Rules of Procedure, and in Article 2 of the OP-CEDAW. The HRCee holds that in such circumstances an intimate personal link between the author of the communication and the alleged victim must exist,[49] whereas at the regional level in Africa[50] and in the Americas[51] no such requirement is deemed to be necessary. Generosity may

---

[47] See final views in *Kitok*, 27 July 1988, [1988] *Report of the HRCee*, UN doc. A/43/40, 221, at 228, para. 6.3; *Lubikon Lake Band*, 26 March 1990, [1990] *Report of the HRCee*, vol. II, UN doc. A/45/40, 1, at 9, para. 13.3; *E. P. et al.*, 25 July 1990, ibid. at 186, para. 8.2.

[48] 22 *HRLJ* (2001) 293.

[49] See decisions on inadmissibility of 6 April 1983, 2 *Selected Decisions* (1990) 40; 25 July 1983, ibid. at 43. Confirmation of the early jurisprudence recently in *Y v Australia*, final views of 27 July 2000, UN doc. CCPR/C/69/D/772/1997, 8 August 2000.

[50] See Viljoen, *supra* n. 20, at 76.

[51] Article 44 ACHR, see IACtHR, judgment in *Castillo Petruzzi v Peru*, 4 September 1998, 20 *HRLJ* (1999) 176, at 183–184, paras 75–85.

appear as a courageous step in the right direction, but it may discredit the system of complaints if a NGO submits short pieces of information gleaned from a perusal of newspapers without being able to provide more precise details on the substance of the cases it has submitted. The agenda of the body concerned may then become a huge burial ground for cases that can never be disposed of effectively.

Standing can even be conceived in such wide terms that the applicant may challenge *in abstracto* the compatibility of general national measures with the standards established by the instruments concerned, the applicant acting as guardian of legality. It is clear that the system established under the Additional Protocol to the European Social Charter serves precisely this purpose. In Africa, NGOs also seem to be authorized to play such a role.[52] On the other hand, it was already pointed out that currently no clear answer can be given as to the exact scope *ratione materiae* of Article 2 OP-CEDAW.

Exhaustion of Local Remedies

Generally, the complaint procedures provide that an applicant must have exhausted all available remedies before taking his/her case to a competent international body.[53] The rationale behind this rule is very clear. States are given an opportunity to correct any irregularities they may have committed before being made accountable at the international level. In this connection, all the exceptions which are well known from the mechanism of diplomatic protection apply. To exhaust local remedies cannot be a requirement where such remedies hold no tangible prospect of relief or where they have been unduly prolonged. These exceptional clauses were explicitly incorporated into Article 22(5)(b) CAT and Article 4(1) OP-CEDAW. In Article 5(2)(b) OP-CCPR and Article 14(7)(a) CERD mention is made only of unreasonable delay in domestic proceedings. Notwithstanding these textual differences, the requirement of exhaustion of local remedies is generally interpreted in the same way by all monitoring bodies.

The HRCee has added to the classical rules the requirement for states to specify exactly the available remedies in its response. Otherwise, the Committee will assume that the applicant had no opportunity to assert his/her rights before a domestic court in an effective way. This complement was evolved in connection with numerous Uruguayan cases where the Uruguayan government, at the relevant time a right-wing dictatorship, claimed routinely by way of a form attached to all of its response submissions that the victims could have made use of a vast array of remedies to vindicate their rights.

---

[52] See Viljoen, *supra* n. 20, at 76.
[53] For a recent assessment of the practice of the HRCee see Ghandhi, 'Some Aspects of the Exhaustion of Domestic Remedies Rule Under the Jurisprudence of the HRCee', 44 *GYIL* (2001) 485.

However, since the victims were held in detention under the worst possible conditions, it would have been incumbent upon the government to indicate which remedies under such circumstances the victims could have filed. A domestic remedy must be both available and effective. Since the government was unable to contend with any degree of plausibility that there was a real opportunity to seize any one of the Uruguayan tribunals, the objection of non-exhaustion of local remedies was unhesitatingly rejected.[54]

Other International Procedures of Settlement

Care must also be taken regarding parallel international proceedings. Legal protection by international bodies is a scarce resource. Therefore, although an applicant should certainly have the opportunity to submit his/her case to international review once, he/she has no legitimation to demand that the case be handled by all the bodies which may have some power of review. For that reason, provision is generally made for the exclusion of a second or third review at the international level. In the first text, the complaint mechanism established under the CERD, this was not mentioned. Article 14 CERD does not contemplate the eventuality that an applicant has already made use of other remedies. This oversight was quickly corrected. The OP-CCPR states in Article 5(2)(a) that the HRCee is debarred from entertaining communications which are 'being examined' under another procedure of international investigation or settlement. Although the English text indicates fairly well that this is an obstacle of litispendence and not an obstacle of *res judicata*, it was necessary to look into the *travaux préparatoires* to obtain absolute clarity since the French version as well as the Spanish text[55] could have been construed differently. Eventually, after it had been confirmed that the drafting process had been conducted on the basis of English texts and that all the other texts had been established as translations after the conclusion of negotiations on formulations acceptable to all parties involved, it turned out that indeed the drafters had said what they wanted to say.[56] To construe Article 5(2)(a) as only prohibiting an applicant vindicating his/her rights in two international proceedings at the same time means that indeed two

---

[54] See, for instance, final views in *Torres Ramírez*, 23 July 1980, HRCee, *Selected Decisions under the Optional Protocol*, UN doc. CCPR/C/OP/1 (New York, 1985), 49, at 50, paras. 5, 9(b); *Altesor*, 29 March 1982, ibid. at 105, at 106, para. 4(b): 'in the absence of more specific information concerning the domestic remedies said to be available to the author of this communication and the effectiveness of those remedies as enforced by the competent authorities in Uruguay, the Committee was unable to accept that he had failed to exhaust such remedies.'

[55] 'El Comité no examinará ninguna comunicación de un individuo a menos que se haya cerciorado de que: a) El mismo asunto no ha sido sometido ya a otro procedimiento de examen o arreglo internacionales.'

[56] See *Second Annual Report of the HRCee*, UN doc. A/33/40, *Yearbook of the HRCee (1977–1978)*, vol. II, 300, para. 584.

international proceedings could be instituted one after the other. On reflection, this appeared to many governments to constitute an exaggeration of international relief opportunities. The Council of Europe, accordingly, recommended to its members to enter a reservation when ratifying the OP-CCPR,[57] with a view to excluding such a two-stage review mechanism which would have meant that the HRCee could sit as an appeal body to evaluate the conclusions reached by the European Commission or the ECtHR. The majority of the states members of the Council of Europe followed this recommendation. Some countries, however (e.g., Belgium, Cyprus, Ireland, Netherlands, Portugal) have refrained from entering such a reservation. Hence, after a person has unsuccessfully appealed a governmental act before the ECtHR in Strasbourg, he/she can still try to obtain satisfaction with the HRCee. In several cases, applicants have gone through that experiment.[58] On the whole, the results have been largely similar. Only in the case of *Coeriel and Aurik*, where the European Commission of Human Rights had dismissed the application as 'manifestly ill-founded', did the HRCee find a violation of the applicants' rights under the CCPR.[59]

All the later instruments corrected this apparent oversight. Article 22(5)(a) CAT specifies that a communication is admissible only if 'the same matter has not been, and is not being, examined under another procedure of international investigation or settlement'. Similar language has been included in Article 4(2)(a) OP-CEDAW. When making its proposals for a procedure of individual communications in 1996, the CESCRCee was not aware of this new development. In the text suggested by it (Article 3(3)(b)), the relevant ground of inadmissibility is stated in terms of litispendence: a communication would be inadmissible only if 'being examined' at the same time under another international procedure.

Unsubstantiated Communications

All of the international treaty-based bodies receive many communications characterized by a high degree of superficiality. Allegations are made without any *substantiation*, legal conclusions are drawn which are in no way related to the relevant international treaty instrument, and sometimes it may even be difficult to understand the reasoning which the author is intending to convey. For that reason, a system of pre-screening has become a general practice. At the United Nations, letters are channelled through the office of the High Commissioner for Human Rights, where the communications unit is engaged in finding out to which procedure every single incoming letter

---

[57] Res. 635 of the Parliamentary Assembly of the Council of Europe, 17 September 1976.
[58] First case: *Hendriks v Netherlands*, final views of 27 July 1988, [1988] *Report of the HRCee*, UN doc. A/43/40, 230.
[59] Final views of 31 October 1994, [1995] *Report of the HRCee*, vol. II, UN doc. CCPR/C/57/1, 23.

should be assigned. Thereafter, if need be, the communications unit seeks to enter into contact with the author of the communication in order to suggest to him/her to amplify and concretize his/her submissions. On many occasions, proceedings end at this juncture because the author does not bother to reply.

Any communication that contains a modicum of serious substance is brought to the attention of the competent body, however. If that body nonetheless finds that the complaint has very weak factual or legal foundations, it is of course inclined to dismiss the case *a limine*, without going into a detailed study of its admissibility and merits. Under the ECHR, provision was made from the very outset for the rejection of 'manifestly ill-founded' applications. No hint of such a hurdle can be found in Article 14 CERD, and the drafters of the OP-CCPR likewise forgot to take care of the issue which pertains more to practicality than to principle. And yet, individuals filing a communication under the OP-CCPR have to 'claim' that they are victims of a violation of their rights (Articles 1, 2). Taking this requirement as its starting point, the HRCee has developed a jurisprudence according to which communications lacking sufficient substantiation may be rejected as inadmissible. It holds that a 'claim' as required by the two introductory Articles of the OP-CCPR is 'an allegation supported by a certain amount of substantiating materials'.[60] This is more or less a test of plausibility. To be sure, in some instances one may disagree on whether the minimum requirements were or were not fulfilled. On the whole, however, it is to be welcomed that the HRCee can thus fairly quickly reject communications which do not deserve to be looked into within the framework of a formalized procedure. Indeed, right from the beginning of its practice of rejecting communications lacking the necessary substance as being, in essence, manifestly ill-founded, the HRCee pursued a guiding concept: it did not wish to overburden states with baseless allegations the processing of which according to formalized procedures would have entailed useless administrative expenditure.

It is understandable that the few lines of Article 22 CAT devoted to the individual complaint procedure do not deal with the problem of manifest ill-foundedness. However, when the OP-CEDAW was drafted, all the available international experiences were carefully taken into consideration. On the basis of that evaluation, the drafters decided to include in Article 4(2)(c) the rule that communications are inadmissible if they are 'manifestly ill-founded or not sufficiently substantiated'. In other words, there exists now an unchallengeable legal basis for dealing in a summary fashion with communications that are prima facie devoid of the necessary supportive elements.

---

[60] [2001] *Report of the HRCee*, vol. I, UN doc. A/56/40, 110, para. 113.

Absence of Oral Hearings

Proceedings before the treaty-based bodies for the protection of human rights are all characterized by features which distinguish them from judicial proceedings proper. Whereas judicial proceedings are, in principle, to be held in public (Articles 6(1) ECHR, 14(1) CCPR), the UN monitoring expert bodies are all enjoined to conduct their proceedings in private meetings.[61] This rule reflects, on the one hand, respect for the respondent state, which may be attacked without any valid reasons. On the other hand, however, it corresponds to the logic of an imperfect adversarial procedure. Although there are two litigant parties, the applicant and the respondent government, these parties do not appear before any of those bodies. Hitherto, their role is confined to making submissions in writing. No oral hearings are provided for. No evidence is taken from witnesses or experts. Thus, the committee members deliberating on the materials submitted to them are acting alone. What they are doing corresponds to the final stage of a judicial proceeding where normally, with the exception of Switzerland, the judges deliberate confidentially on the final outcome of a case. Thus, a rule providing for openness of the meetings of the expert bodies would make little sense in the given circumstances. Judicial proceedings are open to the public because its presence is viewed as a democratic control mechanism for the rights of the defence, respect for the principle of equality of arms and in particular respect for due process in taking evidence. All this, however, is done in writing in proceedings under all the complaint procedures.

It is not impossible that the pattern just described may change in the future. While Article 5(1) OP-CCPR specifically provides that the HRCee shall consider the communications it has received 'in the light of all written information made available to it', any reference to 'written' evidence has been deleted in Article 22(4) CAT as well as in Article 7(1) OP-CEDAW. Theoretically, this determination, which certainly is not an oversight, could open the door for oral hearings as well as for testimony by witnesses. No provision for such a radical shift in the procedure has been made as yet by the CATCee, while the CEDAWCee must first of all face up to this issue in drafting the new rules of procedure which henceforth it will need. On closer examination, it would appear that structural difficulties would stand in the way of introducing some elements of a true judicial process into the procedures for the examination of individual complaints by the expert bodies under the UN human rights treaties. To hold oral hearings and to hear witnesses would take huge amounts of time which none of these bodies, which are all conceived of as bodies which meet for a few weeks each year, has at its disposal. Additionally, the principle of equality of arms would have to be respected. While

---

[61] Article 14(6)(a) CERD (implicit, since the identity of the petitioner must not be revealed); Articles 5(3) OP-CCPR; 22(6) CAT; 7(2) OP-CEDAW.

governments would have no difficulties in being represented at oral hearings in Geneva or New York, many of the applicants simply could not afford the costs of travelling to the places where the HRCee meets in session. No system of legal aid exists, and there are no prospects that it could ever come into being.[62] Similar problems would arise with regard to witnesses. Conversely, it could be imagined that it would not be the parties, the witnesses, and the experts who travel, but the committee concerned together with its staff. This, however, would require transforming all the relevant expert bodies into permanent institutions, the members of which being paid full salaries for their activities. For the time being, all this sounds rather speculative.

Interim Relief

In many cases, applicants seek provisional or interim relief, given the danger that the respondent state may cause them irreparable harm. However, in none of the first legal texts governing the handling of individual complaints by the competent expert body was there any reference to a power to indicate provisional measures or to order interim relief. And yet, upon a proposal of the UN Secretariat, which had prepared for it a first draft of its Rules of Procedure,[63] the HRCee decided to include in the definitive text of those Rules a provision that permits it to convey to any respondent state its assessment of the situation and a set of recommendations deriving from such assessment. This provision, which has remained unchanged—with the exception of one word—since 1977, reads (Rule 86, first clause):

The Committee may, prior to forwarding its views on the communication to the State party concerned, inform that State of its views as to whether interim measures may be desirable to avoid irreparable damage to the victim of the alleged violation.[64]

Judging from the text of this provision, one would have to conclude that Rule 86 decisions are not binding. Indeed, the HRCee does no more than convey its 'views' to the respondent state as to what measures that state should take in order to avoid irreparable harm. In recent years, however, the HRCee has clearly manifested its conviction that states are bound to comply with such interim decisions. Consequently, it has on several occasions expressed 'great concern' in instances where a government, in disregard of an Article 86 ruling, had executed a person while the application challenging the correctness of the conviction and sentencing was still pending before it.[65] Its line of

---

[62] A strong plea for the introduction of such a system has been made by Butler, 'Legal Aid Before Human Rights Treaty Monitoring Bodies', 49 *ICLQ* (2000) 360, at 369–389.

[63] Reprinted in *Yearbook of the HRCee (1977–1978)*, vol. II, 1, at 7.

[64] [2001] *Report of the HRCee*, vol. I, UN doc. A/56/40, 168, at 187.

[65] Unfortunately, [2001] *Report of the HRCee*, 115–116, paras 128–130, lists three such instances: *Piandiong et al. v The Philippines*; *Mansaraj et al. v Sierra Leone*; *Saidov v Tajikistan*. Another case of an execution contrary to a Rule 86 decision, *Ashby v Trinidad and Tobago*, is mentioned in [2002] *Report of the HRCee*, vol. I, UN doc. A/5740, 94, para. 134.

reasoning is indeed sensible. To be sure, on the one hand one can argue that interim decisions can have no higher degree of authoritativeness than the final result of a proceeding, which the OP-CCPR classifies as 'views' (Article 5(4)), a term which according to general linguistic usage as well as according to current legal terminology designates an act which is not binding. On the other hand, however, a proceeding which has been instituted and in which the respondent state is obligated to cooperate in good faith, loses its very raison d'être if that state during the course of the proceeding takes measures which settle the matter once and for all, making the subject matter moot. A person on death row who alleges that his/her trial was marred by grave violations of the relevant guarantees of the CCPR (Article 14), can no longer benefit from a finding of the HRCee that indeed those allegations were well-founded if in the meantime he/she has been executed. In such instances, a Rule 86 decision serves to preserve not only the (alleged) rights of the (alleged) victim, but also, and in the first place, the integrity of the procedure.

Interim measures of protection have also gained considerable importance under the CAT. The Rules of Procedure of the CATCee allow for requests to be made to states under the same conditions as provided for under the Rules of Procedure of the HRCee (Article 108). Mostly, the CATCee had to deal with cases of imminent expulsion of a person to a country where he/she might be in danger of being subjected to torture (Article 3 CAT). According to the latest annual report of the CATCee, all states addressed in such instances acceded to the Committee's requests for deferral.[66]

In the OP-CEDAW, the construction of the OP-CCPR by the HRCee has found a clear confirmation. Article 5(1) of the OP-CEDAW reads:

At any time after the receipt of a communication and before a determination on the merits has been reached, the Committee may transmit to the State party concerned for its urgent consideration a request that the State party take such interim measures as may be necessary to avoid possible irreparable damage to the victim or victims of the alleged violation.

This provision makes clear, in the first place, that the CEDAWCee is empowered to address states with a view to obtaining interim relief for the benefit of an applicant. Regarding the main issue, it does not explicitly specify that such a request must be heeded by the respondent state. The phrase that the request will be transmitted to that state for its 'urgent consideration' would even appear to militate against any interpretation that might attach a binding character to the request. From a teleological viewpoint, however, the reasoning deployed by the HRCee is persuasive. It is further buttressed by the case law of the ICJ. As is well known, the ICJ decided in the *LaGrand* case[67]

---

[66] [2002] *Report of the CATCee*, UN doc. A/57/44, 73, para. 205.
[67] Judgment of 27 June 2001 (not yet published in the ICJ Reports).

that the indication of provisional measures under Article 41 of the Court's Statute brings into being true legal obligations for the addressees. Although the ICJ relied mainly on a comparison of the different linguistic versions of Article 41, it should not be overlooked that a powerful argument supporting the interpretation eventually chosen was the concern by the ICJ that legal relief cannot be provided in the form of half-hearted measures. This consideration applies also, and perhaps even a fortiori, to individual complaint procedures. More than states, which generally have other means at their disposal to defend their rights, individuals may be in dire need of a pronouncement of one of the relevant expert bodies in order to preserve the enjoyment of rights that allow a life of physical integrity and dignity.

The IACionHR has also been vested with the power to make interim requests to 'the State concerned'.[68] In the case of the detainees at the American military base of Guantánamo, captured during the armed conflict in Afghanistan, a dispute emerged on whether this power extends to all members of the OAS as a consequence of the general mandate imparted to the Commission in the Charter of the OAS (Article 106) or is limited to states parties to the ACHR. Whereas the Commission itself affirmed its competence by issuing a request for precautionary measures on 12 March 2002,[69] the United States challenged the authority of the Commission in its response of 15 April 2002.[70] According to the view defended by the American authorities, the detainees enjoy neither the protection of American domestic law, including the guarantees flowing from the US Constitution, nor the protection of international humanitarian law or international human rights law, but are located in a total limbo as long as the 'fight against terrorism' continues.

Outcome

Non-binding Views

There can be no doubt that *final views* under Article 5(4) OP-CCPR are not binding as such. The same is true of the other procedures at universal or regional level. Nowhere is the final outcome of a proceeding characterized as a decision or an order. Deliberately, the drafters speak of 'views' (in the case of CERD of 'suggestions and recommendations', Article 14(7)(b)), which the

---

[68] Article 25(1) of the Commission's Rules of Procedure (22 *HRLJ* (2001) 293) provides: 'In serious and urgent cases, and whenever necessary according to the information available, the Commission may, on its own initiative or at the request of a party, request that the State concerned adopt precautionary measures to prevent irreparable harm to persons.'

[69] 41 *ILM* (2002) 532; 23 *HRLJ* (2002) 15; comment by Shelton, 'The Legal Status of the Detainees at Guantánamo Bay: Innovative Elements in the Decision of the IACionHR of 12 March 2002', 23 *HRLJ* (2002) 13.

[70] 41 *ILM* (2002) 1015.

body concerned shall transmit to the litigant parties. This means that a state may reject such views as not corresponding to the true legal position. To recognize such a right of objection is not tantamount to saying that the views expressed have no legal relevance at all. Whenever a state has submitted to an international procedure, it must participate in that procedure bona fide until its very end. This final point is not yet reached at the moment when the expert body concerned has transmitted its views to the litigant parties. As in the case of the recommendations of the UN General Assembly, those parties, and in particular the respondent state, have to examine the views addressed to them carefully, with due respect to their author.[71] Generally, there exists a presumption in favour of substantive correctness of such views. No better expertise as to the scope and meaning of any of the human rights treaties can be found than in the expert bodies set up to monitor their observance by states. If a state disagrees with the views expressed on a given case, it must present detailed observations specifying its counter-arguments.

In fact, there are a number of famous cases where the respondent state unequivocally manifested its disagreement with the findings of the HRCee. After the HRCee had handed down its views in *Broeks, Danning*, and *Zwaan-de Vries*, wherein for the first time it applied the equality clause enunciated by Article 26 CCPR to social rights, the Dutch government considered denouncing the OP-CCPR in order to ratify it again with a reservation excluding the controversial case law from its scope. As pointed out above,[72] when ratifying the OP-CCPR, Germany, later followed by Liechtenstein, made such a reservation. The case law relating to Article 26 CCPR has also been rejected by the French Conseil d'Etat. When it had to adjudicate an action brought on the basis of the views handed down by the HRCee in *Gueye*,[73] it stated,[74] contrary to the opinion of the commissaire du gouvernement Philippe Martin who had suggested respecting the views in *Gueye*,[75] that the HRCee had no competence to rule on issues located outside the field of civil and political rights. To date, this latter conflict remains unresolved.

Follow-up

None of the human rights bodies is satisfied with the response given by states to the views expressed by them. The deficiencies more often than not found to exist call for a *follow-up mechanism*. Since its early days, the HRCee recognized that steps should be taken to improve compliance by states with

[71] See separate opinion of Judge Lauterpacht regarding the advisory opinion of the ICJ in *South West Africa—Voting Procedure*, 7 June 1955, ICJ Reports (1955) 90, at 119.
[72] See *supra* p. 170.
[73] [1989] *Report of the HRCee*, UN doc. A/44/40, 189.
[74] Opinion ('avis') of 15 April 1996, *Doukouré, Revue française de droit administratif*, 12 (1996) 817.
[75] Ibid. at 808–817.

its views. However, as long as its members from central and eastern Europe were committed to the political doctrine of socialism, no institutional solution was conceivable. Those members held that the task of the HRCee was fully completed as soon as it had handed down its views. To establish a follow-up mechanism was not within its competence.[76] This explains why the system as it exists today took shape step by step only as from 1990.[77] In fact, in 1990 the function of a Special Rapporteur on follow-up to communications was established.[78] At the same time, the HRCee began inserting into all its final views a clause in which it stated that it wished to be informed by the respondent state within 90 days on the measures taken as a consequence of the views. Unfortunately, all these constructive efforts have not been able to increase significantly the effectiveness of final views. The extensive documentation included in the annual reports of the HRCee reveals that many states have neither heeded the views nor deemed it necessary to transmit any information on the decisions they have taken on the cases handled by the HRCee. Concerning information provided, only 30 per cent is considered satisfactory by the HRCee.[79] In sum, the effectiveness of the procedure under the OP-CCPR leaves ample room for improvement. An expert body alone does not enjoy sufficient authority to prevail upon states to heed and implement its views. After the HRCee has completed its work, a political body should step in to press for implementation. To date, this has occurred very rarely.

Publication of the Case Law

It was by no means obvious that the final views handed down by the HRCee and the other expert bodies would be publicized as part of their annual reports. Since individual communications have to be dealt with in private meetings, it could also have been argued that the procedure as a whole, with all its results, must be kept confidential. On the basis of that approach, it would have been a reasonable option to view the individual complaint procedure as essentially comparable to international conciliation or mediation, where a third party seeks to bring about a friendly settlement. No one exercising such functions would set out in detail what the factual bases of a

---

[76] See the representative voice of Graefrath, 'Reporting and Complaint Systems in Universal Human Rights Treaties', in Allan Rosas and Jan Helgesen (eds), *Human Rights in a Changing East–West Perspective* (London and New York, Pinter, 1990), 290, at 326.

[77] See Ando, 'The Follow-up Procedure of the Human Rights Committee's Views', in *Liber Amicorum Judge Shigeru Oda* (The Hague, Kluwer Law International, 2002), vol. 2, 1437; Tomuschat, 'Making Individual Communications an Effective Tool for the Protection of Human Rights', in *Recht zwischen Umbruch und Bewahrung: Festschrift für Rudolf Bernhardt* (Berlin, Springer, 1995), 615.

[78] Decision of 24 July 1990, [1990] *Report of the HRCee*, vol. II, UN doc. A/45/40, Annex XI, 205.

[79] [2001] *Report of the HRCee*, vol. I, UN doc. A/56/40, 131, para. 178.

dispute committed to its efforts are and which grounds permit the conclusion that specific human rights were indeed violated. The HRCee, however, which was the first expert body to assess individual communications, did not embark on such a course of 'diplomatic softness'. From the very outset, it viewed its task of handing down views under the OP-CCPR as a quasi-judicial function. Rightly, it considered that its views must be accessible to everyone wishing to file a communication. If the HRCee had decided against publicizing its views, some kind of secret case law would have developed, known only to an intimate circle of persons within the United Nations. On the other hand, no applicant is under an obligation not to make available to other persons the views handed down in his/her case. Thus, reports collecting the case law could have been organized by private initiative, probably with a low degree of reliability. Given these considerations, it was more or less imperative to organize the publication of the jurisprudence of the HRCee under the OP-CCPR officially under the auspices of the United Nations.

The decision in favour of a quasi-judicial concept in evaluating individual communications explains also the format chosen for the final views under Article 5(4) OP-CCPR. As from the very first case, the HRCee set out the facts, summarized the submissions of the parties (sometimes even too extensively), presented its own reasoning, and said in a concluding paragraph which Articles of the CCPR, if any, had been breached by the respondent state. Given this format, the views of the HRCee can indeed be characterized, as to their substance, as the nucleus of a world jurisprudence on human rights. As long as no human rights tribunal exists at the universal level, the case law of the HRCee, and of the other expert bodies, will serve as the most authoritative source for universally applicable human rights standards.

Quantitative Assessment

In quantitative terms, at the universal level the balance sheet of the HRCee is the most impressive one. During a quarter of a century, 1,107 communications concerning 71 countries were received (registered). The HRCee handed down 404 final views, and 313 of these found violations.[80] Under the CAT, 209 individual communications have been received since the inception of its activity: 50 final views were handed down, of which 21 found violations.[81] Most of these cases concern Article 3 CAT, which means that generally communications were not directed against a tortfeasing state practising torture, but against states that were about to send an alien to a country where he/she could be in danger of being subjected to torture.

---

[80] See [2002] *Report of the HRCee*, vol. I, UN doc. A/57/40, 81, paras 88, 89.
[81] See [2002] *Report of the CATCee*, UN doc. A/57/44, 73–74, para. 206.

Qualitative Assessment

It is not only difficult, but indeed impossible to provide a substantive account of the case law of the HRCee under the OP-CCPR. However, we will not refrain totally from commenting on the substantive work of the HRCee— just one highlighted case should be mentioned.

During its first years of activity, the HRCee received many communications complaining of massive violations of the rights under the CCPR to the detriment of political prisoners in Uruguay. Quite naturally, the HRCee had to criticize these abuses. The rule of law had been abolished in Uruguay. Members of the political opposition were denied the most basic rights. Unfortunately, the jurisprudence of the HRCee was not able to change very much. The Uruguayan government took note of the views expressed on individual cases, but it disregarded their recommendations. And yet, the consistent jurisprudence of the HRCee had a long-term effect. As the cruel treatment of many prisoners became known to the world at large through the views on individual cases, the authority of the Uruguayan government suffered a progressive process of erosion. After a few years, it had to give up power and the country returned to democracy. It certainly would be somewhat difficult to establish a causal link with unchallengeable precision. Yet it is clear that the government lost any kind of moral recognition not only at home, but also abroad. Given this moral degradation, its factual power basis, too, evaporated.

II FACT-FINDING

General Considerations

Fact-finding has many great advantages specifically in the field of human rights. While by filing a complaint an individual has the opportunity to establish a direct contact with the competent review body, that remedy may not provide effective relief, in particular because of the hurdles that have to be overcome before access to the international level is open. Many years may pass before all the available domestic remedies have been exhausted, despite the fact that all supervisory bodies are prepared to apply the rule generously that excessive delays in national proceedings must not hinder a communication from being accepted. In any event, an applicant is normally confined to denouncing a violation which has actually occurred. By contrast, fact-finding by international bodies has an important preventive function. During a fact-finding mission, the persons entrusted with the mission can prevail on national authorities to stop any abuses which they may find to exist. Such contacts with officers and authorities at the grass-roots level are able directly to address the actual deficiencies causing injury to the victims, whereas any views formulated in a conference room in Geneva or New York first have to pass through the entire network of a complex governmental and administrative system before they reach the place where remedial action is needed.

Even though the official mandate of a fact-finding mission is generally limited to collecting evidence, those involved in such a mission inevitably have a broader spectrum of opportunities to press for immediate steps to be taken by the government concerned, just by virtue of the fact that he/she is present on the ground. This applies also to the country rapporteurs, whatever their official title, and even to thematic rapporteurs who invariably will conduct extensive talks on the results of their mission with the responsible governmental officers.[82] For that reason, fact-finding may be called the most effective method of international protection of human rights.

Existing Procedures

Fact-finding by the Inter-American Commission on Human Rights

The IACionHR has a long tradition of visits to countries with a human rights record deserving closer examination. Long before the ACHR came into being, it carried out visits to Member States of the OAS.[83] Article 41 ACHR does not specifically mention that function. It refers in general terms to the preparation of 'such studies or reports' as the Commission may consider advisable in the performance of its duties. But visits to individual countries still form an essential part of the spectrum of tasks which the Commission discharges in actual practice.[84]

Fact-finding by the Committee Against Torture

The first of the UN treaties for the protection of human rights which specifically provided for country visits to be carried out was the CAT. Article 20 CAT establishes an extraordinary procedure for situations apparently characterized by the systematic practice of torture in the territory of a given country. If the CATCee receives reliable information to that effect, it can institute proceedings with a view to establishing the veracity of the allegations. Interestingly enough, Article 20 abstains from specifying who is entitled to provide such information, which means in practice that a NGO may play the role of author who triggers the setting into motion of a proceeding. According to Article 20(3), in such circumstances an inquiry may (even) include a visit to the territory of the state concerned, provided that its government agrees. This

---

[82] See *supra* p. 124.

[83] See our study on the initial stage of the Commission: 'Die Interamerikanische Menschenrechtskommission', 28 *ZaöRV* (1968) 531, at 546–547.

[84] Thus, in 2001 the Commission carried out on-site visits to Panama and Colombia, see *Annual Report of the Inter-American Commission on Human Rights* (2001), doc. OEA/Ser./L/V/ II.114 doc. 5 rev.,16 April 2001, Chapter II, section D.

requirement of specific consent makes such visits subject to a double conditionality. First of all, Article 20 must be accepted by states parties. In order to gain approval for the CAT back in 1984, it was necessary to insert a clause according to which the competence of the CATCee under Article 20 may be excluded by a simple declaration.[85] Secondly, whenever an actual visit is envisaged, the state concerned must again give its consent. Lastly, Article 20(5) CAT prescribes that the proceedings must be confidential. Only after they have ended can a summary be published in the Committee's annual report after consultation with the state party concerned.

It is an interesting group of states which has made the declaration under Article 28.[86] The former German Democratic Republic was so worried by the prospect of visits to places of detention where torture might occur that in its declaration under Article 28, it not only excluded the right of the CATCee to make such inquiries on the spot, but stated additionally that it would not contribute to financing any of the missions of the Committee in accordance with Article 20(3). When carrying out such missions, the CATCee can do a great deal to improve the situation of potential victims. In its 2001 annual report, it describes in detail the inquiry which it carried out between 1995 and 1999 with regard to Peru, which included a two-week visit to the country in August/September 1998, after having been apprised of systematic torture practices allegedly in its fight against terrorism.[87] It came to the conclusion that torture was not an occasional occurrence, but had been systematically used as a method of investigation.[88] Much more positive are the conclusions of an inquiry on Sri Lanka, which had been triggered by five London-based NGOs. The inquiry lasted three years (April 1999 to May 2002). Sri Lanka cooperated in an exemplary fashion by responding accurately to all the recommendations formulated by the CATCee. The favourable outcome was of course facilitated by the ceasefire agreement which in February 2002 was reached between the government of Sri Lanka and the rebel group (Tamil Tigers).[89]

Fact-finding by the European Committee for the Prevention of Torture

A much more elaborated system of visits to places of detention was ushered in by the European Convention against Torture of 1987.[90] According to Article

---

[85] Obviously, states ratifying the CAT could also have excluded the procedure under Article 20 by a reservation. But any reservation makes its author an outsider who departs from the common treaty regime, whereas through Article 28 exclusion of Article 20 has become a normal component of the treaty regime. Secondly, it could have been argued that to exclude the procedure under Article 20 was incompatible with the object and purpose of the CAT.

[86] Afghanistan, China, Cuba, Indonesia, Israel, Kuwait, Monaco, Poland, Saudi Arabia.

[87] [2001] *Report of the CATCee*, UN doc. A/56/44, 60–70.

[88] Ibid. at 63, para. 163.

[89] For details see [2002] *Report of the CATCee*, UN doc. A/57/44, 59–71.

[90] Of 26 November 1987, *ETS* No. 126.

2 of this Convention, states agree to visits to any place under their jurisdiction where persons are deprived of their liberty by a public authority. Apart from periodic reports, 'other visits' as appear to be required by the circumstances are provided for (Article 7). The practice under this Convention has yielded impressive results. Under the chairmanship of Italian lawyer Antonio Cassese, important precedents were set which have had a continuing effect until today. The control body under the Convention, the European Committee for the Prevention of Torture and Inhuman or Degrading Treatment or Punishment, looked with the utmost care into all the details conditioning the existence of the persons entrusted to the care of the Committee. Whereas according to the text of the Convention the reports of the Committee should in principle be confidential (Article 11(1)), it has now become routine for states to request the Committee to publish those reports together with their own comments. In that way, everyone can fully inform him/herself of the actual conditions in the places of detention visited by the Committee. Unfortunately, the work of the Committee has been hampered by budgetary constraints.[91]

In exceptional circumstances, the European Committee may make a public statement on the matter. The first such statement was issued by it[92] after it had found, in a room of the Ankara Police Headquarters, a stretcher-type bed with four straps on each side, obviously destined to subject persons to electric shocks, and in a police station in Diyarbakir the equipment necessary for suspension of a human being by the arms in place and ready for use. Little has been more damaging for Turkey's reputation than this statement. The third public statement was issued on the treatment of detained persons in Chechnya.[93] The Committee voiced strong concerns over the refusal of the Russian authorities to carry out an investigation into allegations that from December 1999 to early February 2000 physical ill-treatment had been practised in a specific detention facility in the north-west of the Chechen Republic. This statement underscored the general disregard of Russian forces for elementary rules of humanity in the armed conflict ravaging that country.

New Optional Protocol to the UN Convention Against Torture

At a global level, attempts to create a similar procedure took an entire decade. In 1992 the Commission on Human Rights established an open-ended working group mandated to draft an optional protocol to that effect. Thereafter, the Vienna World Conference on Human Rights endorsed that aim.[94]

---

[91] See Kelly, 'Perspectives from the European Committee for the Prevention of Torture and Inhuman or Degrading Treatment or Punishment (CPT)', 21 *HRLJ* (2000) 301, at 303.

[92] 15 December 1992, 14 *HRLJ* (1993) 49. For the second public statement on Turkey of 6 December 1996 see 18 *HRLJ* (1997) 292.

[93] 22 *HRLJ* (2001) 338.

[94] Programme of Action, para. 61, 32 *ILM* (1993) 1663, at 1682.

However, many states were clearly opposed to such direct control by an international body. It is mainly due to the efforts of a few NGOs and also to the energy of Costa Rica, which had linked its name with that initiative, that eventually the Protocol could be drafted and that it was adopted by the HRCion by Res. 2002/33 on 22 April 2002. The vote was 29 to 10, with 14 abstentions. The 'noes' came from China, Cuba, Japan, Libya, Malaysia, Nigeria, Republic of Korea, Saudi Arabia, Sudan, and Syria. Similarly, the United States, which in 2002 was not a member of the HRCion, voiced strong dissent when it commented on the draft text as an observer. It argued that the authority to be granted to the new Subcommittee on Prevention would be 'incompatible with principles of accountability and the need for reasonable checks and balances on any grant of power'.[95] This assertion completely misses the point. First of all, the Subcommittee entrusted with conducting the required visits will have to present a public annual report to the CATCee (Article 16(3)), which epitomizes its accountability. Secondly, the whole thrust of such a mechanism of protection by visits lies precisely in the power of the monitoring body to have access to any place where human beings are held against their will. No harm could be done to any law-abiding state by such visits, only to states which fail to apply minimum standards of humanity. Fortunately, on 18 December 2002 the General Assembly approved the draft by a vote which was again contested, but which put an end to 10 years of untiring efforts for its adoption.[96]

III CONCLUSION

Individual complaints, combined with on-site inspections, constitute an effective tool for the protection of human rights. Although none of the procedures examined above ends with a binding decision, they can be expected to remedy deficiencies found to exist as long as the government concerned cares about its international reputation, and wishes to heed the standards evolved by the international community. Essentially, acceptance of a complaint procedure or on-site inspections testifies to the will of a state to remain faithful to those standards. Mistrust is warranted if a state submits to the substantive contents of a human rights treaty, but refrains from likewise submitting to its procedural mechanisms, keeping aloof, in particular, from any available complaint procedure. Such half-hearted steps reflect either a self-righteous attitude or constitute an implicit acknowledgement that the record of compliance is far from satisfactory.

---

[95] United States Mission Geneva, *Press Releases* (2002), 22 January 2002.
[96] GA Res. 57/199, adopted by 127 votes in favour to four against (United States, Marshall Islands, Nigeria, Palau), with 42 abstentions.

9

Supervision by International Tribunals

I INTRODUCTORY CONSIDERATIONS

Mostly, when dealing with judicial protection of human rights, writers refer to the existing international courts specifically entrusted with adjudicating disputes about the interpretation and application of the relevant rules. But this approach is too narrow. Human rights has become a genuine component of international law. It cuts across all regimes which traditionally were deemed to be outside of its scope. When the United Nations was established in 1945, no one would have thought that one day the Security Council would concern itself with the issue of compliance by states with minimum human rights standards. Even in 1995, when the WTO Agreement was drafted and the new GATT came into being, no provision was made for human rights as a possible factor to be taken into account when assessing the lawfulness of trade restrictions.[1] Experience has shown, however, that human rights now belong to the key principles determining the framework within which international law is operating and evolving. This must also find its reflection in the case law of international tribunals that have no specific mandate in the field of human rights. Indeed, one does not encounter any reluctance on the part of judicial bodies at the international level to 'trespass' on that field.

II WORLDWIDE LEVEL

There exist currently three international courts with a worldwide scope of jurisdiction *ratione materiae*. The International Criminal Court (ICC), which

---

[1] See the controversy between Petersmann, 'Time for a United Nations "Global Compact" for Integrating Human Rights into the Law of Worldwide Organizations: Lessons from European Integration', 13 *EJIL* (2002) 621, and Alston, 'Resisting the Merger and Acquisition of Human Rights by Trade Law: A Reply to Petersmann', ibid. at 815, with a rejoinder by Petersmann, 'Taking Human Dignity, Poverty and Empowerment of Individuals More Seriously', ibid. at 845. See also Marceau, 'WTO Dispute Settlement and Human Rights', ibid. at 753.

is based on the Rome Statute, will be dealt with in a later chapter. The International Tribunal for the Law of the Sea has a limited field of action. In disputes regarding law of the sea matters, human rights issues will not frequently arise, but may crop up from time to time. In any event, however, due to its short existence (it came into being in 1996), the Tribunal has not yet had to face legal questions that would deserve to be classified under the rubric of human rights.[2] The International Court of Justice (ICJ), on the other hand, has had to pronounce from time to time on human rights issues, although such issues have almost never been the central point in any judgment. With the exception of recent cases centring on charges of genocide,[3] when the argument was relied upon by the ICJ, it served to support findings which eventually resolved disputes over other matters. This merely auxiliary character of the statements of the ICJ on human rights does not detract from their importance. They have become signposts that generally orient the thinking of international lawyers on the impact of human rights on the traditional rules, which emerged from the understanding of international law as a complex web of interrelationships between states.[4]

Advisory Opinions of the ICJ

The ICJ has first of all made a contribution to determining the strategic place of human rights in the international legal order by a number of advisory opinions. Never has it been requested to say whether an alleged human rights principle does exist or how it has to be understood. Thus, human rights has never occupied the centre stage in a legal proceeding with which it was seized. But in its advisory opinions one finds a number of the crucial propositions which fix the coordinates for any discussion on the relevance of human rights.

The first advisory opinion that deserves special attention had to deal with the issue of *Reservations to the Convention on Genocide*.[5] A number of states, in particular states belonging to the former socialist bloc, did not accept the compromissory clause in Article IX of the Convention. Generally reluctant to submit to the jurisdiction of the ICJ, they did not even want to become subject to judicial review regarding factual occurrences susceptible of being

---

[2] However, in cases of prompt release under Article 292 of the Convention on the Law of the Sea, the flag state acts for the protection of the patrimonial rights of the owner of the vessel that has been detained and possibly also for the release from detention of the crew of the vessel.

[3] See *infra* p. 196.

[4] For an overview see Bedjaoui, 'A propos de la place des droits de la personne humaine dans la jurisprudence de la Cour internationale de justice', in *Protecting Human Rights: The European Perspective: Studies in Memory of Rolv Ryssdal* (Köln, Heymanns, 2000), 87; Gros Espiell, 'Les droits de l'homme et la Cour internationale de Justice: une vision latino-américaine', in *Liber Amicorum Judge Shigeru Oda* (The Hague, Kluwer Law International, 2002), vol. 2, 1449.

[5] *Reservations to the Convention on Genocide*, ICJ Reports (1951) 15.

scrutinized from the viewpoint of genocide. At that time, back in 1951, the prevailing view in legal doctrine and practice still considered the consent of all states parties to be a requirement for a reservation to produce legal effects.[6] The ICJ departed from that view, taking into account the need to show some flexibility in order to ensure for treaties established at the universal level the broadest possible participation. It held that only reservations contrary to the object and purpose of the treaty concerned were inadmissible[7]—a formula which some years later found its way into Article 19 of the Vienna Convention on the Law of Treaties. Concerning the substantive provisions of the Genocide Convention, the ICJ found that 'the principles underlying the Convention are principles which are recognized by civilized nations as binding on States, even without any conventional obligation'.[8] For positivists who remain attached to the formal sources of law as circumscribed in Article 38(1) of the Statute of the ICJ this bold statement still comes as an irritating challenge.[9] The ICJ, however, has never reneged on this proclamation of faith. If the ban on genocide is part and parcel of the international legal order, even without any foundation in conventional stipulations and even absent any specific link to customary law, which today it certainly has, the conclusion cannot be escaped that the international legal order has roots in a layer constituted by the moral conscience of mankind, as also borne out by the famous Martens clause in the preamble to the 1907 Hague Convention IV Respecting the Laws and Customs of War on Land.[10]

The advisory opinion on the status of *Namibia*,[11] which was handed down five years after the ICJ had dismissed the action brought by two of the former three African members of the League of Nations (Ethiopia and Liberia) as being inadmissible,[12] stands out as one of the richest in legal consequences. Called upon to decide whether the mandate concluded between the League of Nations and South Africa continued to exist, the ICJ had to determine whether the United Nations had relied upon valid grounds in denouncing the mandate by GA Res. 2145 (XXI), 27 October 1966. According to the General Assembly, the introduction of the system of Apartheid in Namibia

---

[6] See *Report of the League of Nations Committee for the Progressive Codification of International Law*, 24 March 1927, reproduced in Lord McNair, *The Law of Treaties* (Oxford, Clarendon Press, 1961), 173, at 176; L. Oppenheim and H. Lauterpacht, *International Law: A Treatise* (8th edn, London, Longmans, 1955), vol. I, at 914.

[7] Ibid. at 24.

[8] Ibid. at 23.

[9] See, for instance, Georg Schwarzenberger, *International Law* (3rd edn, London, Stevens, 1957), vol. 1, 52.

[10] Reprinted in Adam Roberts and Richard Guelff (eds), *Documents on the Laws of War* (3rd edn, Oxford, Oxford University Press, 2000), 69.

[11] *Legal Consequences for States of the Continued Presence of South Africa in Namibia (South West Africa) Notwithstanding Security Council Resolution 276 (1970)*, ICJ Reports (1971) 16.

[12] *South West Africa, Second Phase*, ICJ Reports (1966) 6.

was contrary 'to the Mandate, the Charter of the United Nations and the Universal Declaration of Human Rights'. The Court endorsed this line of reasoning. It held that:

to establish . . ., and to enforce, distinctions, exclusions, restrictions and limitations exclusively based on grounds of race, colour, descent or national or ethnic origin which constitute a denial of fundamental human rights is a flagrant violation of the purposes and principles of the Charter.[13]

This sentence made clear that the different references in the UN Charter to human rights (in particular, Article 1, para. 3; Articles 55 and 56), the significance of which is by no means free from ambiguities, establish a binding obligation on states to ensure and protect human rights. There was no need for the ICJ to go into details. Obviously, no more can be derived directly from the UN Charter than a commitment of Member States to comply with human rights in principle. That commitment, however, must be understood to embrace a minimum threshold. In the view of the ICJ, which was foreshadowed by the judgment in the *Barcelona Traction* case,[14] a system of Apartheid, in any event, runs diametrically counter to the philosophy of equality which lies at the heart of human rights. Consequently, the ICJ held that the material violation perpetrated by South Africa amply justified the denunciation of the mandate by the General Assembly. Before this authoritative pronouncement, most writers were of the view that the provisions of the Charter mentioning human rights as one of the purposes of the World Organization were of a purely hortatory character and did not establish truly binding obligations. Thus a quantum leap forward in the understanding of the Charter was achieved, which prompted the General Assembly henceforth to embark on formally criticizing states involved in grave violations of human rights. As from 1971, it had a reliable legal basis to sustain such evaluations.

The second advisory opinion that clarified essential issues regarding the relevance of human rights within the general context of the international legal order had for its subject matter the *Legality of the Threat or Use of Nuclear Weapons*.[15] For a layperson, it would seem almost self-evident that any use of nuclear devices amounts to a violation of the right to life, given the vast destructive potential of such devices. In fact, some of the proponents of the illegality of the use of nuclear weapons argued that Article 6 CCPR as well as a corresponding rule of international customary law stood in the way of such use. Rightly, however, the ICJ argued that no determination could be made solely on the basis of the right to life in isolation. In order to know whether deprivation of human life had to be stigmatized as 'arbitrary' under the terms of the international rule that seeks to forestall any violation, recourse was

---

[13] *Supra* n. 11, at 57, para. 131.
[14] ICJ Reports (1970) 3.
[15] *Legality of the Threat or Use of Nuclear Weapons*, ICJ Reports (1996) 226, at 239, para. 24.

necessary to the law governing permissible conduct in armed conflict which constituted *lex specialis* for that purpose. In fact, during an armed conflict the killing of human beings is allowed within certain limits, in derogation from the regime applicable in time of peace. Combatants may attack combatants from the enemy camp. In other words, the ICJ rejected the contention that a solution could be found directly on the basis of the right to life, emphasizing instead that the specific features of armed conflict could not be disregarded. No matter how disappointing this approach may sound at first glance for a human rights lawyer, the opinion is remarkable because of its firm assertion that the general protection of human life does not disappear completely in a period of armed conflict, but is covered in modified form by a specialized legal regime, the *jus in bello*. Never before had the ICJ made such a clear statement on the relationship between human rights law and humanitarian law. Beforehand, many writers considered that the two disciplines were totally distinct from one another. Since the advisory opinion of the ICJ of 1996, it has become clear that the right to life remains the general foundation of the entire system of humanitarian law.

Judgments of the ICJ in Contentious Proceedings

As far as the case law of the ICJ in contentious matters is concerned, the most influential pronouncement is certainly the judgment in *Barcelona Traction*.[16] Essentially, the ICJ had to determine whether Belgium was entitled to assume the protection of the Belgian shareholders of a company, Barcelona Traction, Light and Power, which allegedly had been driven into bankruptcy by the Spanish authorities shortly after the Second World War. The company, incorporated in Canada, had been the major electric power provider for the entire region of Catalonia. For reasons which could not be elucidated, Canada refrained from defending the interests of the company and of its shareholders. Belgium then endorsed the claims of the great number of shareholders who had Belgian nationality. To be sure, these investors had suffered large economic losses, but the Spanish measures, which allegedly had violated the rule under aliens' law that foreign property must be respected, did not directly affect the shareholders, being directed against the company. In these circumstances, the ICJ held that a distinction had to be drawn between the traditional law of aliens, the infringement of which was a bilateral matter between the acting state and the home state of the individuals claiming to be victims, and the law of human rights within which some rules were of paramount importance for the entire international community. It held that, given the importance of this latter group of rights, all states had a legal interest in their protection: they were obligations 'erga omnes'. Particularizing

---

[16] *Barcelona Traction, Light and Power Company,* ICJ Reports (1970) 3.

this concept, the ICJ noted that the ban on aggression and genocide as well as the 'principles and rules concerning the basic rights of the human person, including protection from slavery and racial discrimination', had to be classified as such obligations.[17]

It is this dictum of the ICJ which stimulated the debate among jurists on the hierarchization of the sources of international law. One year earlier, through the adoption of the Vienna Convention on the Law of Treaties (Articles 53, 64), the international community had recognized the category of *jus cogens*, i.e. of norms of higher rank capable of invalidating a treaty approved by two or more states but repudiated by the international community at large. Now again, a differentiation was suggested according to which a number of elementary norms of human rights protection were granted higher status, their breach authorizing any third state to take up the matter in a way which, however, was not specified in detail. Clearly, the two concepts of *jus cogens* and of obligations *erga omnes* are closely related. Many efforts have been undertaken aimed at distinguishing between the two categories, in particular with a view to establishing which one of the two is the broader category. We are of the view that this debate is founded on erroneous premises since most commentators have failed to realize that the relevant primary rules must be separated from the legal consequences which are entailed by their breach.[18] No matter how this debate will be settled, however, the decision in *Barcelona Traction* has evinced that the international community is founded on a set of common values the transgression of which it cannot accept if it wishes to remain faithful to its basic philosophy. If, for instance, genocide is permitted and/or does not encounter any legal response, the whole edifice of the international legal order collapses. Genocide is the denial of the notion of human justice. A community which condones genocide abandons itself.

In a number of recent cases, the ICJ has relied upon its categorical condemnation of genocide to require states to do everything in their power to prevent the commission of genocide by military or security forces under their orders. In a proceeding brought by *Bosnia-Herzegovina against Yugoslavia (Serbia and Montenegro)*,[19] the ICJ confirmed the statement it made in its advisory opinion of 1951 that genocide 'shocks the conscience of mankind . . . and is contrary to moral law and to the spirit and aims of the United Nations'. Basing itself on this proposition, it enjoined the government

---

[17] *Barcelona Traction, Light and Power Company*, ICJ Reports (1970) 3, at 32, paras 33, 34.

[18] For a short demonstration of this necessary distinction see Tomuschat, 'International Law: Ensuring the Survival of Mankind on the Eve of a New Century', 281 *Recueil des cours* (1999) 81.

[19] *Application of the Convention on the Prevention and Punishment of the Crime of Genocide, Provisional Measures*, ICJ Reports (1993) 3, at 24.

of the Federal Republic of Yugoslavia, in accordance with Article 41 of its Statute, to ensure that no act of genocide be committed. A similar request was made in May 2002 by the Democratic Republic of the Congo in a case brought against Rwanda on account of the invasion of Congolese territory by Rwandan troops and the atrocities committed against the Congolese population in that connection.

Mention must also be made of the *LaGrand* case before the ICJ.[20] In issue was Article 36 of the Vienna Convention on Consular Relations.[21] It is common knowledge that the competent US authorities had failed to comply with their duties under that provision so that Germany learned only in 1992 of the detention, trial, and sentencing of the LaGrand brothers. This lack of respect for the requirements of the Consular Convention was all the more dramatic since each of the brothers was sentenced to death. The question was debated during the proceeding whether this breach of an international obligation towards Germany constituted at the same time a violation of the individual rights of the LaGrand brothers. Basing itself on the wording of Article 36(1)(b) of the Consular Convention ('The ... authorities shall inform the person concerned without delay of *his*[22] rights') and a similar phrase in subparagraph (c) of that same provision, the ICJ answered this question affirmatively.[23] In the dispositif of its judgment it stated twice that the United States had breached its obligations 'to the Federal Republic of Germany and to the LaGrand brothers'.[24] In other words, the Consular Convention contains human rights accruing directly to individuals, but the assertion of these rights is committed to governments according to the traditional mechanisms of diplomatic protection.[25]

The *LaGrand* case was followed by the *Avena* case brought by Mexico also against the United States on similar grounds.[26] Granting a Mexican request, the ICJ, by an order of 5 February 2003, indicated provisional measures. Basing itself on its findings on the merits of the *LaGrand* case, it formulated its requests (para. 59) this time in terms which make it clear that these requests are truly binding ('The United States of America shall take all measures necessary to ensure that ... are not executed pending final judgment

---

[20] Judgment of 27 June 2001, 40 *ILM* (2001) 1069.

[21] Of 24 April 1963, 596 *UNTS* 261.

[22] Emphasis added.

[23] *Supra* n. 20, at para. 77.

[24] Ibid. at para. 128. Comment by Pinto, 'De la protection diplomatique à la protection des droits de l'homme', 106 *RGDIP* (2002) 513.

[25] See comment by Mennecke, 'Towards the Humanization of the Vienna Convention of Consular Rights: The *LaGrand* Case Before the International Court of Justice', 44 *GYIL* (2001) 430, at 449–455.

[26] Case concerning *Avena and Other Mexican Nationals (Mexico v United States of America)*, filed 10 January 2003.

in these proceedings'). Nonetheless, it has been reported that the Texan authorities are not willing to heed this decision of the ICJ.[27]

III REGIONAL LEVEL

European Court of Human Rights

General Features

Of all the specialized regional courts for the protection of human rights, the European Court of Human Rights (ECtHR) is the most important institution not only because of its long existence (it was established in January 1959) and its large membership (it holds jurisdiction over 44 states (as at September 2003)), but also and mainly because of its widely extended case law and the effectiveness of its implementation mechanism. Having become the frontrunner which predates all other regional experiments, it has quite naturally become the model which serves as the point of orientation for any similar initiative.

The first of November 1998 was the great turning point in the history of the ECtHR. Until that date, its jurisdiction was not compulsory. States had a free choice whether to accept the remedy of individual application according to Article 25 ECHR and whether to accept the jurisdiction of the ECtHR according to Article 46 ECHR (former version). Applications filed in Strasbourg were first reviewed as to their admissibility by the European Commission of Human Rights and could then be transmitted, at a second stage of the proceedings, to the ECtHR if the state concerned had submitted to its jurisdiction. This two-stage arrangement reflected the thinking of a period when it was completely inconceivable that individuals could appear before a truly international tribunal. Pursuant to that intellectual scheme, the Commission not only served to facilitate the work of the ECtHR, but also kept individual applicants away from the ECtHR, access to which was originally reserved to the states parties closely related to the case at hand and to the Commission. By virtue of the Eleventh Protocol to the ECHR, this complicated institutional structure was abolished.[28] The European Commission of Human Rights was suppressed.[29] All the work to be carried out on applications lies now in the hands of the ECtHR. Since the Eleventh Protocol has made the remedy of individual application compulsory for all states parties to the ECHR, one can say without any exaggeration that the

[27] *International Herald Tribune*, 8–9 February 2003, 3.
[28] See, e.g., Drzemczewski, 'The ECHR: Protocol No. 11: Entry into Force and First Year of Application', 21 *HRLJ* (2000) 1.
[29] But it operated until 31 October 1999 to process nearly 500 pending applications which had been declared admissible before 1 November 1998.

ECtHR has become the constitutional court of Europe. Regarding the traditional Western group of members of the Council of Europe, the ECtHR succeeded in having its jurisprudence prevail over national laws and practices to the contrary.[30] The difficulties to be overcome in eastern Europe, however, are much weightier. It remains to be seen whether the ECtHR will emerge as the winner in the struggle against the remnants of authoritarian thinking as was prevalent in socialist states.[31]

The ECtHR is composed of as many judges as the ECHR has parties. Each state party may propose three candidates from whom one will then be elected by the Parliamentary Assembly of the Council of Europe (Article 22(1)). Normally, the first person on the list will be chosen. It stands to reason that the ECtHR must meet all the requirements laid down in the ECHR itself (Article 6(1)) which specify the substantive criteria of a court or tribunal that adjudicates disputes over civil rights and obligations or criminal charges. Formally, there can be no doubt that the ECtHR stands in full conformity with those demands. However, it is intriguing that judges are elected for a short period of six years only. Under the original version of the ECHR, the mandate had a duration of nine years. In connection with the reform ushered in by the Eleventh Protocol, this period was reduced to its current length. Since judges may be re-elected not only once, but several times until they reach the (new) age limit of 70 years (Article 23(6)), their independence can in fact be jeopardized because the first act in the selection process is a nomination by the state party concerned. It is of course to be hoped that persons 'of high moral character' (Article 21(1)) are immune against the temptation to discharge their mandate in consonance with the explicit or tacit wishes of their national governments. Institutionally, however, it is a thoroughly bad solution to make judges dependent on the favour of their governments. A formula pursuant to which judges would be elected for a longer period, but could not run for re-election, would provide much better objective safeguards.[32] Unfortunately, the current system cannot easily be criticized because the same short duration of the judicial mandate is provided for in Article 223 EC and has been practised for decades without any obvious failures. Nonetheless, it cannot be denied that it may invite

---

[30] An outstanding example of this rise to the top level of the normative hierarchy is the judgment of the French Conseil d'Etat in *Lorenzi*, 30 October 1998, 115 *Revue du droit public et de la science politique* (1999) 649, where the incompatibility of a parliamentary statute with the procedural guarantee of Article 6 ECHR (oral hearing in judicial proceedings) was censured.

[31] See Walter, 'Die Europäische Menschenrechtskonvention als Konstitutionalisierungs-prozess', 59 *ZaöRV* (1999) 961, at 962–966.

[32] An 'Evaluation Group' established by the Committee of Ministers of the Council of Europe has in fact recommended the reintroduction of a mandate of a minimum nine years, which would not be renewable, see *Report of the Evaluation Group to the Committee of Ministers on the European Court of Human Rights*, 22 *HRLJ* (2001) 308, at 326, para. 89.

abuses, in particular in states not used to respecting judicial independence and impartiality.

Interstate Applications

Two types of applications are provided for in the ECHR, individual applications (Article 34) and interstate applications (Article 33). The experience of many decades has shown that interstate complaints are rarely lodged in practice.[33] In fact, states can normally assume that a person who is a victim of a human rights violation may take his/her fate into his/her own hands by filing an individual application. Only when a 'consistent pattern of gross and reliably attested human rights violations' can be deemed to exist in a given country may a state feel prompted to initiate a proceeding for the protection of the affected group of persons. In the past, interstate applications were mostly filed in situations where a government felt that the application was necessary for the defence of its own rights or for the defence of the rights of persons sharing a common ethnicity but living as a minority in another country. This latter alternative characterizes the cases of *Greece v United Kingdom*,[34] *Austria v Italy*,[35] and *Ireland v United Kingdom*.[36] The case of *Greece v United Kingdom* concerned the colonial regime which the United Kingdom maintained at a time when many Third World countries had already gained their independence; obviously, Greece supported the cause of the Greek Cypriots. In *Austria v Italy*, Austria came to the support of the ethnic Germans living in the province of South Tyrol, which had belonged to Austria until 1919. The Austrian government believed that unfair methods were used by Italy in proceedings against young Tyroleans who allegedly had committed terrorist acts. In *Ireland v United Kingdom*, Ireland sought to protect the rights of presumed terrorists in Northern Ireland who had been subjected to doubtful interrogation methods. In fact, the ECtHR found that the United Kingdom had resorted to inhuman and degrading treatment in trying to extract information from a number of suspects, but stopped short of qualifying those methods as torture.

Only rarely have states acted as true champions of the European public order as it is embodied in the ECHR. Two cases may be referred to as examples in this connection. In 1967 Denmark, the Netherlands, Norway, and Sweden brought an application against Greece at a time when that country had fallen under the dictatorship of a military junta. There were plausible reports to the effect that the military power-holders used torture

---

[33] For a complete overview see Sören C. Prebensen, 'Inter-State Complaints under Treaty Provisions: The Experience under the ECHR', 20 *HRLJ* (1999) 446.

[34] 2 *Yearbook of the European Convention on Human Rights* (*YBECHR*) (*1958–1959*) 182, at 186 (two applications).

[35] 4 *YBECHR* (1961) 116; 6 *YBECHR* (1963) 742.

[36] Judgment of 18 January 1978, A 25.

and other inhumane methods against anyone contesting their rule. In 1982, after a military coup had toppled the civilian government in Turkey, the same countries, this time supported also by France, instituted proceedings against Turkey. Again, credible evidence seemed to show that massive violations of all political freedoms were routinely committed. For the respondent country, that type of configuration is much harder to come to terms with than instances where its opponent just defends its own interests. The circumstances show that the state has fallen into the position of an isolated outsider. On the other hand, the decision to make use of the right enshrined in Article 33 ECHR is never taken lightly. No government likes such a formalized confrontation before a human rights body. Invariably, diplomats and their advisers believe that quiet diplomacy is a more effective method. In fact, to institute an interstate proceeding is tantamount to acknowledging that a deep gap exists between the litigant parties, a gap that cannot be bridged by 'normal' methods of diplomatic settlement. This is probably the reason why the traditional members of the Council of Europe have hitherto refrained from placing the methods employed by the Russian military in Chechnya before the ECtHR. Lastly, it has also to be realized that logistical difficulties are not easily overcome. Any state wishing to file an interstate application must produce hard evidence in order to sustain its case. It may take long weeks and months before allegations reproduced in newspapers have been verified. For that purpose, a whole taskforce may be necessary. Given the usual staff shortages in the competent ministerial departments, it may prove extremely difficult to establish the required working unit. It is clear that an interstate application against Russia on account of the tragedy in Chechnya would require a lengthy period of careful preparation. On the other hand, there can be no doubt that to initiate a proceeding under Article 33 ECHR would be infinitely more effective than the individual applications which have reached the ECtHR.[37] The governments opting for that judicial course would confirm that they take their commitment to the cause of human rights seriously, irrespective of a favourable or unfavourable political context.

The class of cases where a state has used Article 33 ECHR for the defence of its own rights and those of its citizens is represented by a number of applications filed by Cyprus against Turkey. Two applications were lodged with a view to denouncing the invasion of the island by Turkish troops, the first one on 19 September 1974 and the second one on 21 March 1975. This proceeding did not make its way to the ECtHR since at the relevant time neither Cyprus nor Turkey had accepted the jurisdiction of the ECtHR. The

---

[37] By recommendation 1456 (2000), 6 April 2000, 21 *HRLJ* (2000) 286, at 287, para. 18, the Parliamentary Assembly of the Council of Europe made an urgent appeal to Member States to make use of Article 33 ECHR with regard to the armed conflict in Chechnya.

Committee of Ministers declared the proceeding closed by a resolution of 20 January 1979.[38] It could not agree on any substantive demands to be addressed to Turkey, confining itself to inviting the two parties to resume their talks. A further application followed on 6 September 1977. Curiously enough, the report established by the Commission on 4 October 1983 was made public only eight years later by a resolution of the Committee of Ministers of 2 April 1992.[39] The Commission concluded that in particular the rights under Article 8 ECHR (protection of the family) as well as under Article 1 of the [First] Protocol to the ECHR (protection of property) had been violated. In 1994 Cyprus again attempted to obtain relief for its claim that massive violations of human rights continued to be committed by Turkey in the northern part of the island. This application (of 22 November 1994) reached the ECtHR after having been processed by the European Commission of Human Rights, since as from 1 November 1998 the jurisdiction of the Court was obligatory for all states parties to the ECHR. According to the judgment of 10 May 2001,[40] Turkey was responsible for a considerable number of violations of human rights on account of the living conditions in northern Cyprus. But no palpable improvement of the situation in Cyprus has emerged from these proceedings. Turkey maintains its view that it does nothing else than defend the rights of the Turkish Cypriots who would be threatened if the former state of affairs with its predominance of the Greek part of the population were restored. It does not appear that it pays any great heed to the latest pronouncement of the ECtHR. One cannot fail to note that it seems, whenever a situation has become as entangled and violent as in Cyprus, the specific remedies of human rights protection are of little avail.

Individual Applications

The great majority of applications is brought by individuals seeking to vindicate rights which they feel have been infringed by the respondent state. During its first years of existence, the ECtHR had very little to do. On the one hand, the opportunities provided by seizing the Strasbourg bodies were for a long time very little known among lawyers. On the other hand, the Commission took pride in rejecting almost any application that was not inadmissible on other grounds as 'manifestly ill-founded'. The first matter the Court had to deal with was the *Lawless* case in 1960 and 1961.[41] However, during the entire period of the 1960s the number of cases referred to the ECtHR was extremely low. As from 1970, the Commission showed greater preparedness to cooperate in a supportive fashion with the ECtHR, from thereon leaving the determination of issues of principle to the superior

---

[38] *EuGRZ* (1979) 86.
[39] 13 *HRLJ* (1992) 154.
[40] 22 *HRLJ* (2001) 217.
[41] Judgments of 14 November 1960, A 1: Preliminary objections; 1 July 1961, A 3: Merits.

body. Gradually, the number of cases increased. Clearly, the extension of the ECHR to central and eastern Europe brought another boost to individual applications. In 2001 the ECtHR dealt with roughly 10,000 cases. It delivered 889 judgments; 8,989 cases were either declared inadmissible or struck off the list. In 683 cases a violation was found to exist. During the same period the registry of the ECtHR had to open 31,398 provisional files, and 13,858 were registered as genuine cases deserving examination as to their admissibility and merits. In 2001 it was reported that the Court receives 700 letters and 200 telephone calls from abroad every day.[42] By 2005 more than 20,000 complaints are expected annually.[43]

No special gifts of fortune-telling are needed for the inference that this state of affairs is worrying. The ECtHR has been conceived as a judicial body of last resort mandated to correct any mistakes that might still occur notwithstanding the obligation of each state party to apply the ECHR itself—or national guarantees of similar scope and effect—within its domestic legal system.[44] If states complied with their duty to respect and ensure the rights set forth by the ECHR, there would be little left that the ECtHR would have to remedy. However, if a legal system is fundamentally in disarray, the ECtHR finds itself confronted with a Herculean task that should have been discharged at the national level. To date, the ECtHR is still faced essentially with its traditional clientèle, the Western European states. But applications are arriving in ever greater numbers from the former socialist states. It is certainly extremely difficult to find ways and means permitting the ECtHR to increase its output even further. If the judgments are to remain solid pieces of legal craftsmanship and if the general line of the case law of the Court is to be kept without any major inconsistencies, sufficient time for reflection and deliberation must be set aside. There exists a definite danger that the ECtHR might become a victim of its own success. To forestall a dramatic loss of its effectiveness and credibility, the responsible authorities of all states parties must now engage their best endeavours in order to prevent a complete standstill of the judicial machinery. The Strasbourg judges cannot possibly render their judgments years after the relevant applications have been registered. A judicial body that has the duty—and the privilege—to criticize national judges because of the slowness of their handling of disputes, would lose any credibility if it followed the same pattern of unreliability. Justice delayed is justice denied, irrespective of the causes adduced to explain

---

[42] Parliamentary Assembly of the Council of Europe, Committee on Legal Affairs and Human Rights, *Report on Structures, Procedures and Means of the ECtHR*, doc. 9200, 17 September 2001, 22 *HRLJ* (2001) 303, at 304, para. 16.

[43] See Wildhaber (President of the ECtHR), 'A Constitutional Future for the European Court of Human Rights', 23 *HRLJ* (2002) 161, at 163.

[44] Rightly, in the *Report of the Evaluation Group*, *supra* n. 32, at 7, 319, para. 43(a), the main responsibility of states parties—or the principle of subsidiarity—is emphasized.

the delay. The current President of the ECtHR, the Swiss lawyer Luzius Wildhaber, has recently suggested that the Court's role should be limited to rendering 'constitutional decisions of principle'.[45] This idea had already been included in the Report of the Evaluation Group to the Committee of Ministers on the ECtHR of 27 September 2001.[46] At the present juncture, it cannot be predicted whether this suggestion will rally sufficient support among the states parties to the ECHR.

A look at the statistical breakdown of the judgments rendered in 2001 is highly instructive. Italy occupies the front position with 359 findings of a violation. This certainly does not mean that Italy is a lawless country. But Italy does not seem to be capable of organizing its judicial system in a reasonably efficient manner. One case of those decided in 2001 stands out where a civil case lasted 38 years and one month,[47] with other cases close behind with 26, 25, 23, 21, and 19 years. In its *Bottazzi* judgment, the ECtHR held that such an accumulation of breaches, which had gone on for more than a decade, 'constitutes a practice that is incompatible with the Convention'.[48] The Committee of Ministers also adopted a specific resolution on the issue of excessive length of proceedings before the civil courts in Italy.[49] Governmental authorities have pledged to take remedial action. It remains to be seen whether the reforms already undertaken and still envisaged are in fact capable of putting an end to a flawed practice unworthy of a country with a rich legal tradition.

More serious are the many cases against Turkey as the respondent party. In 2001 Turkey was found to be in breach of its obligations under the ECHR in not less than 169 cases. Mostly, the applicants had charged their country with curtailment of political freedoms, brutal conduct by military and police forces, and destruction of property in the Kurdish region. Judging by that record, Turkey is still far away from reaching a normal standard of compliance. Precisely regarding political freedoms, true clashes seem to have occurred at a conceptual level. Pluralism is still a word largely unknown in Turkey. Promoting the rights of minorities by peaceful means is easily seen as an offence punishable by harsh penalties.

The other countries which in 2001 figured on the lists of respondents found guilty of violations of their obligations under the ECHR are France (32 cases), the United Kingdom (19 cases), Poland (17 cases), Austria and Greece (14 cases each), and Germany (13 cases). In none of the relevant

---

[45] *Supra* n. 43, at 164.

[46] *Supra* n. 32, at 327, para. 98. President Wildhaber was one of the three members of that Group.

[47] Judgment of 25 October 2001, *Antonio Rosa*.

[48] Judgment of 28 July 1999, 20 *HRLJ* (1999) 480, at 481, para. 22.

[49] Interim Resolution DH (99) 437, 15 July 1999, 20 *HRLJ* (1999) 501.

judgments were fundamental inconsistencies revealed.[50] Yet, the fact in particular that France succumbed in a relatively large number of instances demonstrates that even a well-organized judicial system may not sufficiently ensure full respect for the rights under the ECHR. Concerning Germany, on the other hand, it is obvious that the remedy of constitutional complaint has the potential to take care of most of the cases where basic rights of the individual have been infringed. The few judgments finding against Germany do not raise fundamental issues, but concern differences of interpretation on issues of small detail.

On 7 May 2002 the first judgment against Russia was handed down by the ECtHR.[51] The applicant had been granted financial compensation for his participation in clearing the site of the exploded Chernobyl nuclear reactor, but for years the judgments of the competent Russian tribunals had not been executed for lack of funding. The ECtHR held that this conduct by state authorities amounted to a violation both of Article 6(1) ECHR and Article 1 [First] Protocol to the ECHR. The judgment highlights one of the specific features of the European system, which it has in common with all other complaint procedures, namely the requirement of prior exhaustion of local remedies. Russia has been subject to the ECHR since 1 November 1998, but it took three and a half years before the first judgment in a Russian case could be rendered. Ascending the judicial hierarchy in the national state of the applicant requires an enormous amount of energy. Additionally, the ECtHR needs adequate time to deal with a case. Of course, the two periods are cumulative. It can therefore take years before a victim eventually receives reparation for the harm suffered. In many instances, the original victim has already died at the time when the final judgment in his/her case is delivered. In the case of *Burdov*, the harm to the applicant's health due to radiation exposure occurred in 1986 and 1987. In 1991 he was awarded compensation. However, since no payments were made to him, he seized the Russian courts in 1997. The application to the ECtHR was filed in 2000. Although the ECtHR dealt with his case very expeditiously, it took 11 years before the case came to its end.

In these circumstances, the issue of interim relief is of great importance. There is no provision in the text of the ECHR itself allowing for injunctions to be addressed to the parties, in particular the respondent state. However, Article 39(1) of the Rules of the ECtHR provides that the competent Chamber or its President may 'indicate to the parties any interim measure which it considers should be adopted in the interests of the parties or of the proper conduct of the proceedings before it'.[52] The cautious wording of this

---

[50] But see, in the case of France, the *Krombach* judgment, 13 February 2001, about trials *in absentia*.

[51] *Burdov v Russia*.

[52] See Garry, 'When Procedure Involves Matters of Life and Death: Interim Measures and the European Convention on Human Rights', 7 *European Public Law* (2001) 399.

text makes clear that the drafters did not view Article 39 as establishing a rule with binding effect. In former years, when the European Commission of Human Rights still existed, this was also the understanding of the Commission itself regarding a similar article in its Rules (Article 36). The most spectacular use of Article 39 of the ECtHR's Rules was made in the *Ocalan* case, where the Court first requested Turkey to respect Ocalan's rights of defence (4 March 1999), and where later, after Ocalan had been sentenced to death, it issued another interim measure indicating that the death penalty should not be carried out until it had heard the case (30 November 1999). In light of the judgment of the ICJ in *LaGrand*, where a text couched in similar language had to be assessed,[53] it may well be that the ECtHR will construe Article 39 as embodying a true legal commitment.[54] Valid reasons can be adduced to support such a 'progressive' understanding of Rule 39. States should not be given the licence to frustrate the outcome of a proceeding by taking measures that cause irreparable damage. Since the final outcome of a proceeding before the ECtHR is a judgment with binding effect, it can well be argued that interim orders must have the same kind of binding effect.

The cases where the applicants have requested the European Commission of Human Rights and the ECtHR to grant interim relief are numerous. As of 20 July 2000 not less than 1,457 such applications had been registered. In about 20 per cent of these instances, provisional measures of protection were indeed indicated, mostly in an informal way by telephone calls to the competent authorities. As reported by Hannah R. Garry, the applicants mostly challenged their expulsion or extradition to another country outside the circle of the states parties to the ECHR, alleging that they would suffer treatment contrary to the ECHR if sent to the foreign country concerned.[55] The need for protection against measures of prosecution not fully in keeping with the standards of conduct established by the ECHR was illustrated in an exemplary fashion by the case of *Soering v United Kingdom*.[56] Here, the extradition of the applicant to the US State of Virginia was in issue. First the President of the Commission indicated to the British government that it was 'desirable' not to proceed to the extradition as long as the case had not been examined,[57] and afterwards the Court informed the government that extradition would not be 'advisable' pending the outcome of the proceedings.[58] These requests were complied with by the United Kingdom. On the other hand, in the case of *Cruz Varas and others v Sweden*, the government of

[53] ICJ, judgment of 27 June 2001, paras 98–109.
[54] This has now happened in the judgment of *Mamatkulov and Abdurasulovic v Turkey*, 6 February 2003, para. 110.
[55] *Supra* n. 52, at 415.
[56] Judgment of 7 July 1989, A 161.
[57] Ibid. at 31, para. 77.
[58] Ibid. at 9, para. 4.

Sweden chose not to heed a request by the European Commission of Human Rights not to deport the applicants.[59] A few hours after this request had been communicated to the government, Cruz Varas was sent back to Chile. This disregard for the wishes of the Commission led to considerable friction between the Strasbourg bodies and Sweden. It was not the first time that a government had not complied with a request from the European Commission, but it was the first time in an expulsion case. The two other earlier cases related to extradition proceedings where the requested government owed an obligation to the requesting state under an extradition treaty, while in *Cruz Varas* Sweden enjoyed unfettered discretion to suspend the expulsion proceedings until the case had been duly examined in Strasbourg.[60] Together with the first interim order in the *Ocalan* case, which Turkey rejected as going beyond the scope of jurisdiction of the ECtHR, and a French[61] as well as a Belgian[62] case, the Swedish decision in *Cruz Varas* has hitherto been the only case of open contempt for an interim injunction of the two Strasbourg bodies for the protection of human rights. In a more positive light, this conclusion amounts to saying that the balance sheet of the mechanisms of the ECHR is fairly satisfactory, notwithstanding the formal lack of binding force of the relevant decisions[63] which are now under the exclusive responsibility of the ECtHR.

Whenever the ECtHR concludes that a violation has been committed by the respondent state, it must, if the internal law of that state allows only for partial reparation to be made, afford 'just satisfaction' to the injured party if necessary (Article 41).[64] In this regard, the ECtHR enjoys a wide measure of discretion. Within the present context, we confine ourselves to noting that for many years the ECtHR itself doubted its power to enjoin the state party concerned to take measures of reparation amounting to *restitutio in integrum*. According to this line of reasoning, the Strasbourg judges could do no more than make findings of violation and were additionally authorized to grant financial compensation as 'just satisfaction'.[65] This self-limitation would have shown its intellectual weakness in instances such as a judgment finding that an innocent person was serving a prison term on account of miscarriage of justice or, even worse, that an innocent person was about to be executed on the basis of a similarly flawed judgment. In the recent past, the ECtHR has

[59] Judgment of 20 March 1991, A 201, 25–26, paras 52–64.

[60] Garry, *supra* n. 52, at 418–419.

[61] *DS, SN, and BT v France*, Application No. 18560/91.

[62] *Conka v Belgium*, Application No. 51564/99.

[63] The legal position has now been clarified by the ECtHR in the sense that requests under Art. 39 of its Rules are binding, see *supra* n. 54.

[64] As far as financial compensation is covered by this formula, see *infra* p. 299.

[65] Confirmation of this position was recently given in *Lavents v Latvia*, judgment of 28 November 2002, para. 147.

cautiously moved away from its former rigid stance. In 1995 for the first time it stated in a judgment (*Papamichalopoulos v Greece*) that a judgment in which it finds a breach:

imposes on the respondent State a legal obligation to put an end to the breach and make reparation for its consequences in such a way as to restore as far as possible the situation existing before the breach . . . If the nature of the breach allows of *restitutio in integrum*, it is for the respondent State to effect it.[66]

This proposition even found its way into the operative part of the judgment.[67] By contrast, in the later judgment in *Akdivar*, the ECtHR repeated the statement on the obligation of the respondent state to make reparation in the body of its judgment,[68] but refrained from setting forth that proposition in the operative part. The applicants had demanded that any obstacle should be removed which prevented them from returning to their village. The judges shied away from pronouncing on that claim, holding that in practice compliance with that demand was impossible. In a recent judgment (*Brumarescu*),[69] the ECtHR returned to the model it had used in *Papamichalopoulos*. Again, this was a case of restitution of property. In order to 'soften' its decision, it specified exactly as in *Papamichalopoulos* that failing such restitution, the respondent state was to pay to the applicant a certain amount of money in respect of pecuniary damage.[70] In sum, although the ECtHR has embarked on a new course, it seems still to nurture some doubts regarding the power it enjoys to address truly binding injunctions to states for the purpose of *restitutio in integrum*. Future decisions will show how the ECtHR will definitively deal with this issue.[71]

Enforcement of Judgments

No case is terminated at the moment when judgment has been delivered—the question then arises whether the judgment will in fact be executed. Within a national context, state authorities normally do everything in their power to effectuate judicial pronouncements since otherwise the concept of the rule of law would be seriously jeopardized. A state in which final judicial decisions can be disregarded by the parties at their whim, risks falling into anarchy and chaos. International judgments do not partake of the same

---

[66] Judgment of 31 October 1995, A 330-B, 59, para. 34.

[67] Ibid. at 64: '*Holds* that the respondent State is to return to the applicants, within six months, the land in issue of an area of 104,018 sq.m, including the buildings on it.'

[68] Judgment of 1 April 1998, *Reports of Judgments and Decisions* (1998-II), 711, at 723, para. 47.

[69] Judgment of 23 January 2001.

[70] This jurisprudence seems now to be firmly consolidated, see recently *Savulescu v Romania*, 17 December 2002.

[71] For a comment see Tomuschat, 'Reparation for Victims of Grave Human Rights Violations', 10 *Tulane Journal of International and Comparative Law* (2002) 157, at 164–165.

automatic effect. They must be accepted by the state concerned, and in many instances the defendant in a proceeding under the ECHR may feel that he has been unjustly treated by the ECtHR. Therefore, arrangements had to be made to ensure that judgments rendered by the ECtHR do not remain a dead letter.

First of all, the ECtHR itself has conceived of a number of devices designed to accelerate the payment of 'just satisfaction' that may have been awarded to an applicant under Article 41 ECHR. Having been apprised of some long delays in the payment of such financial compensation, the ECtHR began in August 1991 inserting a clause into its judgments according to which the payment must be effected within three months.[72] Since January 1996 the relevant judgments contain a clause which provides that interest begins to run if the deadline of three months is not respected. These determinations alone do not suffice to ensure a correct and timely execution of judgments. A provision included in the ECHR itself (Article 46(2), formerly Article 54) entrusts the Committee of Ministers with discharging that task.

Fortunately, the Committee of Ministers does not hide behind closed doors. Its annotated agenda is made public and can be accessed via the Internet.[73] Detailed indications are given on each and every case dealt with by the ECtHR so that some pressure can be brought to bear on states not in compliance with their obligation to implement what the ECtHR has determined.[74] The general picture gives rise to concern. Whereas during the initial years of the application of the ECHR, respect for judgments rendered was not a serious issue deserving closer consideration, the picture is no longer so positive. The situation has become so critical that the debate has even spilled over to the political plane in the Parliamentary Assembly of the Council of Europe.[75]

In the first place, execution of a judgment may require measures of reparation in the individual case which was adjudicated. Where 'just satisfaction' has been awarded, the Committee of Ministers must see to it that the

---

[72] Judgment of 28 August 1991, *Moreira de Azevedo,* A 208-C.

[73] See Rules adopted by the Committee of Ministers for the Application of Article 46, paragraph 2, of the ECHR, 22 *HRLJ* (2001) 472, Rule I. The following indications are based on the annotated agenda of the 792nd (DH) meeting of the deputies of the Ministers of 16 to 19 April 2002, http://cm.coe.int/stat/E/Public/2002/agendas/2002cmdelojot792.htm (visited December 2002).

[74] Harman, 'Complementarity of Mechanisms within the Council of Europe: Perspectives of the Committee of Ministers', 21 *HRLJ* (2000) 296, at 297, has reported that 'all too often, the proceedings of the Committee of Ministers take the form of a dialogue between the Directorate General of Human Rights (of the Council of Europe) and the representative of the respondent State, without necessarily involving others'.

[75] See Report of the Committee on Legal Affairs and Human Rights of the Parliamentary Assembly on the execution of judgments of the ECtHR, 28 September 2000, 21 *HRLJ* (2000) 275.

three months time limit set by the ECtHR is indeed respected. Unfortunately, in April 2002 there were many instances in which the payment owed to the applicant was delayed for more than six months (France: 9 cases; Italy: 32 cases; Poland: 11 cases; Turkey: 10 cases). Governments also refrained many times from paying the default interest owed to the applicant; here, Italy took the lead with 264 cases. In order not to leave any doubts open, the Committee of Ministers demands of Members States written confirmation of the payment. Regarding Turkey, many controversies arose on account of the correctness of the method of currency conversion employed.

Not all the violations found can be made good simply by financial compensation. Specifically with regard to non-respect of the procedural guarantees contained in Article 6 ECHR, the system of reparation is marred by a glaring gap in that states are not bound to allow for the reopening of proceedings vitiated by such defects.[76] In the case of *Hakkar v France*, the accused, who had been sentenced to life imprisonment in violation of fundamental guarantees of due process, received reparation in the form of suspension of his sentence which, as such, was not set aside.[77] In such instances, the Committee of Ministers tries its best to obtain the most suitable reparation that can be obtained in the circumstances.

Many judgments do not disclose defective conduct of state authorities in the case at hand, but conclude that the encroachment suffered by the applicant was due to an unsatisfactory state of the internal law. The Committee of Ministers is perfectly aware of this problem. It does not feel constrained to look solely into the individual case decided by the ECtHR, but urges the government concerned to take general measures suited to eliminate the deeper causes of the violation found. The ECtHR itself has established a list of 294 cases where the shortcomings could be traced back to a general inconsistency of the domestic normative system with the requirements of the ECHR and where, accordingly, the law should have been amended and was in fact mostly amended to deal with the criticisms expressed by the ECtHR.[78] In many instances, on the other hand, when bad practice has crept into a legal system, it may be sufficient just to disseminate the judgment widely so that any relevant authorities are made aware of the position of the ECtHR.

Since 1998 the greatest challenge to the authority of the ECtHR has come from the negative attitude of Turkey regarding the judgment in the *Loizidou*

---

[76] On 19 January 2000 the Committee of Ministers of the Council of Europe adopted a recommendation (No. R (2000) 2) on the re-examination or re-opening of certain cases at domestic level following judgments of the ECtHR, see 21 *HRLJ* (2000) 272.

[77] But Hakkar could be kept in custody on the basis of other convictions, see ECtHR, decision of 8 October 2002.

[78] See the Memorandum 'Effects of Judgments or Cases 1969–1998', http://www.echr. coe.int/Eng/EDocs/EffectsOfJudgments.html (visited December 2002).

case. Ms Loizidou, a Greek Cypriot, lost access to her property located in the northern part of the island as a consequence of the Turkish invasion in 1974. In the opinion of the ECtHR, that denial of access amounted to a violation of Article 1 of the [First] Protocol to the ECHR (protection of property).[79] Turkey has refused to pay the compensation which was set by the ECtHR at quite a high level.[80] Obviously, the Turkish government is afraid that compliance with the *Loizidou* decision would set a precedent for the many more cases the essential features of which are identical. Unsurprisingly, the obstinate refusal of Turkey has been brought to the attention both of the Committee of Ministers and the Parliamentary Assembly of the Council of Europe.[81] All these efforts have hitherto failed.[82]

Inter-American Court of Human Rights

General Features

The Inter-American Court of Human Rights (IACtHR) is based on the ACHR of 1969, which came into force on 18 July 1978. It has its seat in San José (Costa Rica) and is composed of seven judges. The first election was carried out on 22 May 1979, and the first meeting of the newly elected judges took place in June 1979. The mandate of the judges has a duration of six years. Re-election is permissible only once. Soon, the IACtHR will have existed for a quarter of a century. Consequently, it is not too early to try to establish a provisional balance sheet.

Generally, the IACtHR follows the example set by the ECtHR before the reform brought about by Protocol No. 11. It cannot be seized directly. Only the states parties and the IACionHR may submit a case to the Court after the procedures before the IACionHR have been completed (individual 'petition' in accordance with Article 44 or interstate communication in accordance with Article 45 ACHR). In contrast to the legal position now prevailing under the ECHR, the jurisdiction of the IACtHR is not compulsory, but must be specifically accepted (Article 62(1) ACHR). Once given, such consent cannot be withdrawn unilaterally, as determined by the IACtHR in

---

[79] Judgment of 18 December 1996, *Reports of Judgments and Decisions* (1996-IV), 2216, at 2239.

[80] Judgment of 28 July 1998, *Reports of Judgments and Decisions* (1998-IV), 1807, at 1821.

[81] See the Report of the Committee on Legal Affairs and Human Rights, *Implementation of Decisions of the European Court of Human Rights by Turkey*, Doc. 9537, 5 September 2002 (with references to earlier resolutions of the Committee of Ministers and the Parliamentary Assembly of the Council of Europe).

[82] At the European level, the Human Rights Chamber for Bosnia and Herzegovina is mandated by the Dayton Peace Agreement to apply *inter alia* the ECHR. Given the fact that the Human Rights Chamber is partially made up of international members, it can under functional aspects be considered as an international judicial body.

two decisions of 24 September 1999 (*Peruvian Constitutional Court* case[83] and *Ivcher Bronstein v Peru*).[84] Only by denouncing the ACHR as a whole can a state escape the jurisdiction of the IACtHR. Unfortunately, the IACtHR received only little political support for its firm position from the Organization of American States.[85]

The IACtHR can also deliver advisory opinions. This latter power has played an important role in the history of the Court,[86] while to date the ECtHR has not been requested once to assess a legal issue *in abstracto*.

Although jurisdiction covering contentious cases is still the weightier power, the IACtHR has not been able to reach the degree of effectiveness of its European counterpart. In the first place, it must be noted that the IACtHR has a limited working capacity, given the small number of judges as well as the fact that it is not a permanent institution. Secondly, the IACtHR reflects still the pre-1998 structure of the European system for the protection of human rights. Any complaint must first be submitted to the IACionHR and no direct access to the Court is possible. Seizure of the IACtHR is reserved to the states parties and to the Commission.

Quantitative Balance Sheet

As during the first years of the operation of the European system, the relationship between the IACtHR and the IACionHR is not free from tensions.[87] The practice of the Commission to refer to the Court only a few selected cases has provided astounding results. A number count encompassing all the proceedings dealt with by the IACtHR from its inception until the end of February 2002 yields no more than 37 cases with 92 judgments. It would appear that some of the cases received excessive attention. Thus, in *Loayza Tamayo* and *Cesti Hurtado v Peru*, the IACtHR delivered each time six judgments. Given the fact that judicial settlement of human rights disputes is a scarce commodity, this extravagance is hardly justifiable: either the system as such is not well structured, or the judges have failed to operate the system as efficiently as possible. As can be gleaned from the Internet information provided by the IACtHR, 17 more cases are pending (December 2002). In comparison with the ECtHR, this is a meagre record. But the situation may soon change since according to the revised Rules of Procedure of the

---

[83] 21 *HRLJ* (2000) 430, at 433–435.

[84] 21 *HRLJ* (2000) 436.

[85] See Cassel, 'Peru Withdraws from the Court: Will the Inter-American Human Rights System Meet the Challenge?', 20 *HRLJ* (1999) 167; Frumer, 'Dénonciation des traités et remise en cause de la compétence par des organes de contrôle', 104 *RGDIP* (2000) 939, at 956–962.

[86] No less than 16 advisory opinions were delivered.

[87] See *supra* p. 166.

IACionHR[88] (Article 44) the Commission 'shall' refer a case to the IACtHR if the state concerned has accepted the jurisdiction of the Court and has failed to heed the recommendations of the Commission.

Interim Relief

In one aspect the Inter-American system is clearly distinct from the European system for the protection of human rights. Almost in a routine fashion, the two competent bodies grant interim relief to applicants living under serious threat in their home countries. The Rules of Procedure of the IACionHR provide (Article 25) that precautionary measures may be taken for the protection of persons having filed a petition. In 2001 alone, the IACionHR granted such measures in 54 cases. Concerning the IACtHR, the relevant power is set forth in the ACHR itself. Article 63(2) provides:

In cases of extreme gravity and urgency, and when necessary to avoid irreparable damage to persons, the Court shall adopt such provisional measures as it deems pertinent in matters it has under consideration. With respect to a case not yet submitted to the Court, it may act at the request of the Commission.

It is clear from the wording of this rule that provisional measures adopted by the IACtHR are binding on the parties to which they are addressed. The Court not only enjoys a competence to take action, but is bound to do so. Consequently, states would breach their conventional commitments if they acted contrary to such an order. In numerous cases, protection of witnesses deposing before the Court was ordered. No data are available showing the effectiveness of such provisional measures.

Consequences Attaching to the Finding of a Violation

One of the highlights of the case law of the IACtHR was the very first proceeding it had to handle, the case of *Velásquez Rodríguez*. The next of kin of the victim, who had 'been disappeared' in Honduras, charged the government of that country with having orchestrated the disappearance. Preliminary objections raised by the respondent government were dismissed by the IACtHR. In the judgment on the merits,[89] it found a violation of a number of key provisions of the ACHR, in particular the right to personal freedom, the right to humane treatment, and the right to life. Synthesizing its view of a state's duty to respect and ensure the rights under the ACHR, it held:

The State has a legal duty to take reasonable steps to prevent human rights violations and to use the means at its disposal to carry out a serious investigation of violations committed within its jurisdiction, to identify those responsible, to impose the appropriate punishment and to ensure the victim adequate compensation.[90]

---

[88] 22 *HRLJ* (2002) 293.   [89] Judgment of 29 July 1988, 28 *ILM* (1989) 294.
[90] Ibid. at 325, para. 174.

Essentially, the IACtHR has indicated the right direction in setting forth this proposition. However, its reasoning is marred by some degree of rigidity.[91] The statement quoted should not be taken out of its context, the commission of a horrific atrocity. In such circumstances, the demands by the IACtHR are fully justified.

Notwithstanding the praise the IACtHR deserves for this bold decision, it seems that the IACionHR is still the preponderant element in the institutional structure of the Inter-American system for the protection of human rights. As a latecomer, the IACtHR suffers from a natural handicap. It may well be, additionally, that the IACionHR enjoys much better logistical resources than its fellow institution. To a greater extent than the European system, the bodies operating under the ACHR would appear to lack sufficiently strong support from the states parties concerned. In situations of major tension, the pronouncements of the IACtHR do not easily prevail over short-sighted considerations of political expediency.

African Court on Human and Peoples' Rights

On 9 June 1998 the Assembly of Heads of State and Government of the Organization of African Unity adopted a Protocol to the African Charter on Human and Peoples' Rights on the Establishment of an African Court on Human and Peoples' Rights.[92] To be sure, the initiative as such deserves praise.[93] The Protocol provides for complaints to be submitted both by the AfHPRCion and by states; individuals may bring cases if the respondent state concerned has made a special declaration to that effect (Article 34(6)). But it appears that a plan to compete with Europe and the Americas is somewhat premature. Up until May 2002 only five states (Burkina Faso, Gambia, Mali, Senegal, Uganda) had ratified the Protocol. Its entry into force requires the deposit of 15 instruments of ratification. There is no real chance currently that this threshold will be reached soon. Seemingly, no consideration has been given to organizing in practice the future work of the Court. It stands to reason that oral hearings entail considerable costs which, on the African continent, private applicants would hardly ever be able to assume.

---

[91] On the duty of criminal prosecution see *infra* p. 271.

[92] Reprinted in Ian Brownlie and Guy S. Goodwin-Gill (eds), *Basic Documents on Human Rights* (4th edn., Oxford, Oxford University Press, 2002), at 741; 20 *HRLJ* (1999) 269.

[93] For first comments see Krisch, 'The Establishment of an African Court on Human and Peoples' Rights', 58 *ZaöRV* (1998) 713; Mutua, 'The African Human Rights Court: A Two-Legged Stool?', 21 *HRQ* (1999) 342; Mubiala, 'La Cour africaine des droits de l'homme et des peuples: mimétisme institutionnel ou avancée judiciaire?', 102 *RGDIP* (1998) 765.

Court of Justice of the European Communities

The mandate of the Court of Justice of the European Communities (CJEC) has been set forth in Article 220 EC, which directs the Court to 'ensure that in the interpretation and application of this Treaty the law is observed'. Human rights constitutes one of the many elements of the complex legal order of the European Communities, but not the defining key element. As is well known, the Luxemburg judges originally were quite reluctant to accept human rights as an applicable standard of conduct within a system the hallmark of which was a market philosophy.[94] Step by step, however, their case law acknowledged that within a legal order overarching a number of democratic states attached to the rule of law, human rights were an indispensable ingredient.[95] Progressively, this realization also made its entry into the founding legal instruments. Since the coming into force of the Amsterdam Treaty on 1 May 1999 the CJEC has a firm mandate to uphold human rights and fundamental freedoms. To date, the main sources of human rights within the legal order of the European Union are the ECHR as well as the 'constitutional traditions common to the Member States, as general principles of Community law' (Article 6(2) TEU). However, the European Union has embarked on a major legislative undertaking with a view to better protecting human rights in their complex interrelationship between traditional freedoms, on the one hand, and economic and social rights, on the other. In December 2000 the Charter of Fundamental Rights of the European Union was adopted, and according to the existing programme for the deepening of the European Union this Charter should be included in the future Constitution of the Union.[96] Accordingly, human rights will gain an even more prominent place in the jurisprudence of the CJEC. Obviously, if the mandate of the CJEC is extended to protecting human rights as a primary task, it will be necessary to coordinate its jurisdiction with that of the ECtHR. The ECtHR should not fall into disrepute as an institution just for those states that are not seen fit for admission to the European Union.

---

[94] *Präsident, Geitling, Mausegatt, Nold v High Authority,* Judgment of 15 July 1960, [1960] ECR 885, at 921.

[95] *Stauder* [1969] ECR 419, at 425; *Internationale Handelsgesellschaft* [1970] ECR 1125, at 1135; *Nold* [1974] ECR 491, at 507.

[96] See European Convention, *Final Report of Working Group II*, doc. CONV 354/02, 22 October 2002, 2: '*all* members of the Group either support strongly an incorporation of the Charter *in a form which would make the Charter legally binding and give it constitutional status* or would not rule out giving favourable consideration to such incorporation.'

10

Enforcement by States and the Role of Non-Governmental Organizations

I GENERAL CONSIDERATIONS

As shown in the preceding chapters, most of the special procedures for the protection of human rights come to their termination once the body concerned has made its findings and formulated its recommendations as appropriate. At the universal level, generally no formalized enforcement procedures are provided for. This applies to the relevant resolutions of the General Assembly and the HRCion as well as to the concluding observations of the various expert bodies after the examination of a state report or to the views adopted on an individual complaint. Although the expert bodies have attempted to organize some follow-up on their own initiative, such makeshift arrangements on uncertain legal bases do lack the necessary clout. While the evaluation of a given factual situation constitutes a legal exercise for which no more than expertise and authoritative legitimacy are required, enforcement cannot be delinked from factual power. Expert bodies alone are not in a position to compel reluctant states to heed their views. Consequently, the international community should establish mechanisms and procedures that bring all the monitoring procedures to their desirable end, namely compliance with the legal standards of which non-respect has been noted.

It is well known that the international legal order finds itself currently in a transitional stage. Although the concept of international community has been largely acknowledged, as opposed to the earlier system the pivotal element of which was constituted by the principle of sovereignty, the framework that deserves to be labelled as international community consists mainly of substantive rules.[1] This is true, in particular, of the commitments assumed by states for the protection of human rights. While institutions have been

---

[1] See Andreas Paulus, *Die internationale Gemeinschaft im Völkerrecht* (München, Beck, 2001), passim; Tomuschat, 'International Law: Ensuring the Survival of Mankind on the Eve of a New Century', 281 *Recueil des cours* (1999) 72.

established to monitor, supervise, and control, states have been rather reluctant to accept some form of institutionalization for purposes of enforcement.

Within the World Organization, the General Assembly is in principle entrusted with discharging all the tasks listed in Article 1 of the Charter, with the exception of those functions which the Charter specifically assigns to the Security Council.[2] Article 13(1)(b) invites the General Assembly to assist in the realization of human rights and fundamental freedoms for all without distinction as to race, sex, language, or religion, and Article 68 directs the Economic and Social Council to set up a commission for the promotion of human rights. In that sense, it is highly significant that the Security Council has been vested with enforcement powers only in the field of international peace and security. According to the text of the Charter its mandate does not explicitly extend to upholding and protecting human rights. In 1945, after the horrors of the Second World War, there was a clear awareness of all the leading figures in world politics that common institutions for the maintenance of international peace and security were indispensable. From the very outset, the Security Council was charged with not only framing general principles or even issuing binding injunctions in an individual case, but also with intervening by force if necessary and appropriate. By contrast, human rights were seen as a subject matter where the United Nations should be confined to a more modest role. The two key provisions already referred to, Article 1(3) and Article 68, mention only promotion of human rights as a task to be fulfilled by the Organization. This choice of words was deliberate and cannot be discarded as an oversight. In fact, Article 2(7) prevents the UN from intervening in matters 'essentially' within domestic jurisdiction. During more than two decades after the founding of the United Nations, human rights were considered as falling within that rubric. But even after this intellectual hurdle had been overcome,[3] there was no escaping the realization that the General Assembly, the body that primarily has to shoulder responsibility for human rights, is not endowed with true powers of decision and/or enforcement. Therefore, the international community has to rely on the power of states willing to act *pro bono commune*.

II ACTION BY STATES

In order to understand the general framework within which individual states may take action for the defence of human rights, different situations have to be distinguished.

---

[2] ICJ, *Certain Expenses of the United Nations (Article 17, paragraph 2, of the Charter)*, advisory opinion of 20 July 1962, ICJ Reports (1962) 151, at 167–168.

[3] See *supra* p. 125.

Diplomatic Protection

From the very outset, it should be noted that states have kept their traditional right of diplomatic protection. This right permits them to protect their citizens who have been injured by unlawful conduct on the part of a foreign government. It does not matter whether a person has suffered a breach of the rules that guarantee his/her status as an alien or whether he/she invokes any of the rights enshrined in specific human rights instruments that apply to everyone, regardless of his/her nationality. Diplomatic protection is particularly important vis-à-vis states that have not recognized any of the relevant individual complaint procedures so that the victims themselves are unable to assert their rights before an international body.

Representations by Diplomatic Means

In order to afford protection to persons regardless of their nationality, states may make representations to other states that are in breach of their human rights commitments. Such representations are today a commonly accepted instrument of foreign policy. A great deal of such diplomatic activities remain hidden to the general public. As already pointed out, governments more often than not believe that quiet diplomacy is more effective than anything that is publicly displayed. In many states, public opinion expects their governments to take a forceful stance against massive violations of human rights in other countries. No legal objections may be raised against such attempts to resolve through open dialogue human rights issues that because of their gravity transcend a purely national dimension. Such *démarches* have also become a frequently used tool of the Common Foreign and Security Policy of the European Union.[4]

Interstate Complaints

In the preceding chapter, it has already been explained that some human rights instruments have established special procedures of interstate complaints that allow third states lawfully to concern themselves with situations outside their boundaries. It should be recalled that Article 33 ECHR grants every state party to the ECHR the right to refer to the ECtHR any alleged breach of the ECHR by another state party. This provision is the clearest expression of the role of *custodes legalitatis* which all states parties are expected to play as guarantors of unimpaired application of the ECHR. While the concept sustaining this legal device deserves unrestricted praise, is has been

---

[4] See King, 'Human Rights in European Foreign Policy: Success or Failure for Post-modern Diplomacy?', 10 *EJIL* (1999) 313, at 316–318, 325.

shown that in practice the interstate complaint has led a marginal existence to date.

Measures of Retortion

Instead of engaging in negotiation and dialogue, or after having fruitlessly pursued the aim of remedying a situation contrary to generally acknowledged human rights standards, a state may decide to take against an alleged tortfeasor actual measures which, in and by themselves, do not interfere directly with the rights held by that other state under international law. Thus, in particular the United States has developed a system of clauses in legislative acts regulating assistance to foreign countries, according to which the provision of such assistance is to be dependent on the country's performance in the field of human rights.[5] Such unfriendly measures or measures of retortion that seek to induce the tortfeasing state to desist from further violations do not require any specific justification. Decades ago, it might have been argued that steps which at face value appear to pertain to the realm of foreign policy with its normal interplay of action and counter-action become unlawful if they are designed to induce another state to change the course of its domestic policies. In fact, the former socialist states maintained consistently that any outside criticism of their internal human rights policies constituted unlawful interference with their domestic affairs. But this charge failed for at least two reasons.

First of all, according to GA Res. 2625 (XXV), which the ICJ has recognized as an authoritative statement of the law as it stands,[6] the actions complained of must in fact interfere with matters which are committed to the sole competence of the targeted state. Since the two Covenants entered into force and since the ICJ determined that states are bound, under the UN Charter, to respect human rights, the issue of compliance with human rights has lost its character as an exclusive area of national jurisdiction. The international community has become the watchdog that is expected to ensure respect for human rights. Hence, a state which attempts to induce another

[5] See, in particular, the Foreign Assistance Act, as amended in 1974, 22 U.S.C. para. 2151n(a): 'No assistance may be provided under subchapter I of this chapter to the government of any country which engages in a consistent pattern of gross violations of internationally recognized human rights, including torture or cruel, inhuman, or degrading treatment or punishment, prolonged detention without charges, causing the disappearance of persons by the abduction and clandestine detention of those persons, or other flagrant denial of the right to life, liberty, and the security of person, unless such assistance will directly benefit the needy people in such country', and para. 2304(a)(2): 'Except under circumstances specified in this section, no security assistance may be provided to any country the government of which engages in a consistent pattern of gross violations of internationally recognized human rights.'
[6] *Military and Paramilitary Activities in and against Nicaragua (Nicaragua v United States of America), Merits*, ICJ Reports (1986) 14, at 100, para. 188.

state to abide by its commitments under customary international law or under international conventional law does not pursue an illegitimate objective. Rather, it assumes a function that is acknowledged as socially desirable and by no means objectionable.

Secondly, unlawful interference is characterized by coercion. Coercion is explicitly mentioned in the elaboration on the principle of non-intervention in GA Res. 2625 (XXV). According to the second paragraph of that commentary, 'no State may use or encourage the use of economic, political or any other type of measures to coerce another State in order to obtain from it the subordination of the exercise of its sovereign rights and to secure from it advantages of any kind'. A high degree of intensity is required for a measure to be classifiable as coercion. In its judgment in *Nicaragua v United States*, the ICJ held that the decision of the United States to reduce the sugar quota for imports from Nicaragua by 90 per cent did not amount to forbidden intervention.[7] In general, economic measures cannot easily be classified as infringement of the principle of non-intervention as long as no specific obligation exists to permit a free exchange of goods and services. There may be extreme circumstances where abrupt severance of economic ties might entail such disruptive effects that the question of unlawful interference can be raised with some degree of plausibility. A sudden halt of oil exports to Western countries, for instance, would bring these countries down to their knees and would mean a deadly blow to their economic activity. In general, however, no state can trust that established patterns of economic exchange will continue forever if they lack firm conventional foundations. In sum, there exist hardly any legal obstacles that would impede the use of economic weapons for the promotion and protection of human rights.

Countermeasures

A next level of intensity is reached if a third state takes measures which under normal circumstances would have to be judged as unlawful, inasmuch as they interfere with protected legal rights of a targeted state. It is in this field that dramatic changes of the legal position have occurred in recent decades. Obviously, it is easier in theory to draw a distinction between measures of retortion, which as such do not adversely affect the rights of another state, and countermeasures, which *per se* are unlawful, than in practice. Given the vast expansion of the field of interstate relations governed by international law, it may be hard to say whether a given form of economic contacts between the countries concerned is subject to a specific legal regime. Even development aid, which in principle the donor states are free to accord or to deny, can

---

[7] *Military and Paramilitary Activities in and against Nicaragua (Nicaragua v United States of America), Merits*, ICJ Reports (1986) 14, at 126, para. 244.

materialize as a legal entitlement if firm promises have been made to that effect. Thus, depending on the circumstances, the cutting-off of financial assistance may either have to be classified as no more than an unfriendly act, a measure of retortion, or a countermeasure proper.

Under normal circumstances states wishing to endorse the cause of human rights in a third country will not even think of military operations. If measures that are *per se* lawful (measures of retortion) are unavailable, they might instead envisage taking steps short of war that run counter to their obligations towards the targeted state without infringing the principle of non-use of force. In the present-day world of global networks states no longer sit isolated in their territories, but have widespread connections beyond their boundaries. Back in 1945 the drafters of the UN Charter were already fully aware of the opportunities provided by this new factual pattern of trans-national interrelationships. Thus, Article 41 UNCh empowers the Security Council to enact a 'complete or partial interruption of economic relations and of rail, sea, air, postal, telegraphic, radio, and other means of diplomatic relations'. Additionally, foreign assets might be frozen, ships and aircraft might be placed under seizure.

May a third state take such measures when it does not act for the protection of its own rights and interests, but purports to alleviate the suffering of a population which at the hands of its own government has become the victim of massive human rights violations? According to the traditional doctrine of reprisals (countermeasures), only the direct victim of an unlawful act may respond by not complying with its obligations towards the wrongdoer. However, in the case of human rights violations there is normally no other subject of international law that could claim to be a direct victim, unless some of its nationals have also been injured. Conferring on any third state the right to take countermeasures amounts therefore to admitting the remedy of *actio popularis*. Every state is then invited to act for the protection of the common interest.

As already pointed out, many of the universal and regional human rights treaties contain clauses that permit any state party to charge another state party with not living up to its commitments under the instrument concerned. These clauses entrust to every state party a role of guardian of legality. Although, as shown, little use is made in practice of these clauses, they are highly significant as a matter of principle. If and when a human rights treaty provides for interstate complaints, it makes clear that it is not based on reciprocity understood as an economic trade-off, but that the parties have pledged to pursue a common goal for the attainment of which they all share responsibility. It was certainly a breakthrough when in 1950 the ECHR established (Article 24, now Article 33) that every state party may refer to the European Commission of Human Rights any alleged breach of the provisions of the ECHR. It is in fact by relying on this procedural mechanism that the Commission could state that the ECHR reflected a 'common public order of the free democracies of Europe'[8] and that the ECtHR expressed itself in similar terms as follows:

Unlike international treaties of the classic kind, the Convention comprises more than mere reciprocal engagements between contracting States. It creates, over and above a network of mutual, bilateral undertakings, objective obligations which, in the words of the Preamble, benefit from a 'collective enforcement'.[9]

It is a matter requiring careful consideration whether such formal procedures must be understood as a self-contained regime that would exclude recourse to the general remedies provided under general international law. When the CCPR came into force, socialist states contended that its mechanisms were indeed of an exclusive character and prevented other states parties from taking countermeasures in case of human rights violations. This contention had no serious foundations since neither of the two communication procedures under the CCPR—the interstate communication under Article 41 and the individual communication under the OP-CCPR—was accepted by a single one of those states. Clearly, the intention of the drafters of the CCPR had been to strengthen international protection of human rights and not to weaken it.[10] However, under a system which makes interstate applications generally available and which ends with a binding decision, like the current system of the ECHR, it can be argued with a high degree of plausibility that countermeasures must be deemed to be ruled out as long as the relevant proceedings can be pursued with some prospect of success.

Although the right to lodge an interstate complaint constitutes a big step forward on the route to a true enforcement mechanism, it still remains below that threshold. To be sure, enforcement starts out with a determination of the obligations that should be fulfilled and have not been fulfilled. But such a determination cannot be equated with enforcement proper. The taking of countermeasures constitutes the additional step which brings true pressure to bear upon the targeted state. At the current stage of development of the international legal order, countermeasures short of force constitute the maximum of what is permissible as a response to an internationally wrongful act.

On the level of general international law, the judgment of the ICJ in the *Barcelona Traction* case, now dating back more than 30 years, opened the

---

[8] Decision in *Austria v Italy,* 11 January 1961, 4 *Yearbook of the European Convention on Human Rights* (1961) 116, at 138.

[9] *Ireland v UK,* Judgment of 18 January 1978, A 25, para. 239. See also Matthew Craven, 'Legal Differentiation and the Concept of the Human Rights Treaty in International Law', 11 *EJIL* (2000) 489, at 510–513.

[10] For a well-documented discussion see Katrin Weschke, *Internationale Instrumente zur Durchsetzung der Menschenrechte* (Berlin, Berlin Verlag, 2001), at 41–63.

gates for states to concern themselves with human rights violations committed in other states by inflicting upon them disadvantages consisting of breaches of the rules applicable in the mutual relationships. By holding that the prohibition of genocide as well as the basic rights of the human person, including protection from slavery and racial discrimination, are owed towards the entire international community as obligations *erga omnes*,[11] the ICJ suggested that indeed states not directly affected are legitimated to vindicate the rights of the victims, notwithstanding some ambiguous language in another part of the judgment.[12] In any event, states have interpreted the *Barcelona Traction* judgment as authorizing them to take countermeasures with a view to enforcing respect for, and observance of, human rights in instances where, in the words of ECOSOC Res. 1503 (XLVIII), a consistent pattern of gross and reliably attested human rights violations obtains.

The judicial precedent of the *Barcelona Traction* case as well as the practice related to that case prompted the ILC, when it drew up its draft articles on state responsibility, to set forth clauses that indeed provide for *actio popularis* in case of (grave) breaches of human rights. The text adopted in 1996 on first reading[13] gave a broad definition of 'injured State', including any state party to a multilateral treaty for the protection of human rights and fundamental freedoms, and any other state where the right concerned had its roots in customary international law (Article 40(2)(e)). Additionally, the broad description of the injured state in the field of human rights was buttressed by the proposition that in case of commission of an international crime, all other states were deemed to have suffered injury (Article 40(3)). To be sure, the legal consequences flowing from that determination were flawed in that the following provisions did not in any manner distinguish between the rights of the direct victim and those third states which were injured only in a legal sense, without having been exposed to tangible harm. It stands to reason, though, that a third state cannot have a right to reparation for its own benefit. It acts as a guarantor of the international legal order. Consequently, there was an obvious need to introduce a differentiation between the different classes of injured states.

---

[11] ICJ Reports (1970) 3, at 32, paras 33, 34.

[12] Ibid. at 47, para. 91, where the Court emphasizes that the relevant treaties at the universal level 'do not confer on States the capacity to protect the victims of infringements of such rights irrespective of their nationality'. This statement, however, is limited strictly to the field of conventional regimes and does not touch upon the position according to general international law; see Abr. Frowein, 'Die Verpflichtungen erga omnes im Völkerrecht und ihre Durchsetzung', in *Völkerrecht als Rechtsordnung. Internationale Gerichtsbarkeit. Menschenrechte: Festschrift für Hermann Mosler* (Berlin, Springer, 1983), 241, at 245–246; Simma, 'Fragen der zwischenstaatlichen Durchsetzung vertraglich vereinbarter Menschenrechte', in *Staatsrecht— Völkerrecht—Europarecht: Festschrift für Hans-Jürgen Schlochauer* (Berlin and New York, de Gruyter, 1981), 635, at 642–643.

[13] *Yearbook of the ILC (1996)*, vol. II, part 2, 58.

The lack of clarity of the 1996 draft was remedied in the final draft adopted by the ILC in 2001, of which the General Assembly 'took note'.[14] This draft defines an injured state as a state that is actually affected in a negative manner (Article 42). But it does not deny other states the important function of guardians of the integrity of the international legal order. According to Article 48(1), any state may invoke the responsibility of a wrongdoing state if 'the obligation breached is owed to a group of States including that State, and is established for the protection of a collective interest of the group'. This description fits exactly the protection of human rights in the international arena, and quite on purpose: it was precisely the intention of the ILC to consolidate the existing practice according to which states are accustomed to making representations to the wrongdoer, claiming in particular cessation and reparation in the interest of the beneficiaries of the obligation breached (Article 42(2)). On the other hand, regarding counter-measures the ILC sticks to extremely cautious language. Article 54 of the draft specifies that the rules set out in the relevant chapter on countermeasures 'do(es) not prejudice' the right of any state to take lawful measures against the wrongdoer to ensure cessation and reparation. The commentary to Article 54 explicitly explains that the ILC was not sure that indeed a customary rule permitting the taking of countermeasures had evolved. Therefore, it confined itself to setting forth a 'saving clause'. Indeed, the provision serves as a reminder that a right to take countermeasures may exist outside the frame-work of general international law. This hesitancy of the ILC would not appear to be justified in light of the practice which the ILC itself displays in its report. What the ILC has failed to do is relate the specific classes of breaches listed in Articles 40 and 41 (serious breaches of obligations under peremptory norms of general international law) to the issue of counter-measures. In the entire part of the draft articles devoted to the implementa-tion of the international responsibility of a state (Articles 42 to 54), not a single reference is made to those particularly grave breaches which formerly were placed under the heading 'international crimes'. Nobody would con-tend, of course, that just any breach of a human rights obligation may be responded to by countermeasures that any third state could take. Therefore, it is certainly correct to be somewhat prudent as far as a general and compre-hensive right of third states to intervene is concerned. But the ILC was excessively cautious when it abstained from positing any rule. What the ICJ stated back in 1970, namely that any state has a legal interest in the protection of a number of core rights, must be true today as well. The international community has not rowed backwards during the more than 30 years since that pronouncement.

---

[14] Res. 56/83, 12 December 2001, op. para. 3.

Treaty Clauses on Observance of Human Rights

Instead of relying on the somewhat uncertain rules of general international law, states can also try to conclude bilateral treaties which establish a linkage between the provision of economic advantages and compliance with human rights. This is the path embarked upon by the European Community, in particular. According to Article 11 TEU, it is one of the objectives of its common foreign and security policy to 'develop and consolidate democracy and the rule of law, and respect for human rights and fundamental freedoms'. Since 1989 it succeeded in complementing its agreements with the ACP States (African, Caribbean, and Pacific states)[15] by a human rights clause. The Lomé IV Convention of 1995 specified for the first time that this clause constituted an 'essential element' of the entire conventional arrangement.[16] The Cotonou Convention of June 2000 has confirmed that precedent (Article 9(2)(4)).[17] Consequently, any breach of the pledges made by one or the other side—the European partners are of course not immune from criticism—constitutes a violation of the Agreement and entitles the other party to suspend its performance or to take countermeasures as appropriate.[18] A similar strategy was pursued in treaties concluded with OSCE member states in central and eastern Europe. In his comprehensive monograph, Frank Hoffmeister has analysed the relevant practice up to 1996. It has emerged from that study that the European Community more often than not acted in an informal way, shying away from making use of the formal procedures set forth for that purpose.[19] Interestingly enough, Hoffmeister confines himself to appraising the impact of the democracy and human rights clauses 'on

[15] All of these agreements were mixed agreements, comprising on the European side not only the European Community as a specific subject of international law, but also all of the Member States.

[16] Article 5(1)(3): 'Respect for human rights, democratic principles and the rule of law, which underpins relations between the ACP States and the Community and all provisions of the Convention, and governs the domestic and international policies of the Contracting Parties, shall constitute an essential element of this Convention.'

[17] 'Respect for human rights, democratic principles and the rule of law, which underpin the ACP–EU Partnership, shall underpin the domestic and international policies of the Parties and constitute the essential elements of this Agreement.'

[18] For a detailed study of the human rights clauses in the conventions concluded by the EC see Frank Hoffmeister, *Menschenrechts- und Demokratieklauseln in den vertraglichen Außenbeziehungen der Europäischen Gemeinschaft* (Berlin, Springer, 1998), passim. See also Hilpold, 'Human Rights Clauses in EU-Association Agreements', in Stefan Griller and Birgit Weidel (eds.), *External Economic Relations and Foreign Policy in the European Union* (Wien, Springer, 2002), 359, at 361–368, 374–380; Eibe Riedel and Martin Will, 'Human Rights Clauses in External Agreements of the EC', in Philip Alston (ed.), *The EU and Human Rights* (Oxford, Oxford University Press, 1999), at 723–754.

[19] *Supra* n. 18, at 452–559, English summary 609–610.

European and international law' without trying to assess the impact of the policy on the factual situation in the targeted countries.[20]

Military Intervention

Military intervention undertaken with a view to bringing to an end massive violations of human rights by a dictatorial regime is the most drastic strategy ever conceivable. According to the UN Charter, the principle of non-use of force is placed under just two exceptions. On the one hand, the Security Council may authorize military operations if it finds a threat to the peace, a breach of the peace, or an act of aggression to exist (Article 39 UNCh). On the other hand, every state enjoys the 'inherent' right of self-defence (Article 51 UNCh). However, a situation where large-scale violations of human rights are being committed to the detriment of a minority group in a given country does not give rise to a right of self-defence. The UN Charter sets forth self-defence as a right of states and not as a right of groups within a state. If in such circumstances the Security Council fails to come to the assistance of the persecuted group, the question arises whether individual states may attempt to save the lives of the actual and potential victims. Humanitarian intervention is the legal concept which knits together all the considerations that militate for the permissibility of such rescue operations by military means.

It cannot be denied that the UN Charter does not speak of humanitarian intervention, thus abstaining from authorizing it explicitly. It may well be, furthermore, that the drafters of the UN Charter intended to make the ban on the use of force an exclusive principle that overrides any justifications of the use of force that may have existed before the entry into force of the UN Charter. Nevertheless, legal reflection cannot be paralysed by the intentions of the historical law-makers. It is inherent in the concept of law that in a situation of conflict between two legal rules a balancing test must take place. On the one hand, according to a time-honoured rule of international law, which no textbook fails to mention, rights may not be asserted if their exercise amounts to an abuse.[21] This proposition is based on the assumption that any right must be understood, and is exercisable only, within a given social context. Sovereignty and territorial integrity as one of its main legal consequences are dependent on similar societal prerequisites. If a state engages in gross atrocities such as genocide and ethnic cleansing, it commits an abuse of its sovereign rights and may forfeit the protection afforded to it by the general principles of international law. Sovereignty is not a natural, inherent quality of any entity recognized as a state. Rather, it is a distinction conferred on that entity by the international community as a recognition of its ability and

---

[20] *Supra* n. 18, at 452–559, English summary at 610.
[21] See Kiss, 'Abuse of Rights', 1 *EPIL* (1992) 4.

willingness to take care of law and order and to administer justice within the group of human beings organized under its roof. Inevitably, failure to discharge the general function which legitimate the existence of a government must entail certain consequences.

Many learned discussions have taken place on the admissibility of humanitarian intervention, mostly with a great display of legal argument.[22] In the preceding lines, by contrast, the rationale lying behind the concept of humanitarian intervention has been explained in just a few lines. This discrepancy is essentially due to differences of method. The classical method seeking to identify rules of customary law relies primarily on empirical research. Pursuant to Article 38(1) of the ICJ Statute, a 'general practice' is one of the two main elements of customary law. Given the low number of situations that may justify humanitarian intervention, that practice could in no circumstances be very significant in quantitative terms. Additionally, it should not be overlooked that more often than not the Security Council is prepared to seize itself of such situations. Regional organizations may also step in to afford relief in situations of extreme urgency even if the legal justification for their involvement may remain doubtful. Consequently, humanitarian intervention becomes an actual issue only in a few instances where, for some reason, the Security Council abstains from taking action. It is no wonder, therefore, that actual reliance on the concept of humanitarian intervention constitutes a rare occurrence. Hence, it is not difficult to contest the existence of a sufficiently broad empirical basis sustaining the permissibility of humanitarian intervention as a legal concept.

On the other hand, however, humanitarian intervention can also be justified pursuant to a different line of reasoning, by deductive inference. Undeniably, human rights constitute today one of the pillars of international law, on the same level of importance as sovereignty or the principle of non-use of force. From the very outset, it is clear that human rights may conflict with unbridled respect for national sovereignty since the obligation to

---

[22] For the most recent discussion see Flauss, 'La primarité des droits de la personne: licéité ou illicéité de l'intervention humanitaire?', in Christian Tomuschat (ed.), *Kosovo and the International Community: A Legal Assessment* (The Hague, Martinus Nijhoff, 2002), 87; Uerpmann, 'La primauté des droits de l'homme: licéité ou illicéité de l'intervention humanitaire', ibid. at 65–86; J. L. Holzgrefe and Robert O. Keohane (eds), *Humanitarian Intervention: Ethical, Legal and Political Dilemmas* (Cambridge, Cambridge University Press, 2002). Krisch, 'Legality, Morality and the Dilemma of Humanitarian Intervention after Kosovo', 13 *EJIL* (2002) 323, has meticulously reviewed the earlier monographs and collections of essays: Simon Chesterman, *Just War or Just Peace? Humanitarian Intervention and International Law* (Oxford, Oxford University Press, 2002); Christine Gray, *International Law and the Use of Force* (Oxford, Oxford University Press, 2000), at 26–42; Nikolaos K. Tsagourias, *Jurisprudence of International Law: The Humanitarian Dimension* (Manchester, Manchester University Press, 2000); Reinhard Merkel (ed.), *Der Kosovo-Krieg und das Völkerrecht* (Frankfurt/Main, Suhrkamp, 2000). See also the editorial comments on 'NATO's Kosovo Intervention' by Henkin, Wedgwood, Charney, Chinkin, Falk, Franck, and Reisman, 93 *AJIL* (1999), 824.

respect, observe, and ensure them sets definite limits to the space left to the discretionary sovereign power of states. To be sure, to date the international legal order leaves it in principle to states to take in their territories the necessary measures required to heed and implement human rights. But there can be borderline cases where the tension between the two principles reaches such a high degree of intensity that, on the basis of a balancing exercise, one of them must yield. The international community has on many occasions affirmed and confirmed its condemnation of genocide, in particular. It would run counter to this determination of principle to abandon a group of human beings to extermination if the Security Council does not assume its responsibility on account of a veto cast by one of its permanent members, just because territorial sovereignty is regarded as a fetish that must under no circumstances be touched.

An example may suffice to buttress what has been stated. It is common knowledge that during the reign of terror of National Socialism in Germany, anyone of Jewish faith or origin was persecuted. Not just thousands, but millions of human beings were deported and killed in gas chambers. Could one seriously argue that in such circumstances the international community must take the role of an idle bystander if, because of complicity of one of the permanent members of the Security Council with the wrongdoing regime, an authorization to use military force cannot be obtained? The law would make a mockery of itself if it did not acknowledge that in such a situation the protection of human life must be given precedence. This is not only an issue of a conflict between law and morals as assumed by Antonio Cassese[23] or Nico Krisch, for instance.[24] Those who have argued that NATO's air operations against Yugoslavia were separated by a 'thin red line' from full lawfulness[25] misjudge the full potential of law as a system which is based on, and deeply permeated by, moral principles. Under conditions of normalcy, there will be no need to refer directly to moral principles as an integral element of the international legal order. But when the defences against the arbitrary taking of human life break down, it must be permissible to resort to extraordinary remedies. Humanitarian intervention is the primary example of such a remedy of last resort.[26]

Significantly, NATO's air operations against Yugoslavia, carried out with a view to bringing to a halt the atrocities committed by Serbian forces against

---

[23] 'Ex iniuria ius oritur: Are We Moving towards International Legitimation of Forcible Humanitarian Counter-measures in the World Community?', 10 *EJIL* (1999) 23.

[24] *Supra* n. 22, at 327.

[25] Simma, 'NATO, the UN and the Use of Force: Legal Aspects', 10 *EJIL* (1999) 1, at 22. Essentially the same view was defended by Antonio Cassese, although he 'respectfully disagree(d)' (*supra* n. 23, at 24).

[26] See Tomuschat, 'International Law: Ensuring the Survival of Mankind on the Eve of a New Century', 281 *Recueil des cours* (1999) 224 (with ample references).

the Kosovo Albanians, was controversial when it started. Criticism was voiced both in the General Assembly and in the Security Council. But implicitly the international community approved the military enforcement of the resolutions previously adopted by the Security Council which Yugoslavia had flatly disregarded. If there had not been such a tacit recognition of the well-foundedness of NATO's strategy, it could hardly be explained that immediately at the end of the bombing raids the Security Council adopted almost unanimously[27] SC Res. 1244 (1999). This resolution establishes that Kosovo shall enjoy 'substantial autonomy'. Thereby, it supported the political objectives pursued by the Western alliance. If NATO, by launching its attacks on Yugoslavia, had committed a major international crime, namely aggression, the other Member States of the Security Council could not possibly have given their approval to the results imposed on Yugoslavia by military force. The Kosovo operation has reminded the entire international community that respect for human rights and fundamental freedoms, in particular for human life, lies at the heart of the present-day international legal order.

It stands to reason that humanitarian intervention can only be a means of last resort when grave violations of human rights have taken place—such as genocide or ethnic cleansing—and if all other avenues have proved to be of no avail. Sporadic occurrences could never provide a sufficient justification. Obviously, humanitarian intervention will have a higher degree of legitimacy if it is carried by a collective effort of a group of states and not just by an individual state. Contrary to many fears nurtured in particular by Third World countries, it will never be a strategy lightly resorted to by powerful—or more powerful—states. To engage in armed conflict invariably entails high costs, not only in monetary terms. Generally, loss of human lives must also be taken into account on both sides. Hardly ever can humanitarian intervention come down to a 'surgical strike', which hits only at the heart of the evil without taking also innocent lives and without claiming lives on the side of the intervenor. However, these grounds should not lead to an outright condemnation of humanitarian intervention. Territorial integrity cannot be the supreme value of the international legal order. We conclude, therefore, that under extreme circumstances humanitarian intervention can be justified and not only excused (mitigated), as recently submitted by Thomas M. Franck.[28]

Human Rights Enforcement in Practice

There is no guarantee, on the other hand, that the right of states to lend their assistance to the fight for human rights is actually exercised by many or just

---

[27] Only China abstained; there was no negative vote.

[28] *Recourse to Force: State Action Against Threats and Armed Attacks* (Cambridge, Cambridge University Press, 2002), at 191.

one other state. Katarina Tomasevski has carried out a comprehensive study of all the instances where during the years from 1946 to 1999 states not only posed, but also acted as champions of the cause of human rights. The pattern of condemnations and sanctions which she establishes provides a picture of inconsistency. More often than not, unilateral 'sanctions'[29] by individual states were imposed on political grounds and not because of genuine concern over human rights. Political friends were protected, whereas the tiniest mote in the eyes of political foes was discovered and could serve as a pretext for denying the alleged wrongdoer the enjoyment of certain rights.[30] A study of the human rights element in the common foreign and security policy of the European Union concludes that the Union's response to grave violations of human rights in Rwanda, Zaire, Nigeria, Burma, and East Timor 'has been minimal and ineffectual'.[31] For many years, the United States sought to promote human rights in China by linking in particular most-favoured nation treatment to certain human rights conditions, but there were ups and downs in the vigilance shown by Washington.[32] The current debate on the fight against terrorism shows how volatile the international political climate is. Although according to all available reports Russia massively violates the applicable rules of humanitarian law in Chechnya, it encounters no active opposition to its military strategies. Likewise, the denial of the most elementary procedural rights to the persons interned at the US base at Guantánamo (Cuba) has not motivated other states to take up the cause of those interned. Relying only on publicly available information, it is impossible to know whether the treatment of the Guantánamo prisoners has been referred to in diplomatic conversations behind closed doors. It is mostly smaller states that have been targeted. The easiest measure of retaliation is, of course, the cutting-off of aid, which entails no tangible costs, whereas the interruption of economic relations inevitably implies economic disadvantages. In spite of this unsatisfactory state of affairs, the principle should not be called into question: where a state engages in a consistent pattern of grave and reliably attested violations of human rights, other members of the international community enjoy a right to take countermeasures with a view to bringing about cessation of the unlawful conduct.

---

[29] In principle, the word 'sanction' should be reserved for collective measures imposed by an international organization.

[30] *Responding to Human Rights Violations 1946–1999* (The Hague, Martinus Nijhoff, 2000), in particular at 369–390; see also Katrin Weschke, *Internationale Instrumente zur Durchsetzung der Menschenrechte* (Berlin, Berlin Verlag, 2001), at 98–125.

[31] King, 'Human Rights in European Foreign Policy: Success or Failure for Post-Modern Diplomacy?', 10 *EJIL* (1999) 313, at 335.

[32] See Kent, 'States Monitoring States: The United States, Australia, and China's Human Rights, 1990–2001', 23 *HRQ* (2001) 583, at 587–608.

Although outside specific conventional frameworks it does not matter whether just one state acts for the defence of human rights breached massively by another state, or whether a group of states embarks on that path, the rule of law is of course much better ensured by a collective strategy. Counter-measures individually imposed invariably smack of arbitrariness. Within a group of states, careful preparation of any action is necessary. No decision can be taken merely according to the whims and fancies of domestic public opinion. Measures taken by the Member States of the European Union or of the Council of Europe, for instance, are always preceded by intense diplomatic deliberations. More often than not, the lowest common denom-inator constitutes the solution eventually found. Caution dominates and rash determinations are not likely ever to occur. For this reason, the charge that can be brought against the European Union is generally rather timidity than excessive boldness.

III ACTION BY NON-GOVERNMENTAL ORGANIZATIONS

Definition of NGOs

In view of the reluctance of states to take up the cause of human rights regarding other countries, non-governmental organizations (NGOs) can play an important subsidiary role. Although NGOs may have widely different agendas, in the field of human rights they essentially pursue altruistic goals. Their general status is normally that of associations under the domestic law of a given country.[33] Although they have been endowed with some rights under international law, they can be classified as subjects of international law only to the same limited extent as individuals.[34] It is also clear from the very outset that NGOs lack any real power in economic or military terms. They have no armies, and they depend as to their financing on financial contributions by private donors—and also on states.[35] But they can remind governments of the tenets they have pledged to uphold. In a democratic society, where the principle of freedom of expression and of speech obtains, governments must take seriously any criticism directed against them. Neither domestic nor foreign policies can be pursued against the prevailing trends in public

---

[33] For a study of their status see Kamminga, 'The Evolving Status of NGOs under International Law: A Threat to the Inter-State System?', in G. Kreijen (ed.), *State, Sovereignty, and International Governance* (Oxford, Oxford University Press, 2002), at 387.

[34] See Delbrück, 'Prospects for a "World (Internal) Law?": Legal Developments in a Changing International System', 9 *Indiana Journal of Global Legal Studies* (2002) 401, at 412–413; Hobe, 'Der Rechtsstatus der Nichtregierungsorganisationen nach gegenwärtigem Völkerrecht', 37 *Archiv des Völkerrechts* (1999) 152; Tomuschat, *supra* n. 26, at 155–160.

[35] Truly government-controlled NGOs are called GRINGOs in UN parlance.

opinion. Potent NGOs know how to avail themselves of the inherent logic and the mechanisms of democratic opinion-making.

As a rule, NGOs set themselves limited goals. There are NGOs with a fairly broad spectrum of tasks, like Amnesty International, Human Rights Watch, or the International Commission of Jurists, and NGOs which concentrate on a small sector in the variegated field of human rights. Thus, the Swiss Association for the Prevention of Torture, whose mandate is indicated in its title, fought for years for the adoption of the Optional Protocol to the UN Convention against Torture. There are groups with an even narrower window to the world. All of them seek to induce states to support the policies pursued by them.[36]

Legitimacy of NGOs

The restricted terms of reference of the NGOs active in the human rights field constitute a strength, but also a weakness. No NGO has to shoulder a comprehensive responsibility for the society where it has its roots, nor for the societies to which it devotes its attention. Thus, there is no need to balance diverging interests. A NGO can always claim unreserved respect for the interests which it defends. Sometimes, NGOs therefore lose sight of the societal context in which their concerns are embedded. Occasionally, their world view tends to be somewhat simplistic. They believe that a governmental apparatus can achieve anything it determines should be done, without taking into account the difficulties of implementation. On the other hand, one can view this stubborn single-mindedness as a precious asset, which leads to a certain division of labour between governments and NGOs. The NGOs denounce, they present claims, and press for action. Governments, by contrast, evaluate these demands, examine whether they can be translated into reality, and emphasize the difficulties to be surmounted in practice.

A more difficult point is the question of accountability. All NGOs have their programme of action. But they may be small groups of persons, and both their management as well as the articulation of their concerns are generally in the hands of a small élite. No accountability exists towards the public at large, and sometimes even accountability towards the membership is poorly organized. Thus, the legitimacy of NGOs is not beyond doubt, depending on the circumstances of each case.[37] This also means that it can

---

[36] An overview is given by Laurie S. Wiseberg, 'Human Rights NGOs', in Alex Geert Casterman et al. (eds), *The Role of NGOs in the Promotion and Protection of Human Rights* (Leiden, Stichting NJCm Boekerij, 1989), at 23–44.

[37] See Onuma, 'Towards an Intercivilizational Approach to Human Rights', 7 *Asian Yearbook of International Law* (1997) 21, at 38–42; Tomuschat, *supra* n. 26, at 155–156. Excessively critical is Sur, 'Vers une Cour pénale internationale: la Convention de Rome entre les O.N.G. et le Conseil de Sécurité', 103 *RGDIP* (1999) 29.

hardly be said that the positions defended by a NGO are necessarily better in tune with the philosophy of human rights than the official position of a government.[38] NGOs have to convince their audiences by the intrinsic value of their views and practices. The label 'NGO' as such is not a label of quality. But the claim that NGOs must be placed under a system of control seems to be grossly overstated.[39]

Activities of NGOs

NGOs may deploy their activities within domestic frameworks, or they may seek to influence international decision-making procedures. Many of them combine both approaches. Since at the level of the UN the defining concepts are shaped that later require to be translated into practice, it is understandable that it is attractive for NGOs to be present when in the fora of the HRCion or the General Assembly codification proceedings are carried forward. Of course, the same considerations apply to any legislative projects at a regional level.

The Domestic Field of Action

According to the simplest scenario, NGOs speak out on human rights violations in the country where they have their seat and of which most of their members are nationals. Although simple in conceptual terms, this configuration encounters many obstacles in practice. Dictatorships generally do not accept being criticized by opponent groups. They invariably aspire to have a complete command over civil society. When, after the ratification by Czechoslovakia of the CCPR, an independent group sprang up ('Charter 77') that had no other aim than to remind the government of the country of the commitments which it had thereby undertaken, persecution was merciless. Members of the group were dismissed from their jobs, and the harassment was so relentless that some of them suffered a complete physical breakdown. Members of the HRCee confronted the Czechoslovak representative with these realities. Although they did this in a polite and diplomatic manner,[40] the Czechoslovak delegation were shocked on that occasion by the simple fact that such occurrences were openly mentioned by an official body. In their answer to the questions put, they avoided making any reference to the taboo title 'Charter 77'.[41] Likewise, the former German Democratic Republic was at loggerheads with non-state-controlled groups which pursued their own

[38] Emphasized by Onuma, *supra* n. 37, at 24–25.
[39] See González, 'El control internacional de las organizaciones no-gubernamentales', 25 *Revista IIDH* (1997) 29.
[40] See the summary record of the examination of the first Czechoslovak report on 27 January 1978, *Yearbook of the HRCee (1977–1978)*, vol. I, 207–215.
[41] Ibid. at 219–224.

agenda of human rights. Thus, the words 'Swords into plowshares', the motto of the peace movement, was viewed by its government as a signal of sedition, the expression of which it persecuted by means of criminal law.[42] It has also been reported that in the Arab region, NGOs face 'systematic harassment by the majority of the governments'.[43]

On the whole, it is not uncommon for an NGO to have a different concept of the true value system of its country and people than the government concerned. This divergence has become particularly visible in Asian countries. Whereas the governments of Singapore and Malaysia have on many occasions emphasized the specific nature of the national community concept, the NGOs established in these countries have constantly proclaimed their attachment to the common values embodied in the relevant UN instruments, in particular the UDHR and the two International Covenants. But it is nowhere easy to assume a watchdog function. Even governments emerging from truly democratic societies tend to react angrily when they are confronted with charges of human rights violations.

Because of the well-known difficulties one may encounter in one's own country by making public claims for strict compliance with human rights, some transnational NGOs have adopted rules of strategy which direct national groups to focus their attention primarily on occurrences in other countries. Amnesty International, in particular, invariably assigns responsibility for political prisoners to groups outside the state where the prisoner concerned is held in detention. By inviting its members and friends to express by letters and other messages their dissatisfaction with unacceptable practices, it is in a position both to bring individual cases to the attention of the public at large and to exert considerable pressure on the targeted governments. Letter campaigns may, however, become a blunt instrument after a while. What appears as a routine exercise will soon be ignored. Subordinate civil servants may then be entrusted with throwing incoming messages into the wastebin. Therefore, NGOs must constantly search for new and effective instruments of action. Experience has shown that comprehensive reports on a given country appeal to the media and are deemed to constitute an event worth being mentioned. Greater trustworthiness is attributed to Amnesty International's country reports or similar reports of Human Rights Watch than to the reports of the US government which are never free from political prejudice. In sum, NGOs have become a potent force in the struggle for human rights. But there are certain limits to their influence. All they can do is orchestrate shame. When any government has relinquished all principles of

---

[42] See the summary record of the examination of the GDR report on 19 July 1984, *Yearbook of the HRCee (1983–1984)*, vol. I, 537, para. 53.

[43] An-Na'im, 'Human Rights in the Arab Word: A Regional Perspective', 23 *HRQ* (2001) 701, at 723.

civilized behaviour, and is no longer listening to admonishments addressed to it by the international community, the method of persuasion through compiling a balance sheet of evil and exposing the atrocities that have been committed to the light of the day will fail.

The International Field of Action

In international fora, NGOs have found a promising field of activity as well. Right from its inception, the United Nations provided for cooperation between diplomatic circles and civil society. Article 71 UNCh provides that ECOSOC may make 'suitable arrangements for consultation with non-governmental organizations'. Admission of NGOs to consultative status is governed by ECOSOC Res. 1996/31, which particularizes Article 71 UNCh. According to the rules contained therein, the conferment of such status is decided by ECOSOC upon a recommendation of the Committee on Non-Governmental Organizations, a standing committee of ECOSOC.[44] Many criticisms have been directed against this Committee which allegedly has sometimes pursued a policy of rejecting groups which too blatantly declare their dissatisfaction with governmental policies.[45] The Council of Europe, too, has issued rules for the granting of consultative status to NGOs. A limited number of NGOs have even been admitted as observers to the intergovernmental Steering Committee for Human Rights.[46] NGOs are also involved in the work of the AfHPRCion.[47]

Within the HRCion, NGOs may sit as observers and may also be heard if the Secretary-General so recommends and the Commission so decides.[48] Similar rules have been framed for the world conferences organized under

---

[44] There are three different classes of consultative status: general consultative status for organizations that are concerned with a broad spectrum of tasks corresponding to the activities of ECOSOC, special consultative status for organizations dealing with only a few of the activities of ECOSOC, and listing on a list known as the Roster for other organizations which can make occasional useful contributions to the work of ECOSOC.

[45] See Aston, 'The United Nations Committee on Non-governmental Organizations: Guarding the Entrance to a Politically Divided House', 12 *EJIL* (2001) 943, with the caustic remark: 'the fox is guarding the hen-house' (at 950).

[46] In 1996 these were Amnesty International, the International Commission of Jurists, and the International Federation of Human Rights, see Nowicki, 'NGOs before the European Commission and the Court of Hunman Rights', 14 *Netherlands Quarterly of Human Rights* (1996) 289, at 292; see also Roth, 'Zur Mitwirkung von Nichtregierungsorganisationen—Gemeinsames Engagement zum Schutz der Menschenrechte', in Uwe Holtz (ed.), *50 Jahre Europarat* (Baden-Baden, Nomos, 2000), 159, at 161–165.

[47] About this somewhat uneasy relationship see Murray, 'Report on the 1998 Session of the AfHPRCion', 21 *HRLJ* (2002) 374, at 375–377; for the relevant resolutions of the AfHPRCion of 31 October 1998 see ibid. at 467–468.

[48] See Articles 75, 76 of the Rules of Procedure of the Functional Commissions of ECOSOC.

the auspices of the United Nations.[49] Thus, at the World Conference against Racism, Racial Discrimination, Xenophobia and Related Intolerance, held in Durban from 31 August to 7 September 2001, NGOs were allowed to make oral statements on questions in which they have special competence, subject to an invitation of the presiding officer and the approval of that body (Article 66(2)).[50] It is well known that NGOs had indeed a great impact on that conference, setting the tone for sharp attacks against the human rights policies of the State of Israel.[51]

As recognized participants of international meetings, NGOs can effectively stimulate international law-making in the field of human rights.[52] It stands to reason that they have no formal right to initiate a standard-setting process. But by establishing good contacts with delegations and providing them with briefs or even draft texts of a new desirable instrument they can in fact launch such processes for which a state or a group of states has to assume responsibility. At world level, in 1983 not less than 23 NGOs established the Informal NGO Ad Hoc Group on the Drafting of the Convention on the Rights of the Child. By submitting to governmental delegations detailed proposals, they were able to exert considerable influence on the ongoing negotiating process.[53] Reference has already been made to the efforts of a similar coalition of not less than 11 human rights groups undertaken with a view to complementing the CAT by an optional protocol providing for visits to persons deprived of their liberty. After years of labour which was frequently quite frustrating, this Optional Protocol was finally adopted in December 2002.[54] At the regional level, the International Commission of Jurists was particularly successful. Together with the Swiss Committee against Torture, it was the driving force behind the initiative to adopt a European convention against torture, an initiative that came to a positive conclusion in 1987.[55] It was also

[49] See the reference document on the participation of civil society in United Nations conferences and special sessions of the General Assembly during the 1990s, www.un.org/ga/president/55/speech/civilsociety1.htm (visited December 2002).

[50] UN doc. A/CONF.189/2, 14 August 2001.

[51] See José L. Gómez del Prado, *La Conferencia Mundial contra el Racismo*, Durban, Sudáfrica 2001 (Bilbao, Universidad de Deusto, 2002), at 39–43.

[52] For an overview see van Boven, 'The Role of NGOs in International Human Rights Standard-Setting: Non-Governmental Participation a Prerequisite of Democracy?', in Casterman et al., *supra* n. 36, at 53–69; Gordenker, 'NGOs and Democratic Process in International Organisations', in *The Role of the Nation-State in the 21st Century: Human Rights, International Organisations and Foreign Policy: Essays in Honour of Peter Baehr* (The Hague, Kluwer Law International, 1998), 277; Otto, 'Nongovernmental Organizations in the United Nations System: The Emerging Role of International Civil Society', 18 *HRQ* (1996) 107.

[53] See Price Cohen, 'The Role of Nongovernmental Organizations in the Drafting of the Convention on the Rights of the Child', 12 *HRQ* (1990) 137.

[54] GA Res. 57/199, 18 December 2002.

[55] European Convention for the Prevention of Torture and Inhuman or Degrading Treatment or Punishment, 26 November 1987, *ETS* No. 126; see Kamminga, *supra* n. 33, at 396.

instrumental in prompting African nations to accept the idea of a regional treaty for the protection of human rights. Due to its tireless work, with the well-known international lawyer Kéba Mbaye as its president, the AfChHPR was drawn up in 1981 and eventually came into force on 21 October 1986.[56] In fact, many delegations at international conferences are grateful for input that has been carefully prepared. Smaller states may be much less well-equipped than an NGO that is able to concentrate on specific goals, whereas a small delegation has to deal with a vast array of issues, having little time for any individual topic. Now that the codification work is nearly completed, this aspect of the activity of NGOs tends to recede into the background. The last great success of NGOs was their presence at the world conference where the Rome Statute of the ICC was drafted. The NGO Coalition for an International Criminal Court, which comprised more than 800 groups, emerged as one of the most influential actors, precisely because of their vast and solid expertise.[57]

NGOs have furthermore played an essential role in making the examination of state reports submitted to expert bodies meaningful, as already pointed out.[58] For the legitimacy of an NGO in this field, it is essential that it act with consistency and free from any bias. Whenever an expert body discovers that an NGO acts selectively, being interested only to assist its political friends while doing everything to denigrate its political foes, its views will automatically fall into disrepute. NGOs operating within the structural framework of the UN must adapt to the philosophy of equality that permeates the entire activity of the UN in the field of human rights.

Rarely are NGOs endowed with formal rights to initiate proceedings. However, as shown in Chapter 8 above, such instances do exist. Two different situations may be distinguished.

In the first place, NGOs may attempt to bring individual cases before an international body by acting as the representative of the victim concerned. On the basis of Article 44 ACHR, the IACionHR has granted NGOs standing to file complaints for alleged victims even in instances where no prior personal contact has been established.[59] In a similar fashion, the new

---

[56] For details see MacDermot, 'The Role of NGOs in the Promotion and Protection of Human Rights', in Casterman et al., *supra* n. 36, at 47; Kéba Mbaye, *Les droits de l'homme en Afrique* (2nd edn., Paris, Pedone, 2002), at 169–183; Howard B. Tolley, *The International Commission of Jurists: Global Advocates for Human Rights* (Philadelphia, University of Pennsylvania Press, 1994), at 178–181.

[57] See Kamminga, *supra* n. 33, at 398; Pace and Schense, 'The Role of Non-Governmental Organizations', in Antonio Cassese, Paola Gaeta, and John R. W. D. Jones (eds), *The Rome Statute of the International Criminal Court: A Commentary* (Oxford, Oxford University Press, 2002), vol. I, 105.

[58] See Kooijmans, 'The NGOs and the Monitoring Activities of the United Nations in the Field of Human Rights', in Casterman et al., *supra* n. 36, at 15–22.

[59] See González, *supra* n. 39, at 37.

Protocol to the African Charter on Human and Peoples' Rights on the Establishment of an African Court on Human and Peoples' Rights provides for complaints by NGOs (Article 5(3)), subject to the condition that the respondent state has made a special declaration to that effect (Article 34(6)). It will depend on the construction of that provision what connotation it will have. On the one hand, the future practice might follow the example of the Inter-American system. On the other hand, however, complaints brought by NGOs could also be understood as complaints legitimated to raise certain general concerns *in abstracto*, without any direct relationship to actual cases.

It is such a power of general scrutiny which has found its expression in the Additional Protocol to the European Social Charter Providing for a System of Collective Complaints.[60] This Protocol deals primarily with organizations of employers and trade unions, but extends also to other NGOs which have consultative status with the Council of Europe. Obviously, its adoption was motivated by a number of pertinent considerations. First, the denial of a right of complaint to individuals makes clear that according to the conception prevailing with the drafters individuals have no subjective entitlements according to the European Social Charter, an assumption which confirms what was said above. Secondly, the drafters were of the view that states parties were not sufficiently interested in defending the pledges set forth in the Social Charter. If they had felt that states parties were vigilant enough, they would have refrained from establishing a specific procedural mechanism which has NGOs as its pivotal element. Lastly, the drafters must have been of the view that NGOs were an appropriate advocate of the common interest embodied in the Social Charter. The establishment of the Additional Protocol is a clear sign indicating that in order to reach the goals of the Social Charter the voice of the groups concerned must be heard. Or to put it bluntly: state bureaucracies are deemed unable to define the common interest of Europe on their own.

Lastly, NGOs have been granted the right to file *amicus curiae* briefs both before the ECtHR (Article 36(2) ECHR)[61] and before the ACtHR.[62] Thus, they may raise points of general interest in proceedings that might otherwise be focused on more specific issues. No conclusive answer can be given as to whether this right of judicial participation may from time to time lead to conflicts with the interests of the applicant, who may not be anxious to discuss points of principle that could jeopardize his/her claim, preferring instead to have the case adjudicated on the narrowest possible grounds.

---

[60] Of 9 November 1995, *ETS* No. 158.

[61] Nowicki, *supra* n. 46, at 297; Ascensio, '*L'amicus curiae* devant les juridictions internationales', 105 *RGDIP* (2001) 897, at 901–902.

[62] Ascensio, ibid.; Shelton, 'The Participation of Nongovernmental Organizations in International Judicial Proceedings', 88 *AJIL* (1994) 611.

Outside the formal and informal mechanisms of international organizations, NGOs have sometimes established their own international procedures for the attainment of their goals. In this regard, the setting up of 'peoples' tribunals' ('Russell tribunals') may be called the culmination of their strength. The activity of such self-appointed judges raises complex problems. If they conclude their proceedings by statements which they call 'judgments', such attempted usurpation of official authority must cause uneasiness to any lawyer attached to the rule of law. If, however, such a body confines itself to organizing a public forum in order to give a voice to the victims of abuses and atrocities to be clarified, the legal perspective changes. Such exercises are supported by freedom of expression. No criticism could, therefore, be directed against the 'Women's International Tribunal on Japanese Military Sexual Slavery' which convened in December 2000 in Tokyo.[63]

It is true indeed that NGOs are less prone than states to play the game of power politics. They do not have to take into account economic interests, in contrast to what governments have inevitably to do. Nor do they have to follow other patterns of amity or enmity. It remains, though, that at world level most NGOs are of Western inspiration. Many of them are funded by governmental monies. Therefore, they are often portrayed as a 'fifth column' of the states that support them. One can hardly deny, however, that most NGOs stand for the values embodied in the international instruments adopted by the United Nations. In this sense, it is crucial to note that these values do not have an exclusively Western background, but have their roots in all civilizations of the world. Since universality of human rights is a concept borne out by any serious study of the issue, most attacks on NGOs constitute no more than political strategies resorted to by governments desperately in need of some pretext as justification for their deviant conduct.

The high degree of appreciation of NGOs active in the field of human rights is also demonstrated by the unanimous adoption, by the General Assembly, of the Declaration on the Right and Responsibility of Individuals, Groups and Organs of Society to Promote and Protect Universally Recognized Human Rights and Fundamental Freedoms in 1998.[64] This Declaration has become the Charter of NGOs in that it not only covers individuals, but also associations for the promotion and protection of human rights (Article 5). Unfortunately it shares the fate of all resolutions of the UN General Assembly in that—as a non-binding instrument—it is neither self-executing nor enforceable. However, it will serve as a yardstick for the HRCee when examining compliance by states with the political freedoms set forth in

[63] See Chinkin, 'Women's International Tribunal on Japanese Military Sexual Slavery', 95 *AJIL* (2001) 335.
[64] GA Res. 53/144, 9 December 1998. On the difficulties surrounding its adoption see Dennis, 'The 54th Session of the UN Commission on Human Rights', 93 *AJIL* (1999) 246, at 246–247.

the CCPR. Likewise, the General Assembly itself and the HRCion will measure the overall performance of a country in the field of human rights by the degree to which it allows advocacy of compliance with the standards binding on that country. Among the factors which induce states to abide by their obligations, NGOs occupy today a leading position.

11

Mitigating the Effects of Armed Conflict: Humanitarian Law

I GENERAL CONSIDERATIONS

Jus ad Bellum, Jus in Bello

In a community of nations which remains attached to basic concepts of peace and human rights, war, if and when it occurs, cannot simply be regarded as a fact of life which lasts as long as it lasts with whatever consequences it may entail. In the same manner as great efforts have been made to ban and effectively eradicate war, it should be a supreme objective of the international community to reduce as far as possible the detrimental and often atrocious corollaries of armed conflict. With this objective in mind, two strands of rules have been developed: *jus ad bellum* governs the lawfulness of resort to force, and *jus in bello* connotes the rules applying to the actual conduct of warfare. There is no absolute watertight division between the two branches. The right of self-defence, for instance, is placed under the requirements of necessity and proportionality. Actions of self-defence may not be extended beyond what is necessary and appropriate for the attainment of the aim pursued, namely cessation of an armed attack.[1] Consequently, if in a given situation this borderline is crossed, the action concerned becomes unlawful. In general, however, *jus in bello* must be distinguished from *jus ad bellum*.

It has already been explained that formerly among the rules of *jus in bello* the Hague law was distinguished from the Geneva law (or humanitarian law), the former one containing the regime for the conduct of hostilities and the latter one establishing rules for the protection of victims of war. Since the coming into force of the two Additional Protocols to the four Geneva Conventions of 1949 this delimitation has become obsolete since the two Protocols set forth at the same time rules pertaining to both

---

[1] ICJ, *Legality of the Threat or Use of Nuclear Weapons*, Advisory Opinion, ICJ Reports (1996) 226, at 245, para. 41.

subject matters. Today, *jus in bello* in its entirety is called international humanitarian law.[2]

Since international humanitarian law aims to maintain a modicum of civilization amid the worst of all cataclysms human communities can experience, namely war, it may be classified as one of the branches of international human rights law.[3] During an armed confrontation, human rights suffer by necessity. In particular, the killing of combatants cannot be avoided. Therefore, special rules had to be evolved in order to adapt the normal regime of human rights to the specificities of armed warfare, rescuing whatever possible of its core substance.[4] The international community has always sought to prevent armed conflict from degenerating into an orgy of killing where death and destruction are the only guidelines.

Non-discrimination

The differentiation between *jus ad bellum* and *jus in bello* is particularly important in view of the question whether an aggressor state can invoke for itself the benefits of *jus in bello*. One could argue that a deeply vitiated armed action, such as aggression, should not be covered by humanitarian rules since these rules would provide the protection of the law to an action contrary to the law, which at first glance would appear to be an inconsistency. Indeed, it was contended in the past that the law on warfare should be split, better treatment being deserved by a victim than by an offender. In *United States v List*,[5] a case from the time of the Second World War dealing with the treatment to be accorded to hostages, the prosecution took the view that, because of Germany's unjustified invasion of the Balkan states, any conduct of the German Army during the Second World War had to be adjudged as unlawful and that consequently the German command could not invoke the powers normally granted under the Hague Rules to an occupation force, an argument which was rejected by the tribunal. Indeed, many weighty reasons militate against this interpretation.[6]

---

[2] ICJ, *Legality of the Threat or Use of Nuclear Weapons*, Advisory Opinion, ICJ Reports (1996) 226, at 256, para. 75. See also Bugnion, 'Droit de Genève et droit de La Haye', 83(844) *IRRC* (2001) 901; Meron, 'The Humanization of Humanitarian Law', 94 *AJIL* (2000) 239.

[3] See also Caflisch, 'The Rome Statute and the ECHR', 23 *HRLJ* (2002) 1, at 2.

[4] See ICJ, *Legality, supra* n. 1, at 240, para. 25; see also Meron, *supra* n. 2, at 266–273.

[5] 15 *Annual Digest, Year 1948* (1953), 632, at 636–637.

[6] Persuasive arguments against any discrimination in the applicability of humanitarian law were previously advanced by L. Oppenheim and H. Lauterpacht, *International Law* (7th edn, London, Longmans, 1952), vol. 2, at 218.

First of all, empirical experience shows that respect for the rules of humanitarian law is to a large extent dependent on reciprocity.[7] No state observes rules which its enemy states do not comply with. One of the most effective motives for law abidance is the expectation that all the parties will behave in the same way and that any departure from the standard intended to establish the applicable discipline will entail immediate retaliation. In particular for that reason, during the Second World War no poisonous gas was used as weapon, although such gas was found in the stocks of all belligerent parties. Denying a criminal state the shield of humanitarian law would impel it to strike back by the same or similar means. Thus, nothing would be gained. Any possible immediate advantage would be largely outweighed by a harmful long-term disadvantage, namely a vicious spiral of violence and counter-violence depriving the conflict concerned of any residue of a legal framework suited to maintain elements of civilization even during war. Additionally, there is a simple truth. In many instances, it is difficult, if not impossible, to determine in a given conflict before it has come to its end who bears responsibility for commencing hostilities. As a rule, charges are met by counter-charges. If both sides identify the other one as the culprit, *jus in bello* would be eliminated from the very outset.

Essentially, it is not states as abstract entities that would bear the brunt of a denial of *jus in bello*, but the persons in its service, the members of its armed forces and also its civilians, not only men, but also women and children. Looked at realistically, recourse to discrimination in the application of humanitarian law would thus amount to collective punishment based on an assumption of collective guilt, which flies in the face of the presumption of innocence which is a centrepiece of the edifice of modern human rights law. Dictators and high military commanders, precisely those persons who decide on issues of war and peace, always know how to protect themselves. They would not be hurt if the cover of *jus in bello* were torn away. It is the common human being who suffers if armed conflict is left without any restraining rules. Instead of punishing those who deserve punishment, one would more often than not strike at innocent people.

In fact, the persuasive weight of these considerations is such that today the principle of non-discriminatory application of the rules of humanitarian law prevails without any serious objection. In GA Res. 2162 (XXI), 5 December 1966, the General Assembly declared:

---

[7] See Wolfrum, 'Enforcement of International Humanitarian Law', in Dieter Fleck (ed.), *The Handbook of Humanitarian Law in Armed Conflicts* (Oxford, Oxford University Press, 1995), 517, at 525–526, para. 1202. Doubts have been expressed, however, by Doswald-Beck, 'Implementation of International Humanitarian Law in Future Wars', in Michael N. Schmitt and Leslie C. Green (eds), *The Law of Armed Conflict: Into the Next Millennium* (Newport, Rhode Island, Naval War College, 1998), 39, at 41.

that the strict observance of the rules of international Law on the conduct of warfare is in the interest of maintaining these standards of civilization,

and this guideline determined the work of the Geneva Diplomatic Conference on the Reaffirmation and Development of International Humanitarian Law Applicable in Armed Conflicts which, from 1974 to 1977, met in Geneva to modernize the traditional rules of *jus in bello*. Protocol I on international armed conflict, one of the two instruments adopted by that Conference, provides in its preamble that there may be no adverse distinction based on the nature or origin of the armed conflict or on the causes espoused by or attributed to the parties to the conflict. This proposition seemed so evident in 1977 that the author explaining the preamble in the official commentary of the International Committee of the Red Cross does not even find it worthwhile to mention that in the past there existed views which differed from the line now definitively approved.[8]

It is obvious that the rules of humanitarian law must also govern military operations within the context of humanitarian intervention. Rightly, the President of the International Committee of the Red Cross, Cornelio Sommaruga, warned on the occasion of the 50th anniversary of the signing of the four Geneva Conventions of 1949 of distinguishing between 'good' victims of the 'humanitarian' side and 'bad' victims among those who oppose a humanitarian intervention.[9] Indeed, such a rescue operation would find itself intrinsically perverted if, on its part, non-respect of the applicable regime were to result in the commission of war crimes.

II BRIEF HISTORICAL SURVEY

Before the First World War

Humanitarian law proper has a tradition which does not go as far back as the majority of the rules of modern international law. It was the nineteenth century only which set out to civilize war by establishing rules designed to protect, to the extent possible, potential victims. To be sure, there had always been calls by lawyers and philosophers underlining the necessity to uphold certain standards of human decency even in armed conflict. But these exhortations did not reach the level of positive law. Eventually, in 1863, under the impression of the suffering of the soldiers wounded on the battlefields of northern Italy during the Italian war of national liberation,

[8] See Zimmermann, in Yves Sandoz, Christophe Swinarski, and Bruno Zimmermann (eds), *Commentary on the Additional Protocols of 8 June 1977 to the Geneva Conventions of 12 August 1949* (henceforth: *ICRC Commentary*) (Geneva, Martinus Nijhoff, 1987), at 29.
[9] 'Renew the Ambition to Impose Rules on Warfare', *International Herald Tribune*, 12 August 1999.

the Red Cross movement began life with the conclusion of a treaty founding an organization mandated to care for the victims of war, and at an ensuing conference for the neutralization of medical services in the field the first Geneva Convention for the Amelioration of the Condition of the Wounded in Armies in the Field was elaborated (22 August 1864). At the same time, the famous Lieber Code took shape, a set of rules on warfare in the form of a manual which had been prepared by an American professor of German origin, Francis Lieber, at the request of President Lincoln, who put that Code into effect as General Order 100 during the civil war with the Confederate states.[10] These instruments, in particular, created a general awareness of the need to fill in the existing lacunae. The Institut de droit international, at its Oxford session in 1880, adopted a Manuel des lois de la guerre sur terre,[11] which comprised not less than 86 Articles. However, truly binding international instruments were required. With a view to realizing this objective, at the initiative of the Russian government the 1899 Peace Conference at The Hague was convened.[12]

The most outstanding achievement of the 1899 Conference was to reach agreement on the Convention with respect to the Laws and Customs of War on Land[13] with its annexe, the Regulations respecting the Laws and Customs of War on Land, which contained the bulk of the substantive provisions. For the first time in the history of humankind, a comprehensive legal regime for warfare (with the exception of maritime and air warfare) had thus been established, a regime aiming to find universal application. In 1907 at the Second Peace Conference, the Convention was improved by a number of amendments, but its general thrust remained unchanged;[14] additionally, no less than 11 other agreements were concluded, all related to issues of warfare. Of course, the universality of the Regulations and the other agreements was a term which did not correspond to the true picture inasmuch as all of them were intended to apply solely in wars between states mutually recognizing one another as such. When the European powers established and consolidated their colonial empires in Africa and Asia at that time, they did not consider themselves bound by any legal rules. In fact, from Asia only Japan and

---

[10] Reprinted in Dietrich Schindler and Jiri Toman (eds), *The Laws of Armed Conflicts: A Collection of Conventions, Resolutions and other Documents* (3rd edn, Dordrecht and Geneva, Martinus Nijhoff and Henri Dunant Institute, 1988), at 5. For a recent comment see Vöneky, 'Der Lieber's Code und die Wurzeln des modernen Kriegsvölkerrechts', 62 *ZaöRV* (2002) 423.

[11] Reprinted in Institut de droit international, *Tableau général des résolutions (1873–1956)* (Basel, Verlag für Recht und Gesellschaft, 1957), at 180.

[12] For the historical context see Caron, 'War and International Adjudication: Reflections on the 1899 Peace Conference', 94 *AJIL* (2000) 4; Pictet, 'La formation du droit humanitaire', 84(846) *IRRC* (2002) 321.

[13] Reprinted in A. Pearce Higgins, *The Hague Peace Conferences* (Cambridge, Cambridge University Press, 1909), at 207.

[14] For a careful analysis see Aldrich, 'The Laws of War on Land', 94 *AJIL* (2000) 42.

Thailand were among the states parties, and Liberia was the only African state participating. To date, this meagre record has not improved significantly. Ratification of the Hague instruments of 1907 lags far behind the response which the later Red Cross conventions have encountered in the community of nations. On the one hand, this can certainly be explained by the fact that Additional Protocol I of 1977 has largely overtaken the somewhat outdated regime of the Regulations in particular. But another factor has also to be taken into account. Since most of the Third World countries were not yet in existence in 1899 and 1907 and since they never benefited from the advantages provided by the Hague instruments in their relations with the then colonial powers, they resent these instruments on political grounds as dishes of an exclusively European kitchen prepared without any regard for their concerns.

Between the Two World Wars

As from the time of the two Hague Conferences, humanitarian law separated into two branches. On the one hand, the 'Hague law' set forth rules on the conduct of hostilities, addressed to everyone engaged in combat. On the other hand, the 'Geneva law' comprised rules for the protection of persons not or no longer participating in armed operations, outside the ambit of active hostilities.[15] It was naturally the International Committee of the Red Cross which took care of this second branch. After the First World War, in light of the experiences gathered during that confrontation, a Conference convened in Geneva succeeded in establishing two conventions on the condition of the sick and wounded members of armed forces in the field and on prisoners of war.[16] But no significant review of the rules on warfare proper, of the Hague rules, occurred, with only one important exception. In 1925, the Protocol for the Prohibition of the Use in War of Asphyxiating, Poisonous or Other Gases, and of Bacteriological Methods of Warfare[17] was concluded, an instrument which also had as its background the practices of the First World War where Germany had first attempted to break through the enemy defence lines by releasing chlorine gas. For the rest, however, the Hague Regulations remained the applicable standard although it was clear that the Regulations did not provide adequate answers to the many challenges of warfare with modern technological means.

[15] Article 21 of the Regulations Respecting the Laws and Customs of War on Land, Annexed to Hague Convention (IV) Respecting the Laws and Customs of War on Land, 1907, made explicit reference to the then applicable Geneva Convention of 1906.

[16] Conventions of 27 July 1929: Geneva Convention Relative to the Treatment of Prisoners of War, 118 *LNTS* 343; Geneva Convention for the Amelioration of the Condition of the Wounded and Sick in Armies in the Field, 118 *LNTS* 303.

[17] 94 *LNTS* 65.

After the Second World War

It was only after the Second World War that major reforms could be carried out. At another Red Cross Conference in Geneva in 1949, four conventions were adopted, covering sick and wounded on land (I), sick and wounded at sea (II), prisoners of war (III), and civilians as victims of armed conflict (IV). Of these four instruments, Convention No. IV affects only slightly the rules on warfare since it contains some vague general principles on the treatment to be accorded to civilians which have a limited bearing on strategies and tactics of warfare. However, a true convergence of the Hague law and the Geneva law came about only in 1977 when a Diplomatic Conference, after four rounds of sessions during more than three years, produced the two Additional Protocols to the four Geneva Conventions of 1949, Protocol I regulating international armed conflict, and Protocol II regulating internal armed conflict.

III PROHIBITION OF SPECIFIC WEAPONS

The current regime of *jus in bello* is complemented by a number of treaties which ban certain types of weapons. The most important of these are the 1972 Biological Weapons Convention,[18] which in a narrow sense does not belong to the *jus in bello* because it does not deal with the use of biological means of warfare, but only prohibits their development, production, and stockpiling; the Convention on Conventional Weapons of 10 October 1980,[19] which rules out the use of certain weapons which 'may be deemed' to be excessively injurious or to have indiscriminate effects;[20] and the Chemical Weapons Convention,[21] which unequivocally bans the use of chemical weapons. The most recent achievement is the Convention on the Prohibition of the Use, Stockpiling, Production and Transfer of Anti-Personnel Mines and on their Destruction of 3 December 1997.[22] As far as nuclear weapons are concerned, no prohibition by way of treaty law exists. In 1996 the ICJ gave an advisory opinion on the *Legality of the Threat or Use of Nuclear*

---

[18] Convention on the Prohibition of the Development, Production and Stockpiling of Bacteriological (Biological) and Toxin Weapons and on Their Destruction, 16 December 1971, 11 *ILM* (1972) 310.

[19] 19 *ILM* (1980) 1524.

[20] According to the annexed protocols: Protocol on Non-Detectable Fragments (Protocol I); Protocol on Prohibitions or Restrictions on the Use of Mines, Booby Traps and other Devices (Protocol II); Protocol on Prohibitions or Restrictions on the Use of Incendiary Weapons (Protocol III).

[21] Convention on the Prohibition of the Development, Production, Stockpiling and Use of Chemical Weapons and on Their Destruction, 13 January 1993, 32 *ILM* (1993) 804.

[22] 36 *ILM* (1997) 1507.

Weapons[23] in which it held that the threat or use of nuclear weapons would 'generally' be contrary to the rules of international law applicable in armed conflict. However, said a deeply divided Court, it could not conclude definitively whether the use of nuclear weapons would be lawful or unlawful in an extreme circumstance of self-defence, 'in which the very survival of a State would be at stake'.[24] This escape clause sets a dangerous precedent in that it may seem to suggest that in any grave emergency situation the law ceases to lose its normative force, in accordance with the German saying: '*Not kennt kein Gebot*' ('Necessity knows no law'). A draft providing for a total ban on nuclear weapons has been pending for many years in the General Assembly of the United Nations, but has never been definitively approved.[25]

IV LAW-MAKING

Necessity of Humanitarian Law?

In the very first years after the setting up of the United Nations, the question could legitimately be raised whether humanitarian law was necessary at all in a world governed by a general prohibition on the use of force. In fact, if war disappears as a factual phenomenon, humanitarian law becomes obsolete. It could even be argued that to focus on humanitarian law accepts war as a natural component of international relations, thereby undermining the strictness of Article 2(4) UNCh. It is for this reason that the ILC, during its very first session when it considered its programme for the future, declined to include humanitarian law as one of the relevant topics in its work schedule.[26] Today, however, the hopes which may have attached to the consequences of the ushering in of a new world order have largely faded away. After half a century of practical experiences, one must conclude today that the collective security system of the Charter of the United Nations has not been—and will certainly not be—able definitively to eradicate armed conflict as a form of confrontation between human groups and societies. Therefore, adequate rules of humanitarian law are as urgent in our time as they were before the First World War, and probably even more so since the destructive power of modern armament has increased to such an extent that indeed humankind could be wiped out from this planet within a few hours.

---

[23] ICJ Reports (1996) 226. For comments see Weil, 'L'avis consultatif sur la licéité de la menace ou de l'emploi d'armes nucléaires possibles: deux lectures possibles', in *Liber Amicorum Mohammed Bedjaoui* (The Hague, Kluwer Law International, 1999), 545.

[24] Ibid. at 266, para. E.

[25] See GA Res. 52/39 C, 9 December 1997, Annex: Draft Convention on the Prohibition of the Use of Nuclear Weapons.

[26] *Yearbook of the ILC (1949)*, at 51–53.

Legal Sources

Treaties

Considering the techniques of law-making in this sector of *jus in bello*, one is struck that here the most orthodox principles apply. States insist on the necessity of acceptance by explicit consent. In contrast to what has been introduced in the law of the environment, the adoption of new rules taking into account new technological developments has in no way been facilitated. The opting-out model is entirely ignored. Quite obviously, issues of national defence are closely related to an archaic, but immensely vital concept of national independence and sovereignty. Governments wish to take the relevant decisions in absolute freedom, without being put under pressure by any technical devices which might push them without their full knowledge into commitments which they do not approve unrestrictedly. In spite of this reluctance to submit to any streamlined procedures of acceptance of treaty obligations, humanitarian law has amazingly strong support in the international community. The Geneva Conventions of 1949 today count on quasi-universal membership. As far as the two Additional Protocols of 1977 are concerned, the balance sheet is less positive. France, fearing that the use of nuclear weapons might come within the purview of Protocol I, had for many years refused its ratification, but eventually overcame its hesitations in April 2001.[27] By contrast, the United States has decided to remain aloof from both of them, and Israel and Japan share this negative approach together with four other Asian countries: India, Indonesia, Iran, and Iraq.

Custom

In contrast to the process of treaty-making, which remains cumbersome and slow, customary law has advanced at a rapid pace in recent years. Custom, closely intertwined with considerations of morality, has always played a leading role in international humanitarian law. As has already been pointed out, in the preamble of the Convention with respect to the Laws and Customs of War on Land of 1899 the so-called 'Martens clause' appeared, a deliberate rejection of the positivist doctrine.[28] In a slightly modified form, the Martens clause has been included in Article 1(2) of Additional Protocol I of 1977, where reference is made to principles derived from 'established

---

[27] Comment by Laucci, 'La France adhère au protocole 1 relatif à la protection des victimes des conflits armés internationaux', 105 *RGDIP* (2001) 677, who specifically focuses on the 18 (!) reservations entered by France.

[28] 'Until a more complete code of the laws of war has been issued, the High Contracting Parties deem it expedient to declare that, in cases not included in the Regulations adopted by them, the inhabitants and the belligerents remain under the protection and the rule of the principles of the law of nations, as they result from the usages established among civilized peoples, from the laws of humanity, and the dictates of the public conscience.'

custom, from the principles of humanity and from the dictates of public conscience', as well as in the preamble to Additional Protocol II (para. 4).

Similar ethical forces are driving a growing tendency to contend that treaty rules, once the relevant treaty has entered into force and the circle of states parties has expanded beyond the minimum requirements, have crystallized as custom.[29] Two judicial pronouncements should be mentioned in this connection. In the case of *Nicaragua v United States*, the ICJ held that Article 3 common to the four Geneva Conventions of 12 August 1949 constituted 'a minimum yardstick' for the assessments of armed conflict within a domestic setting, encapsulating 'elementary considerations of humanity'.[30] Similarly, in its advisory opinion on the *Legality of the Threat or Use of Nuclear Weapons* the ICJ took the view that even states not having ratified the Hague or Geneva Conventions were bound by the rules contained therein 'because they constitute intransgressible principles of international customary law'.[31] In view of the massive adherence to the four Geneva Conventions, bridging the gap between treaty and custom was not too bold a step to take.

However, when the Secretary-General of the United Nations presented to the Security Council his report setting out a draft statute for the planned international criminal tribunal for the former Yugoslavia,[32] far greater difficulties had to be faced. Since the Security Council has no mandate to legislate in the field of criminal law, and since any law-making activity in this field is constrained by the prohibition of retroactive application, it had to be assumed that the substantive rules to be applied by the Tribunal, which the draft statute mentioned as falling within its jurisdiction, had a firm customary basis. In order to reach this conclusion, two intellectual operations had to be performed. In a first step, it had to be argued—and shown—that the provisions of the Hague Regulations of 1907 which underlay Article 3 of the draft ('Violations of the laws or customs of war') had crystallized as customary law. Furthermore, it had to be shown that any violation of these rules constituted a criminal offence punishable by penalties, although the Hague Regulations do not provide for criminal sanctions to be imposed.[33] The Appeals Chamber in the *Tadic* case saw no obstacle to affirming these two propositions, holding additionally that the scope of violations of humanitarian law punishable under customary law had widened by the inclusion of breaches of Article 3 common to the four Geneva Conventions of 1949.[34] Many more examples could be cited of situations where the two existing international criminal

---

[29] See Meron *supra* n. 2, at 244.

[30] ICJ Reports (1986) 14, at 114.

[31] ICJ Reports (1996), 226, at 257, para. 79. See also Mani, 'The International Court and the Humanitarian Law of Armed Conflict', 39 *IJIL* (1999) 32.

[32] UN doc. S/25704, 3 May 1993.

[33] Ibid. at paras. 41–44.

[34] Judgment of 2 October 1995, 35 *ILM* (1996) 32, paras. 87–137.

tribunals have enforced humanitarian law through the meting out of punishments, not hesitating to affirm the customary law nature of the rules in issue and their suitability as legal norms permitting the imposition of criminal sanctions. To date, the judges have never hesitated to make full use of the powers bestowed upon them within the scope of jurisdiction delineated by the relevant resolutions of the Security Council.

V MAIN ISSUES

War and Armed Conflict

It is since 1949 that the term 'war' has generally been supplanted by the term 'armed conflict'. On many occasions, controversies had arisen as to the applicability of *jus in bello* because one side at least contended that an armed confrontation did not have the characteristics of a war, the term which stood at the centre of the Hague Regulations. Such a power to exclude humanitarian law by denying the existence of its factual foundations cannot be reconciled with the general philosophy of humanitarian law, which is to protect human beings dragged into an armed confrontation without or against their will. Therefore, the four Conventions of 1949 all provide (Article 2(1)) that they shall apply not only to all cases of declared war, but also to any other armed conflict between two contracting parties 'even if the state of war is not recognised by them'. Thus, if still today one speaks of the law of war or of war crimes, this is strictly speaking a misnomer. Even the Hague Regulations are now deemed to govern not only war proper, but armed conflict in the broader sense. This extension of the scope of *jus in bello* is to be welcomed wholeheartedly since it benefits the victims of interstate violence.

Internal Armed Conflict

It is a relic of the past that humanitarian law focuses primarily on international armed conflict. At the turn of the last century, when the first Peace Conference convened, it would have been unthinkable to frame rules for purely internal conflicts, and it is highly doubtful whether the Martens clause was ever intended to protect persons involved in a domestic insurgency against a ruling government. A first step recognizing the needs of victims in internal disturbances was taken in 1921 when the Xth International Conference of the Red Cross in Geneva adopted a resolution relating to civil war, which established the right of all victims of civil wars or social or revolutionary disturbances to receive aid in accordance with the general principles of the Red Cross, and gave the International Committee of the Red Cross a mandate to intervene in a supporting role in relief matters.[35] But the decisive breakthrough came in 1949 when an identical clause was inserted into all of the four Conventions according to which even in armed conflicts of a non-international character certain minimum guarantees are to be respected (Article 3). These guarantees are not spelled out in great detail ('mini-code'). But it was acknowledged by the states parties that a domestic conflict, too, is a matter which does not fall exclusively within domestic jurisdiction.[36]

When the Diplomatic Conference reviewing the rules of humanitarian law in the 1970s established its work programme, the intention was to strengthen the protection afforded to persons involved in internal armed conflict. The final result, however, was only a half-hearted victory for this plan. On the one hand, the Conference drew up an instrument which expanded considerably the scope *ratione materiae* of the rules, which until then had been merely sketched out. On the other hand, fears by governments that any internal disturbances might rise to a level bringing them under the umbrella of international protection led to a marked lifting up of the threshold conditioning the applicability of the relevant rules. While common Article 3 of the four Geneva Conventions requires no more than the existence of an armed conflict, Article 1(1) of Protocol II provides that the instrument is intended to govern armed activities between the armed forces of a state party:

and dissident armed forces or other organized armed groups which, under responsible command, exercise such control over a part of its territory as to enable them to carry out sustained and concerted military operations and to implement this Protocol.

In order to dispel any possible remaining doubts, Article 1(2) complements this restrictive clause by setting forth that the Protocol shall not apply to situations of internal disturbances and tensions, such as riots as well as isolated and sporadic acts of violence.

Understandable as the anxieties assailing governmental military experts may be, the consequences of the raising of the triggering threshold may be called completely disastrous. In the world of today, a situation meeting the criteria of Article 1 will hardly ever come into being. Normally, government troops are much better equipped than insurgent units. Guerrilla troops, in particular, mostly lack any air forces, air power being exclusively in governmental hands. For that reason, more often than not guerrilla troops cannot pretend to be in control of a given area in the sense required by Article 1. As a whole, the provision is reminiscent of the situation as it prevailed during the Spanish civil war, where front lines existed which separated the two parts of

---

[35] See Junod in *ICRC Commentary supra* n. 8, at 1322.

[36] For a brief historical survey see Moir, 'The Historical Development of the Application of Humanitarian Law in Non-International Armed Conflicts to 1949', 47 *ICLQ* (1998) 337, at 353–361.

the country. Such configurations have become a rare exception in civil wars of our time at the beginning of a new century. In many instances, a region will be controlled during daylight time by the security forces of the state, while during the night the guerrillas will be the masters. Protocol II appears never to have been applied in a single armed conflict since its entry into force. This is a serious flaw of the instrument inasmuch as most of the conflicts taking place today are indeed internal conflicts.

Two routes may lead out of this dilemma. To begin with, it is tempting to argue that Protocol II constitutes nothing more than an elaboration of the principles laid down in common Article 3 of the four Conventions of 1949 so that it can be considered a reflection of the customary law in force. In part this intellectual leap may well be warranted.[37] As far as protection of the civilian population is concerned, the Rome Statute of the ICC, whose lists of crimes are supposed to codify rules applicable as customary law, has visibly drawn on Protocol II in particular by establishing rape and enforced prostitution as war crimes.[38] Ample evidence to this effect is also afforded by the judgment of the Appeals Chamber in the *Tadic* case.[39] Or else, in another bold leap forward, it could be maintained that the distinction between international and internal armed conflicts has become outdated and obsolete, given the guiding idea that humanitarian law reflects precisely the same values on which international protection of human rights is predicated, adjusting the relevant rules to the specific context of armed conflict where, in contradistinction to any other situation, it is not considered unlawful in principle to kill a human being.[40] It has been convincingly demonstrated by the *Tadic* judgment that indeed the borderline between the legal regime of internal armed conflict on the one hand, and international armed conflict on the other, has undergone constant erosion. Nonetheless, it would be premature to speak of perfect coincidence. Some core elements of classical humanitarian law have now also found *droit de cité* in the body of customary law governing internal armed conflict. Above all, no one would challenge the proposition that the civilian population shall not be made the object of attack. But the more detailed rules, as laid down in Protocol I, cannot automatically be transferred to internal conflicts. Summing up the results of its inquiry, the Appeals Chamber of the ICTY held in the *Tadic* case that the applicable rules:

[37] Article 1(1) of Additional Protocol II states that it 'develops and supplements' Article 3 common to the Geneva Conventions.

[38] Protocol II (Article 4(2)(e)) forbids 'outrages upon personal dignity, in particular humiliating and degrading treatment, rape, enforced prostitution and any form of indecent assault'; the Rome Statute lists as a war crime in armed conflicts not of an international character (Article 8(2)(e)(vi)) 'rape, sexual slavery, enforced prostitution, forced pregnancy'.

[39] 35 *ILM* (1996) 35, at 67, para. 117.

[40] See *supra* p. 242.

cover such areas as protection of civilians from hostilities, in particular from indiscriminate attacks, protection of civilian objects, in particular cultural property, protection of all those who do not (or no longer) take active part in hostilities, as well as prohibition of means of warfare proscribed in international armed conflicts and ban of certain methods of conducting hostilities.[41]

This view is also reflected in the Rome Statute of the ICC where, much beyond the scope of Articles 13 to 18 of Protocol II, a number of specific actions of warfare are declared war crimes (Article 8(2)(e)).

There is one area, in particular, where the protection provided by humanitarian law with regard to internal armed conflict remains far below the standards applicable to international armed conflict. Prisoners of war, if caught during a classical interstate conflict, cannot be made responsible for serving in the army of an enemy state. They may be brought to trial for committing breaches of humanitarian law, but taking part in organized fighting as a combatant does not constitute an offence for which the relevant rules would allow punishment. On the other hand, Protocol II does not afford any guarantees against criminal prosecution to participants in an internal uprising. Article 6 confines itself to stating that any kind of penal prosecution must comply with standards of fair trial. It does not restrict the power of states to make participation in an insurgent movement a punishable offence. Even death sentences may be pronounced on account of participation in an insurgent movement.[42] Since the written law is markedly reticent on this point, obviously in deference to a general stance taken by governments, it would be hazardous to contend that the existing lacuna has been filled in by customary law.

One specific type of armed conflict which has no cross-boundary element has been placed by Additional Protocol I of 1977 under the regime of international armed conflict, namely wars of national liberation (Article 1(4)). When the Geneva Diplomatic Conference opened in 1974, the demands of Third World countries to adopt this kind of provision first met with stiff resistance on the part of many Western countries. Eventually, however, the opponents gave up their resistance. The victory thus achieved is to be welcomed wholeheartedly as a victory for the principle of humanity. On the other hand, the actual relevance of Article 1(4) was shortlived since after 1977 the last bastions of colonialism quickly fell.[43] No one wished that the special regime for wars of national liberation be extended at a later stage to any secessionist movements.

Although one should be content with the swift progress of the rules imposing constraints upon warfare in internal armed conflict, custom has a

---

[41] See *supra* at 34, para. 127.

[42] In that regard, Additional Protocol II of 1977 appears to be in need of review, see Sandoz, 'Le demi-siècle des Conventions de Genève', 81(834) *IRRC* (1999) 241, at 247.

[43] See Aldrich, *supra* n. 14, at 45.

serious disadvantage. In contrast to written law embodied in international treaties, its scope *ratione materiae* can never be identified with the same accuracy, and therefore also it is less suitable than written law as a basis for the understanding of humanitarian law. A great part of the directive force of humanitarian law derives from the knowledge which members of armed forces have of its requirements. It is much better to work on the basis of unchallengeable texts. It might therefore be a good idea to convene an international conference on humanitarian law in 2007 to be celebrated on the centennial of the Second Hague Peace Conference, three decades after the successful conclusion of the Geneva Diplomatic Conference which elaborated the two Additional Protocols of 1977.

Distinction between Combatants and Civilians

The distinction between combatants and civilians is crucial for the entire regime of *jus in bello*. Humanitarian law seeks to confine armed activities to persons and objects serving armed activities. Likewise, combatants who have ceased to participate in armed activities—being sick or wounded or having become prisoners of war—are placed under its protection. On the other hand, humanitarian law takes care of combatants as well. They are shielded from penal sanctions for taking up and using arms. In this connection, the treatment to be accorded to *francs tireurs* or guerrilla fighters has been a highly disputed matter at all times. The Hague Regulations of 1907 sought to strike a balance between the demands of larger states, keen on being able clearly to identify any member of adversarial forces, and the interests of smaller states to be able to rely on informal armed units. Article 1 granted the special rights of combatant status not only to members of duly organized armies wearing a uniform, but also to militia and corps of volunteers under four conditions, namely to be under a responsible commander, to have a distinctive emblem fixed and recognizable at a distance, to carry arms openly and to conduct their operations in accordance with the laws and customs of war. In addition, it was recognized in Article 2 that the population of a territory not yet under foreign occupation has the right to take up arms in a spontaneous movement of *levée en masse*; if that occurred, the population was to enjoy all the rights of belligerency. Whereas Article 2 covers a situation which even in theory would constitute a rare exception, practice has shown that the requirements of Article 1 are so exacting that almost no resistance movements have ever been able to live up to them.

It was one of the demands of Third World countries at the Geneva Diplomatic Conference reviewing the body of humanitarian law in the 1970s to depart from the rigours of Article 1 of the Hague Regulations. This claim was directly related to the treatment of struggle for national liberation in the exercise of the right to self-determination. Under the traditional rules, guerrilla warfare against a colonial power would have been considered as pertaining to the realm of internal conflict. After protracted deliberations, which at the initial stage threatened the continuance of the Conference, it was eventually agreed to acknowledge armed struggle for national liberation as a form of international armed conflict (Protocol I, Article 1(4)). However, this achievement would have meant very little; the activities of freedom fighters would generally have fallen outside the ambit of the special protection gained by their inclusion in Protocol I if the traditional rules governing armed combat by non-members of regular armies had been maintained. The dispute unleashed by this additional demand was also one of the most controversial issues the Conference had to deal with. Eventually, the Conference decided to lower the standard required. According to Article 44(3) Protocol I, combatants must carry their arms openly (a) during each military engagement, and (b) during such time as they are visible to the adversary while they are engaged in a military deployment preceding the launching of an attack in which they are to participate.

It is hard to say what the second requirement actually means. Above all, the formula eventually chosen provides guerrilla forces with the opportunity to disappear in the civilian population once an operation carried out by them is terminated. This lowering of the standard is not to the liking of states which do not contemplate that they would ever be in need of resorting to this special type of combat, the war of the poor. Article 44(3) is one of the provisions which the United States has referred to as preventing it from ratifying Protocol I. Indeed, any blurring of the dividing line between combatants and non-combatants is likely to reduce or annihilate the protective effect of humanitarian law. The organized military forces of one side will then suspect the entire civilian population of their adversary as being involved in armed activities, a suspicion which does not strengthen strict compliance with the applicable rules. Experiences of the past show that under such circumstances hostage-taking may become a common practice, another violation of the applicable rules, so that eventually the law breaks down totally in a vicious circle of violence and counter-violence.[44]

Distinction between Military and Civilian Targets

It is a ground rule of humanitarian law, applicable both in international and in internal armed conflict, that attacks must be limited strictly to military objectives (Protocol I, Articles 48, 52). In practice, to distinguish between military and civilian objects raises considerable difficulties. The core of Article 52 is not difficult to identify. Armed military units in combat or during transport, barracks, airfields, or military fuel stations clearly consti-

---

[44] For a defence of the formula see Aldrich, *supra* n. 14, at 46–48.

tute military targets. However, Article 52 contains also a penumbra which reaches far out into the normal life of a society. According to the wording of paragraph 2, it is legitimate to consider as military objectives those objects:

which by their nature, location, purpose or use make an effective contribution to military action and whose total or partial destruction, capture or neutralization, in the circumstances ruling at the time, offers a definite military advantage.

In the armed conflict between NATO and Yugoslavia, the almost unlimited width of this definition became apparent day after day. Not only were bridges and railway tracks destroyed, the air raids targeted also factories, power plants, and water services so that the civilian population suffered considerable hardship.[45] Even according to the commentary edited by the International Committee of the Red Cross, military attacks may be directed against dual use objects, objects which primarily serve the civilian population, but from which the armed forces of the country concerned also derive certain benefits.[46] At one point in time, even the official Belgrade radio and TV station was attacked, the reason given being that in the concomitant war of words it was necessary to silence a voice of constant lies.[47] This was certainly not a day of glory for NATO. Only under exceptional circumstances could a media centre be a legitimate target of military attacks, for instance if it were calling upon its audience to commit war crimes or crimes against humanity.[48]

---

[45] See the Statement by the International Committee of the Red Cross of 26 April 1999, 81(834) *IRRC* (1999) 409, at 410. See harsh criticism of NATO's operation by Egorov, 'The Kosovo Crisis and the Law of Armed Conflicts', 82(837) *IRRC* (2000) 183. Concerning cybertargets see Busuttil, 'A Taste of Armageddon: The Law of Armed Conflict as Applied to Cyberwar', in *The Reality of International Law: Essays in Honour of Ian Brownlie* (Oxford, Clarendon Press, 1999), 37, at 50–51.

[46] Claude Pilloud and Jean Pictet, on Article 52, in *ICRC Commentary, supra* n. 8, at 636, marginal no. 2023. For an analysis of the Kosovo war see de Mulinen, 'Distinction between Military and Civilian Objects', in Christian Tomuschat (ed.), *Kosovo and the International Community: A Legal Assessment* (The Hague, Kluwer Law International, 2002), 103; Weckel, 'Les devoirs de l'attaquant à la lumière de la campagne aérienne en Yougoslavie', ibid. at 129.

[47] James A. Burger, a former US Army Judge Advocate, 'International Humanitarian Law and the Kosovo Crisis: Lessons Learned or to be Learned', 82(837) *IRRC* (2000) 129, at 131, writes that it was legitimate to destroy installations spreading 'Serbian propaganda'. See also questions raised by Rowe, 'Kosovo 1999: The Air Campaign', ibid. at 156.

[48] The Prosecutor of the ICTY, who had serious doubts about the lawfulness of the attack, established a special committee which came to the conclusion that a justification could be found since the TV station was a pivotal element in the Serbian military command and control system, see report of 8 June 2000, 21 *HRLJ* (2000) 267, at 269, para. 76. For critical comments see Benvenuti, 'The ICTY Prosecutor and the Review of the NATO Bombing Campaign against the Federal Republic of Yugoslavia', 12 *EJIL* (2001) 503; Bothe, 'The Protection of the Civilian Population and NATO Bombing on Yugoslavia: Comments on a Report to the Prosecutor of the ICTY', ibid. at 531–535; Ronzitti, 'Is the *non liquet* of the Final Report by the Committee Established to Review the NATO Bombing Campaign Against the Federal Republic of Yugoslavia Acceptable?', 82(840) *IRRC* (2000) 1017.

In the competition of opinions, however, military force is an extraneous element. The truth cannot be established by guns, and it is precisely for this reason that military targets are defined by their closeness to military action.[49]

Protection of the Environment, Protection of Human Habitat

It is one of the achievements of Protocol I to set forth rules designed to protect the environment during armed conflict. The rule that no means of warfare may be used which are intended or may be expected to cause widespread, long-term, and severe damage to the environment has even been set forth twice, first as a general principle governing methods and means of warfare (Article 35(3)) and second as a principle specifically protecting the civilian population (Article 55(1)). In addition, Protocol I bans attacks on installations containing dangerous forces, namely dams, dykes, and nuclear power plants, if such attacks may cause the release of dangerous forces which are likely to entail severe losses among the civilian population. In the case of Article 35, it is the environment as such which has been placed under protection. As far as Article 55(1) is concerned, harm to the natural environment is taken only as a link in a causal chain which ultimately leads to prejudicing the health or the survival of the affected population. In the war between Iraq and Kuwait, the proposition that inflicting injury upon the natural environment constitutes a breach of applicable standards of humanitarian law was applied for the first time in history. By SC Res. 687 (1991) the Security Council determined that Iraq is liable under international law for any direct loss, damage, or injury to foreign governments, 'including environmental damage and the depletion of natural resources' (para. 16). No matter how encouraging this decision of the Security Council is, the amounts involved are of such magnitude that the harm done will probably never be repaired. The consequences of nuclear war would be so disastrous that humankind would have to rejoice if it could only survive.

Threshold of Armed Conflict

As far as internal conflict is concerned, one of the major issues relates to the threshold criterion of armed conflict. Protocol II specifies explicitly that it shall not apply to 'situations of internal disturbances and tensions, such as riots, isolated and sporadic acts of violence and other acts of a similar

---

[49] By declaring the application lodged in *Bankovic* inadmissible (judgment of 12 December 2001, not yet published), the ECtHR dispensed itself from having to deal with the substantive issue (see *supra* p. 107).

nature'. Common Article 3 of the four Geneva Conventions has the same conceptual basis. Before the Geneva Diplomatic Conference, the International Committee of the Red Cross had given a definition of internal disturbances, predicated on its own experience, which served as a guideline for participants in their later deliberations. Although it may generally be warranted to adopt a liberal interpretation of the concepts relied upon by humanitarian law, extreme caution is required in defining armed conflict. If the threshold is lowered excessively, one runs the risk of favouring banditry and common crime by withdrawing the elements involved from the unrestricted reach of internal police and criminal laws. It is particularly difficult to classify isolated acts of an urban guerrilla force which kidnaps and assassinates representatives of the government in power, in response to similar strategies pursued by the government itself. In principle, humanitarian law is not designed to afford a special regime of legal protection to activities which on neither side have anything to do with organized armed struggle, but must simply be characterized as criminal acts. The International Committee of the Red Cross itself has found tremendous difficulties in correctly appraising such situations where armed operations do take place, but are mainly directed, on political grounds, against non-combatants. Terrorism must be distinguished from armed conflict in the understanding of humanitarian law.

Applicability of Common Article 3

Of course, the applicability of common Article 3 is not dependent upon specific recognition by the government concerned that the disturbances in its territory have reached the triggering level of intensity. The existence of armed conflict constitutes an objective standard, and the International Committee of the Red Cross has an important function to discharge in persuading the competent authorities that as from a given moment they are bound by the relevant rules of international law. Understandably, governments are reluctant to admit that they have lost absolute control in their territory, which politically amounts to a loss of face. Furthermore, to be under an obligation to apply the rules governing internal armed struggle seriously reduces their freedom of action. In fact, they may particularly appreciate situations just below the level of armed conflict where, under the rules of the human rights treaties they have subscribed to, they are allowed to suspend most of the guarantees owed to their citizens, without humanitarian law becoming automatically applicable. The relevant clauses of the human rights treaties refer to 'public emergency which threatens [threatening] the life of the nation'[50] or to 'time of war, public danger, or other emergency that threatens the independence or security of a state party'.[51] An 'emergency' is a situation which need not bear

[50] Article 4 CCPR; Article 15 ECHR.   [51] Article 27 ACHR.

the features of an armed conflict. Thus, a gap in the protection of citizens may occur: human rights guarantees may be suspended, but the specific guarantees of humanitarian law do not yet apply.

Declaration on Minimum Humanitarian Standards

With a view to closing this gap, a number of scholars have prepared, as a private initiative, the text of a 'Declaration on Minimum Humanitarian Standards'[52] which is intended to apply to all situations of internal violence, disturbances, tensions, and public emergency.[53] Although such a private paper does not constitute a source of law in a formal sense, it reflects better than the lists of non-derogable rights in the existing human rights treaties the essence of legal norms that should be recognized as having a peremptory character.[54]

The 'Declaration on Minimum Humanitarian Standards' deals at the same time with a problem which increasingly gives rise to concern. States, represented by governments, are the normal addressees of rules of international law, and this basic proposition applies also to humanitarian law. However, with regard to internal armed conflict there can be no relationship between two or more states in the classical sense of international law. Governments find themselves opposed to armed groups which more often than not lack a clearly recognizable identity. On the other hand, because of the underlying logic of reciprocity, humanitarian law would collapse if it imposed its duties only on one of the parties to an internal conflict. Hence, insurgent forces must be brought into the system so that a network of mutual rights and duties may come into being. According to the prevailing doctrine, ratification by a state of the four Geneva Conventions entails for any insurgent movement the obligation to respect common Article 3, and likewise it is assumed that ratification of Protocol II produces a similar binding effect. This conclusion can be justified in theory by the power of any government to exercise jurisdiction for the entire national territory. It remains, though, that insurgent movements may totally ignore the contention that they are bound by legal rules established without any actual participation on their part.

Lacunae in the Legal Regime of Internal Armed Conflict

Notwithstanding these efforts of legal institution-building, the scope *ratione personae* of the rules applying to internal armed conflict is still marred by

---

[52] 85 *AJIL* (1991) 377.

[53] For a comment see Rosas and Meron, 'A Declaration of Minimum Humanitarian Standards', 85 *AJIL* (1991) 375, and Petrasek, 'Moving Forward on the Development of Minimum Humanitarian Standards', 92 *AJIL* (1998) 557.

[54] For an earlier suggestion to establish a set of rules applicable to internal disturbances below the level of armed conflict see Gasser, 'A Measure of Humanity in Internal Disturbances and Tensions: Proposal for a Code of Conduct', 28(262) *IRRC* (1988) 38.

serious deficits. During such a situation, armed activities taking place between governmental troops and insurgent movements do come within the ambit of the legal regime as described. As far as armed confrontation between different insurgent movements is concerned, no explicit rules have been framed, but it is assumed that common Article 3 applies.[55] Secondly, humanitarian law is designed to protect military opponents, but it does not apply to the treatment of a party's own population or its own combatants. Atrocities committed by military units in their own territory may be crimes against humanity, but they do not infringe rules of humanitarian law. Yet, as experience amply demonstrates, human life is in need of protection also against abusive acts by 'friends'. Lastly, if the degree of intensity of an armed conflict has not been reached, the question arises what standards must be observed by an insurgent movement. Technically, during that stage humanitarian law does not apply. The 'Declaration of Humanitarian Standards' provides (Article 2) that its precepts:

shall be respected by, and applied to, all persons, groups and authorities, irrespective of their legal status and without any adverse discrimination.

It thus purports to subject everyone involved in internal disturbances or tensions to the same rigorous requirements of conduct.

The Security Council and the General Assembly have embarked on a different course. When dealing with countries engulfed in civil strife, they have in recent times consistently called upon governmental forces and insurgent forces alike to respect the human rights of the population concerned. For orthodox thinking, this practice is almost shocking. For a long time, it seemed to be an unassailable axiom that it is incumbent upon governments only to respect and ensure human rights, so that it was inconceivable that groups without any official position could also violate human rights. Here again, the argument of reciprocity is of great weight. Not to subject insurgent movements to any obligation owed to the international community before an armed conflict may be found to exist would leave them exclusively under the authority of domestic law, favouring them, but also discriminating against them at the same time. It was one of the great challenges of the Guatemalan Historical Clarification Commission to determine the legal yardstick by which conduct of the different guerrilla groups could be measured even in times when one could hardly speak of an armed conflict. The Commission decided, somewhat ambiguously, that the standards common to human rights and international humanitarian law were also binding upon an insurgent movement at any time.[56]

---

[55] Junod, in *ICRC Commentary, supra* n. 8, at 1351, marginal no. 4461.

[56] Comisión para el Esclarecimiento Histórico (ed.), *Guatemala, Memoria del Silencio*, (Guatemala, UNOPS, 1999), vol. 2, at 308–313, paras. 1679–1700.

In conclusion, however, it is not a lack of normative standards which constitutes today the crucial problem of international humanitarian law. Although with the coming into force of the two Additional Protocols of 1977 the body of legal rules was brought *à jour*, the record of compliance is dismal. In no other sector of international law is lack of respect for the law as common as here. In particular, internal armed conflict is rarely fought according to the established rules. Consequently, the great challenge is not to give another twist of perfection to the law in force, but to devise ways and means suited to ensure that the level of compliance is raised.[57]

VI ENSURING OBSERVANCE OF, AND RESPECT FOR, HUMANITARIAN LAW

A Culture of Compliance

On the occasion of the ceremonies celebrating the 100th anniversary of the first Hague Peace Conference, Christopher Greenwood underlined the need for creating a 'culture of compliance'.[58] For this to happen, preparations have to begin before actual hostilities break out. It was one of the key insights of military lawyers, gained in the course of many decades, that in the first place the existence of the applicable rules and their contents must be widely known. For this reason, the four Geneva Conventions of 1949 all contain identical clauses to the effect that the contracting parties pledge themselves to disseminate the text of the conventions as extensively as possible and to include the study thereof in their programmes of military and possibly also of civil instruction. In this way, at least the official armed forces of the state can be reached. It is far more difficult, if not completely impossible, to spread the knowledge of humanitarian law to the entire population in good time. There is no other alternative than to instruct rebel groups about humanitarian law after they have taken up arms. Of course, the best institution to carry out this task in a neutral fashion and objectively is the International Committee of the Red Cross.

Monitoring

During an armed conflict, Protocol I provides for a sophisticated system of monitoring compliance with all the applicable rules. According to Article 5,

---

[57] For an inventory of the gaps in the legal position see Sandoz, 'Le demi-siècle des Conventions de Genève', 81(834) *IRRC* (1999) 241.

[58] 'International Humanitarian Law (Laws of War). Revised Report for the Centennial Commemoration of the First Hague Peace Conference 1899', in F. Kalshoven (ed.), *The Centennial of the First International Peace Conference 1899* (The Hague, Kluwer, 2000), 161, at 241.

each party to an armed conflict is obligated to designate without delay a Protecting Power, whose task it is to safeguard its interests vis-à-vis its adversaries. It appears, however, that this system with its similar precedents has never operated as originally envisioned.[59] Instead, the International Committee of the Red Cross has assumed the functions of a Protecting Power. Due to its large experience spanning the entire world, the ICRC can indeed achieve a great deal for the benefit of everyone and everything under the protection of humanitarian law. It is its constant practice to keep in close touch with all the nations engaged in armed conflict, but almost never to speak publicly about the findings it has made during its missions. Thus, the ICRC has been able to gain the confidence of governments. On this basis, it has regularly found access to the detention centres where prisoners of war were held. For the ICRC, therefore, confidential methods of monitoring occupy pride of place among all the mechanisms which are available for the enforcement of humanitarian law standards.

It was felt during the Diplomatic Conference that a special mechanism should be established for the purpose of fact-finding in cases where a state party to Protocol I charges another state party with not abiding by its obligations. This mechanism, an International Fact-Finding Commission, was indeed included in Article 90. Although fact-finding would seem to constitute a fairly innocuous activity, a system of unilateral declarations of acceptance conditions the applicability of the system. In other words, states may accept international inquiry, but they are not bound to do so. In 1991 the Commission came into existence after the deposit of the 20th instrument of acceptance. But it has not yet attracted much sympathy. To date, it has never been called on to discharge its functions.[60] In appraising its usefulness, it should not be overlooked that it was established exclusively with a view to clarifying occurrences in international armed conflict. There is no analogous institution for internal armed conflict, where it would be required infinitely more urgently. There is no real prospect, however, that the mechanism might be extended to cover internal armed conflict as well. States would regard this as too intrusive an inroad on their sovereignty. It was difficult enough to obtain the necessary support for the inclusion of the Commission in Protocol I. Adoption of Article 90 took place by majority vote.[61] In spite of lying dormant up to the present time, the usefulness of the Commission should not

[59] See Aldrich, *supra* n. 14, at 56.

[60] Condorelli, 'La Commission internationale humanitaire d'établissement des faits: un outil obsolète ou un moyen utile de mise en oeuvre du droit international humanitaire?', 83(842) *IRRC* (2001) 393, at 394.

[61] See Jean de Preux in *ICRC Commentary, supra* n. 8, at 1040, marginal no. 3602. See also Frits Kalshoven, 'The International Humanitarian Fact-Finding Commission: its Birth and Early Years', in *Reflections on International Law from the Low Countries in Honour of Paul de Waart* (The Hague, Martinus Nijhoff, 1998), 201.

be underrated since it establishes for the first time a permanent non-political and impartial international commission of inquiry to which the parties to a conflict can turn at any time.

As far as internal armed conflict is concerned, it has not been possible to establish a system of monitoring suited to induce the parties concerned to abide by the rules binding upon them. It is not so much (or at any rate not only) the reluctance of governments to recognize the existence of an armed confrontation on their soil which has impeded the creation of such a mechanism. The greatest difficulty stems from the simple fact that in general the identity of insurgent movements is hard to define. More often than not, there exists no spokesperson who could commit his/her movement for good. The technique used in Article 96(3) of Additional Protocol I, according to which a national liberation movement may undertake to apply the Geneva instruments by means of a unilateral declaration, can hardly be generalized to cover all situations of internal armed conflict.

Countermeasures

Under the general regime of state responsibility, any breach of its international obligations by a state gives rise to a right for the state whose corresponding rights have been infringed to take countermeasures. Countermeasures are designed to induce the wrongdoer to desist from its unlawful conduct and to observe the law in future. As far as humanitarian law is concerned, countermeasures have an utterly ambiguous character. On the one hand, the effectiveness of humanitarian law largely depends on reciprocity. If an evil government decides not only to wage aggression, but also to disregard any standards of *jus in bello*, there are very few deterrents available if it is not permissible to retaliate by committing the same kind of breach. According to the logic of assumed reciprocity, it was possible, during the Second World War, to prevent attacks with gas. The Protocol of 1925 received its effective strength from the fear that any use of gas by one side would immediately trigger an analogous response. On the other hand, countermeasures might undermine the very essence of humanitarian law. If during an armed conflict one party begins killing prisoners of war instead of treating them as required by the Third Geneva Convention, the other side will be quite naturally tempted to commence a similar practice in order to bring to an end the abuses to the detriment of its own people. This, however, could lead to an abysmal spiral of death and destruction, rendered all the more painful since objective findings on the facts can hardly ever be made during an armed conflict.[62]

---

[62] See Aldrich, *supra* n. 14, at 57–58. For the relevant British reservation to Protocol I see ibid. at 58. Laucci, *supra* n. 27, at 688–690, discusses the French reservations in this regard.

In balancing these two strands of arguments, states have increasingly rallied to the position that the negative effects of countermeasures by far outweigh their usefulness as a remedy of enforcement. Since the conclusion of the four Geneva Conventions of 1949, international law has evolved a system affording immunity from retaliation to specific groups or objects in order, above all, to forestall any abuses. Prisoners of war, as well as persons no longer taking part in active combat—the sick, wounded, and shipwrecked—have thus been provided with a protective shield which leaves few, if any, gaps.[63] The development of the law has reached its peak with Article 51(6) Protocol I which forbids any attacks against the civilian population by way of reprisals.[64] Pursuant to a leading authority on the issue, such reprisals were considered lawful before the entry into force of Protocol I.[65] With regard to the use of nuclear weapons, Article 51(6) is of cardinal importance. As already noted, the ICJ held in its advisory opinion of 1996 that the use of this type of weapons would be generally incompatible with the rules of humanitarian law.[66] Therefore, at the most, resorting to nuclear warfare could be justified as a countermeasure. To the extent, however, that because of their indiscriminate effects nuclear devices necessarily affect the civilian population or neutral countries, the ban to which they are subjected must be deemed to be of rigorous strictness, not leaving any loopholes.[67]

State Responsibility

Lastly, state responsibility could be thought of as a remedy to enforce respect for the rules of humanitarian law. From the very outset, it is clear that state responsibility can be available only in interstate relations, i.e. if an international armed conflict occurs. But state responsibility comes by definition too late. Normally, in peace negotiations violations of the rules of humanitarian law are not considered as an item deserving specific attention. Under the aegis of the United Nations, the picture has recently changed. As determined by the Governing Council of the United Nations Compensation Commission, Iraq's duty to compensate the victims of its invasion of Kuwait comprises also the harm caused by its breaches of the applicable standards of

[63] Balancing the pros and cons of such far-reaching prohibitions is Meron, *supra* n. 2, at 249–251.

[64] For an extensive discussion of the pros and cons of prohibitions of reprisals see Kalshoven, 'Belligerent Reprisals Revisited', 21 *Netherlands Yearbook of International Law* (1990) 80.

[65] Frits Kalshoven, *Belligerent Reprisals* (Leiden, Sijthoff, 1971), at 353–361.

[66] *Supra* n. 1 at 266, conclusion E.

[67] For a discussion of this issue see Cassese, 'On the Current Trends towards Criminal Prosecution and Punishment of Breaches of International Humanitarian Law', 9 *EJIL* (1998) 2; Oeter, 'Methods and Means of Combat', in Fleck, *supra* n. 7, 105, at 204–207.

humanitarian law. [68] It remains to be seen whether this new development will lead to a general reorientation in the practice of reparation. The more deterrents international law can mobilize against war, the better it is.[69]

[68] 109 *ILR* 612.
[69] As far as criminal prosecution is concerned, see Chapter 12 below.

12

Criminal Prosecution of Human Rights Violations

I GENERAL CONSIDERATIONS

It has already been pointed out that to comply with human rights obligations is not confined to abstaining from interference with such rights. While the ECHR only provides that the states parties shall 'secure' the rights and freedoms which it sets forth (Article 1), the CCPR makes clear that the duty of states consists of two elements, an undertaking to 'respect' and an undertaking to 'ensure' (Article 2(1)).[1] This careful choice of words underlines that states cannot remain passive with regard to threats endangering the effective enjoyment of human rights by their holders, but that they are additionally obligated, if need be, to take active steps for the protection of the rights concerned. The ACHR, too, uses the double formula 'to respect...and to ensure' (Article 1), whereas the African Charter (Article 1) lacks a similar degree of precision ('The Member States...shall recognize the rights, duties and freedoms'). Irrespective of slight variations in drafting, however, there is broad agreement not only in legal doctrine as to the scope of the obligations states assume in ratifying a human rights treaty. Their duties go much beyond simple non-interference. Instead, they have to play an active role in seeing to it that everyone may effectively benefit from the legal propositions describing specific advantages that should accrue to him/her under the guarantee of human rights.

Some of the provisions of the relevant human rights treaties repeat once again the need for states parties to take measures of protection. This has happened in particular with regard to the right to life, the cardinal right, which is the precondition for the enjoyment of all other rights. Thus, not only the CCPR, but also the ECHR and the ACHR state that the right

---

[1] Highlighted by the HRCee as early as 1981, see General Comment No. 3, para. 1, reprinted in *Compilation of General Comments and General Recommendations by Human Rights Treaty Bodies*, UN doc. HRI/GEN/1/Rev.5, 26 April 2001, 112.

to life 'shall be protected by law'.[2] Only the African Charter remains one step behind by determining that every human being shall be entitled 'to respect for his life'. In its case law, the AfHPRCion has made good this intellectual gap by holding that indeed the general pattern characterizing the substance of human rights obligations applies here as well. In *Commission Nationale des Droits de l'Homme et des Libertés v Chad* it stated that a violation can be attributable to a state even if its agents are not the immediate cause of that violation but failed to take the measures necessary for effectively protecting a guaranteed right against threats coming from third parties.[3]

The duty of protection applies to the core rights to be enjoyed by every human being. Somewhere, however, a line has to be drawn. States are not almighty machines capable of taking care of every detail of an individual's life and existence. Overemphasizing the duty of protection could become tantamount to ushering in an Orwellian type of Leviathan who, in order fully to discharge its mandate, would as a first step establish a comprehensive system of intelligence in order to monitor the activities of its citizens in all fields of life. Some of the measures currently taken by states in their 'war on terrorism' illustrate that danger. Although a wide margin of discretion must be left to individual states, the principle of proportionality, a defining element of the entire branch of human rights law, must not be discarded. Otherwise, the most abominable encroachments on individual freedom could be legitimized. Generally, the competent human rights bodies have found reasonable solutions for establishing an equilibrium between the principle of individual freedom, on the one hand, and the necessity to ensure that freedom by restricting other freedoms. Neither the HRCee[4] nor the ECtHR or the ACtHR[5] are easily impressed by the argument that terrorism could only be fought effectively by measures derogating from the general standards applicable under the rule of law.

It stands to reason that 'protection by law' cannot be taken to mean that states have no more to do than to enact laws. Protection must be effective protection. Laws that would not be implemented would not serve their purpose. In other words, states must ensure that the laws in force are executed

---

[2] Article 6(1) CCPR; Article 2(1) ECHR; Article 4(1) ACHR.

[3] Referred to by Heyns, 'Civil and Political Rights in the African Charter', in Malcolm Evans and Rachel Murray (ed.), *The African Charter on Human and Peoples' Rights* (Cambridge, Cambridge University Press, 2002), 137, at 138–139.

[4] See the final views handed down in two cases against Peru where convictions had been pronounced by 'faceless judges': *Polay Campos*, 6 November 1997, [1998] *Report of the HRCee*, vol. II, UN doc. A/53/40, 36, at 43, para. 8.8; *Arredondo*, 27 July 2000, [2000] *Report of the HRCee*, vol. II, UN doc. A/55/40, 51, at 60, para. 10.5.

[5] The IACtHR, too, has held trial by 'faceless judges' to be in violation of fundamental procedural guarantees, see judgment of 30 May 1999, *Castillo Petruzzi v Peru*, 21 *HRLJ* (2000) 143, at 162, para. 133.

according to their letter and spirit.[6] For that purpose, administrative agencies and judicial institutions must be established so that attacks on protected core rights are actually sanctioned by criminal prosecution. A country where even attacks on the right to life would elicit no official response from public authorities would have to be classified as a failed state, a crippled member of the international community.

The threat of criminal proceedings may act as a potent deterrent.[7] Within the context of a human rights policy, its preventive function is more important than its repressive counterpart, which are the two sides of the same coin. Lastly, if all other remedies fail, states must indeed resort to their most effective weapon, which is criminal law. Thus, criminal law constitutes a necessary ingredient of any coherent human rights policy.

On the other hand, it should not be overlooked that criminal prosecution has time and again been abused as a weapon against political opponents of governments. Seen from a historical viewpoint, it can even be said that the doctrine of human rights emerged from the struggle first of the nobility during the feudal epoch, later of peoples against their princes in monarchical times against the arbitrary use of state power. In a central passage of its rich contents, the Magna Charta of 1215 enunciates guarantees against unlawful arrest and detention,[8] and later codifications are also mainly concerned with procedural safeguards against such interference with personal freedom. In democratic states placed under the rule of law, criminal prosecution is viewed mainly as an instrument designed to shield the public at large from any attacks on their rights and goods. But measures taken under that heading can easily be diverted from their legitimate purpose. Furthermore, notwithstanding the best of intentions, it may prove extremely arduous to abide fully by all the standards prescribed for the conduct of proceedings. It is in particular the right to a speedy trial, a key element of all human rights instruments, which causes great difficulties even in well-developed systems. It is not a rare occurrence, therefore, that suspects have to spend excessively long periods of pre-trial detention precisely because of the abundant availability of legal remedies. This problem has arisen even in the practice of the ICTY. Thus, criminal prosecution is Janus-faced. Although in principle defused as a political weapon in a world dominated by human rights, it can at any moment become again, deliberately or inadvertently, an instrument of oppression. It must therefore be held under strict scrutiny.

---

[6] See *supra* p. 46.

[7] For an optimistic view see Akhavan, 'Can International Criminal Justice Prevent Future Atrocities?', 95 *AJIL* (2001) 7.

[8] Section 39: 'No free man shall be seized or imprisoned, or stripped of his rights or possessions, or outlawed or exiled, or deprived of his standing in any other way, nor will we proceed with force against him, or send others to do so, except by the lawful judgement of his equals or by the law of the land.'

II NATIONAL PROSECUTION

Since the obligations deriving from human rights propositions are mainly addressed to states, states bear the main burden of instituting criminal proceedings against alleged offenders. No such comprehensive responsibility rests on international organizations. Apart from the fact that until a few years ago, international organizations had been denied any jurisdiction for criminal proceedings, their obligation to respect human rights is only a sectoral one. Within their fields of competence they have to comply with the human rights standards binding upon them, but this duty concerns their own conduct. They have not been vested with personal jurisdiction over the citizens in their member countries, or have received only partial delegations of power to that effect (which is the case of the European Communities). Consequently, they would be unable to secure human rights by initiating criminal proceedings against persons who, in other respects, may be under their jurisdiction. As far as criminal jurisdiction is concerned, states are generally fairly reluctant to divest themselves of the powers which they hold as sovereign states.

Territorial Jurisdiction

In the first place, states are responsible for occurrences within their territories. According to traditional thinking, they had to ensure that within their borders nothing happened which might have injurious consequences for other states. Thus, foreign nationals had to be treated in accordance with the rules of aliens' law, harmful transboundary effects of human activities had to be prevented or curbed, and foreign diplomats in particular were entitled to claim special immunities and privileges. In case of grave violation of these commitments, criminal sanctions had to be taken against the responsible perpetrators.[9] Since, however, human rights did not yet exist before 1945 as a distinct legal discipline, it was entirely left to states how to respond to criminal attacks which had no transnational aspects. Inasmuch as only citizens of the same state were involved, international law had no say. To be sure, no state is viable without an effective system of criminal prosecution. Thus, in their own interest, and remaining within the logic which underlies the creation of governmental structures for the benefit of all citizens, governments took care to respond to criminal activities by tracking down their

---

[9] See examples from the earlier practice given by Clyde Eagleton, *The Responsibility of States in International Law* (New York, New York University Press, 1928), at 185–187; an account of the contemporary practice by Arangio-Ruiz, 'Second Report on State Responsibility', UN doc. A/CN.4/425 and Add. 1, *Yearbook of the ILC (1989)*, vol. II, part 1, 39–40. See also the *Rainbow Warrior* case, where the transfer of the two responsible French officers to a French military facility on an isolated island outside of Europe, as determined by the UN Secretary-General in his award of 6 July 1986, 20 *RIAA* 224, boiled down to a quasi-punishment.

authors and imposing repressive sanctions. But it was their sovereign decision how to handle such matters.

With the emergence of human rights, the picture has changed. The duty of protection implies that even in circumstances where all the actors involved have the same nationality states must take all the measures necessary for the purpose of effective protection, including the imposition of adequate penalties. The IACtHR has gone very far by stating that in case of human rights violations a state must:

> prevent, investigate and punish any violation of the rights recognized by the Convention [and] . . . use the means at its disposal to carry out a serious investigation of violations committed within its jurisdiction, to identify those responsible, to impose the appropriate punishment and to ensure the victim adequate compensation.[10]

This statement cannot apply to any infringement of human rights. Fortunately, most violations are of much lesser gravity than what had happened in the *Velásquez Rodríguez* case (disappearance and killing at the hands of the Honduran security forces). Therefore, normally it will not be necessary to initiate criminal proceedings against the responsible governmental agents. Disciplinary measures may be fully sufficient, and on many occasions even that may not be the appropriate response if, for instance, until a decision of the competent judicial body legitimate doubts were entertained as to the scope and meaning of the relevant human rights guarantee.

In its recent case law, the ECtHR has also stated its view that in appropriate cases states are under an obligation to carry out an investigation which should be capable of leading to the identification and punishment of those responsible for the violation in issue.[11] As far as can be seen, this legal inference has never been set out as a general proposition being applicable to any case of a violation, but merely added as a sentence reflecting the conclusions to be drawn in the case at hand. Furthermore, to date this inference has never appeared in the operative part of a judgment, the ECtHR interpreting its mandate under Article 41 ECHR in a narrow fashion as an obstacle to granting to individuals anything more than financial compensation if a violation has been found to exist. It would be interesting to make a careful assessment of all the cases hitherto decided in this extensive fashion in order to identify the instances where, because of the gravity of the violation, the

---

[10] Case of *Velásquez Rodríguez*, Judgment of 29 July 1988, 28 *ILM* (1989) 294, at 324, para. 166, 325, para. 174.

[11] First articulated in the *McCann* case, 27 September 1995, A 324, 47–49, paras 157–161; from the more recent jurisprudence see *Assenov v Bulgaria*, 28 October 1998, *Reports* (1998–VIII), 3264, at 3290, para. 102; *Ogur v Turkey*, 20 May 1999, *Reports* (1999–III), 519, at 551, para. 88; *Selmouni v France*, 28 March 1999, *Reports* (1999–V), 149, at 175–177, paras 76–79; *Mahmut Kaya v Turkey*, 28 March 2000, para. 102; for an overall assessment see Mowbray, 'Duties of Investigation under the ECHR', 51 *ICLQ* (2002) 437.

Strasbourg judges have seen criminal prosecution as a necessary complement of the consequences to be shouldered by the respondent state.

How difficult it may be to draw the exact borderline is illustrated in an exemplary fashion by two decisions of the German Constitutional Court on the issue of abortion. In the first judgment, the Court, proceeding from the premise that even growing human life constitutes human life as protected by Article 2(2) of the Basic Law (the German Constitution), held that the life of the unborn must be protected by all reasonably available means, including criminal law.[12] In its second judgment, it gave up that strict position. Having realized that the existing criminal provisions against abortion had proved largely ineffective, it stated that in these circumstances other means, in particular advisory services, could be deemed to provide a valid alternative to penal sanctions.[13] In sum, the outcome of the appraisal hinged on the degree of effectiveness which a provisional forecast could attribute to the different means which, in the circumstances, could be considered serious alternatives.

Reference may also be made to the case law of the HRCee under the Optional Protocol to the CCPR. Originally, when it delivered its first views in accordance with the OP-CCPR, it abstained from pronouncing on the issue of possible criminal prosecution of perpetrators of grave human rights violations. The first case where it addressed this issue was the case of the two brothers *Dermit Barbato*. In the views it handed down on 21 October 1982, it stated, regarding one of the brothers who had died while being imprisoned, that Uruguay was:

under an obligation to take effective steps . . . to establish the facts of Hugo Dermit's death, to bring to justice any persons found to be responsible for his death and to pay appropriate compensation to his family.[14]

Similar pronouncements were made in later cases. Thus, for instance, in the case of *Muteba v Zaire*, where torture had been committed, the HRCee stated that Zaire was obligated:

to conduct an inquiry into the circumstances of his torture, to punish those found guilty of torture and to take steps to ensure that similar violations do not occur in the future.[15]

Likewise, in a case concerning Surinam, where the entire leadership of the political opposition had been assassinated in a sweeping raid against dissident voices, the Committee urged the respondent state:

---

[12] Judgment of 25 February 1975, *Entscheidungen des Bundesverfassungsgerichts* (*BVerfGE*) 39, 1, at 51–66.

[13] Judgment of 28 May 1993, *BVerfGE* 88, 203, at 257–263.

[14] Views of 21 October 1982, *Selected Decisions*, vol. 2, 112, at 116, para. 11.

[15] Views of 24 July 1984, ibid. 158, at 160, para. 13

to bring to justice any persons found to be responsible for the death of the victims.[16]

This jurisprudence now seems to be firmly settled. In the more recent cases of *Nydia Bautista de Arellana* and *Arhuacos v Colombia*, the HRCee clarified its position as to the duties of states where grave violations have been perpetrated:

the Committee has repeatedly held that the Covenant does not provide that private individuals have a right to demand that the State criminally prosecute another person. The Committee nevertheless considers that the State party has a duty to thoroughly investigate alleged violations of human rights, particularly enforced disappearances and violations of the right to life, and to criminally prosecute, try and punish those deemed responsible for such violations.[17]

Similar statements can be found in the concluding observations by which the HRCee terminates the examination of a state report. Thus, for instance, in October 2001 it addressed to Ukraine the recommendation:

to ensure that all allegations of torture are effectively investigated by an independent authority, that the persons responsible are prosecuted, and that the victims are given adequate compensation.[18]

In sum, according to the HRCee criminal prosecution as a remedy suited to redress legitimate grievances depends on the gravity of the violation in issue. In its practice, it suggests initiating penal proceedings against the responsible persons only if serious crimes against the life, the physical integrity, or the dignity of human beings have been committed. It would appear that with these guiding criteria the HRCee has found a well-balanced solution which should be acknowledged as a general principle determining the consequences of breaches of human rights violations in the field of criminal law.

Extraterritorial Jurisdiction

The duties of states are much more limited where actions alleged to amount to criminal offences have occurred outside their boundaries. Even in such instances, national authorities are not powerless. According to the active personality principle, a state holds jurisdiction over its nationals wherever they may be. But it stands to reason that, having to respect the territorial

[16] Views of 4 April 1985, ibid. 172, at 176, para. 16.
[17] Views of 29 July 1997, [1997] *Report of the HRCee*, vol. II, UN doc. A/52/40, 173, at 182, para. 8.8. From the more recent case law see *Jiménez Vaca v Colombia*, 25 March/15 April 2002, UN doc. CCPR/C/74/D/859/1999, para. 9.
[18] [2002] *Report of the HRCee*, vol. I, UN doc. A/57/40, 34, para. 15. Similar statements can be found in the concluding observations regarding Azerbaijan, ibid. at 49, paras 9, 10; Georgia, ibid. at 54, para. 8, 55, para. 15.

sovereignty of their peers, states are prevented from arresting and putting on trial a person residing or sojourning in a foreign country. Nonetheless they should be able to institute proceedings where one of their nationals has committed a grave crime abroad and is subsequently extradited to them or is otherwise found in their territory. The CAT can be deemed to reflect the complex legal position in an exemplary fashion. Tailored to increase the obligations of states in any instances where persons are charged with committing torture, the Convention had to take into account the limits of general international law. Thus, while it establishes a duty of every state party 'to take such measures as may be necessary to establish its jurisdiction' over torture when the alleged offence is committed in its territory or by one of its nationals (Article 5(1)), a duty to arrest arises only with regard to persons in its own territory (Article 6(1)).

A new dimension is added to the legal edifice providing for effective repression of serious crimes against human rights by universal jurisdiction. Universal jurisdiction means the authority of a state to prosecute and punish offenders, irrespective of the place of commission of the crime and regardless of the link of nationality or any other factual relationship tying the suspect to the prosecuting state. No lengthy arguments are needed to explain the raison d'être of universal jurisdiction. In the first place, it flows from the empirical knowledge that not all states live up to their duty to combat serious crime as they are required to do. In many instances, when large-scale crimes are committed, this happens with the connivance of the government or is directly attributable to the government. In this sense, the thousands of crimes committed during the wars in the former Yugoslavia were mostly part of an official strategy to expel and/or exterminate persons of a different ethnic identity. Secondly, universal jurisdiction is intended to enable third states eager to assist in the repression of grave crimes to conduct such trials before their tribunals, even if the crimes were perpetrated abroad in foreign countries. In essence, therefore, universal jurisdiction is a legal concept suited to strengthen the protection of human rights once it has become a matter of general knowledge that not even authors of state-sponsored crimes have a chance to escape to third countries in order to gain impunity. Obviously, this presupposes that there exists a tight network of mutual obligations which leaves no major loopholes open.

One of the best-known examples of universal jurisdiction is provided by the CAT. The *Pinochet* case has highlighted the vast potential of this principle. Former Chilean President Augusto Pinochet, who had come to the United Kingdom for a medical visit, was arrested and faced extradition to Spain until he was sent back to Chile on humanitarian grounds after a forced stay of many months in his host country. As the commander-in-chief of the Chilean Armed Forces during the time of his dictatorship, he was charged with mercilessly hunting down all political opponents of his rule and subjecting many of them to brutal forms of physical mistreatment (= torture). Indeed, the CAT sets forth a duty for states to establish their jurisdiction over the crime of torture without any regard for the place of the commission of the crime if the alleged offender is found in their territory and they do not extradite him (Article 5(2)). This acknowledgement of the universal principle is typical of the numerous treaties based on the legal proposition 'to try or to extradite' (*'aut dedere, aut prosequi'*), which have been concluded above all for the purpose of combating terrorism. All of these treaties may be classified as treaties for the protection of human rights since terrorist acts are essentially directed against the life and limb of innocent human beings outside a situation of armed conflict. We need refer, in this connection, only to a few of these treaties, in particular the Convention on the Prevention and Punishment of Crimes against Internationally Protected Persons, including Diplomatic Agents,[19] the International Convention against the Taking of Hostages,[20] and the International Convention for the Suppression of Terrorist Bombings.[21] All of these conventions seek to establish such a tight network of obligations that not a single one of the acts summarily indicated in their titles and more precisely circumscribed in their operative provisions goes unpunished. It is true that their Member State status is impressive.[22] It is difficult to say, though, whether in practice they have yielded all the results expected of them. In many cases, the agreement which states have reached in principle to ban by all means certain forms of violent attacks is overshadowed by political sympathy for the motives of the perpetrator(s). In such circumstances, it cannot be expected that the legal mechanisms operate smoothly.

It is one of the big questions which to date remain unresolved whether universal jurisdiction exists for all the offences which the international community has taken to calling 'international crimes'. It is well known that the first list of such crimes, which was contained in the Charter of the International Military Tribunal at Nürnberg, comprised three classes, namely crimes against peace, war crimes, and crimes against humanity, the latter group being linked to war crimes, not being recognized as a class on a level of parity with the other two. Currently, the most authoritative list can be found in the Rome Statute of the ICC, which enunciates four groups of crimes, namely genocide, crimes against humanity, war crimes, and the crime of aggression. There exists broad international agreement to the effect that indeed this is a complete inventory of the most atrocious acts that adversely affect human rights.

---

[19] Adopted by GA Res. 3166 (XXVIII), 14 December 1973.
[20] Adopted by GA Res. 34/146, 17 December 1979.
[21] Adopted by GA Res. 52/164, 15 December 1997.
[22] In October 2002 there were 122, 112, and 76 states respectively.

Curiously enough, the international community has refrained from clearly setting forth the universal principle for all of these crimes. Even the ICC has not been vested with automatic jurisdiction for their prosecution. According to Articles 12 and 13 Rome Statute, certain conditions must be met for the jurisdictional clauses to take full effect. The fact alone that the state of custody of a suspect is a party to the Statute does not entitle the Court to commence proceedings. Rather, its jurisdiction depends on either the state of commission of the crime or the state of nationality of the suspect having accepted the Statute. This extreme caution of the drafters puts the statement in the preamble to the Statute, according to which 'it is the duty of every State to exercise its criminal jurisdiction over those responsible for international crimes', seriously in doubt.[23] Such doubts are strengthened by a close look at the different offences.[24]

The Genocide Convention does not establish universal jurisdiction for the prosecution of the crime of genocide, despite the fact that genocide is the most horrendous form of attack on human values.[25] In a carefully drafted clause (Article VI), it provides that genocide shall be tried by a competent tribunal of the state in the territory of which the act was committed, or by an international penal tribunal. This formula was originally meant to exclude universal jurisdiction.[26] But in legal doctrine it was soon pointed out that Article VI did not do away with the other grounds of jurisdiction recognized by general international law, in particular the personality principle, the effects principle, and the protective principle. Later, the *Eichmann* judgment of the Supreme Court of Israel went even one step further by arguing that, because of its abhorrent character, genocide must be prosecutable in accordance with the universal principle.[27] In recent years, the applicability of the universal principle to genocide has been affirmed by the ICJ.[28] In fact, this restrictive reading of Article VI does not divest it of any substance. Article VI may be construed—in perfect harmony with the plain meaning of its terms—in the sense that it deals with no more than the duty to prosecute genocide, without specifying the conditions under which genocide

[23] But this statement is accepted *tel quel* by Condorelli, 'La Cour pénale internationale: Un pas de géant (pourvu qu'il soit accompli . . .)', 103 *RGDIP* (1999) 7, at 19. Charney, 'Progress in International Criminal Law?', 93 *AJIL* (1999) 452, at 455, also believes that universal jurisdiction exists for all international crimes.

[24] For the reluctant French practice see Stern, note on the *Javor* and the *Munyeshyaka* case, 93 *AJIL* (1999) 525.

[25] See Verdirame, 'The Genocide Definition in the Jurisprudence of the Ad Hoc Tribunals', 49 *ICLQ* (2000) 578.

[26] See William A. Schabas, *Genocide in International Law: The Crime of Crimes* (Cambridge: Cambridge University Press, 2000), at 355–358.

[27] *Attorney General of Israel v Eichmann*, judgment of 29 May 1962, 36 *ILR* 277, at 304.

[28] *Application of the Convention on the Prevention and Punishment of the Crime of Genocide, Preliminary Objections*, ICJ Reports (1996) 595, at 616, para. 31.

may be prosecuted.[29] This reading of the jurisdictional clause now enjoys universal support inasmuch as it corresponds to the inherent logic of the system which has taken shape for the repression of 'international' crimes, i.e. of crimes which affect the interests of the entire international community. The application of universal jurisdiction is one of the main tools in that battle. If, however, universal jurisdiction did not apply to genocide, the whole system would lose its most significant signpost.

Concerning crimes against humanity,[30] the second class of crimes listed by the Rome Statute, no general international treaty exists apart from that Statute itself. The international community has produced only a number of specific international instruments that deal with certain of the crimes enunciated by the Statute. Thus, slavery, a practice which has been combated by European nations since 1815,[31] has found its regulation in the Slavery Convention of 1926[32] and two additional treaty instruments,[33] torture became the subject matter of a separate instrument in 1984; the General Assembly adopted a comprehensive resolution regarding enforced disappearance;[34] and lastly Apartheid was proscribed by the International Convention on the Suppression and Punishment of the Crime of Apartheid.[35] Other offences mentioned in the Rome Statute, however, remain rather controversial. Thus, it would be somewhat bold to suggest that 'deportation or forcible transfer of population' (Article 7(1)(d) Rome Statute) is solidly founded on international consensus.

Of all the four examples referred to in the preceding paragraph, only torture is clearly subject to universal jurisdiction, as pointed out earlier. All the other crimes, however, have a status which may be adequately described as unsettled. The clause of the Slavery Convention dealing with criminal jurisdiction (Article 6) was framed at a time when the international community had not yet reaped sufficiently broad experiences with the universal principle. The relevant sentence, according to which states parties 'undertake

---

[29] However, the ICJ has stated—as an *obiter dictum*—that 'the obligation each State . . . has to prevent and to punish the crime of genocide is not territorially limited by the Convention', ibid.

[30] See McAuliffe de Guzman, 'The Road from Rome: The Developing Law of Crimes against Humanity', 22 *HRQ* (2000) 335; Robinson, 'Defining "Crimes against Humanity" at the Rome Conference', 93 *AJIL* (1999) 43; Zakr, 'Approche analytique du crime contre l'humanité en droit international', 105 *RGDIP* (2001) 281.

[31] See Trebilcock, 'Slavery', 4 *EPIL* (2000) 422.

[32] 60 *LNTS* 253.

[33] Protocol amending the Slavery Convention, adopted by GA Res. 794 (VIII), 23 October 1953, 182 *UNTS* 51; Supplementary Convention on the Abolition of Slavery, the Slave Trade, and Institutions and Practices Similar to Slavery, 7 September 1956, 266 *UNTS* 3.

[34] GA Res. 47/133, Declaration on the Protection of all Persons from Enforced Disappearance, 18 December 1992.

[35] Adopted by GA Res. 3068 (XXVIII), 30 November 1973, 1015 *UNTS* 243.

to adopt the necessary measures in order that severe penalties may be imposed', does not specifically address the issue of jurisdiction to prosecute, and Article 3(1) of the Supplementary Convention is marred by the same lack of clarity. Understandably, the Declaration on the Protection of All Persons from Enforced Disappearance, being a resolution having the legal value of a recommendation, is couched in rather guarded language in that it exhorts (Article 14) all states 'to bring to justice all persons presumed responsible for an act of enforced disappearance, who are found to be within their jurisdiction or under their control' ('All States should take any lawful and appropriate action available to them'). Lastly, it is a well-known fact that the Apartheid Convention, which contains the most rigourous jurisdictional clause providing for universal jurisdiction (Article IV(b)), has never been ratified by any state of the Western group. To date, its acceptance among the international community remains significantly low. Additionally, the Apartheid Convention has had little, if any, impact in practice. It would appear, above all, that it has never been applied by the so-called 'frontline' states, which on the political level continually attacked South Africa, but which on the level of economic exchanges consistently cooperated with their southern neighbour, who during the time of the Apartheid regime was and today still is the only important industrial power in the whole of southern Africa. In sum, the few examples given do not support the conclusion that every state is entitled to commence criminal proceedings against anyone charged with a crime against humanity, irrespective of the specific nature of the crime and irrespective of the place where it allegedly was committed.[36]

Concerning war crimes, the legal position is different, due to the wise political leadership exercised by the International Committee of the Red Cross. The four Geneva Conventions of 1949 each contain a clause, which is literally the same in all of them, according to which allegations of grave breaches of the applicable norms must be looked into by the competent territorial state (I: Article 49; II: Article 50; III: Article 129; IV: Article 146). States are even under the obligation to search for persons responsible for such breaches and to bring them, if found, before their own courts. Additional Protocol I of 1977 extended that obligation to the new grave breaches set forth therein (Article 85). As pointed out by authors who sought to verify the real significance of these clauses, little heed was paid by states to their duties during the first four decades of the existence of the Geneva Conventions.[37] It

---

[36] Cassese, 'Crimes Against Humanity', in Antonio Cassese, Paola Gaeta, and John R. W. D. Jones (eds), *The Rome Statute of the ICC: A Commentary* (Oxford, Oxford University Press, 2002), vol. 1, 353, at 376, openly acknowledges that by including Apartheid in Article 7 the Rome Statute went beyond the existing rules of general international law.

[37] Cassese, 'On the Current Trends towards Criminal Prosecution and Punishment of Breaches of International Humanitarian Law', 9 *EJIL* (1998) 2, at 7; Charney, 'International Criminal Law and the Role of Domestic Courts', 95 *AJIL* (2001) 120, at 120; Maison, 'Les

is only after the outbreak of the wars in the former Yugoslavia that third states started bringing to trial persons involved in atrocities who afterwards had moved to other European countries.

It is not only lack of goodwill which explains this shortcoming. The difficulties of conducting a trial based on facts which have occurred far away in another country or even continent are of a tremendous magnitude and cannot easily be overcome. No tribunal in Europe would be able to clarify in an individual case what happened during the hostilities in the Great Lakes district in Central Africa. A small country could not even bear the costs of a proceeding which would imply hearing witnesses from far-away countries with the help of interpreters. Thus, until recently, the obligation to institute criminal proceedings in all instances of grave breaches regardless of the place of the commission of the crime has largely remained a dead letter.

The crime of aggression disturbs again a picture in which the concept of international crime would be viewed as inextricably linked to universal jurisdiction. It is true that aggression has been inserted in Article 5(1)(d) Rome Statute as one of the crimes within the jurisdiction of the ICC. But Article 5(2) immediately adds that the ICC shall 'exercise' its jurisdiction only after a definition has been hammered out and agreement has been reached on the conditions determining the procedural modalities of that exercise. One does not need to be a prophet in order to predict that for decades the crime of aggression will lie dormant. None of the great powers has any interest in seeing its military actions reviewed in light of the concept of international crimes, which means that individuals can be made accountable and not just the state as an abstract entity.

In conclusion, it can be said that universal jurisdiction is a highly complex concept, resort to which should not be blindly advocated. The international community has shown great reluctance in accepting it. Almost without exception, universal jurisdiction has its roots in conventional instruments. As the example of aggression makes clear, states are afraid of granting access to complex factual situations to judges who either know little of the contextual background or who may be biased from the very outset against the suspected perpetrators. Indeed, such fears have solid foundations. Although it is a general requirement of a fair proceeding that judges must be independent and impartial (see, for instance, Article 14(1) CCPR), the factual situation in many countries differs greatly from that normative model. Wherever a dictatorship comes into power, one of its first concerns is to streamline the

premiers cas d'application des dispositions pénales des Conventions de Genève par les juridictions internes', 6 *EJIL* (1995) 260, at 263. Ziegler, 'Domestic Prosecution and International Cooperation with Regard to Violations of International Humanitarian Law: The Case of Switzerland', 7 *Revue suisse de droit international et de droit européen* (1997) 561, at 586, underlines the almost insurmountable difficulties which efforts at prosecution of crimes committed in foreign countries have to face.

judiciary so that no major political decision can be challenged. But even in countries where in principle the rule of law is upheld, judges can never escape the *Zeitgeist* which links them to the societies in which they are operating. On the one hand, universal jurisdiction seems ideally suited to prevent authors of despicable crimes finding safe havens. On the other hand, it subjects persons who at an initial stage are only alleged criminals to the whims and fancies of judiciaries, some of which act as the long arm of the political power in their countries. In this regard, judges Higgins, Kooijmans, and Buergenthal, who wrote a concurring opinion in the *Arrest Warrant* case,[38] showed a certain degree of naiveté when they said that 'charges may only be laid by a prosecutor or juge d'instruction who acts in full independence without links to or control by the government' of his state.[39] In postulating a rule of general international law, a jurist must take into account all possible configurations. If and when universal jurisdiction is affirmed and exists, it may be relied upon by all states. It is precisely the threat of judicial arbitrariness which to date has prevented states from being generous in accepting such jurisdiction which denies to an accused the benefit of the legal system with which he/she is familiar. Writers who approach this delicate issue exclusively from the viewpoint of human rights activism, without reflecting on the possible negative consequences, act unthinkingly and close their eyes to political realities.

III INTERNATIONAL PROSECUTION

For the reasons just explained, an international tribunal brought into being by the international community is much to be preferred to national tribunals which are inevitably caught within the framework of their national culture and political thinking. International prosecution constitutes not just a specific organizational modality, but is substantively predicated on the premise that individuals may incur criminal liability directly under international law.[40] Where prosecution takes place on the basis of general international law, the states concerned holding jurisdiction over an accused do not even have to state their acceptance. Their domestic law is completely discarded, and for good reasons since in most countries where grave breaches of international law occur such breaches are perfectly lawful under the applicable national law.

---

[38] ICJ, judgment of 14 February 2002.

[39] Ibid. at para. 59.

[40] See Greppi, 'The Evolution of Individual Criminal Responsibility under International Law', 81 (835) *IRRC* (1999) 531.

International Military Tribunal at Nürnberg

The first international criminal tribunal of modern history was the International Military Tribunal established at Nürnberg for the prosecution of the major war criminals of the German Third Reich, the evil Nazi empire. Its foundation was an international agreement between the victorious powers United States, France, United Kingdom, and the USSR.[41] No participation from neutral states was provided for, which would have helped the Tribunal shed the suspicion that it constituted nothing else than an embodiment of victors' justice. Thus, it essentially was a multinational rather than an international judicial body.[42] Additionally, the trial suffered from another deficiency in that its jurisdiction was strictly limited to crimes committed by German nationals, whereas war crimes committed by the Allied Forces could not even be touched upon. At the same time, when the Nürnberg Tribunal held its hearings, massive murderous repression of political opponents of the regime took place in the USSR. Hence, the Soviet judge was hardly suited to act in defence of the rule of law. Despite these structural weaknesses, the trial was conducted fairly, and all the penalties meted out by the Tribunal, including the death sentences, were fully deserved by the accused. The general degree of objectivity of the Tribunal was demonstrated in particular by the fact that no less than three of the accused were acquitted.

Having been established after the defeat of Germany, the Nürnberg Tribunal could not do anything to prevent the commission of human rights violations, the primary objective of international criminal prosecution. The same can be said of the Tokyo trial, where the main representatives of imperialist Japan were made accountable for their criminal conduct during the Second World War. In the following years and decades, it seemed that the concept of international criminal jurisdiction had outlived itself, given the prevailing circumstances of the Cold War between East and West. Attempts to generalize the Nürnberg experience failed at the United Nations. The reference in the 1948 Genocide Convention (Article VI) to an 'international penal tribunal' remained a dead letter. In 1973 the Apartheid Convention (Article V) repeated the same formula, but again no actual steps were taken to establish such a judicial body. On the whole, it could be assumed that the grandiose idea of making perpetrators of grave human rights violations directly responsible under international law had fallen into obsolescence.

---

[41] Agreement for the Prosecution and Punishment of the Major War Criminals of the European Axis, 8 August 1945, reprinted in Ingo von Münch (ed.), *Dokumente des geteilten Deutschland* (Stuttgart, Alfred Kröner, 1968), at 43.

[42] See Greenwood, 'The Development of International Humanitarian Law by the International Criminal Tribunal for the Former Yugoslavia', 2 *Max Planck UNYB* (1998) 97, at 100.

Ad Hoc Tribunals Established by the Security Council

It was the progress of history which made the international community aware of the evident truth that for some historical situations, in any event, international criminal tribunals were a suitable instrument of effective repression—and hopefully also prevention. The ILC worked again on a Code of Crimes against the Peace and Security of Mankind as from 1982, after the topic had been provisionally abandoned in 1954. But during the early 1980s no one really believed in the possible success of these endeavours. The big change came about in 1990, together with the demise of socialism as a political doctrine. For the first time, precisely in that year, concrete suggestions were made to elaborate, together with the Code, the statute of an international criminal court.[43] A number of exceptional international occurrences helped pave the way to a more fruitful outcome of the work that progressively moved away from its traditional slowness. On 21 December 1988 an American jetliner exploded over the Scottish town of Lockerbie, raising the question of who should try the perpetrators if it should ever be possible to issue an indictment against an individual. The defeat of Iraq after its invasion of Kuwait could have ended with the arrest of Iraqi dictator Sadam Hussein, but there existed no judicial body that could have charged him with the crime of aggression. The wars in the former Yugoslavia, which started in 1991, became soon known in the whole world on account of their brutality and disregard of all applicable rules of humanitarian law. For a long period of time, the international community remained essentially passive, contenting itself with sending peacekeeping forces to the embattled zones which had no mandate to put an end to the massive violations of human rights by both sides, in particular by the Serbian forces. Lastly, the Caribbean countries, which felt submerged by drug-related crime, supported strongly all initiatives for the establishment of an international criminal court.[44]

Against this background, fully aware of its disastrous handling of the Yugoslav crisis, the Security Council decided to establish the International Criminal Tribunal for the former Yugoslavia (ICTY). SC Res. 808, 22 February 1993, made the determination of principle, requesting the Secretary-General to work out the details. SC Res. 827, 25 May 1993, thereafter took the definitive step by adopting the report of the Secretary-General which contained the Statute of the ICTY.[45] In the following year, by SC Res. 955, 8 November 1994, the Security Council brought into being the International Criminal Tribunal for Rwanda (ICTR), a move which was again prompted

---

[43] For the discussion in the ILC see *Yearbook of the ILC* (*1990*), vol. II, part. 2, 19–25, paras. 93–157.

[44] See Cassese, 'From Nuremberg to Rome: International Military Tribunals to the ICC', in Cassese, Gaeta, and Jones, *supra* n. 36, 3, at 16.

[45] UN doc. S/25704, 3 May 1993.

by the recognition that the international community had failed to respond adequately vis-à-vis the threat of genocide which had visibly loomed over Rwanda many months before it actually materialized.

International Criminal Court

The establishment of these ad hoc tribunals prepared the ground for the creation of the ICC.[46] Since the two judicial bodies had successfully stood their first tests of reality, it seemed not only possible, but entirely feasible to broaden the experience thus acquired by setting up a criminal tribunal with comprehensive jurisdiction for all classes of international crimes. Obviously, this could not be effected again by a resolution of the Security Council. The Security Council is empowered to maintain and restore international peace and security. But it can make use of these powers only in a situation where there exists as a minimum an actual threat to peace and security. It would by far exceed its area of competence if it decided to set up new institutions with a mandate to combat abstract dangers that could arise even outside a context of international peace and security. In the former Yugoslavia and in Rwanda, massive disturbances of public order had prevailed. In the former Yugoslavia, these disturbances had undoubtedly an international character since the former component units of the Socialist Federal Republic of Yugoslavia had been recognized by the international community as sovereign states. In Rwanda, it was the fact of the genocide which imprinted an international hallmark on the situation prevailing in the country. In both instances, it was felt necessary to set up an international mechanism of criminal prosecution in order to bring the hostilities to a formal closure and to consolidate peace. Article 41 UNCh grants the Security Council a broad margin of discretion as to the appropriateness of the measures required for the restoration of a peaceful situation. The Security Council is under no obligation to stop its intervention as soon as actual hostilities have ended. But an ICC with comprehensive jurisdiction over all kinds of international crimes does not serve primarily the cause of international peace and security. It is designed generally to protect human rights through the preventive effect which is expected to attach to its judgments. There is certainly a partial overlap. But the mandate of the ICC as outlined in the Rome Statute is much wider than the mandate of the two ad hoc tribunals established by the Security Council. It was therefore necessary to resort to the traditional technique of treaty-making—with the great disadvantage that any state could evade membership just by refusing to ratify the Rome Statute.

[46] On the ICC see, for instance, Arsanjani, 'The Rome Statute of the ICC', 93 *AJIL* (1999) 22; Cassese, Gaeta, and Jones, *supra* n. 36; Otto Triffterer (ed.), *Commentary on the Rome Statute of the International Criminal Court* (Baden-Baden, Nomos, 1999).

It is well known that among all the opponents of the Rome Statute the United States has embarked on a path not only of distancing itself from the ICC by 'unsigning' the Rome Statute which President Clinton had signed on the last day of his term of office (31 December 2000),[47] but of actively combating it,[48] even attempting to bring pressure to bear on third states by concluding with them agreements that provide for non-surrender of their mutual nationals to the ICC.[49] Although the Rome Statute entered into force on 1 July 2002, the battle for the ICC is not yet over. The fact that the United States keeps aloof from it, and that consequently China and Russia will for the time being do the same, cannot but negatively affect its authority.[50] The United States has already obtained an important victory in prompting the Security Council to adopt SC Res. 1422 (2002), according to which for a period of one year (starting 1 July 2002) the ICC is requested not to take measures of prosecution against nationals of states parties not having ratified the Rome Statute if the acts in issue relate to an operation established or authorized by the United Nations.[51]

Whereas the Statute of the ICTY as well as the Statute of the ICTR provide for jurisdiction to prosecute individual breaches of the applicable standards of humanitarian law, the ICC has not been conceived of as an institution designed to engage in such exercises where isolated acts would become the subject matter. Rather, the ICC is called upon under Article 8 of its Statute to pronounce on war crimes 'in particular when committed as part of a plan or policy or as part of a large-scale commission of such crimes'. Thus, in cases of particular significance the ICC might try a person whose criminal conduct was not enmeshed in a general pattern, but this would certainly only happen in exceptional circumstances. The ICC will be placed under the principle of subsidiarity or complementarity (Article 17). It is expected to step in after the normal mechanisms are shown to have failed, in spite of the wide reach of the

[47] See letter by US Under-Secretary of State for Arms Control and International Security, John R. Bolton, of 27 April 2002, 41 *ILM* (2002) 1014. The American viewpoint is presented by Wedgwood, 'The International Criminal Court: An American View', 10 *EJIL* (1999) 93; contra: Hafner, Boon, Rübesame, and Huston, 'A Response to the American View as Presented by Ruth Wedgwood', ibid. at 108.

[48] The American Servicemembers' Protection Act, H.R. 4775, reprinted in 23 *HRLJ* (2002) 275, threatens resort to military force in case a criminal trial should be conducted before the ICC against a person member of the US armed forces. For a critical response to that Act see letter by Benjamin B. Ferencz, former prosecutor at the Nürnberg trial, of 24 June 2002, http://www.globalpolicy.org/intljustice/icc/2002/0624ben.htm (visited December 2002).

[49] Such bilateral arrangements would be unlawful for a state party to the Rome Statute, see opinion of EU Commission, 23 *HRLJ* (2002) 158. The first country where such a treaty on a mutual obligation of non-surrender to the ICC was definitively approved by the competent legislative body was Sierra Leone (6 May 2003), see Amnesty International News Release, 8 May 2003 (http://www.amnestyusa.org/news/2003/sierraleone05082003.html).

[50] See Charney, *supra* n. 37, passim.

[51] For background information see 96 *AJIL* (2002) 725.

principle of universal jurisdiction. Indeed, the ICC would simply be over-burdened if it had to look into each and every charge of violation of humanitarian law.

Very rarely in actual life will the Nürnberg or Tokyo situation reoccur in the sense that a country has been defeated and that its entire leadership can be put on trial for war crimes systematically committed during a preceding armed conflict. Consequently, international prosecution of war crimes remains largely dependent on cooperation by states for purposes of surrender of indicted persons or retrieval of documentary evidence. Events in the former Yugoslavia have amply demonstrated that the requisite assistance is not automatically forthcoming, notwithstanding existing legal commitments. Antonio Cassese, the former President of the ICTY, has compared his institution to 'a giant without arms and legs'.[52] Although this observation may seem somewhat exaggerated, the dilemma can hardly be denied. All the crimes falling within the scope of jurisdiction of an international criminal tribunal constitute essentially state crimes, involving not only the individual under indictment, but the entire State machinery. Therefore, reluctance to cooperate with an international criminal tribunal must be viewed as an almost natural attitude of a state involved in such criminal practices. Nonetheless, there is no other avenue available. Despite all the foreseeable difficulties, the establishment of the ICC will not only give effect to humanitarian law, but will also mean a considerable gain in objectivity in better ensuring equality before the law.[53]

Hybrid Criminal Tribunals

Criminal tribunals of a hybrid character, composed of both national and international judges, have been or were planned for Cambodia and Sierra Leone. Their task would be to deal with the atrocities committed in the civil wars that plagued both countries for long periods. While the envisaged Criminal Tribunal for Cambodia has conclusively failed to materialize,[54] the differences of opinion between the United Nations and the government of Cambodia not being susceptible of being bridged, there seems to be still some hope that the 'Special Court' for Sierra Leone[55] will come into being

[52] *Supra* n. 37, at 13.

[53] Inevitably, however, it will face the same problems of enforcement, see Cassese, 'The Statute of the ICC: Some Preliminary Reflections', 10 *EJIL* (1999) 144, at 164–167; Wedgwood, 'The ICC: An American View', ibid. 93, at 106.

[54] However, in January 2003 new negotiations took place between the Cambodian government and the United Nations.

[55] Cryer, 'A "Special Court" for Sierra Leone?', 50 *ICLQ* (2001) 435–446; Frulli, 'The Special Court for Sierra Leone: Some Preliminary Comments', 11 *EJIL* (2000) 857; McDonald, 'Sierra Leone's Shoestring Special Court', 84(845) *IRRC* (2002) 121. The legal foundations were laid by SC Res. 1315 (2000), 14 August 2000.

in the not too distant future. Indeed, the first judges were sworn in on 2 December 2002.

IV A SUMMARY BALANCE SHEET OF THE TWO AD HOC TRIBUNALS

Given the fact that the ICC has not yet become operative, the election of the judges being scheduled for February 2003, it is of course too early to establish a balance sheet of its activities. However, the ICTY and the ICTR may already be assessed as to the contribution which they have made to the cause of human rights. In this regard, two aspects need to be considered. On the one hand, the effectiveness of the two tribunals must be examined. On the other hand, it is no less interesting to inquire whether their functions have been discharged in full conformity with the requirements of the rule of law.

Authority of the Security Council

In the first place, the question arose of whether the Security Council was empowered to establish judicial bodies for the prosecution of genocide, war crimes, and crimes against humanity. The defence in one of the first cases, the *Tadic* case, argued that Chapter VII of the UN Charter did not confer such far-reaching authority on the Security Council. In a carefully drafted and entirely persuasive decision of its Appeals Chamber of 2 October 1995,[56] the ICTY, however, rejected all of these objections. It held that Article 41 UNCh provided a sufficient legal basis for its establishment, that among other measures the creation of a judicial body, too, was permissible, and that in the circumstances a resolution of the Security Council could be equated with a 'law' as generally required by human rights instruments for the establishment of a criminal tribunal.[57] Yet one difficulty remains. It is certainly true that criminal prosecutions may be necessary in order to restore peace in a country ravaged by war. On the other hand, a post-conflict regime cannot continue forever. At some point in time, normalcy must return. This is an issue which the Appeals Chamber did not have to address back in 1995, but which will become ever more urgent as time goes by. Generally, the ICTY has become aware of the actual time constraints. According to a provisional time schedule, the Office of the Prosecutor aims to finalize its work of investigation by 2005, and the last decisions by the Trial Chambers are expected for 2008.

---

[56] 35 *ILM* (1996) 35, at 42–48.
[57] But see critical comments by Greenwood, *supra* n. 42, at 104.

Customary Nature of International Criminal Law

The next question concerned the legal foundations of the crimes within the jurisdiction of the ICTY and the ICTR. The Security Council proceeded on the premise that it was empowered to bring into being a judicial body, but it never thought of creating new substantive rules establishing offences for which individuals may directly incur criminal responsibility under international law. Such legislative authority would not have been covered by Article 41 UNCh. Conceiving of the Security Council as a body competent to enact substantive criminal law would have been all the less acceptable since the rule *nullum crimen, nulla poena sine lege* belongs to the core elements of criminal justice in consonance with the rule of law. The ICTY was mandated to prosecute persons who had committed crimes since 1991, well before the date of its establishment. Since the *nullum crimen* rule forbids retroactive legislation, the Security Council had to assume that all of the offences listed in Articles 2 to 5 of the ICTY Statute and Articles 2 to 4 of the ICTR Statute were recognized as crimes under customary international law.[58] No doubts could be entertained as to the punishable character of genocide and the grave breaches listed in the four Geneva Conventions of 1949 and in Additional Protocol I of 1977 (Article 85). It was far less obvious that other violations of the laws or customs of war and crimes against humanity had reliable bases in general international law.

Non-international Armed Conflicts

The most serious doubts arose in connection with violations of the rules applicable to non-international armed conflicts. The ICTY Statute does not mention such violations as punishable offences, but the ICTR Statute does so quite openly. Article 4 bears the heading 'Violations of Article 3 common to the Geneva Conventions and of Additional Protocol II'. Yet, neither common Article 3 (of 1949) nor Additional Protocol II (of 1977) declare in any manner whatsoever that acts contrary to the legal regime governing internal armed conflict shall entail criminal responsibility of the responsible actors. At the Geneva Conference of 1949, which drafted common Article 3, no suggestion was made to that effect. The official commentary of the International Committee of the Red Cross does not contain any reference to criminal sanctions. Probably, since the introduction of the new regime was utterly controversial, common Article 3 would not have received the necessary approval if it had been complemented from the very outset by a provision establishing penal consequences.[59] Likewise, a provision on grave

[58] This was confirmed by the ICTY in *Delalic*, case IT-96–21–AR72.5, decision of the Appeals Chamber, 15 October 1996.
[59] See Condorelli, *supra* n. 23, at 11.

breaches is conspicuously absent from Additional Protocol II. While Additional Protocol I ties in with the regime provided for in the four 1949
Conventions which it is designed to complement, this was a clear message
to the effect that the participating states did not wish to see their sovereign
freedom in handling internal conflicts restricted by a tight system of international responsibility.

Notwithstanding this data, which seemed to block any prosecution of
violations of the rules governing non-international armed conflicts, the
ICTY and the ICTR did not hesitate to conclude that the dividing line
between international and non-international conflicts had been blurred
over the course of time and that sufficient practice had accumulated to
support the punishment of authors of grave breaches of the applicable legal
regime, irrespective of the nature of the conflict at hand. Also in the *Tadic*
case (Jurisdiction), the ICTY held that:

customary international law imposes criminal liability for serious violations of
common Article 3, as supplemented by other general principles and rules on the
protection of victims of internal armed conflict, and for breaching certain fundamental principles and rules regarding means and methods of combat in civil strife.[60]

It goes without saying that the ICTR had to follow this precedent in order
to maintain consistency within the system of prosecution established by the
Security Council. Indeed, in *Akayesu*,[61] it adhered to the *Tadic* doctrine,
stating that it found the reasoning of the ICTY Appeals Chamber 'convincing
and dispositive of the issue'.[62] Since that time, the issue is indeed considered
as closed by the two ad hoc tribunals.[63] This has not prevented voices in legal
doctrine, though, voicing dissent, arguing that the materials relied upon by
the Appeals Chamber in the *Tadic* case did not really seem to corroborate
what they were made to say.[64]

Amnesties

One of the big problems which the ICC will have to deal with is the granting
of amnesties by the national state of an accused person. Neither for the ICTY
nor for the ICTR has there been any need to pronounce on this issue since the
successor states of the former Yugoslavia as well as Rwanda have refrained

[60] 35 *ILM* (1996) 32, at 71, para. 134.
[61] Judgment of 2 September 1998.
[62] Ibid. at para. 615.
[63] The Appeals Chamber confirmed its ruling in the *Tadic* jurisdiction decision in the case
of *Celebici Camp v Delalic et al.*, IT–96–21, 20 February 2001, paras 153–174.
[64] See Fox, 'The Objections to Transfer of Criminal Jurisdiction to the UN Tribunal', 46
ICLQ (1997) 434, at 442. By contrast, Greenwood, *supra* n. 42, at 130–133, defends the
reasoning in *Tadic*. For a somewhat cautious statement see Bothe, 'War Crimes', in Cassese,
Gaeta, and Jones, *supra* n. 36, 379, at 417.

from enacting any amnesties. Logically, it would seem to follow from the concept of international prosecution that the state of nationality has no right to block or impede proceedings conducted on behalf of the international community. Yet the example of South Africa has shown that there may be other means of reckoning with the past than to impose punishments on persons found guilty of committing atrocities.[65]

Pre-trial Detention

Another one of the difficulties facing the ICTY as well as the ICTR is the length of time suspects may have to spend in pre-trial detention before the proceedings against them actually start. Thus, the proceeding against Dragan Nikolic[66] was still at its pre-trial stage at the end of 2002 although Nikolic had been apprehended in April 2000, and the same was true of the proceeding commenced against Momcilo Krajisnik.[67] According to the latest report of the ICTR, at the beginning of July 2002, 60 persons were held in custody in its detention facility, of whom 29 were waiting for the commencement of their trials, some for three years.[68] Such delays affect the reputation of the system of international criminal jurisdiction which is expected to set an example of good administration of justice. To be sure, the difficulties of a trial far away from the places where the crimes were committed are tremendous, not least because of the need for translation of all documents and oral statements. Nonetheless, resolute efforts should be undertaken to reduce the span of time suspects have to wait for their trial to start.[69]

Reparation for Persons Erroneously Prosecuted

An unresolved problem is reparation for persons erroneously prosecuted. The statutes of the two ad hoc tribunals do not address this issue. According to Article 14(6) CCPR, any person victim of 'miscarriage of justice' shall be

---

[65] On this issue see, for instance, Gavron, 'Amnesties in the Light of Developments in International Law and the Establishment of the ICC', 51 *ICLQ* (2002) 91, at 106–108 (without a definitive stance); Hafner, Boon, Rübesame, and Huston, 'A Response to the American View as Presented by Ruth Wedgwood', 10 *EJIL* (1999) 108 at 109–113 (denying the relevance of national amnesties); Roht-Arriaza and Gibson, 'The Developing Jurisprudence on Amnesty', 20 *HRQ* (1998) 843 (rejecting amnesties); Stahn, 'United Nations Peace-Building, Amnesties and Alternative Forms of Justice: A Change in Practice?', 84 (845) *IRRC* (2002) 191; Tomuschat, 'Current Issues of Responsibility under International Law', *Bancaja Euromediterranean Courses of International Law*, IV (2000), 515, at 595–596.

[66] Case IT–94–2.

[67] Case IT–00–39 & 40.

[68] *Seventh Annual Report of the ICTR for the period from 1 July 2001 to 30 June 2002*, UN doc. A/57/163–S/2002/733, 2 July 2002.

[69] See on that issue Caflisch, 'The Rome Statute and the ECHR', 23 *HRLJ* (2002) 1, at 3.

compensated 'according to law', which means that the CCPR enjoins states parties to enact domestic legislation for that purpose. The most famous case in this regard is the case of the *Kupreskic Brothers*, two of whom were in custody in The Hague for not less than four years before being acquitted by the ICTY. Thereafter, they demanded financial compensation, a claim which generated confusion and to date (December 2002) has not been satisfied. It stands to reason that a judicial body established by the United Nations must comply with the judicial guarantees as they are laid down in the human rights treaties established under the auspices of the World Organization. Otherwise, its authority would be greatly affected.[70]

Statistics

Both the ICTY and the ICTR are relatively small institutions. Originally, the ICTY, comprising 11 judges, was made up of just two Trial Chambers and one Appeal Chamber, and the same configuration was chosen for the ICTR. In view of the augmenting workload, the ICTY Statute was amended by the Security Council three times,[71] while the ICTR Statute was adapted to the exigencies of the situation four times.[72] Both institutions are now made up of three Trial Chambers, while there is still just one Appeals Chamber in each case. Corresponding to this extension, the number of permanent judges was pushed up to 16, and furthermore allowance was made for the addition of *ad litem* judges, in the case of the ICTY much earlier than in the case of the ICTR.[73] This strengthening of the judicial staff made it possible, at the same time, to provide for the splitting of the Trial Chambers into sections of three judges each of which may discharge the functions of a Trial Chamber. In this fashion, it may be possible significantly to reduce the number of pending cases.

In spite of all the efforts undertaken with a view to making the two tribunals more effective, their balance sheet is far from attracting unrestricted applause. The latest report of the ICTR, its Seventh Annual Report, reveals that at the end of June 2002 no more than eight persons had been convicted and sentenced, while on the other hand one acquittal had occurred. In the case of the ICTY, an official 'Fact Sheet on ICTY Proceedings' of December 2002[74] shows that no more than 20 cases were settled by final judgments: 15

---

[70] See Beresford, 'Redressing the Wrongs of the International Justice System: Compensation for Persons Erroneously Detained, Prosecuted, or Convicted by the Ad Hoc Tribunals', 96 *AJIL* (2002) 628.

[71] SC Res. 1166, 13 May 1998; 1329, 30 November 2001; 1411, 17 May 2002.

[72] SC Res. 1165, 30 April 1998; 1329, 30 November 2001; 1411, 17 May 2002; 1431, 14 August 2002.

[73] SC Res. 1431, 14 August 2002.

[74] http://www.un.org/icty/glance/index.htm (visited December 2002).

persons received their final sentences, and five persons were found not guilty. But these figures do not represent the whole truth. Regarding the ICTY, 12 cases were pending on appeal, while two persons still had the opportunity to file an appeal. Additionally, some indictments were withdrawn; other persons died during the proceedings conducted against them.

On the whole, this statistical breakdown cannot be comforting to the observer's eye. It amply demonstrates the difficulties surrounding trials before international tribunals. Almost 1,300 persons are at the service of the ICTY, and its annual budget amounts to roughly US $100 million. Administering justice within an international context constitutes a tremendously expensive undertaking. This is one of the reasons why the ICC will operate in accordance with the principle of complementarity.[75] Moreover, it should not be overlooked that no less than 24 arrest warrants of the ICTY have not been executed, some of the successor states of the Socialist Federal Republic of Yugoslavia, in particular the Federal Republic of Yugoslavia (Serbia and Montenegro), refusing to comply with their duty to cooperate with the ICTY. To be sure, it was a great success for the concept of international criminal justice when Slobodan Milosevic, the former President of the FRY, was surrendered to the ICTY. But Ratko Mladic and Radovan Karadzic, the two main suspects charged with organizing the genocide in the Bosnian town of Srebrenica, where 7,000 Bosniaks were murdered in cold blood, are still at large notwithstanding the arrest warrants issued by the ICTY many years ago. As long as these two persons, who symbolize the brutal reality of impunity, have not been brought to trial, the work of the ICTY will appear fragmentary and unsatisfactory.

V CONCLUSION

Yet these critical comments should not be regarded as totally eclipsing the positive side of the balance sheet. The work of the ICTY has made clear that individual criminal responsibility does exist and cannot be brushed aside as a hollow word.[76] One may take it that the ongoing process of criminal prosecution has largely contributed to stabilizing the situation in Bosnia-Herzegovina. Even ethnic fanatics know that they are well-advised to refrain from engaging in criminal activities since otherwise they might end up before the judges in The Hague. Never has it been contended that the ICTY might be able to deal with all of the crimes that were committed during the years of cataclysm, when ethnic hatred superseded all considerations of human solidarity and tolerance.

[75] Article 17 Rome Statute: in principle, prosecution is committed to national courts.
[76] See also optimistic appraisal by Akhavan, 'Justice in The Hague, Peace in the Former Yugoslavia? A Commentary on the UN War Crimes Tribunal', 20 *HRQ* (1998) 737.

For an outsider, it is hard to say whether the activity of the ICTR may be assessed in similarly positive terms. In Rwanda, tens of thousands of people were involved in the mass killings during the fatal months in 1994. Compared to these figures, the number of cases tried by the ICTR seems almost irrelevant. It is true that the ICTR has succeeded in convicting and sentencing a number of politicians who held prominent positions in the structure of the state. Among them are Jean Kambanda, the Prime Minister, and Jean-Paul Akayesu, the Mayor of Taba, both sentenced to life imprisonment.[77] Additionally, among the detainees still being held one finds the names of no less than 11 Ministers. Generally, however, one must conclude that for the future of human rights in Rwanda it is much more important to achieve fairness of proceedings for the thousands of suspects who are still being held by the current government of the country. Local justice by laymen, to which recourse is increasingly had (the system of *'gachachá'*), may not constitute an ideal solution in light of the fundamental guarantees set forth by Article 14 CCPR. But it is a simple fact that the ICTR would be simply overwhelmed and submerged if it had to deal with all the cases requiring an assessment from the viewpoint of criminal law.

The ICC according to the Rome Statute will encounter even greater difficulties than the two ad hoc tribunals. Since for the time being it lacks the support of the three permanent Security Council members China, Russia, and the United States, its effectiveness will be seriously curtailed. International criminal justice can be successful only if it is supported by the entire international community. Currently, a human rights lawyer can only express the wish that the United States may be able to revise its opposition to an institution which, in an environment of bona fide international understanding and cooperation, is certainly capable of making a significant contribution to real enjoyment of human rights for the benefit of every human being.

In sum, to date international criminal law has made only a modest contribution to upholding the standards of human rights and humanitarian law. Since loss of human life can never be repaired, emphasis must be placed on prevention. To create a culture of humanity may be the best safeguard. Yet, once the ICC has come into actual operation, the sole fact of its existence may act as another deterrent factor capable of inducing all of the actors involved in armed conflict to abide by the standards evolved by the international community.

---

[77] See ICTR Detainees, Status on 21 November 2002, http://www.ictr.org.

13

Civil Suits against Human Rights Violators

I GENERAL CONSIDERATIONS

Although states are obligated to respect and ensure human rights, it is trivial to note that violations occur time and again. Even if administrative or judicial remedies are available to the aggrieved individual, the successful conclusion of a proceeding brought against the body or person responsible for the act or omission complained of may not suffice as reparation for the harm caused. A victim of torture does not recover his health simply because the perpetrator has been convicted and sentenced. A person unlawfully imprisoned for a time not only wishes to be released, but also to be compensated for the time spent in prison. Likewise, somebody discriminated against on account of his race does not receive full satisfaction by a simple finding that he/she was indeed affected by racial prejudice. Justice seems to require that the effects of such unlawful actions be wiped out to the greatest extent possible. If restoration of the situation as it existed beforehand is impossible, financial compensation would seem to be the adequate means of redress. Indeed, under general international law financial compensation is due to an injured state if the damage is not made good by restitution.[1]

Many obstacles impede justice taking its course according to such ideal signposts. Satisfaction of claims for financial redress is, of course, easy if the wrongdoing state is prepared to take remedial action under its national law, assuming that responsibility for torts operates effectively within its jurisdiction. If, however, the rules of the national legal system concerned regarding state liability for torts caused to private citizens remain a theoretical construct, which may not be enforced in practice, the question arises how such

---

[1] ILC Articles on Responsibility of States for Internationally Wrongful Acts, taken note of by GA Res. 56/83, 12 December 2001, Article 36(1).

deficiencies at national level can be corrected or compensated at the level of international law.[2]

It is clear that in the field of human rights the traditional rules of diplomatic protection also apply. Inasmuch as a state has violated the human rights of a foreign national, it incurs responsibility vis-à-vis the home state of that person. Such instances occur from time to time.[3] But in the great majority of cases infringements of human rights are perpetrated by state agents against their own nationals. In such circumstances, the classical rules on state responsibility are of no avail. Traditionally, international law has been concerned with interstate relations and not with internal relationships existing between a state and its citizens. New ways would therefore have to be found to accommodate the emerging need for a regime of secondary rules on reparation designed to complete and support the regime of primary rules on human rights protection which is now firmly in place.

As already pointed out, international humanitarian law can also be said, in a wider sense, to constitute human rights law, adapted to the particular circumstances of armed conflict. This branch of the law essentially protects members of enemy forces against violations of the basic rules governing situations where, in principle, arms may be used to destroy human life. Any such violation entails state responsibility according to the traditional connotation. Individuals negatively affected thereby do not have direct claims against the enemy state. To be sure, it has been contended in particular by Frits Kalshoven[4] that Article 3 of the Hague Convention (IV) Respecting the Laws and Customs of War on Land was intended to confer a right of reparation directly on victims of breaches of the Convention and its Annex, the Regulations Respecting the Laws and Customs of War on Land. But the text of Article 3 does not say so, and the alleged meaning has not been confirmed by any relevant practice.[5] In its commentary on Additional Protocol I to the 1949 Geneva Conventions the International Committee of the Red Cross observes with extreme caution that 'since 1945 a tendency has emerged to recognize the exercise of rights by

---

[2] Kirgis, 'Restitution as a Remedy in U.S. Courts for Violations of International Law', 95 *AJIL* (2001) 341, does not clearly distinguish between remedies under national and remedies under international law.

[3] See, for instance, the case of Ahmadou Sadio Diallo (*Republic of Guinea v Democratic Republic of the Congo*), pending before the ICJ since 1998 (allegations of unlawful imprisonment and deprivation of all financial assets).

[4] State Responsibility for Warlike Acts of the Armed Forces, 40 *ICLQ* (1991) 827, at 830–832.

[5] For a strong advocacy of individual rights flowing from any violation of the rules of humanitarian law see Bernhard Graefrath, 'Schadensersatzansprüche wegen Verletzung humanitären Völkerrechts', 14 *Humanitäres Völkerrecht* (2001) 110.

individuals'.[6] Of course, individual rights may be brought into being by specific treaty instruments. Under general international law, however, states have generally insisted on the need to settle the consequences of armed conflict by global arrangements.[7]

II REDRESS AFFORDED BY THE INTERNATIONAL COMMUNITY

Since the international community has brought into being an impressive array of rules for the protection of human rights, it might additionally have established a system for the indemnization of victims of violations of these rights. An impeccable logic could support the creation of such a system for righting the wrongs suffered by innocent persons: the international community having assumed responsibility for the life, the physical integrity, and the wellbeing of every human person, regardless of his/her nationality, regional affiliation, or any other feature, it should also provide the victims of unlawful conduct with remedies suited to assuage their distress. However, hard facts should not be overlooked. The international community has not yet reached the stage of a true community of solidarity, where all the members are prepared to share jointly the burdens caused not only by natural disasters, but also by political cataclysms. On the contrary, the gist of the existing system of international responsibility is a different one. In international relations, peoples are made responsible, including in financial terms, for the unlawful acts committed by their governments against foreign states and peoples, even if they themselves have domestically suffered from a regime which in its external relations has engaged in grave breaches of international law. In any event, nations are in general quite unwilling to defray the costs for crime and mismanagement that have occurred in other national settings. To establish such a system at universal level is almost inconceivable not only at the present time, but also in the foreseeable future. Even the European Union has not yet become a social union. Each Member State has its specific system of social security. To grant financial redress for victims of state crime would be even more demanding than running a Community system of social security.

Only timid steps in that direction can be observed. At the level of the United Nations, several trust funds have been established. There is one fund

---

[6] Yves Sandoz, Christophe Swinarski, and Bruno Zimmermann (eds), *Commentary on the Additional Protocols of 8 June 1977 to the Geneva Conventions of 12 August 1949* (Geneva, Martinus Nijhoff, 1987), comment on Article 91, 1057, marginal note 3657.

[7] See Pierre d'Argent, *Les réparations de guerre en droit international public* (Bruxelles and Paris, Bruylant and L.G.D.J., 2002), at 842.

for the victims of torture which receives about US $10 million per year.[8] Another fund for the victims of Apartheid existed during the time of the racist regime in South Africa but has lost any importance since 1995.[9] A third fund, which seeks to provide assistance to victims of slavery, established in 1991,[10] seems to enjoy support from many sides, but has a fairly modest financial dimension.[11] To hope for generalization of these laudable efforts by the international community would be no more than wishful thinking, considering the large amounts of financial resources that would be needed for such purposes. It may be called a great success that in some particularly difficult areas, where human rights violations may totally destroy the physical and mental stability of a person, the international community has seen fit at least to provide some relief to victims.

If it should ever be envisaged to establish a regime of reparation for the benefit of victims of slavery and colonialism, as suggested by some of the participants of the World Conference against Racism, Racial Discrimination, Xenophobia and Related Intolerance (WCAR), held in Durban from 31 August to 8 September 2001,[12] this could only be done in the form of a fund to be established by the international community, in particular states which practised, and benefited from, slavery and colonialism. Today's human rights norms cannot be applied retroactively.[13] Furthermore, it is simply impossible to determine who today could legitimately claim to be a victim of such policies, to the extent that they go back 50, 100, or even 200 years into the past. Countries and people which suffered injustices in the past should roll up their sleeves and make full use of their capabilities under the new conditions of independence and freedom, instead of remaining in a passive role as recipients of foreign aid. Consequently, forward-looking strategies are necessary and legitimate, in particular investment in education and vocational training.

III THE GAPS IN EXISTING INTERNATIONAL SYSTEMS

A major difficulty results from the fact that many states are not parties to any international system under which adequate redress can possibly be obtained.

---

[8] United Nations Voluntary Fund for Victims of Torture, established by GA Res. 36/151, 16 December 1981.

[9] Trust Fund for the Programme of Action for the Third Decade to Combat Racism and Racial Discrimination, established by GA Res. 38/14, 22 November 1983.

[10] Established by GA Res. 46/122, 17 December 1991.

[11] In 2001 grants of less than US $200,000 were disbursed.

[12] See, in particular, the Dakar Declaration of the regional African Preparatory Conference of the WCAR, 24 January 2001, available at http://www.unhchr.ch/html/racism/02–recomdak.html (visited December 2002), para. 20.

[13] Cogently demonstrated by Bossuyt and Vandeginste, 'The Issue of Reparation for Slavery and Colonialism and the Durban World Conference against Racism', 22 *HRLJ* (2001) 341, at 342–343.

As will be discussed below, general international law has not yet evolved a right of financial compensation for victims of gross human rights violations. It is only within the framework of international treaties that an aggrieved individual may obtain relief to make good the injury he/she has suffered. As already pointed out, to date there exists no instrument for the protection of human rights in the Asian region. As far as the OP-CCPR is concerned, which provides some, albeit weak, foundations for granting relief to victims, it has still many important gaps in the circle of its states parties.[14] In general, it is especially the 'good' countries which have had the courage to submit to the control exercised by the HRCee through the consideration of individual communications addressed to it. Additionally, it is a simple fact of life that very few cases come before the competent international bodies. Under normal circumstances, nobody can expect that he/she will be able to benefit from the compensation schemes laid down in these treaties.

Additionally, many individual complaints/communications refer to occurrences that happened before the relevant instrument entered into force for the country concerned. More often than not, a new democratic government, committed to the rule of law, which has come into power after a period of dictatorial lawlessness, accepts international review of its actions as a tangible sign of its will strictly to comply with the obligations under international law which are binding upon it. Then, quite naturally, victims of the former regime feel encouraged to present claims seeking to obtain reparation for the harm they suffered during the earlier period of arbitrary exercise of public power. However, these grievances cannot be satisfied under international mechanisms which are generally based on the principle of non-retroactivity, as generally stipulated in Article 28 of the Vienna Convention on the Law of Treaties or specifically in the relevant agreements.[15]

IV A CAUSE OF ACTION UNDER INTERNATIONAL LAW

Reparation under Human Rights Treaties

International Covenant on Civil and Political Rights
Whenever national or international remedies hold no prospect of success, victims may attempt to institute civil proceedings before the ordinary courts of other countries in order to obtain at least financial redress for the injury

[14] As of 9 December 2002, the number of states parties stood at 104.
[15] It is understandable that many applicants have tried to recover the properties which were confiscated under socialist regimes. But both the HRCee and the ECtHR have ruled that, in principle, expropriation produces its effects the moment it is enacted and has no continuing effect, see HRCee, *Koutny v Czech Republic*, views of 20 March 2000, [2001] *Report of the HRCee*, vol. II, UN doc. A/55/40, 215, at 217, para. 6.2.; ECtHR, *Prince Hans-Adam II of Liechtenstein v Germany*, judgment of 12 July 2001, para. 85.

they have suffered. Many requirements must be met by such claims. In the first place, the plaintiff must be able to invoke a cause of action, ideally a cause of action deriving directly from international law. Secondly, he/she must find a forum which has jurisdiction over the case and which is prepared to adjudicate his/her claim. And lastly, there remains of course the problem of enforcement. Even the best judgment is not worth much if no real opportunity exists to see it satisfied.

General treaties for the protection of human rights are mostly extremely discrete regarding the 'secondary' rights which should accrue to victims of breaches of the rights they set forth. Thus, the CCPR contains only two clauses which specifically address the issue of compensation. Article 9(5) provides that anyone who has been the victim of unlawful arrest or detention shall have an enforceable right to compensation. Similarly, Article 14(6) stipulates that persons who have been punished as a consequence of a miscarriage of justice shall be compensated 'according to law'. In both instances, it is assumed that such compensation should be granted on the basis of domestic legislation which the state concerned is required to enact.[16] However, there is no general provision governing the issue of reparation. According to Article 2(3), everyone whose rights under the CCPR have been violated shall have an 'effective remedy'. Seen in context, this provision addresses remedies as a procedural means to obtain redress, but does not say anything about the substance of redress owed to the victim of a violation. This construction of Article 2(3) is confirmed by the other linguistic versions of the text. In French, the word 'recours' is employed, and the Spanish text uses the word 'recurso'. Both terms designate procedural devices but do not connote substantive remedial rights to which an aggrieved individual may be entitled.

Notwithstanding this lack of clear indications as to the way in which human rights violations should be made good, the HRCee has had no doubts as to the obligation of a wrongdoing state to provide relief. At an early stage of its jurisprudence, it began including in the concluding paragraphs of its views that the state concerned was to desist from the unlawful practice found to exist, not only as regards the case at hand, but also with regard to other similar cases, and further to compensate the victim for any damage sustained.[17] This jurisprudence reached its high point when the HRCee stated that persons who had been convicted and sentenced to death under irregular circum-

---

[16] See Pisillo-Mazzeschi, 'International Obligations to Provide for Reparation Claims?', in Albrecht Randelzhofer and Christian Tomuschat (eds), *State Responsibility and the Individual: Reparation in Instances of Grave Violations of Human Rights* (The Hague, Martinus Nijhoff, 1999), 149.

[17] See the *Weismann* case, Communication No. 8/1977, final views, 3 April 1980, HRCee, *Selected Decisions under the Optional Protocol*, UN doc. CCPR/C/OP/1 (1985), 45, at 49, para. 17.

stances and had additionally spent long years on death row should be granted the benefit of a commutation of their sentence or even be released.[18] In evolving this straightforward jurisprudence, the Committee was obviously led, apart from the flawed literal construction of Article 2(3) CCPR, by the general customary law governing the consequences of internationally wrongful acts in an interstate context.[19] The record of achievement is a fairly mixed one, however.[20] The response by states parties to the views handed down by the HRCee does not prove conclusively that states have an obligation to make good any harm caused by a violation of human rights.

European Convention on Human Rights

At the regional level, the ECtHR is empowered, under Article 41 ECHR, to afford 'just satisfaction' to an injured party if it has found that a measure taken by a state party was in conflict with its obligations under the ECHR. This is a discretionary power. Examination of the case law of the Court shows many inconsistencies. The Court does not feel obligated to compensate an injured party under all circumstances. On the contrary, it has many times exercised its discretion by holding that a judicial pronouncement determining a breach of its commitments by a state party constitutes sufficient redress.[21] In a few cases, this has produced even shocking results. Thus, in *McCann*, adjudicated in 1995,[22] the Court denied any financial compensation to the families of three persons who had been shot dead by a British anti-terrorist unit in Gibraltar in violation of the right to life protected in Article 2 ECHR.

More recently, the ECtHR seems to have followed a less erratic course, a course less permeated by motives of moral reprobation.[23] But it remains faithful to its position that not every violation found should give rise to a compensation claim.[24] It feels that in many instances its decision provides sufficient redress to the victim. In other words, the successful applicant may win a moral victory, but he/she is not compensated for all of the economic

---

[18] For the first cases see *Earl Pratt and Ivan Morgan v Jamaica*, Communications 210/1986 and 225/1987, final views, 6 April 1989, *Official Records of the HRCee* (1988/89), vol. II, 419, at 423, para. 14; *Daniel Pinto v Trinidad and Tobago*, Communication 232/1987, final views, 20 July 1990, *Official Records of the HRCee* (1989/90), vol. II, 405, at 407, para. 13.2.

[19] The Articles on Responsibility of States for Internationally Wrongful Acts (*supra* n. 1) provide in Article 34 that 'full reparation for the injury caused by the internationally wrongful act shall take the form of restitution, compensation and satisfaction, either singly or in combination'.

[20] See *Supra* p. 184.

[21] For a review of the relevant case law see Tomuschat, 'Just Satisfaction under Article 50 of the European Convention on Human Rights', in *Protecting Human Rights: The European Perspective, Studies in Memory of Rolv Ryssdal* (Köln et al., Carl Heymanns, 2000), 1430.

[22] Judgment of 27 September 1995, PECHR, Series A, vol. 324, 63, para. 219.

[23] But see the judgment in *Craxi v Italy*, 5 December 2002, para. 112.

[24] See recently the case of *Kingsley v UK*, judgment of 28 May 2002, para. 43.

injury, in particular the non-pecuniary damage, he/she has suffered.[25] It may well be that the rule now enunciated in Article 41 dates back to the early stages of the emergence of human rights in international law. But when the states parties amended the ECHR in 1998 through the Eleventh Protocol,[26] they refrained from amending in any manner whatsoever what had been in force for nearly 50 years. In other words, they gave their implicit approval to the restrictions inherent in Article 41. We have to note, therefore, that the system which in the field of human rights can boast of being ahead of all other regional and universal systems does not acknowledge a right to financial compensation in all instances of violations of human rights, irrespective of the gravity of the relevant breach. However, recognition of the injury suffered through the breach, amounting to satisfaction for the victim, is a requirement which will invariably be fulfilled through the pronouncement of the Court.

American Convention on Human Rights

The ACHR contains a provision which is very similar to Article 41 ECHR. Article 63 enjoins the IACtHR to:

rule, if appropriate, that the consequences of the measure or situation that constituted the breach of such right or freedom be remedied and that fair compensation be paid to the injured party.

The phrase 'if appropriate' introduces once again a considerable measure of discretion. It is left to the Court to decide that compensation should either be paid or denied to the victim. In another respect, however, Article 63 is more courageous than its model in that it permits remedial measures to be ordered by the Court. What took the ECtHR almost 40 years to accept, and only in a veiled form, was envisaged under the Inter-American system from the very outset of its operation.

It is furthermore a matter of common knowledge that the IACtHR chose a victim-friendly course as from its very first decisions on the merits of an adversarial case. In *Velásquez Rodríguez* of 1988 it held that in instances of human rights violations the state concerned had 'to ensure the victim adequate compensation'.[27] This sweeping statement suffers, though, from its excessive generality. It was certainly justified in the circumstances of the case at hand. Velásquez Rodríguez had disappeared and in all probability had been murdered while being detained. However, it was pointed out at the time that the formulations employed by the Court went too far. The Court seems to have been encouraged into its sweeping statement by the assumption that

---

[25] See, for instance, from the recent past the case of *Sürek v Turkey*, judgment of 8 July 1999, ECHR Reports (1999–IV) 353, at 388 para. 85.

[26] 33 *ILM* (1994) 960.

[27] 38 *ILM* (1989) 291, at 325, para. 174.

Article 63 embodies the customary rule of classical international law, namely interstate law, according to which any damage caused by a breach of a rule of international law must be made good by the wrongdoer. In fact, in its judgment in *Aloeboetoe v Surinam*[28] it refers to the famous *Chorzow* case of the Permanent Court of International Justice.[29] However, neither the Permanent Court of International Justice nor its successor, the ICJ, have ever said that states are under an obligation to compensate their own citizens where they have suffered harm at the hands of public authorities. Thus, one may conclude that the jurisprudence of the Court is predicated on a basic misunderstanding.[30] Where the victim has essentially suffered moral injury by a breach of his or her rights, a finding to that effect by the IACtHR will provide adequate redress in the same way as within the European system. To date, the Court has not handled many cases, and almost all of them had an extremely serious character.[31] No trivial matters have been considered by it. Therefore, it would seem that it has not had the opportunity to introduce the necessary distinctions according to the gravity of the cases dealt with by it. In any event, one should note that the factual basis it had to appraise was invariably constituted by egregious violations of an abhorrent character.

Conclusion

Drawing the requisite inferences from this short overview, one may state that in the first place the granting of compensation to a victim is linked to a proceeding being handled by one of the competent bodies, a committee of experts (e.g. HRCee) or an international tribunal (ECtHR, IACtHR). It cannot be gleaned from the relevant texts that there exists a right of compensation also independently of such an actual proceeding. In fact, as explicitly laid down in the clauses governing the power of the two international tribunals to grant reparation, it is entirely left to their discretion to award financial compensation or to refer the winning party to the moral value of a judgment that finds a violation to have been perpetrated. Given this strong

---

[28] Judgment of 10 September 1993, paras 43, 44.

[29] P.C.I.J., Ser. A, No. 17, 47.

[30] Francisco Villagrán Kramer, *Sanciones internacionales por violaciones a los derechos humanos* (Guatemala, Ministerio de Cultura y Deportes, 1995), at 216, endorses the jurisprudence of the Court without any comment. Regarding such judgments providing for reparation see also Cançado Trindade, 'Current State and Perspectives of the Inter-American System of Human Rights Protection at the Dawn of the New Century', 8 *Tulane J. of Int'l & Comp. Law* (2000) 5, at 22.

[31] One of the recent examples is the judgment in *Bámaca*, 12 March 1992, where the Court formulated far-reaching demands concerning reparation and prosecution of the perpetrators. For a comment see Hagler and Rivera, '*Bámaca Velásquez v. Guatemala*: An Expansion of the Inter-American System's Jurisprudence on Reparations', 9(3) *Human Rights Brief* (Washington) (2002) 2. For the judgment on the merits of the case of 25 November 2000 see 22 *HRLJ* (2001) 367.

discretionary element, it is hard to speak of a true right to compensation of aggrieved individuals.

Reparation under European Community Law

Only under some specific international treaties does an unconditional right to reparation, including financial compensation, arise. A reparation regime which leaves almost nothing further to be desired has evolved under the treaties on the European Communities. In the text of these instruments, it is explicitly stated that the Communities are liable for damage caused by official acts. Thus, Article 288(2) EC provides:

In the case of non-contractual liability, the Community shall, in accordance with the general principles common to the laws of the Member States, make good any damage caused by its institutions or by its servants in the performance of their duties.

Nothing was said, however, about instances where instead of the Communities and their 'servants' it is the Member States of the two Communities that breach their obligations, thereby causing injury to individuals. In a ground-breaking case, the case of *Francovich*, where the claimant had suffered important financial losses because of the failure of the Italian State to introduce a system of guaranteeing workers' salaries in the event of insolvency of their employer, the CJEC held that Italy was liable to pay compensation to those affected by the Italian delay in establishing the required system.[32] Although originally many voices in legal doctrine attempted to narrow down the scope of this case law to instances where a state has failed to implement a Community directive within the prescribed time limits, it soon became clear that the *Francovich* doctrine applies to any violation of Community law. Likewise, contrary to views expressed immediately after the handing down of the *Francovich* judgment, is has also emerged that the right to reparation concerned has its roots in the Community legal order. No more is left to Member States than to regulate the details of the vindication of this right, in particular to make determinations on which tribunals are competent to adjudicate claims brought by victims. Nowhere else in the world has such a sweeping system of reparation for breaches of international law obligations to the benefit of individuals taken shape. Whereas in the aftermath of the *Francovich* ruling many commentators found the boldness of the European judges shocking, arguing that such decisive steps for the completion of the Community legal system had to remain reserved to determinations by the competent law-making bodies,[33] satisfaction with the state of affairs thereby

---

[32] Judgment of 19 November 1991, [1991] ECR I-5403.

[33] This was particularly the case in Germany. For references see Tomuschat, 'Das Francovich-Urteil des EuGH – Ein Lehrstück zum Europarecht', in *Festschrift für Ulrich Everling*, (Baden-Baden, Nomos, 1995), vol. II, 1584, at 1585–1586.

reached now seems to be general. The *Francovich* doctrine has become a firm element of the Community legal order.[34]

Reparation under the Convention Against Torture

The CAT should also be mentioned in this connection. It establishes (Article 14(1)):

Each state party shall ensure in its legal system that the victim of an act of torture obtains redress and has an enforceable right to fair and adequate compensation, including the means for as full rehabilitation as possible.

The thrust of this provision is very clear. It does not bring into being an individual entitlement under international law, but, just as Articles 9(5) and 14(6) CCPR, enjoins states to enact legislation which on its part provides for individual rights which then can be enforced before domestic tribunals. Obviously, the framers of the Convention found it too difficult to establish a right under international law, given the fact that in instances where an individual asserts a right against his/her own state the dispute requires detailed regulation under domestic law.

Reparation within the Framework of Criminal Prosecution

One could have imagined that in international criminal proceedings the opportunity would be used at the same time to adjudicate civil claims against convicted authors of crimes. However, the relevant rules are characterized by a considerable degree of caution in that regard. The Rules of Procedure and Evidence of the ICTY provide in Rule 106 that the judgment finding an accused guilty of a crime which has caused injury to a victim shall be transmitted to the authorities of the state concerned and that, on the basis of that judgment, but 'pursuant to the relevant national legislation', the victim may bring an action in a national court or other competent body to obtain compensation. In other words, the ICTY itself is bound to refrain from making a determination on such claims, for which, indeed, it has no jurisdiction under its Statute. One may ask whether the cause of action underlying such a suit pertains to international or to domestic law. The phrase 'pursuant to the relevant national legislation' would seem to suggest that the cause of action is rooted in domestic law, the judgment rendered by the ICTY providing no more than a piece of evidence proving the criminal responsibility of the convicted person for such injury. But it could also be argued that, in the same way as under the *Francovich* doctrine, domestic law

---

[34] Recently, the *Francovich* doctrine was introduced by the CJEC into relationships under private law, see *Courage v Crehan*, judgment of 20 September 2001 (not yet published).

has no more to do than to set forth the modalities for the vindication of a right to reparation directly anchored, or codified, in the Rules of Procedure and Evidence of the ICTY. It would appear that no substantial legal consequences flow from choosing which alternative to apply. In any event, it is clear from the determination in Rule 106 that domestic tribunals cannot decline jurisdiction to hear a case for reparation. Secondly, Rule 106 also implies that an accused convicted by the ICTY cannot base his/her defence on the argument that he/she enjoys immunity since he/she acted in the exercise of sovereign powers when committing the relevant crimes. Whoever is debarred from invoking immunity in criminal proceedings, is also prevented from relying on that defence in subsequent civil proceedings designed to obtain compensation for the damage caused.

We have no information as to whether Rule 106 has already been applied in the practice of the ICTY.[35] Realistically, it may be assumed that this provision has no great potential. Normally, persons standing trial before the ICTY are involved in so many crimes that they are simply unable to compensate, by their assets or through the proceeds from their work, all the damage they have caused. If indeed all the victims used the mechanism of Rule 106, an international insolvency procedure would be needed in order to distribute the few available assets of the perpetrators fairly among all those entitled to receive reparation. In the case of a mass murderer like Adolf Hitler, any attempt to make him financially accountable would have been vain from the very outset, failing any assets that could have been attached. It stands to reason that in such circumstances the classical 'collective' methods of settlement are preferable. It is not only the perpetrator himself who is made liable for the injury inflicted upon the victims, but, as a subject of international law, the nation on whose behalf—or better: in whose name—he committed his evil deeds. To individualize responsibility has obvious limits. The most evident limit in this regard is constituted by the financial capacity of the individual responsible for the harm done. Considering the issue of solvency of the debtor, to have a claim against the responsible collectivity is certainly much to be preferred.

It is for this reason that the Rome Statute of the ICC has devised a different system. In Article 77 it sets forth that, in addition to imprisonment, fines may be imposed on a convicted accused and that forfeiture of proceeds, property, and assets derived directly or indirectly from the crime concerned may be ordered. Under Article 79 a Trust Fund is to be established for the benefit of victims of crimes within the jurisdiction of the ICC. This Trust

---

[35] According to Kress and Sluiter, 'Fines and Forfeiture Orders', in Antonio Cassese, Paola Gaeta, and John R. W. D. Jones (eds), *The Rome Statute of the International Criminal Court: A Commentary* (Oxford, Oxford University Press, 2002), vol. II, 1823, at 1833, the issue has arisen in the practice of the ICTY 'only to a very limited extent'.

Fund may, by order of the Court, receive monies and other property collected through fines or forfeiture. It is then a matter of good management to distribute the income of the Fund to the victims concerned.

V LEGAL CONNOTATION OF INDIVIDUAL CLAIMS UNDER INTERNATIONAL LAW

General Framework

To date, the system of international responsibility is essentially a system of interstate responsibility. International organizations, too, have been included in this system since the famous advisory opinion of the ICJ in the *Bernadotte* case.[36] They enjoy a right to claim compensation when their rights under international law have been infringed by another subject of international law; conversely, they can also be made accountable if, through their actions, another subject of international law has suffered damage.[37] All this is now founded on an extensive international practice and does not give rise to major difficulties.

If and to what extent individuals are subjects of international law is still highly controversial. One can interpret in different ways the legal status which human beings enjoy under the treaties for the protection of human rights. Since no such treaty may enter into force for the inhabitants of a given country without its consent, which is normally expressed by its government, it can be argued that the rights enunciated by those treaties are always rights conferred upon them by a sovereign national act. On the other hand, as soon as an international remedy has been established for the vindication of such rights, the individual becomes independent of the will of his/her country. He/she can then assert his/her rights directly, even if the respondent, the state of nationality, may disagree with 'internationalizing' the dispute. As long as the relevant treaty and its procedural mechanism remain in force according to international law, no one can be stopped from availing him/herself of the opportunities provided for by that treaty. Any attempt by a state party to the OP-CCPR to impede access by its citizens to the HRCee constitutes a grave violation of its obligations.[38] One may characterize this situation as a legal status under international law inasmuch as the state to whose jurisdiction the

---

[36] *Reparation for Injuries Suffered in the Service of the United Nations,* ICJ Reports (1949) 174.

[37] See, for instance, Tomuschat, 'The International Responsibility of the European Union', in Enzo Cannizzaro (ed.), *The European Union as an Actor in International Relations* (The Hague, Kluwer Law International, 2002), 177.

[38] HRCee, views in *Ashby v Trinidad and Tobago,* 21 March 2002, [2002] *Report of the HRCee,* UN doc. A/57/40, 94, para. 134.

individual is generally subject is legally debarred from preventing the institution of proceedings against it.[39]

Whatever answer one may find to this doctrinal dispute, it is clear that
international law has not yet evolved to a point where it could be said that,
just as states under the regime of state responsibility, individuals enjoy a full
(secondary) right to reparation, including financial compensation, where
their (primary) rights have been infringed. As pointed out above, no such
right exists under the most highly developed treaties for the protection of
human rights at the universal level as well as at the regional level. While the
CCPR, with the exception of two provisions which refer to national law,
remains absolutely silent with regard to reparation, the two comprehensive
human rights treaties at regional level, the ECHR and the ACHR, commit
the granting of financial compensation to the discretion of the competent
Courts. If no unequivocal individual entitlement exists under these treaties,
no such entitlement can exist under general international law. Customary law
does not go further in scope than the most advanced treaties on that same
subject.

It is significant, in this respect, that an ambitious project promoted by the
Sub-Commission on the Promotion and Protection of Human Rights still
awaits definitive approval by the HRCion. Under the rapporteurship of the
Dutch lawyer Theo van Boven, the Commission established in 1997 a set of
'Basic Principles and Guidelines on the Right to Reparation for Victims of
[Gross] Violations of Human Rights and International Humanitarian
Law'.[40] One year later, a new independent expert was appointed to prepare
a revised version of these 'Basic Principles and Guidelines'. Mr Cherif
Bassiouni, who was entrusted with carrying out this task, submitted his
final report in January 2000.[41] In Part IX of that document (para. 15), the
expert deals with the victims' right to reparation. He suggests that 'adequate,
effective and prompt reparation shall be intended to promote justice by
redressing violations of international human rights or humanitarian law'.
Another long section (Part X) deals with the different forms of reparation by
listing all the forms of reparation which the ILC had included in its draft
articles on state responsibility of 1996, namely restitution, compensation,
rehabilitation, satisfaction, and guarantees of non-repetition. These Principles, being applicable to all kinds of human rights violations, are admirable
in their logical consistency. But the international community hesitates to

[39] See, on the one hand, Randelzhofer, 'The Legal Position of the Individual under Present
International Law', in Randelzhofer and Tomuschat, *supra* n. 16, 231; on the other hand,
Tomuschat, 'International Law: Ensuring the Survival of Mankind on the Eve of a New
Century. General Course on Public International Law', 281 *Recueil des cours* (2001) 149.

[40] UN doc. E/CN.4/1997/104, annex,16 January 1997.

[41] *Civil and Political Rights, Including the Questions of Independence of the Judiciary,
Administration of Justice, Impunity,* UN doc. E/CN.4/2000/62, 18 January 2000.

commit itself to such a far-reaching degree. On the one hand, more flexibility will be needed. The 'Basic Principles and Guidelines' are characterized by a high degree of perfectionism. They also disregard the fact that many grave violations result from cataclysms which engulf an entire nation, such as the coming into power of a criminal dictatorial regime. South Africa during the time of Apartheid provides another example of such a perversion of governmental power, where legislation was used as a method to establish racial discrimination in all fields of life. After the fall of such a regime, all hands must join to rebuild the nation. The damage caused normally reaches such huge dimensions that it is impossible for everyone to obtain full reparation for the injury suffered. By Res. 2002/44, 23 April 2002, the HRCion made another appeal to states to finalize the work on the topic of the 'Basic Principles and Guidelines'. Consultations are to be held, together with intergovernmental organizations and NGOs. But it must be assumed that for the time being the draft will not be approved by the international community, not because the rules it suggests are incomplete and therefore defective, but because they are too complete and defective on that ground.

Competent Forum

It should be clarified, at this juncture, what a claim 'under international law' could actually mean. Regarding relationships between and among states, a legal right or obligation need not be identified in specific terms. Such rights are subject to the entire framework of the rules of general international law. Concerning the relationship between states and individuals, the situation is more complex since in any event national courts would have an important role to play.

In the first place, by characterizing a claim as existing under international law, one would convey the idea that the claim is not dependent on national law. Neither would it be brought into being by domestic legislation, nor could it be extinguished by a national legislative act. In order correctly to understand the legal position, the *Francovich* doctrine of the CJCE could be relied upon. All Member States of the European Union have to accept—and have accepted—that persons harmed by non-respect of any rules of Community law on their part have a right to reparation against them.

In contradistinction to what is the case for interstate relationships, however, there exists no general international forum for the settlement of disputes between states and individuals. In principle, every interstate dispute can be brought before the ICJ, provided only that the litigant parties have submitted to the jurisdiction of the World Court. With regard to disputes between states and private parties, only specialized fora are provided for, in particular on the basis of human rights treaties being complemented by mechanisms for individual applications (complaints, communications) or within the framework of the ICSID Convention.[42] There is no real prospect of the establishment of such a mechanism in connection with the—highly improbable—adoption of the 'Basic Principles and Guidelines' of the Van Boven/Bassiouni project.

Consequently, even a claim under international law would in any event have to be asserted before national tribunals. According to general rules of civil procedure, as they are applied in most countries, a defendant can be sued at his/her place of residence or, in case of tortious responsibility, at the forum where the tort was committed. This is tantamount to saying that claims for reparation seeking to obtain redress for human rights violations by a state or its servants must in principle be brought before the tribunals of that same state, an inference which shows the complexity of the concept of individual reparation claims under international law. The defendant state would necessarily be *judex in re sua*. In a governmental system placed under the rule of law such a configuration does not give rise to concern. Precisely under the rule of law, judges are independent and subject only to the law. In a dictatorship, however, one cannot trust the judicial branch to keep its independence and objectivity. In Nazi Germany, although some judges succeeded in maintaining a modest degree of independence, there was no possibility of any impartial adjudication of cases with political overtones. In socialist countries, the whole judicial machinery was guided by political decisions taken at the highest level. Chile's judiciary followed the lines predetermined by the government during the right-wing dictatorship of President Pinochet. This list could easily be lengthened, but, unfortunately, this would be a waste of time. It is a fact of life proven by many historical examples that an independent judiciary prospers only in countries where democracy, human rights, and in particular a free press, set a general framework stabilizing the rule of law.

It would be illusory to hope that for claims seeking reparation for human rights violations the principle of universal jurisdiction could be introduced. According to this principle, a claimant could institute civil proceedings against the responsible entity or persons even before the tribunals of third countries. Yet, as shown already, universal jurisdiction can by no means be considered a recognized principle in the field of criminal law. It is even less justifiable as a principle governing territorial jurisdiction in civil matters. Additionally, it is hard to see that third states would be willing to adjudicate claims against persons responsible for human rights violations that were committed in other countries. The applicable legal principles and the empirically observable reluctance of states to meddle with internal matters of other states meet here in a perfect match.

---

[42] Convention on the Settlement of Investment Disputes between States and Nationals of Other States, 18 March 1965, 575 *UNTS* 159.

In the European Union, this very same problematique has found an ingenious solution. Concerning reparation claims according to the *Francovich* doctrine, the starting point is the same. There exists no Community forum for asserting such claims. Consequently, persons believing that they have been injured through a breach of Community rules by their own state, are compelled to file claims before their own ordinary courts. But all national judicial bodies are subject to the supervision of the CJEC. If during a proceeding before a national judge an issue of interpretation presents itself, it must be referred to the Luxembourg Court if it raises any serious difficulties (Article 234 EC) and if no remedy lies to a higher court. Thus, the CJCE can ensure that national judges do not attempt to protect the financial resources of their treasury in a biased manner. It is obvious that to establish such a complex mechanism of judicial cooperation in a worldwide framework would require a tight network of cooperation which will not come into being very soon.

In sum, it must be concluded that the concept of reparation claims under international law has fairly weak foundations, given the absence of an international forum where such claims could be filed. This lack of procedural support also explains why the concept has not yet materialized as a rule of positive international law.

VI PROCEDURES UNDER DOMESTIC LAW

Given the absence of rules of international law outside special treaty systems, the victim of a human rights violation seeking redress for the injury he/she has suffered must rely on the domestic law of a given state. Since human rights violations can, in principle, be committed only by states and/or the persons acting on behalf of the state, it is the law regulating state responsibility for tortious action which is applicable. In most countries, special rules have been evolved for this specific subject matter. These rules have a number of particular characteristics.[43]

First of all, tort law is generally territorial law. Every state enacts or evolves rules on tort primarily for its own territory. Exceptionally, states may subject their own nationals to their own regime of tort law for activities conducted abroad. Almost inevitably, however, in such eventuality a conflict arises with the territorially applicable tort law. Secondly, jurisdiction to enact rules

---

[43] For a general, although somewhat outdated, overview see Max-Planck-Institut für ausländisches öffentliches Recht und Völkerrecht (ed.), *Haftung des Staates für rechtswidriges Verhalten seiner Organe—Liability of the State for Illegal Conduct of its Organs* (Köln and Berlin, Carl Heymanns, 1967). The current legal position in the United States is described by Dinah Shelton, *Remedies in International Human Rights Law* (Oxford, Oxford University Press, 1999), at 64–68.

regulating responsibility for unlawful state conduct lies in principle with the state concerned itself. Italy is not empowered to determine under which conditions and how the French State is to be held accountable and what the legal consequences of such accountability should be. Conversely, the same is true. No state would be prepared to accept a regime of responsibility for the conduct of its own authorities set forth by another state. Even if a state were to take such a temerarious step, it could be sure that no judgment based on such a regime with extraterritorial effect would be recognized.

What is true for state responsibility in general may not be true for responsibility flowing from acts to be characterized as crimes under international law. Over the last couple of years, broad consensus has been reached on a list of offences deserving such characterization. The Code of crimes against the peace and security of mankind adopted by the ILC in 1996,[44] the Statutes of the ICTY and the ICTR as well as the Rome Statute of the ICC all define a core area of acts considered by the international community to affect basic values necessary for peaceful coexistence among nations in full respect for human rights and fundamental freedoms. Many of these crimes fall within universal jurisdiction as pointed out in Chapter 12 above.

Although there exists no customary rule permitting the exercise of universal jurisdiction for all crimes under international law, some specific crimes may doubtless be prosecuted by any state. As a follow-up to that premise, it could be argued that there should also exist universal jurisdiction for civil claims brought against an alleged perpetrator by the victim of his/her actions. Leaving aside for a moment the issue of how this question is to be answered, it must be realized that universal jurisdiction does not, as if by a magic stroke, resolve all the procedural difficulties which may arise in proceedings conducted on that basis. In criminal proceedings, it must be clarified whether some contact with the territory of the prosecuting state must exist or whether first measures of prosecution, such as the issuance of an arrest warrant, can be directed against an alleged perpetrator while abroad.[45] Regarding the trial proper, it must always be conducted in the presence of the accused. Otherwise, due process could not be guaranteed. Hence, if the alleged perpetrator remains in freedom in another country which is not prepared to extradite him/her, no trial can take place.

In civil proceedings, likewise due process must be ensured. For that reason, the rules of all countries presuppose a jurisdictional link justifying the exercise of jurisdiction against a respondent. Even if, on account of the commission of an international crime, subject matter jurisdiction could be affirmed,

---

[44] *Yearbook of the ILC* (1996), vol. II, part 2, 17.

[45] See in that regard the joint concurring opinion of judges Higgins, Kooijmans, and Buergenthal in the *Arrest Warrant* case, judgment of the ICJ of 14 February 2002, paras. 53–58.

personal jurisdiction would have to be established additionally. It would run counter to the principles of procedural fairness to sue a defendant, who has allegedly committed an international crime in Ruritania, before the tribunals of Italy or any other European country if that defendant has never had any relationship with Italy or Europe in general. Every party in a civil proceeding is entitled to 'a fair and public hearing by a competent, independent and impartial tribunal established by law' (Article 14(1) CCPR). This rule applies irrespective of the gravity of the offences the defendant has allegedly committed. Fairness prohibits imposing a forum with which the defendant has no link whatsoever; otherwise, serious manipulations of forum shopping might have to be feared.

As far as the legal position can be correctly assessed, the United States is the only country in the world that has enacted legislation permitting the institution of civil proceedings against authors of grave breaches of human rights committed anywhere in the world. The Alien Tort Claims Act (ATCA), enacted in 1789 for reasons which to date remain unexplained,[46] provides:

The district courts shall have original jurisdiction of any civil action by an alien for a tort only, committed in violation of the law of nations or a treaty of the United States.[47]

According to the prevailing interpretation, this provision not only establishes the jurisdiction of US courts, but also creates a cause of action. Since the ATCA grants rights only to non-citizens of the United States, in 1991 the Torture Victim Protection Act (TVPA) was enacted,[48] which provides a cause of action for instances of torture and extrajudicial killings anywhere in the world.[49]

Both provisions presuppose that there has been a breach of a rule of international law. In general, only states are bound by rules of international law. In derogation from that premise, individuals, too, are directly subject to

[46] See d'Amato, 'The Alien Tort Statute and the Founding of the Constitution', 82 *AJIL* (1988) 62; Burley, 'The Alien Tort Statute and the Judiciary Act of 1789: A Badge of Honor', 83 *AJIL* (1989) 461; Rabkin, 'Universal Justice: The Role of Federal Courts in International Civil Litigation', *Columbia Law Review* (1995) 2120.

[47] Codified as 28 U.S.C. 1350.

[48] Codified as 28 U.S.C. 1350.

[49] 'This Act may be cited as the "Torture Victim Protection Act of 1991". SEC. 2. ESTABLISHMENT OF CIVIL ACTION. (a) Liability.—An individual who, under actual or apparent authority, or color of law, of any foreign nation: (1) subjects an individual to torture shall, in a civil action, be liable for damages to that individual; or (2) subjects an individual to extrajudicial killing shall, in a civil action, be liable for damages to the individual's legal representative, or to any person who may be a claimant in an action for wrongful death. (b) Exhaustion of Remedies.—A court shall decline to hear a claim under this section if the claimant has not exhausted adequate and available remedies in the place in which the conduct giving rise to the claim occurred. (c) Statute of Limitations.—No action shall be maintained under this section unless it is commenced within 10 years after the cause of action arose.'

rules of international law regarding all the crimes for which the international instruments referred to have established criminal responsibility. Most of these crimes, however, presuppose that the individual concerned acted within the wider framework of a governmental activity. As can be seen from the text of the TVPA, this precondition is carefully taken into account. It targets individuals who have committed the controversial acts 'under actual or apparent authority, or color of law, of any foreign nation'. Concerning the ATCA, it must likewise be determined under what conditions an individual can commit a 'violation of the law of nations'. In the famous case of *Filártiga v Peña Irala*,[50] the court rightly held that torture belongs to those acts which are banned under the law of nations. It is of course more promising for claimants to sue corporate bodies, since in the event of success they are faced with a solvent respondent. In *Ken Wiwa v Royal Dutch (Shell)*, complicity of the undertaking with the Nigerian authorities in committing grave human rights violations (torture, summary execution, arbitrary detention) was alleged.[51] In another case against an American undertaking (*Doe I v UNOCAL Corporation*) on account of alleged involvement of the respondent in grave human rights violations in connection with the construction of a gas pipeline in Myanmar, the US Court of Appeals for the Ninth Circuit determined that the proceeding may be continued,[52] contrary to a judgment of the district court. In view of the gravity of the allegations (forced labour, murder, rape, torture) the case does indeed seem to have some merit. By contrast, legal actions brought in November 2002 against Western undertakings that were active in South Africa during the time of the Apartheid regime[53] seem to be conspicuously abusive. Apartheid has never been a generally recognized crime under international law, nor does the fact of conducting business under an evil regime automatically amount to complicity in the crimes committed by that regime.

VII IMMUNITY

Even if a substantive cause of action exists or comes into being, civil actions against perpetrators of human rights violations raise considerable procedural difficulties. Immunity is the most formidable obstacle which has to be overcome.

[50] 630 F.2d 876 (2d Cir. 1980).
[51] See US District Court (S.D.N.Y.), 28 February 2002, http://www.derechos.org/nizkor/econ/shell28feb02.html (visited December 2002). Comment by Rau, 'Domestic Adjudication of International Human Rights Abuses and the Doctrine of *Forum Non Conveniens*', 61 *ZaöRV* (2001) 177.
[52] Judgment of 18 September 2002, 41 *ILM* (2002) 1367.
[53] See, for instance, Abraham, 'The Apartheid Lawsuit', http://users.skynet.be/cadtm/pages/english/abrahamslawsuitapartheid.htm (visited December 2002).

Since human rights violations are invariably linked to the state, two classes of respondents can in principle be imagined. In the first place, actions can be directed against a foreign state charged with breaching its obligations under international human rights law. Or else, an action can be directed against a person or persons who were involved in the alleged unlawful action. Obviously, to obtain a judgment which orders the respondent state to pay compensation is more advantageous for the claimant than a similar judgment against the personal perpetrator who, in most cases, will have few assets that might be attached for the satisfaction of the claim. On the other hand, a judgment against a foreign state may be more or less unenforceable if the state simply refuses to respect a judicial pronouncement issued by a court of a foreign country.

Every international lawyer knows that claims brought against foreign states may run against the barrier of state immunity. It is almost generally accepted today that the theory of absolute immunity has disappeared to make room for a distinction between *acta jure imperii* and *acta jure gestionis* (or commercial activities).[54] However, when human rights violations are in issue, the state concerned has almost invariably acted *iure imperii*. Therefore, a civil action in a foreign forum would have to be dismissed for lack of jurisdiction if no other legal justification could be found for overcoming the hurdle of immunity.

In the United States, the case of *Amerada Hess*[55] has settled the issue. The owner of a tanker from a neutral third country (Liberia), which had been hit by Argentine bombs and rockets during the Falklands war and as a consequence of the destruction caused by that attack had to be scuttled in the open sea, introduced an action before US tribunals, arguing that Argentina had acted in violation of the rules on neutrality and was therefore liable to make reparation under the ATCA. The Supreme Court did not accept that line of reasoning. It held that the rules on state immunity, as codified in the United States Foreign Sovereign Immunities Act (FSIA), did not foresee any derogation from immunity in instances of alleged breaches of rules of international law. Therefore, the principle of sovereign immunity applied. The action had to be dismissed.

Many attempts have been made to circumvent this straightforward ruling. Since the US FSIA explicitly mentions waiver of the foreign state as a circumstance permitting an action to be brought, and rightly so, it has been argued in a number of cases that the commission of grave breaches of

---

[54] See, for instance, Ian Brownlie, *Principles of Public International Law* (5th edn., Oxford, Oxford University Press, 1998), at 332–343 (with some doubts); Antonio Cassese, *International Law* (Oxford, Oxford University Press, 2001), at 92; Patrick Daillier and Alain Pellet, *Droit international public* (6th edn, Paris, LGDJ, 1999) at paras 289–290; Robert Jennings and Arthur Watts, *Oppenheim's International Law* (9th edn, Harlow, Essex, Longman, 1992), at 341–363.

[55] 488 U.S. 428 (1989), also reprinted in 28 *ILM* (1989) 384.

international law, amounting to true crimes, constitutes an implicit waiver. Thus, in the *Princz* case against Germany, the *amicus curiae* contended that a state which, like Germany during the Nazi period, had totally disregarded the law of nations by its murderous actions against the Jewish population in Europe, had thereby implicitly waived its right to be treated as a sovereign state which cannot be impleaded before the courts of another country. But waiver is indeed waiver, an intentional manifestation of the will of the state that is the respondent in a proceeding of such nature. States enter into treaties by their own free will, they can also unilaterally consent to acts that would otherwise have to be characterized as unlawful interference with their rights. Article 20 of the ILC Articles on responsibility of States for internationally wrongful acts[56] provides that 'valid consent by a State to the commission of a given act by another State precludes the wrongfulness of that act'. But consent cannot be artificially or even arbitrarily construed. It then becomes a mere fiction. In order to remain in full harmony with the fundamental principle of sovereign equality of states, it must be taken to mean what it actually means according to the plain meaning of the word.

Lawyers advocating the admissibility of reparation claims have also referred to the tort clauses in a number of international instruments and acts of national legislation. As one of the first instruments setting forth such a clause, the European Convention on State Immunity of 1972[57] states (Article 11):

A Contracting State cannot claim immunity from the jurisdiction of a court of another Contracting State in proceedings which relate to redress for injury to the person or damage to tangible property, if the facts which occasioned the injury or damage occurred in the territory of the State of the forum, and if the author of the injury or damage was present in that territory at the time when those facts occurred.

This provision had a significant influence on many later instruments dealing with state immunity. Thus, in particular, the FSIA provides in largely similar terms (§ 1605(a)(5)):

A foreign state shall not be immune from the jurisdiction of the United States or of the States in any case ... in which money damages are sought against a foreign state for personal injury or death, or damage to or loss of property, occurring in the United States and caused by the tortious act or omission of the foreign state or of any official or employee of that foreign state while acting within the scope of his office or employment.

Similarly, the ILC has joined this trend by suggesting, in its draft Articles on Jurisdictional Immunities of States and Their Property, that jurisdictional immunity cannot be invoked by a state in a proceeding:

which relates to pecuniary compensation for death or injury to the person, or damage to or loss of tangible property, caused by an act or omission which is alleged to be

---

[56] See *supra* n. 1.   [57] Reprinted in 11 *ILM* (1972) 470.

attributable to the State, if the act or omission occurred in whole or in part in the territory of that other State and if the author of the act or omission was present in that territory at the time of the act or omission.[58]

But it is clear from the drafting history and from the commentaries on these provisions that the aim was to cover physical damage resulting from accidents during road transport or transport by ship or air, i.e. calculable, insurable risks. Never was it envisaged to do away with immunity completely in all cases of personal injuries and damage to property. This is corroborated, in particular, by clauses in a number of the instruments concerned to the effect that military actions remain covered by immunity.[59]

The most delicate question in this connection is whether *jus cogens* rules, such as the rules criminalizing genocide or the killing of members of a civilian population or prisoners of war, take precedence over the traditional rule of state immunity. Many authors advocate some kind of balancing test, arguing that fundamental values of the international community that have emerged as norms having superior rank within the hierarchy of international law cannot leave traditional rules unaffected.[60] A decision of the Greek Areopag, the Highest Greek Court, implicitly adopted this kind of reasoning in a case (the *Distomo* case) brought by the victims of a barbarous massacre, committed by special forces of the German Army at the end of the Second World War, as retaliation against an attack by a resistance group.[61] Apart from the fact, however, that the juridical methodology followed by this judgment was flawed by superficiality, it failed to draw the requisite distinction between substantive rules of *jus cogens* and their procedural consequences. If a given rule is characterized as pertaining to the body of *jus cogens*, no more is said

---

[58] *Yearbook of the ILC* (1991), vol. II, part two, 13, at 44: Article 12.

[59] For details see Tomuschat, 'Current Issues of Responsibility under International Law', IV *Cursos Euromediterráneos Bancaja de Derecho Internacional* (2000), 515, at 566–573.

[60] See, for instance, Cerna, 'Hugo Princz *v.* Federal Republic of Germany: How Far Does the Long-Arm Jurisdiction of US Law Reach?', 8 *Leiden Journal of International Law* (1995) 377; Johnson, 'A Violation of Jus Cogens Norms as an Implicit Waiver of Immunity under the Federal Sovereign Immunities Act', 18 *Maryland Journal of International Law and Trade* (1994) 259; Levy, 'As Between *Princz* and King: Reassessing the Law of Foreign Sovereign Immunity as Applied to *Jus Cogens* Violators', 86 *Georgetown Law Journal* (1998) 2703, at 2728; McKay, 'A New Take on Antiterrorism: *Smith v. Socialist People's Libyan Arab Jamahiriya*', 13 *American University International Law Review* (1997) 439, at 464–469; Roht-Arriaza, 'The Foreign Sovereign Immunities Act and Human Rights Violations: One Step Forward, Two Steps Back?', 16 *Berkeley Journal of International Law* (1998) 71, at 82–84; Zaffuto, 'A "Pirate's Victory": President Clinton's Approach to the New FSIA Exception Leaves the Victors Empty-Handed', 74 *Tulane Law Review* (1999) 685, at 708–711; Ziman, 'Holding Foreign Governments Accountable for Their Human Rights Abuses: A Proposed Amendment to the Foreign Sovereign Immunities Act of 1976', 21 *Loyola of Los Angeles International and Comparative Law Journal* (1999) 185, at 204–205.

[61] Judgment of 4 May 2000, summary in 95 *AJIL* (2001), with note by Gavouneli and Bantekas, ibid. at 201–204.

than that the international community attaches great importance to compliance with this rule. It is another question what consequences should flow from the breach of such a rule. The rule of consent, which is an essential component of international dispute settlement, is by no means brushed aside. No state becomes subject to the jurisdiction of the ICJ if it commits an aggression, for instance. To maintain the principle of state immunity is all the more reasonable since no state would recognize judgments rendered by foreign tribunals which order it to pay financial compensation for acting in the exercise of sovereign powers.[62] To lift the ban of immunity would thus open up a bonanza for lawyers, but would not really benefit the victims.

The view that *jus cogens* cannot be understood as a bulldozer suited to flatten the entire edifice of traditional international law is confirmed by the judgment of the ICJ in the case of *Arrest Warrant of 11 April 2000 (Democratic Republic of the Congo v Belgium)*, 14 February 2002. In this judgment, the ICJ stated explicitly that the immunity of an acting Minister of Foreign Affairs was to be respected even though he was alleged to have committed grave crimes.[63] It is certainly true that a balancing test is not inconceivable in international law. In particular, the admissibility of humanitarian intervention can only be established by weighing respect for territorial integrity, on the one hand, and the injury suffered by the entire international community by tolerating massive violations of human rights.[64] However, to disregard state immunity in any case where allegations are made against a state to be in breach of human rights by committing, through its agents, an international crime would do more harm than good in the international legal order. In consonance with the general rules of international law establishing immunity *ratione personae* of a Head of State, American judges rightly upheld the immunity of the Haitian Head of State, Jean-Bertrand Aristide, against claims that sought compensation for alleged killings.[65]

This line of conservative prudence was also confirmed by the judgment of the ECtHR in the case of *Al-Adsani v Government of Kuwait*.[66] The respondent in that case, the United Kingdom, was charged by the applicant with denying him appropriate judicial remedies in accordance with Article 6 ECHR and thereby with failing to afford him adequate protection against torture. The applicant contended that he had been tortured in Kuwait and

---

[62] In a judgment of 17 September 2002, the Special Highest Court under Article 100 of the Greek Constitution ruled that the customary rule of state immunity prohibits any actions against a foreign state on account of alleged wrongful acts of its armed forces.

[63] For comments see Sassoli, 'L'arrêt Yerodia: Quelques remarques sur une affaire au point de collision entre les deux couches du droit international', 106 *RGDIP* (2002) 790, at 807–817; Schultz, 'Ist *Lotus* verblüht?', 62 *ZaöRV* (2002) 703, at 740–746.

[64] See *supra* pp. 226–229.

[65] 844 F.Supp. 128 (E.D.N.Y. 1994).

[66] Judgment of 21 November 2001, not yet published.

had suffered serious bodily harm. Upon his return to the United Kingdom, he instituted civil proceedings in England for compensation against the Sheikh and the government of Kuwait. All his efforts to obtain redress were unsuccessful. The ECtHR dismissed his claim that the United Kingdom had breached its obligations under the ECHR. It held that the United Kingdom could rely on the rule of state immunity in order to deny access to court to the applicant for his claim. It acknowledged that it was 'unable to discern in the international instruments, judicial authorities or other materials before it any firm basis for concluding that, as a matter of international law, a State no longer enjoys immunity from civil suit in the courts of another State where acts of torture are alleged'.[67]

Lastly, consideration must be given to instances where it is not a foreign state which is chosen as the defendant, but an agent or the agents who was/ were involved in perpetrating the offence complained of. Here, the assessment must be a different one. Public servants of a foreign state, with the exception of the holders of the highest offices like the Head of State or a Foreign Minister, do not enjoy personal immunity. The immunity which they may invoke derives from the nature of the activity they are carrying out (immunity *ratione materiae* or *ratione functionis*). This immunity has a limited scope. It covers of course all lawful acts and even acts which may be unlawful under international law. International criminal law, however, does not grant immunity with respect to acts or omissions that are to be classified as crimes under international law. What applies to international criminal law must also apply to civil proceedings. If a person is unable to protect him/ herself against an indictment by invoking immunity, it would be contradictory to grant that defence on the level of civil proceedings.[68] Thus, a distinction must be drawn between state immunity and immunity of individual persons.[69] Valid grounds support this differentiation. Even a 'criminal' state is still a sovereign state, representing its people. On the other hand, individuals who engage in criminal activities should, as a rule, not be able to benefit from the functional position which they occupy within the structure of governance of the state on whose behalf they are acting. To hold them accountable may also operate as a useful general deterrent from abusing posts of responsibility. Thus, it would be wrong to consider different treatment of state immunity and individual immunity as logically incoherent.

[67] Ibid., at para. 61. In the case of *Doe I v UNOCAL*, the US Court of Appeals also dismissed the actions brought against the Myanmar Military and Myanmar Oil, a state agency, see *supra*, n. 52, at 1380–1381.

[68] Thus, in Belgium and France civil universal jurisdiction is linked to criminal universal jurisdiction, see Reydams, 'Remarks', in Wybo P. Heere (ed.), *Contemporary International Law Issues: New Forms, New Applications* (The Hague, TMC Asser Institute, 1998), 166.

[69] Same approach by Rabkin, *supra* n. 46, at 2150 (but erroneously developing his arguments as implicit waiver of immunity).

Enforcement of judgments rendered against private defendants is also a major problem. It is well known that the famous judgment in *Filártiga v Peña Irala*[70] proved of no avail for the successful claimant. More generally, it was stated a few years ago that none of the plaintiffs suing individual defendants had to date been able to collect even part of the multimillion dollar judgments they had been awarded.[71] Thus, a judicial victory does not necessarily mean a victory in concrete terms on the ground.

The preceding considerations have made it abundantly clear that individual reparation claims against tortfeasors outside the country where the tort was committed have to overcome many hurdles. Only one thing is certain: there will be many attempts in the future to use unorthodox strategies with a view to enforcing rights which are not capable of being enforced in the country of origin.

[70] See *supra* n. 50.
[71] Stephens, 'Civil Remedies in the US Courts for International Human Rights Abuses', in Heere, *supra* n. 68, at 161.

14

Time for Hope, or Time for Despair?

As indicated by its name, human rights protection is a process which cannot be finalized once and for all at some point in time. In the human world, paradise will never make a glorious entry, defeating all the evils that besiege the peoples of this globe. It is the basic fact that human beings live under permanent threat from their environment which makes human rights necessary. To believe that total harmony may emerge some day would disregard human nature: different minds pursue different goals, and in many parts of the world life means little more than to ensure survival to the next day. Such hard realities do not make the concept of human rights useless. It constitutes a grand design for a peaceful society where everyone enjoys everything that permits a life in dignity.

It is an open question whether the existing framework for the protection of human rights, as it has evolved at universal and regional levels for more than half a century, provides sufficiently appropriate weapons for the defence and enforcement of these rights. It can certainly be maintained that occasionally some overlap occurs. Many of the UN expert bodies perform the same or similar tasks. On the other hand, regarding burning issues such as the 'modern' slave trade, all the existing institutions seem too weak, almost naive in their endeavour to put a brake on abhorrent practices. Competences are scattered, and the lack of transparency has reached such a degree that even diplomats sometimes confuse the HRCion and the HRCee. It would be wrong, however, to believe that by establishing centralized mechanisms with comprehensive responsibilities more effectiveness could be achieved. In the last analysis, the complex legal edifice which has been described in the preceding pages can do no more than remind states again and again that very precise duties are incumbent upon them to deal with all those under their jurisdiction in a humane manner, and to urge them to act accordingly. The system rests on confidence and persuasion. Against recalcitrant states, which openly defy universally recognized values, the international community has to resort to other methods, including coercion and ultimately even armed force.

In human rights discourse, the state is the key actor. Its centrality can easily be explained in connection with traditional 'negative' rights that seek to shield the individual against governmental interference. In this traditional concept, the state represents the ever-present potential enemy whose claimed sovereignty has elicited recourse to human rights as a vital defence. But the centrality of the state is by no means as self-evident regarding 'positive' rights, rights of the second generation which enjoin governments to provide vital services to persons requiring assistance. In order to satisfy the needs of a population, governmental institutions and society have to cooperate with one another. The state is never an almighty institution with unlimited resources. Against widespread resistance on the ground, its authorities are hardly able to discharge their functions in an effective way. This applies to a great extent also to rights of the first generation. Enjoyment of human rights can only be the result of concerted efforts by state and society. In order to attain this goal, citizens must share together with all the holders of public office the lofty objectives encapsulated in the lists of human rights as they are laid down in the UDHR or in the two Covenants of 1966. A concept that would visualize human rights exclusively as a burden on the governmental apparatus would be doomed from the very outset. This does not mean that the individual as a holder of rights should concomitantly be subjected to legal duties not only under domestic, but also under international law. Governments have always found ways and means to enforce the policies determined by them for the weal of the polity. No more is suggested than the simple truth that the intellectual frame of society conditions its practices in the field of human rights. Human rights cannot prosper in a climate of hatred and vengeance. The values underlying them, such as tolerance and solidarity, must also be acknowledged by the citizens of the country concerned.

It is of course much easier to guarantee human rights if the basic societal framework corresponds fully to the requirements of democracy and the rule of law. Even under such conditions, where human rights are not placed under a structural threat, violations—which generally resemble more errors and accidents than deliberate departures from the path of legality—do occur time and again. Although true democratic rule prevents governmental institutions from acting in fundamental disregard of their people, it always remains true that those actually entrusted with acting on behalf of the state may alienate themselves from those who entrusted them with taking care of the essential functions of the collectivity, or may succumb to the weaknesses to which human beings are generally prone, even as office holders. As our analysis has shown, Western Europe cannot boast a stainless record notwithstanding the generally favourable conditions which have surrounded its rebirth after the Second World War. It was the fundamental error of the communist doctrine that the state machinery could commit no wrong since according to the laws of history the people had taken over the reigns of power.

In states which fail because of their lack of resources, or in states where governments use public authority for criminal purposes, outside assistance through international mechanisms becomes even more important. Sometimes, like in Afghanistan, the internal situation may degenerate to such a degree that all the hopes of the population concerned may be placed on the international community. It is indeed true that in such extreme instances interference by the international community may bring about decisive change for a fresh start. In the last resort, however, it is always the society concerned that must come to terms with its fate. Self-determination is necessarily accompanied by an assumption of responsibility. Human rights must permeate the whole texture of a given society, and human beings must understand that they must claim and uphold their rights, on the one hand, and that they must also be prepared to recognize the rights and entitlements of their fellow citizens. Governmental authority is a powerful instrument for the enforcement of collective decisions, adopted in the name of the nation, but it does not constitute a panacea for the creation of a state of affairs where all human rights are fully secured to everyone.

Index